Reading Rorty

Critical Responses to *Philosophy and the Mirror of Nature* (and Beyond)

Edited by Alan R. Malachowski

ASSOCIATE EDITOR JO BURROWS

BLACKWELL
Oxford UK & Cambridge USA

Copyright © Basil Blackwell Ltd., 1990
Chapter 8 Copyright © Donald Davidson 1990
Chapter 18 Copyright © Nancy Fraser 1990

First published 1990
Reprinted 1991, 1995

Blackwell Publishers Ltd.
108 Cowley Road, Oxford, OX4 1JF, UK

Blackwell Publishers Inc.
238 Main Street,
Cambridge, Massachusetts 02142, USA

British Library Cataloguing in Publication Data
A CIP catalogue record for this book is available from the British Library.

Library of Congress Cataloging in Publication Data
Reading Rorty: critical responses to Philosophy and the mirror of nature (and beyond) / edited
by Alan R. Malachowski: associate editor Jo Burrows.
p. cm.
Includes bibliographical references.
ISBN 0–631–16148–1—ISBN 0–631–16149–X (pbk.)
1. Rorty, Richard. Philosophy and the mirror of nature.
2. Philosophy. 3. Philosophy, Modern. 4. Representation
(Philosophy) 5. Analysis (Philosophy) 6. Civilization – Philosophy.
I. Malachowski, Alan R. II. Burrows, Jo. III. Rorty, Richard.
Philosophy and the mirror of nature.
B53.R682 1990
191–dc20 89–27035 CIP

Typeset in 10 on 12pt Plantin by
Wearside Tradespool, Fulwell, Sunderland
Printed in Great Britain by
Athenæum Press Ltd, Gateshead, Tyne & Wear

This book is printed on acid-free paper

Contents

List of Contributors

Roy Bhaskar is Research Fellow in Philosophy at Linacre College, Oxford, and The City University, London. His *Philosophy and the Idea of Freedom* is forthcoming from Basil Blackwell.

Jo Burrows is a postgraduate student in philosophy at the University of Essex.

Michael Clark is Reader in Philosophy at the University of Nottingham.

Donald Davidson is Professor of Philosophy at the University of California, Berkeley.

Michael Fischer is Associate Professor of English at the University of New Mexico.

Nancy Fraser is Associate Professor in Philosophy at Northwestern University.

Charles Guignon is Professor of Philosophy at the University of Vermont.

Jane Heal is a Fellow of St John's College, Cambridge.

David Hiley is Professor of Philosophy at Memphis State University.

Martin Hollis is Professor of Philosophy at the University of East Anglia.

Jacek Holówka teaches philosophy at Warsaw University.

David Houghton is Lecturer in Philosophy at the University of East Anglia.

Jennifer Hornsby is a Fellow of Corpus Christi College, Oxford.

Alan Malachowski is a Visiting Fellow at the University of East Anglia and an Adjunct Professor of The Philosophical Foundation For International Thought.

W. V. Quine is Edgar Pierce Professor of Philosophy, Emeritus, at Harvard University.

Richard Rorty is University Professor of Humanities at the University of Virginia.

Tom Sorell is Lecturer in Philosophy at the Open University.

Charles Taylor is Professor of Philosophy and Political Science at McGill University.

Gerald Vision is Professor of Philosophy at Temple University.

Bernard Williams is the White's Professor of Modern Philosophy at Oxford University.

John Yolton is Professor of Philosophy at Rutgers, The State University of New Jersey.

Preface

In *Philosophy and the Mirror of Nature*,[1] Richard Rorty presents us with a scholarly and engaging account of how he thinks modern analytical philosophy has outlived its usefulness and should now make way for something more useful.[2] The account Rorty offers is also peculiarly rich.

It is 'rich' in the sense of attempting to deal with so many important themes – most of which involve far more than the fate of the particular academic discipline of philosophy – and 'peculiarly' so because of its innovative approach to these themes. Large substantive claims and broad impressions of intellectual developments on a grand scale are carefully juxtapositioned with sharp arguments, brief historical interludes and snippets of narrative detail. Rorty's ways with themes carry over to his 'theme-makers'. 'Peripheral' thinkers are alluded to in the company of central figures, and hailed as 'the most important philosophers of our century'. But then, the work of the 'insiders' is given prominence, while the actual achievements of the 'outsiders' are not subjected to much scrutiny.

It is a tribute to Rorty's literary skills that this 'juxtapositioning' of themes and figures is so successful, that potential disparities between contrasting features of the text are unobtrusive, and that, at first sight, the philosophical agenda of *Philosophy and the Mirror of Nature* is familiar. It is perhaps an even greater tribute to Rorty's dialectical prowess that when, under close reading, some tensions beneath the stylish surface do become apparent, and items on the agenda begin to lose their air of familiarity, the attentive reader is more likely to be drawn into creative dialogue than turned away. In this respect, *Philosophy and the Mirror of Nature* is, itself, a shining example of the kind of post-philosophical 'conversation' its author advocates.

The present collection of 'critical responses' is intended to serve as a companion to such dialogues. Indeed, in general, the reader would do well to think of it in terms of a friendly gathering of prospective partners in conversation, each ready and willing to respond to the sort of questions Rorty provokes: 'Was Descartes committed to that concept of ideas?' 'Would Quine agree?' 'Where do Rorty and Davidson differ on truth?' 'Is epistemology really finished for good?' 'Do we need a more substantial conception of the self?' 'Can the notion of "conversation" be a politically benign notion?', and so on. In responding to such questions, the contributors not only tend to raise further questions (thus achieving Rorty's laudable aim of 'keeping the conversation going'), they also explore the different levels on which his text operates.

Readers who are more inclined to view things from the various perspectives of the 'Continental Tradition' in philosophy, and who therefore remain extremely suspicious of attempts to anthropomorphize texts, can ignore the foregoing recommendations. They will need no hints about 'levels'. And, in any case, I am happy to let them make their own questioning points of entry.

Readers who are new to academic philosophy, or whose area of interest is normally exceptionally narrow, should arrange an initial encounter with the first two responses written by Tom Sorell and Bernard Williams respectively. These should be accessible to them, and provide a useful lead into the rest of the collection. Old hands can make their own selection of 'conversational partners', though even some of them might benefit from taking the novice's route; especially if they have not been reading Rorty of late.

Teachers of philosophy, and allied disciplines (a category which probably now has a broader definition thanks to Rorty), might also care to consult the note 'On Teaching Rorty' (p. 365) which offers some brief suggestions – mainly bibliographical – as to how these philosophical responses can be put to use in the presentation of academic course material.

Rorty is not only prolific, but manages to combine 'depth' with an unusually wide range. This makes it unrealistic to try to meet with him on all fronts in a single 'gathering' of responses. Readers will soon find that I have made no such attempt here, even in the case of *Philosophy and the Mirror of Nature* itself. I have concentrated, instead, on what I take to be some key areas of that work, and then on some interesting recent developments out of its final themes. Although the reader will perhaps find this a poor substitute for additional contributions, I have tried to ensure that the scholarly apparatus of notes, references and bibliographical material provides some compensation for the more important omissions.

The well-known American philosopher Hilary Putnam (who is incidentally an admirer of Rorty) likes to remind us of Etienne Gilson's witty claim that 'Philosophy always buries its own undertakers'.[3] It would be far too complacent to invoke any such sentiments on behalf of the present responses to Rorty's thought-provoking work. Nevertheless, my pleasant task of editing them has left me convinced that they do chime well with the related but less self-satisfied contention that the best attacks on philosophy always stimulate its recuperative powers. I hope they have a similar effect on the reader.

Alan R. Malachowski

NOTES

1 Richard Rorty, *Philosophy and the Mirror of Nature*, (Princeton University Press, Princeton, 1979); Basil Blackwell, Oxford, 1980).
2 In fact, as Bernstein points out, 'Rorty's primary object of attack is *any* form of systematic philosophy which shares the conviction that there are real foundations that philosophy can discover and that philosophy as a discipline can transcend history and adumbrate a permanent neutral matrix for assessing all forms of inquiry and all types of knowledge': R. J. Bernstein, 'Philosophy in the Conversation of Mankind', in *Philosophical Profiles* (Polity Press, Cambridge, 1986), p. 39 (my emphasis).
3 See H. Putnam, 'Beyond Historicism', in *Realism and Reason: Philosophical Papers Volume 3*, (Cambridge University Press, Cambridge, 1983), p. 303.

Acknowledgements

This project has its origins in a series of seminars on Richard Rorty's *Philosophy and the Mirror of Nature* which were conducted by members of the philosophy sector in the School of Economic and Social Studies at the University of East Anglia in 1982.

Many individuals helped out at various stages, but I would particularly like to mention Tim O'Hagan, Martin Hollis, Tom Sorell, David Houghton, Nick Everitt, Angus Ross, Alan Hobbs, Sally Elloway and Blackwell's editor Stephen Chambers. Judith Sparks provided some exemplary secretarial assistance.

I owe a great deal too, of course, to each contributor; especially to Richard Rorty himself and Jo Burrows, my associate editor. All these philosophers responded efficiently, enthusiastically and often with uncanny prescience to my directives. Their combined efforts made a very challenging project easier to manage, and yet no less exciting to tackle. What more could an editor wish for?

List of Abbreviations

AT   Descartes, *Oeuvres*, ed. Adam and Tannery, Paris: Vrin, 1974.

CC   Richard Rorty, 'The Contingency of Community', *London Review of Books*, 24 July 1986.

CL   Richard Rorty, 'The Contingency of Language', *London Review of Books*, 17 April 1986.

CP   Richard Rorty, *The Consequences of Pragmatism*, Brighton: Harvester Press, 1982.

CS   Richard Rorty, 'The Contingency of the Self', *London Review of Books*, 8 May 1986.

Hall   Descartes, *Treatise on Man*, tr. Thomas Steele Hall, Cambridge, Mass.: Harvard University Press, 1972.

HR   *Philosophical Works of Descartes*, tr. Elizabeth S. Haldane and G. R. T. Ross, Cambridge: Cambridge University Press, 1972.

K   *Descartes' Philosophical Letters*, ed. and tr. A. Kenny, Oxford: Clarendon Press, 1970.

PMN   Richard Rorty, *Philosophy and the Mirror of Nature*, Princeton: Princeton University Press, 1979; Oxford: Basil Blackwell, 1982.

PON   R. Bhaskar, *The Possibility of Naturalism*, 2nd edn, Hemel Hempstead: Harvester Press, 1988.

RTS   R. Bhaskar, *A Realist Theory of Science*, 2nd edn, Brighton: Harvester Press, 1978.

SR   R. Bhaskar, *Scientific Realism and Human Emancipation*, London: Verso, 1986.

Introduction

Alan R. Malachowski

Richard Rorty had made a significant intellectual contribution to the academic community long before his *Philosophy and the Mirror of Nature* (hereafter, *PMN*) was first published in the United States in 1979.[1] However, that book marked out a very important stage in his thinking. It enabled him to marshal together a number of ideas from different areas of his earlier work, and then develop them into a comprehensive and provocative reappraisal of the cultural role of philosophy. By describing some of the ways in which its traditional concerns are embedded in *historical* contexts, and by challenging the *practical* value of these concerns, Rorty tried to undermine the idea that the academic discipline of philosophy can serve as an ultimate court of appeal in which the claims of other disciplines are adjudicated. In addition to his sustained attempts to show that philosophers are ill-suited to bear such a heavy judicial burden, Rorty used the final sections of *PMN* to sketch out a less rigid, and to his mind *more creative*, model for them to emulate. On this model, the task of the philosopher is to find interesting and useful things to say about human beings and their situation without wasting time trying to make the wishful thinking behind the old, more imperialistic, model come true. Since the publication of *PMN*, Rorty has produced a wealth of elaboration on its different facets, reiterating his case against the pretensions of 'traditional' conceptions of philosophy, and fleshing out his own alternative conception.[2]

Although Rorty is still busy reformulating his earlier ideas, and adding new ones at an impressive rate, the time is ripe for these philosophical responses to *PMN* and its aftermath. An earlier collection would perhaps have elicited too many defensive 'reflex reactions' to do justice to the far-sightedness and integrity of Rorty's views. At the present time, philosophers have had a chance to reflect on the key themes in *PMN*, and to consider where they have led Rorty in his later work. Such, at any rate, was the kind of thinking which moved me to assemble the present collection of responses.

These responses are arranged in parts which match up with Rorty's work in a fairly obvious pattern. However, for those who are not familiar with his 'post-*PMN*' output, or who prefer to have at least some idea of the geography of a book before tackling its terrain, perhaps a few words of explanation will be in order.

The first two chapters, by Tom Sorell and Bernard Williams, are, as I intimated in the *Preface*, introductory. This epithet is earned more by lucidity of prose style than by any lack of 'depth' or 'seriousness', and the reader who skims through these chapters at the outset may well gain more from them on a further reading at some later stage. Sorell leads us through the mirror theme and 'contingency' into poetry and politics, happily anticipating the structure of this book as a whole. His remarks on what it is to cause a sentence to be true will stand a second reading after checking out the chapters by Vision, Houghton and Clark. And, some study of Bhaskar's comments on Rorty and science will probably add similar interest to Sorell's treatment of that topic. Williams's chapter was originally published as a review of Rorty's *Consequences of Pragmatism*. Reprinted here with only cosmetic changes, it covers the broad relationship between the latter work and *PMN* itself in a characteristically zestful manner. Williams opens up lines of criticism and inquiry which are pursued further in many of the contributions which follow on.

The chapters in part II fit in more or less chronologically with *PMN*. Rorty presumably started with 'the mind' because that is where 'the mirror' is supposed to be, and with Descartes as an originator of the tradition he wanted to engage with. Jennifer Hornsby meets Rorty at his starting point. Although she finds a broadly congenial message in what he goes on to say about the Cartesian separation of mind and body, she thinks that the 'historical picture' conveyed by part I of *PMN* is incomplete. Her remarks on Descartes are made by way of putting some of the historical record straight, and then she moves on to suggest why Rorty has not done enough to convince us that we should completely abandon 'the whole idea of the phenomenon of mind'. John Yolton examines Rorty's 'historical picture' in some detail and with the finesse we might expect. He concentrates on the 'epistemological problematic' derived from that picture. Yolton's main aim is to 'present certain considerations about Descartes and Locke which free them from the stereotypes of mirror and veil, of an indirect representative theory of perception, and of the mind as an inner arena where "the intellect inspects entities modelled on retinal images"' (*PMN* p. 45). This takes us well into part II of *PMN*, and prepares us for Gerald Vision's foray into the heartland of the book where Rorty introduces 'Epistemological Behaviourism' and begins to 'deconstruct' modern 'theories of knowledge' and their surrogates within the philosophies of psychology and language. In much of Vision's chapter we find him wrestling with Rorty's attack on the classical Correspondence Theory of Truth, trying to pin down Rorty's views on cognition, knowledge and linguistic matters in the process. Vision concludes that Rorty's conception of 'Correspondence' is flawed, and that 'his attack fails.' Jane Heal also tackles some of Rorty's central concerns in *PMN*, but does so by taking issue with the presupposition (of 'his version of Pragmatism') that we are free to *choose* what we believe, 'free to invent and move on to new and exciting forms of discourse'. In addition, Heal disputes Rorty's interpretation of one of the 'peripheral heroes' of *PMN*: Wittgenstein.

In our third grouping of responses (part III), the focus, as suggested in the section heading, is on knowledge and language. W. V. Quine and Donald Davidson are key figures in Rorty's story of how philosophy can get back on the right (pragmatist) track where epistemological and linguistic issues are concerned. Fortunately, we have their own responses to this part of the story. Quine assesses Rorty's 'favourable account' of some of his views and proffers adjustments, clarifications and corrections. Elegant economy is the watchword here as Quine 'lets truth prevail'. In 'A Coherence Theory of Truth and Knowledge', Davidson pursues a question which he feels Rorty 'must think he [is] making a mistake in trying to answer.' This is the question of 'how, given that we cannot "get outside our beliefs and our language so as to find some test other than coherence", we nevertheless can have knowledge of, and talk about, an objective public world which is not of our making.' Then in 'Afterthoughts', Davidson looks back on 'A Coherence Theory' and suggests some ways in which the views he expressed there might be modified in response to Rorty.[3] Differences with Rorty remain, however, and no doubt the reader will enjoy seeing Davidson spell these out. My own chapter takes up the theme of epistemology again, and tries to show that Rorty's announcement of its demise is somewhat undermotivated.

David Houghton and Michael Clark round off part III with responses to Rorty's treatment of the philosophy of language and the theory of reference in particular. Rorty tends to see philosophy of language – 'the kind of philosophy which stems from Russell and Frege' – as being 'simply one more attempt to put philosophy in the position which Kant wished it to have – that of judging other areas of culture on the basis of its special knowledge of the "foundations" of these areas.' He feels that the 'emphasis on language ... does not essentially change the Cartesian-Kantian problematic, and thus does not really give philosophy a new self-image. For analytical philosophy is still committed to the construction of a permanent neutral framework for enquiry, and thus for all culture'

4 *Introduction*

(*PMN* p. 8). Houghton digs beneath the surface of this rhetoric to examine some of the micro-structure of Rorty's general approach to the philosophy of language. He argues that Rorty has not demonstrated that there is no room for 'theories of reference', and indeed, that 'the apparatus he thinks we can make do with leaves a vacuum which the philosophy of language would have to create a concept to fill were one not already available.' Like Houghton, and harking back to Vision, Clark maintains that Rorty's 'commensensical notion' of 'talking about' is inadequate in a number of ways. He then presses his case against Rorty with some further critical considerations on the dangers of conflating fiction with fact.

Finally, parts IV and V of our book deal with various themes Rorty weaves into the ending of *PMN*, and expands on his more recent writings. It is these sections which take the reader 'beyond' *PMN*.

Jacek Holówka discusses Rorty's emphasis on hermeneutics in *PMN*, and reveals some tensions between that predilection and both his 'materialist outlook' and his notion of 'moral choice'. In his ambitious chapter, Roy Bhaskar argues (*contra* Rorty) for both 'an ontologically-orientated philosophically realist account of science' and 'a critical naturalist account of the human sciences'. In addition, he runs two important subsidiary themes for us. The first amounts to something of a mini-critique of Rorty's 'positivist–instrumentalist' conception of science, while the second delves deeper into a number of the problems of 'freedom and agency' raised earlier by both Heal and Holówka. On this second front, Bhaskar holds that '*PMN* is characterised by a central tension – roughly that of Kant's "existentialist" distinction between people as empirical selves and as moral agents (*PMN* p. 382)', and that, correlatively, Rorty fails 'to sustain an adequate account of . . . freedom as involving *inter alia* emancipation from real and scientifically knowable specific constraints rather than merely the poetic redescription of an already-determined world'. For Rorty, the claim 'merely poetic' presumably constitutes a philosophical solecism encouraged by an entrenched false dichotomy between 'science' and 'literature'. Michael Fischer is a distinguished literary scholar,[4] and thus perhaps well-qualified to comment here on Rorty's 'redefinition of philosophy as literature'. Fischer argues that this 'redefinition' depends too much on an extremely unflattering appreciation of 'literary discourse' which ignores its internal 'rigour'. Indeed, Fischer takes a dim view of Rorty's whole attempt to turn the waters of philosophy into the wine of literature. He sees the danger of Rorty instigating a process of 'appropriation', whereby philosophy still 'decides the fate' of literature, and 'literature does not win; philosophy defaults.' From Fischer's 'defence' of literature against philosophical encroachment along Rortyan lines, it is a smooth transition to the elegant prose of Martin Hollis on 'The Poetics of Personhood'. Hollis deftly contends that Rorty badly needs, and yet lacks, 'a careful and constructive account of "self-creation"'. Despite various criticisms, and his conclusion that Rorty 'has painted himself into a corner' with regard to his notion of 'the self', Hollis pays a warm tribute to the way in which Rorty 'makes us see exactly why the golden age of systematic epistemology, with its confident universality, yielded to a silver age where the view of the world could only be from somewhere within it'. Charles Taylor also pays his respects to Rorty's handling of 'the mainstream epistemological tradition from Descartes to Kant', but, somewhat paradoxically (and perhaps anticipating Rorty's own reading *of him*), Taylor claims that Rorty is 'still very much prisoner of the epistemological world view' they both repudiate. He rejects Rorty's 'non-realism' and tries to, as it were 'out-metamanoeuvre him' in an intricate discussion of the sort of meta-issues Rorty is so fond of invoking.

Our last responses follow Rorty along one of the main paths he has taken since the publication of *PMN*. Rorty, himself, sets the scene with his chapter 'The Priority of Democracy to Philosophy'. Always receptive to the ideas of others, and never slow to spot potential allies, Rorty, in this instance, enlists the aid of John Rawls, the well-known author of 'A Theory of Justice'.[5] Rorty is delighted, it seems, to find Rawls claiming that 'philosophy as the search for truth about an independent metaphysical and moral order . . . cannot provide a workable and shared basis for a political conception of justice in a democratic society.'[6] Rorty takes such claims as a licence to attribute a 'thoroughly historicist . . . anti-universalist' and 'Deweyan' view to Rawls. That is to say, the kind of view which supports his own contentions that liberal democracy does not stand in need of 'philosophical foundations', and moreover, that a resolute lack of pretension in this respect might help 'make the world's inhabitants more pragmatic, more liberal, more receptive to the appeal of instrumental rationality'. In her chapter, Nancy Fraser draws our attention to the 'struggle' between Romanticism and pragmatism in Rorty's writings on the politics of post-philosophical culture. On the 'Romantic' side there are, for instance, Rorty's celebrations of the 'strong poet', 'self-creation', and 'aestheticism'. While on the other side, 'pragmatism' is clearly signalled in his preference for 'practical results' and his naturalistic ideal of 'community solidarity'. Fraser raises objections to Rorty's 'three different views of the relationship between Romanticism and pragmatism', including the private/public, or 'partition', view which he expresses here in his 'Priority' chapter and also elaborates on in his book *Contingency, irony, and solidarity*. She signs off with a sketch of her own 'recipe for an alternative combination, a democratic-socialist-feminist pragmatism'.

Rorty's liberal apologetics and his apparently insouciant approach to politics in general have provoked sharp reactions. In her contribution, Jo Burrows shows some of the reasons why. Without disputing the value of

liberalism itself, she wonders whether Rorty's stance only encourages the
tendency to appeal to liberalism as a 'world-historical alibi'[7] for com-
placency in the face of gross structural inequalities within the 'international economico-political game'. She also finds it surprising that a fan of
Nietzsche should depend on the (empirical) 'facts of the matter' for
guidance in political affairs.[8] To highlight the kind of problems she
perceives in Rorty's views, Burrows attempts to show, a shade ironically
perhaps, how they might look through the eyes of a peripheral figure she
calls 'the political contender'. Charles Guignon and David Hiley complete
our collection of responses by discussing Rorty's 'vision of the ideal liberal
democratic culture, an ideal [he] calls "postmodernist bourgeois liberalism" or "aestheticized culture"'. They admire Rorty for 'the courage,
integrity and clear-sightedness with which he bites the bullet and draws
out the inevitable consequences of anti-foundationalism for moral and
social thought.' But, at the same time, they find some of these consequences disturbing, and proceed to show us the reasons for their concern. In
doing so, they join Hollis in scrutinizing Rorty's conception of 'the self'.

I have more than once alluded to Rorty's versatility. In the present
volume this shows up in a corresponding 'variation' in the responses to his
work, and in a measure of disagreement over exactly what to criticize and
what to praise. But, one general worry unites most of the authors: that the
issues raised by the sort of philosophy Rorty attacks are not the sort of
issues which can simply be dropped from the intellectual menu. For, as
Rorty's friend and commentator Richard Bernstein puts it in the review of
PMN we referred to in the Preface, if 'we are liberated from thinking that
the issues can be resolved by an appeal to permanent epistemological
standards . . . What then? Certainly the issues do not disappear. Our task
is precisely to "hammer out" the relevant issues involved, to clarify them
and to try to sort out what are the better and worse arguments'. Rorty does
not appear to have convinced the present 'respondents' that the latter
should not continue to be one of the main tasks of philosophers.

From Sorell on Galileo and Hornsby on Descartes, to Guignon and
Hiley on Nietzsche, Heidegger and Sartre, the intellectual journey is long,
winding and progressively more adventurous. My 'snap-shots' have
provided no more than a glimpse of some of the interesting scenery along
the way, but I hope they will have given the reader an indication of how
what I earlier called 'the geography' of this book stands in relation to the
territory Richard Rorty has explored so insightfully in *Philosophy and the
Mirror of Nature* and beyond.

NOTES

1 See, for example, his articles on 'incorrigibility', transcendental arguments and the mind–body problem as listed in the bibliography of his works in the present volume.

2 Again, see the bibliography of Rorty's work towards the end of this book.

3 Cf. Richard Rorty, 'Pragmatism, Davidson and Truth', in *Truth and Interpretation*, ed. E. LePore (Basil Blackwell, Oxford, 1986).

4 See his *Does Deconstruction Make Any Difference?* (Indiana University Press, Bloomington, 1985).

5 J. Rawls, *A Theory of Justice* (Harvard University Press, Cambridge, Mass., 1971). See also N. Daniels (ed.), *Reading Rawls* (Basil Blackwell, Oxford, 1975).

6 'Justice as Fairness: Political not Metaphysical', *Philosophy and Public Affairs* 14 (1985). See also Rorty's treatment of Michael Sandel in Chapter 17 ('Priority') of the present volume.

7 The phrase is Berman's: see M. Berman, *All That is Solid Melts into Air: The Experience of Modernity* (Simon & Schuster, New York, 1982).

8 Compare Nietzsche's famous 'There are no facts, only interpretations' with Rorty's 'I think that the very idea of a "fact of the matter" is one we would be better off without' in Chapter 17 below.

Part I

An Overview and a Review

1

The World from Its Own Point of View

Tom Sorell

In *Philosophy and the Mirror of Nature*[1] Richard Rorty takes a metaphor that he thinks has captivated philosophers for a long time and tries to break its spell. He takes the metaphor of the mind as a mirror of nature – a medium for accurate representations of the world – and describes the harmful effects that it has had in philosophy up to the present day. Part of his attack is directed against the idea of accurate representation itself, particularly in the form in which it is used to explain the success of natural science. In this form the idea of accurate representation is the idea of knowledge of, or successful linguistic reference to, a reality underlying the appearances that nature presents. In another form the target of Rorty's attack is the idea that as science develops, it reveals more and more of a previously hidden nature of the world. This is a target also of Rorty's recent Northcliffe lectures.[2] In the Northcliffe lectures the idea that science reveals the world's intrinsic nature is taken as one product of a general tendency 'to see the scientist (or the philosopher, or the poet, or *somebody*) as having a priestly function, as putting us in touch with a realm which transcends the human'.

Rorty not only denies that the scientist puts us in touch with a transcendental intrinsic nature of the world; he doubts that there is an intrinsic nature of the world waiting to be discovered by science. He thinks that the idea of the world's intrinsic nature takes for granted an outmoded conception of the world as God's artefact, as 'the work of someone who has something in mind,[3] who Himself spoke some language in which He described his project'. Either the idea of the world's intrinsic nature commits us to believing in a person who made the world, or to thinking of the world itself as a person, that is, as something with a point of view and preferences about how it is described. Neither of these commitments can be welcome, Rorty suggests, which is why we should think twice about the idea which lands us with them. We should think twice about the world as the product of a divinity or as a quasi-divinity itself; we should also think twice about the idea of human nature as a quasi-divinity revealed by politics and morals. Indeed, we should cease to believe in all such higher entities. According to Rorty we should 'try to get to the point where we treat nothing as a quasi-divinity'.[4]

In this chapter I begin by taking issue with Rorty over what is involved in the idea of the world's intrinsic nature; then I ask whether it really is advisable to dispense with higher entities and, in Rorty's phrase, 'dedivinize' culture.[5] I shall suggest that Rorty caricatures the ideas he seeks to discredit and that, in particular, he gives us no very compelling reason to dispense with the idea of the world's intrinsic nature. Turning from the bad old divinity-worshipping philosophy, science and poetry to their dedivinized successors, I shall suggest that Rorty is without the resources to explain why they are better than what they replace. At the end I shall have some questions about Rorty's distinction between, on the one hand, philosophy that welcomes quasi-divinities and makes science the paradigm of human activity, and, on the other hand, a dedivinizing philosophy that takes art, in particular a certain kind of poetry, to be the pre-eminent form of culture.

I

'[O]nly if we have in mind . . . some picture of the universe as either itself a person or as created by a person', Rorty claims, 'can we make sense of the idea that the world has an intrinsic nature'.[6] In other words, only if we think of the world as a person or as created by a person can content be given to such phrases as 'what the world is like in itself' or 'the world as it objectively is'. We must either take literally talk of the point of view of the world, according to Rorty, or else not make much of objectivity. This claim is far too strong. It insinuates that the only way in which a representation of the world can be a privileged or specially accurate representation is by meshing with a supposed self-image the world has. This is to model the privileged representation of the world on the privileged representation of someone else's mental states. In the latter case it *is* a desideratum that the representation agrees with the description that the person himself would give of his mental states.

The quickest way of showing that this first-person model of the privileged representation of the world is not the only model, is by giving examples of others. One example is the model constructed by Bernard Williams in his commentary on Descartes' *Meditations*.[7] The question which leads Williams to introduce the model is this. How can representations of the world incorporate a point of view and yet be representations that give people knowledge? Knowledge is of 'what is there anyway'; but the medium of knowledge – someone's representation of the world from a certain perspective – is bound to contain things introduced by that perspective, things that are *not* 'there anyway'. From the standpoint of acquiring genuine knowledge, these subjective elements of one's perspective seem unwanted; yet, since it is always a person with a perspective who acquires knowledge, the elements seem ineradicable.

Williams notes that the presence of subjective elements does not necessarily prevent a representation of the world from providing knowledge, even when the elements make one person's representation different from another's. Knowledge may be provided despite the difference in representations, for it may be possible to stand back from the differing representations and understand how a single independent world could have given rise to both. What results from standing back is an inclusive conception that relates the representations to the world. Now, admittedly, if the more inclusive representation in its turn has a representation competing with it and both claim to give knowledge, then a yet more inclusive conception must be found. However, if at some stage in this process a representation is formed that faces no competition from a distinct conception claiming to give knowledge, then this unrivalled conception will have the strongest claim to represent the world as it really is in itself. It will have the strongest claim to play the role of what Williams calls 'the absolute conception', the conception of the reality that is 'there anyway'.

Williams describes the absolute conception without committing himself to its cogency, and since he admits that the possibility of the absolute conception may depend on the illusion that a certain representation of the world can be independent of all representation of the world, it sometimes looks as if he thinks that there is no sense to be made of it. If that thought is correct, then it may be adding obscurity to obscurity to say that the world as it is in itself is the object of the absolute conception. On the other hand, if the world as it is in itself is not the object of a representation that tries to transcend all representation, but only the object of a representation that is relatively inclusive and unrivalled, I do not see that one dark notion is being wrapped up in another. In any case, and returning now to what Rorty thinks must lie behind the idea of the world as it is intrinsically, it is clear that Williams's account does not invoke a person who creates the world or a person who is the world.

Williams's is not the only account that throws light on the idea of the world's intrinsic nature without personalizing the world or taking it to be the artifact of a person. Thomas Nagel provides another such account in describing the partially successful pursuit of objective knowledge –

knowledge of a reality beyond appearance. Nagel thinks that the aim of objective knowledge is 'naturally described in terms that, taken literally, are unintelligible; we must get outside ourselves, and view the world from nowhere within it.'[8] This is reminiscent of what Williams finds doubtful in the idea of the absolute conception – the necessity of eliminating representational character from a representation of the world. Nagel, however, thinks that his problem arises from taking a metaphor too literally:

> Since it is impossible to leave one's point of view behind entirely without ceasing to exist, the metaphor of getting outside ourselves must have a different meaning. We are to rely less and less on certain individual aspects of our point of view, and more and more on something else, less individual, which is also part of us.[9]

This something else turns out to be a rational mind, which cuts across the differences between individual human beings, and even between the human and other intelligent species. Nagel focuses on a particular capacity of such a mind, the capacity, independent of experience, to generate hypotheses about what 'in general the world might possibly be like, and the capacity to reject those possibilities that we see could not include ourselves and our experience'.[10]

Nagel believes that the rational mind has been responsible for such objective advances in human knowledge as have already been achieved. Examples of such advances illustrate what it is to proceed from one level of understanding reality to a different and better level, better in that it enables us increasingly to see what is contributed to our understanding by a world independent of us. One objective advance is embodied in the distinction between primary and secondary qualities. Prior to the drawing of this distinction the explanation of why objects appeared to have colours was that they had colours intrinsically. This naïve explanation, however, was easily shown to clash with facts about the conditions in which objects appear to change or lose colour. It resolved this conflict to suppose that objects did not have intrinsically the colours they appeared to have, but only had shape, position, number and so on, which explained their appearing as coloured to creatures with senses like ours. The new hypothesis that objects had intrinsically only their primary qualities bears all the marks of an objective advance on the hypothesis that objects have colour intrinsically. The new hypothesis said that material things objectively have shape, position, number and so on; that we are constituted to have experiences of colour when viewing material things in certain conditions; that the visual experiences can be fully explained in terms of interactions between our sense-organs and external things with primary qualities and that therefore the appearance of objects having colours intrinsically is pure appearance. In this way the more objective conception of material objects, like any other such conception, contributes to the explanation of '(1) what the world is like; (2) what we are like; (3) why the world appears to us in certain respects as it is and in certain respects as it isn't; (4) how beings like us can arrive at such a conception'.[11]

Nagel compares the new conception resulting from an objective advance with what Williams calls the absolute conception,[12] but it seems to me that Nagel's account is different from Williams's, and also better worked out. Williams thinks that the idea of the absolute conception is latent in the ordinary concept of knowledge, and that as a consequence the ordinary concept of knowledge invites philosophical scepticism. But it seems to be a mistake to look for the source of scepticism in the concept of knowledge or for that matter in any concept. The possibility of scepticism is not written into a concept but into the fact that we believe more than we have reason to believe. It is the gap between our beliefs and our grounds that invites scepticism, not the pretensions of our knowledge-ranking beliefs to be perspectiveless and objective. Nagel appreciates both points. Accordingly, he does not derive the ground of scepticism from the concept of knowledge. He derives the possibility of scepticism, like the possibility of objective knowledge, from the 'capacity to fill out the pure idea of realism with more or less definite conceptions of the world in which we are placed'.[13] Nothing in his account of objective knowledge or of an objective advance commits him to a world-person or a person who made the world. He can make sense of the world as it is intrinsically by reference to a conception that relies less and less on what is peculiar to the conceiver or to conceivers in general.

II

Williams's and Nagel's theories, then, are counter-examples to Rorty's claims about the way in which philosophers must understand the world's intrinsic nature. A third counter-example is any account that identifies the world as it really is with the world that can be described with the primitive (i.e. irreducible) referring terms of the most predictively successful scientific theory. Though this sort of account *may* be put forward with the claim that the world described in the preferred vocabulary is the world as it would describe itself – Rorty often writes as if Galileo was claiming this when he said that the Book of Nature was written in the language of mathematics – it is unclear that such a claim is essential.[14]

Rorty knows of Williams's and Nagel's theories,[15] and knows, too, I take it, that both make room for the idea of the world's intrinsic nature. But neither theory makes use of a world-creator or a world-person. Why, then, does Rorty insist that such a theory must make use of a world-creator or a world-person? The short answer, I think, is that it makes for a good story. It makes for a good story about intellectual change in the West from the seventeenth century to the twentieth. Or perhaps the right phrase is 'edifying story'.

Rorty thinks he is following Hans Blumenberg in unfolding this story, which he summarizes in the first Northcliffe lecture. The summary begins like this:

> [O]nce upon a time we felt the need to worship something which lay beyond the visible world. Beginning in the seventeenth century, we tried to substitute a love of truth for a love of God, treating the world described by science as a quasi-divinity.[16]

Here the idea of the world described by science – alias the 'world's intrinsic nature' – is supposed to be a relic of the seventeenth century. Never mind that present-day writers such as Nagel, Williams and perhaps the Putnam of the 1970s, have gone some way towards rehabilitating the idea: its heyday, according to Rorty, was a time more than 300 years ago. At least one definite stage of 'dedivinization' is supposed to have come since then: 'Beginning at the end of the eighteenth century, we tried to substitute a love of ourselves for a love of scientific truth, a worship of our deep spiritual or poetic nature, treated as one more quasi-divinity.'[17] The poetry of the eighteenth century and the science of the seventeenth century are for Rorty specimens of a single tendency, the tendency to suppose that there is a higher or divine reality not normally available to human beings, which we can have access to only with the priestly mediation of the scientist or the poet.[18]

In urging an end to the divinization of the world and ourselves, Rorty is denying that the scientist or the poet has a priestly vocation. Taking up a suggestion that he finds in Blumenberg, Nietzsche, Freud and Davidson, he says that we ought to 'try to get to the point where we no longer worship anything, where we treat nothing as a quasi-divinity, where we treat everything – our language, our conscience, our community – as products of time and chance.'[19] To treat language in the way Rorty suggests is to treat it not as some successor to the mind – a medium between the self and reality that enables the former to represent the latter – but rather, following Davidson, as a useful pairing of noises and marks between people that enables them to predict one another's behaviour.[20] To treat the self in the way Rorty suggests is to treat it in the style of Freud:

> By associating conscientiousness with cleanliness, and by associating both not only with obsessional neurosis but also . . . with the religious impulse and with the urge to construct philosophical systems, Freud breaks down all the traditional distinctions between the higher and lower, the essential and

the accidental, the central and the peripheral. He leaves us with a self that is a tissue of contingencies.[21]

As for the community – Rorty considers the community in the form of liberal democracy – the right way of treating it is not to find foundations for the values it embodies, but to provide apologetics. Thus, instead of searching for a non-circular defence of the value of freedom in a liberal democracy, one should grant that 'a circular justification which makes one feature of our culture look good by citing still another, or comparing our culture insidiously with others by reference to our own standards, is the only justification we are going to get'.[22]

III

Rorty does not exactly argue for the preferred ways of treating language, the self or the community. Instead, as he admits, he emphasizes problems and questions that he thinks will make the preferred treatments look good, and he tries to undermine the terms in which criticisms of those treatments would be put. His strategy, he says, is to try to make the objectors' vocabulary look bad.[23]

One objection that Rorty tries to undermine goes against his views about language, in particular his views about truth. The objection is that these views express relativism and irrationalism.[24] According to Rorty, this objection is only compelling if one is wedded to a vocabulary that revolves round the notions of absolute truth and rationality, a vocabulary which he thinks can be made to look bad. He inveighs against this vocabulary at considerable length in *Philosophy and the Mirror of Nature*,[25] and he repeats some of his criticisms in the Northcliffe lectures, where he attacks the claim that not only the world but truth exists independently of the human mind.

The attack is two-staged. Rorty begins by noting that it is sentences that are true and human beings who make sentences. Since sentences are human creations there is a clear sense in which, if there were no human mind there would be no bearers of truth-value, hence no truth. The second part of Rorty's attack starts by explaining why people are sometimes blind to the dependence of truth on the human mind. There is a tendency to 'run together the truth that the world sometimes causes sentences to be true or false, with the falsehood that what causes the sentence to be true is, somehow, itself true, that the world splits up, on its own initiative, into sentence-shaped chunks called facts.'[26] The idea that there is a correspondence, true sentence by true sentence, with sentence-shaped chunks of the world called facts is in turn encouraged by 'confining

attention to single sentences as opposed to vocabularies. For we often let
the world decide between alternative sentences (for example, between
"red wins" and "black wins" or between "the butler did it" and "the
doctor did it").'[27] In the case of individual sentences, then, it is easy to
make the conflation:

> But it is not so easy once we turn from individual sentences as wholes. When
> we turn to examples of alternative language-games – the vocabulary of
> ancient Athenian politics as against that of Jefferson, the vocabulary of St
> Paul as against that of Freud, the jargon of Newton versus that of Aristotle,
> the idiom of Blake rather than that of Dryden – it is difficult to think of the
> world as making one of these better than another, of the world as deciding
> between them.[28]

The reason it is difficult, according to Rorty, is that there are criteria for
the decision between 'red wins' and 'black wins' but no criteria for a
choice between vocabularies as wholes.

There is something wrong with Rorty's diagnosis of the belief that the
truth is out there, and something wrong also with his use of the distinction
between sentences and vocabularies as wholes. Rorty thinks that in
forming the belief that the truth is out there – independent of us – people
conflate the fact that the world causes sentences to be true with the fiction
that there are sentence-like things (facts) in the world. What is it, though,
for the world to cause certain sentences to be true? Rorty does not say. But
he does seem to suggest that, at the level of individual sentences, the
world's causing certain sentences to be true coincides with the world's
'deciding' in favour of one sentence rather than another. *This*, however, is
a conflation. For the world to decide that the butler did it rather than the
doctor is *not* for the world to cause the sentence 'The butler did it' to be
true. The cause of the truth of the sentence 'The butler did it' is whatever
made the butler do it, his resentment of the victim, for example. On the
other hand, what decides in favour of the truth of 'The butler did it' and
against the truth of 'The doctor did it' is the fact that the butler did it.
'Decides' in the relevant sense is a term for a semantic relation, not a
causal one, a semantic relation of making true. As for the world's deciding
between sentences, this is a matter of one sentence being made true and
another being made false by the same fact. Now, Rorty says that while the
world may decide between individual sentences, it cannot decide between
vocabularies, and on the interpretation just given of 'decides', this is true.
It is trivially true, however: the world cannot make true vocabularies (or
for that matter language-games) because vocabularies and language-games
lack truth-values.

Leaving aside the conflation of causing to be true with making true,
Rorty sometimes applies the term 'vocabularies' to the wrong things. As a

result, he underdescribes the clash between Aristotle and Newton. It is misleading to say that this clash was merely a clash of vocabularies, merely a clash between one jargon and another. It was a clash of theories, of *assertions* of certain explanations of phenomena, phrased in different vocabularies. Between different theories the world sometimes *can* decide, for example, by making the predictions of one true and of the other false.

The impression that perhaps the world cannot decide between Newton and Aristotle is encouraged by treating the difference between them as a specimen of a difference equally well illustrated by Jefferson and the Athenians, Freud and St Paul, and Blake and Dryden. But that there is not just one kind of difference is shown by the fact that Newton's and Aristotle's 'jargons' can be contrasted in terms of predictive accuracy, whereas the others cannot. No doubt it is true that a clash of vocabularies runs through Rorty's examples. Difference of vocabulary is a lowest common denominator; the point is, it may be *too* low when what is at issue is whether the world can decide between what is said in different vocabularies. No one expects the world to choose between different lexicons, but the world can and does decide between theories. The upshot of these troubles with distinctions is that it is harder than Rorty thinks to discredit the claim that the truth is out there, harder than Rorty thinks to throw doubt on the thesis that truth is discovered.

It is also harder than Rorty thinks to make attractive the rival view that truth is created. In *Philosophy and the Mirror of Nature* and *Consequences of Pragmatism*, as well as the Northcliffe lectures, the idea of redescription is central to Rorty's explanation of the view that truth is created. The sense in which we are supposed to be able to make truth is the sense in which we are able to make new bearers of truth-value out of new vocabulary. When one form of description replaces another and is used to express new truths, what happens, according to Rorty, is not that words for appearance are replaced by words for real things; there is not supposed to be some layer of fact that has been waiting to be described in, and that justifies the use of, the new vocabulary. The succession of vocabularies can have a much less involved explanation: users of the old descriptions die or cease to be listened to; something happens which makes a piece of linguistic innovation catch on. Since on this view there is no basis in the world for a given vocabulary's getting the upper hand, and since human art produces the new descriptions, including the true ones, there is a sense in which the truths are made, not found.

The most obvious objection to all of this has already been anticipated: Rorty's view fits some sorts of intellectual change better than others, and it fits such changes of scientific theory as the shift from Aristotle to Newton least well of all. Rather than to labour this objection, I want to show that Rorty's account turns out to be unappealing even when approached from an angle – a Hegelian angle – that seems at first to show it to advantage.

According to Rorty, Hegelian idealism recognizes an important aspect of cultural change, namely the way in which, in a period of innovation, the language of one innovator seems almost to be designed to lead into the ideas of another innovator. In his second Northcliffe lecture, Rorty claims that Freud's innovations made people receptive to the ideas of a host of intellectuals. It is unlikely, he says, that

> without Freud's metaphors we should have been able to assimilate Nietzsche's, James's, Wittgenstein's or Heidegger's as easily as we have, or to have read Proust with the relish we did. All of the figures of this period play into each other's hands. They feed each other lines. . . . This is the sort of phenomenon which it is tempting to describe in terms of the march of the World-Spirit towards clearer self-consciousness.[30]

Now Rorty's story is able to accommodate this phenomenon without giving it the portentous interpretation it receives from the Hegelians. The figures of the late nineteenth and early twentieth centuries play into each other's hands because they are all embarked on a similar enterprise, namely that of making literal the metaphors of an earlier age while introducing new metaphors themselves, sometimes in competition with one another. By identifying the process of intellectual change with what happens when old metaphors die and new ones take over, Rorty is able to offer a deflationary account of the development of ideas. One man's metaphors make way for the next man's, but not as part of an overall movement towards a fully conscious World-Spirit, still less to some fully accurate representation of reality. Instead, there is only an accumulation of a lot of small contingencies:[31] individuals who happen to have been born at certain times, who have been driven by certain obsessive states, who happen to have had neurons firing in response to certain random stimulations, happen to invent forms of words that are made public at the right time and place and catch on.

But this account of intellectual change may be too deflationary. If all that happens in the history of culture is that certain metaphors become literalized and displaced by new metaphors, if there is no overall purpose, for example, of revealing more and more of an independent reality or of bringing a World-Spirit to greater and greater self-consciousness, what sort of change, if any, counts as progress and why? Rorty plainly implies that the process of dedivinization has been progress, but when it comes to the question of why, he may be unable to go beyond saying that the metaphors that have contributed to divinization have gone stale – as if the development of culture consisted of so many solutions to a recurring problem of boringness in styles of description. This seems an unsatisfactory account.

In a way the problem is foreshadowed in Rorty's treatment of edifying philosophy in *Philosophy and the Mirror of Nature*. The point of edifying philosophy, he says, is to try to keep going a conversation that normal philosophy tries to cut short. He admits that there can be more than one point to keeping the conversation going. One point is to expose the failure of a past philosophy to do what it set out to do: one keeps the conversation going in order to succeed where the old philosophy did not. This is the point of what Rorty calls 'systematic and revolutionary' philosophy.[32] But another purpose is served by revolutionary and edifying philosophers, who are 'reactive and offer satires, parodies, aphorisms. They know their work loses its point when the period they were reacting against is over. They are *intentionally* peripheral.'[33] This type of peripheral philosophy, which simultaneously unsettles and revives a discourse which tries to be conclusive, has, if I understand Rorty, exact counterparts in strong poetry, revolutionary politics, morals and science, all of the things which keep culture alive. The question is, keep culture alive for what? keep the conversation going for what?

Rorty says in *Philosophy and the Mirror of Nature* that the edifying philosophers uphold the value of the infinite striving for truth over 'all of truth',[34] and this seems to me to suggest a point of keeping the conversation going, perhaps even of keeping culture alive. But it is unclear that Rorty can agree that this is a point or the point, and yet hold also that philosophy and culture have no overall aim. Plenty of passages in the Northcliffe lectures, especially the first, suggest that Rorty does not believe in such an overall aim. He thinks of the history of culture not as so many partially successful instalments in an enterprise unified by a global purpose, but as a series of enterprises with local purposes unified only by time, chance and the process by which metaphors at first disrupt a discourse and then settle down in it. On this preferred view of culture its history has a lot in common with the evolutionary history of biological species, which we have also come to understand as a sequence of accidents. I admit that if Rorty's view of culture is accepted, then there is a strong analogy between its evolution and biological evolution; but I do not understand why this analogy should seem liberating to Rorty. To the extent it seems to rule out a purpose that intellectuals perennially have in innovating as they do, the analogy seems disabling. However good they are at explaining how culture moves, time and chance seem insufficient for explaining how culture moves *forward*.

IV

Rorty says that in abandoning the vocabulary of accurate representation, intrinsic natures and the rest, he is indicating an allegiance to a poetic as against a scientific culture. This allegiance and Rorty's way of describing it raise a number of questions with which I should like to conclude. First, how stable is the distinction between poetry and science and the co-ordinate distinction between discovering truth and inventing truth? Second, can Rorty's dedivinized conception of poetry – his conception of poetry as the outcome of time and chance – be squared with his belief that poets are active in the process that results in poetry? Third, can the politics of a poetic culture really be as staid as liberal politics?

(1) To readers of *Consequences of Pragmatism* Rorty's distinction in the Northcliffe lectures between poetry and science is familiar as a variation on the distinction between literary and scientific culture, which he adapts from C. P. Snow. Snow's distinction proves useful to Rorty in classifying different styles of philosophy, and different styles of intellectual work generally. In applying it Rorty tends to mark not just a difference but an antagonism between the scientific and the literary, and he tries to promote an outcome of the antagonism which leaves literature in the dominant, and science in the subservient, position. Why the tension between the two cultures cannot end up in some sort of accommodation – for example, in good science fiction or in a *genre* of literary science (arguably pioneered already by Primo Levi) – is never made clear. It seems that Rorty is so keen to overturn the usual ranking of science over literature that he never wonders whether the antagonism between science and literature is deep after all.

On the other hand, the distinctions that Rorty uses to spell out the antagonism have the unintended effect of weakening it. Thus the distinction between the practice of redescription (literary) and the practice of revealing the contours of an external reality (scientific), which Rorty evidently takes for a firm distinction, turns out to be frail because redescription can be for the *purpose* of revealing the contours. The redescription in primary-quality vocabulary of facts stated in secondary-quality vocabulary is a case in point. Again, and now ignoring the alleged tension between revealing and redescribing, isn't it just a fact that there is a variety of prose and poetry, by no means yet extinct, that is realistic or dedicated to realism, that tries to reveal reality as it is? If so, isn't this further evidence of the softness of the poetry/science or literature/science distinction?

(2) Rorty takes a dim view of divinizing poetry – poetry that assumes that it is mediating between human beings and their intrinsic nature. He prefers dedivinizing poetry, which knows that intrinsic natures are illusory and which accepts itself as the product of time and chance. In his second Northcliffe lecture Rorty is trying to give a description of poetry in the spirit of dedivinization when he indicates how slight a dividing line there is between what is called 'fantasy' and what is called 'poetry'. It is a mistake to suppose that poetry reveals something universal and real whereas fantasy reveals something private and unreal. Rather, poetry is a species of fantasy, but one that means something to a whole community in the way that a mere humdrum fantasy means something only to an individual. That a fantasy does mean something to a community – that it catches on – is an accident, according to Rorty, a coincidence of a private obsession with a public need.[35]

One question about this story is whether it only banishes one divinity to introduce another. Even if we accept that poetry is not distinguished from fantasy by getting at or expressing something real and universal – an intrinsic nature of the human being – we may feel dissatisfied with the suggestion that amazing coincidence makes the fantasy answer a public need. If someone is *that* lucky with his fantasy, it might be thought, someone up there has to like him, maybe even use him to speak through. On the other hand, if coincidence is all that it is, and poetry is only fantasy welling up and being expressed at the right time, can the poet really be the figure that makes truth or that makes anything? Might not a fantasy over which someone has no control suggest a metaphor that catches on? If so, then the poet is only a vehicle for a metaphor rather than its inventor. Either the poet's work is inspired – a case of the gods speaking through him – or a case of a psychopathology working itself out. Where in all of this is there room for what Rorty so firmly contrasts with discovery, namely making or invention?

(3) My last question is raised by what Rorty implies in his third Northcliffe lecture, namely that in some sense *liberalism* and the poetic culture are made for one another. He writes that 'liberal politics is best suited to a culture whose hero is the strong poet rather than the truth-seeking, "logical", "objective" scientist'.[36] The reason, if I understand Rorty, is that, 'it is central to the idea of a liberal society that, in respect of words as opposed to deeds, persuasion as opposed to force, anything goes'.[37] Rorty thinks this means that no topics of discussion, and no vocabulary for conducting this discussion, no agenda for discussion, are able to be ruled out in advance. In particular, he seems to think that for liberals there is no outlawing a contribution or a vocabulary on the ground that it is illogical, inconsistent or that it breaks with an order of introducing topics agreed in advance. 'That would be just the sort of society which liberals are trying to avoid – one in which "logic" (and,

perhaps, philosopher kings) ruled and rhetoric were outlawed'.[38]

To say that liberalism tolerates many forms of persuasion, however, is *not* to say that according to liberalism anything goes. *Not* anything goes, because not all forms of speech can be interpreted as persuasive speech. In particular, it is unclear that the particular *outré* forms of speech Rorty so admires in philosophy can be recognized as persuasive. Rorty confuses the real invitation that liberalism extends to different forms of persuasive speech with an imaginary invitation liberalism is supposed to extend to different vocabularies. The latter invitation is far wider than the former, and only the former seems to be derivable from liberalism. 'Anything goes so long as it is in the sphere of persuasion' does not mean that anything goes so long as it is in the sphere of words or that any new vocabulary deserves an encounter with a going vocabulary. To put it another way, it is only the upshots of certain linguistic encounters that liberalism takes to matter to truth. Encounters between arguments fit the bill; encounters between language-games do not. They are at the wrong level of generality. In any case, it would have been odd if liberalism had been made for the poetic culture. Rorty's picture of this culture as one in which new linguistic forms are continually killing off old ones, seems better suited to a politics of permanent revolution than to liberalism.

Rorty has yet to make us see clearly the distinctive characteristics of the poetic culture, let alone its distinctive charms. Until our vision of their successors is improved, we should not abandon the old divinities.

NOTES

1   Richard Rorty, *Philosophy and the Mirror of Nature* (Basil Blackwell, Oxford, 1980).
2   The three lectures, under the titles 'The Contingency of Language', 'The Contingency of Selfhood' and 'The Contingency of Community', were published in *London Review of Books*, vol. 8, on 17 April 1986, 8 May 1986 and 24 July 1986, respectively.
3   Rorty, 'The Contingency of Language', p. 6.
4   Ibid.
5   Ibid.
6   Ibid.
7   Bernard Williams, *Descartes: The Project of Pure Equity* (Penguin, Harmondsworth, 1978), pp. 64–5.
8   Thomas Nagel, *The View from Nowhere* (Oxford University Press, Oxford, 1986), p. 67.
9   Ibid.
10 Ibid., p. 83.
11 Ibid., p. 74.
12 Ibid., p. 70.
13 Ibid., pp. 70–1.
14 See Richard Rorty, 'Method, Social Science and Social Hope', reprinted in *Consequences of Pragmatism* (Harvester, Brighton, 1982), ch. 11.
15 See *Consequences of Pragmatism*, p. 190, n. 4.
16 Rorty, 'The Contingency of Language', p. 6.

17 Ibid.
18 Ibid.
19 Ibid.
20 Ibid., p. 5.
21 Rorty, 'The Contingency of Selfhood', p. 12.
22 Rorty, 'The Contingency of Community', p. 13.
23 Ibid., p. 10.
24 Ibid.
25 Ch. 6, pp. 277–311. A complementary discussion occurs at pp. 322–32.
26 Rorty, 'The Contingency of Language', p. 3.
27 Ibid.
28 Ibid.
29 Examples of Rorty's over-assimilation of science to other intellectual activities are also to
    be found in *Mirror of Nature*, pp. 340–1, and *Consequences of Pragmatism*, p. 192.
30 Rorty, 'The Contingency of Selfhood', p. 14.
31 Rorty, 'The Contingency of Language', p. 6.
32 Rorty, *Mirror of Nature*, p. 369.
33 Ibid.
34 Ibid., p. 377.
35 Rorty, 'The Contingency of Selfhood', p. 14.
36 Rorty, 'The Contingency of Community', p. 11.
37 Ibid.
38 Ibid.

2

Auto-da-Fé: Consequences of Pragmatism

Bernard Williams

Richard Rorty's *Philosophy and the Mirror of Nature* is an original and sustained attack on the idea that it can be the aim of philosophy, or even of science, to represent the world accurately. Neither activity can reveal, as he sometimes puts it, a vocabulary in which the world demands to be described. The book is remarkable for its learning and for its powers of critical exposition. At the same time, some of it is slapdash, and its programme for what philosophy should do when robbed of its traditional conceptions of truth and objectivity is, to put it mildly, schematic.

The Consequences of Pragmatism consists of twelve already published essays written between 1972 and 1980, together with a new introduction. The jacket says that it fills in the details of the story told in *Philosophy and the Mirror of Nature*, but it actually does something more interesting than that. It reveals Rorty's attitude towards questions bearing on the central theories of the earlier book, and offers his view of other philosophers and traditions, including Heidegger, about whom he says that he would now want to revise his view upward. The essays here also have a hero, who was less explicitly seen as one in *The Mirror of Nature*. This is John Dewey; and the pragmatism of the title is above all that of Dewey.

Rorty claims to free Dewey from dated associations, and to find him already waiting at the end of a road on which Michel Foucault and Jacques Derrida are now travelling. Dewey's 'chief enemy' Rorty writes, 'was the notion of Truth as accuracy of representation, the notion later to be attacked by Heidegger, Sartre, Foucault. Dewey thought that if he could break down this notion ... we would be receptive to notions like Derrida's – that language is not a device for representing reality but a reality in which we live and move.'

The new book shares some failings with *The Mirror of Nature*, and at the end we still do not know much about how philosophy should go on without its old illusions. Rorty's style also provides some minor irritations, such as his tendency to parade lists of great names and of turning points in the history of philosophy (something that could be a legacy from his early days at the University of Chicago). But the essays are wide-ranging, informed and above all interesting. Rorty has an unsettling vision of philosophy, science and culture, and it matters to what extent he is right. Like others who have a large view, he sometimes seems to the analytical critic to have run different questions together. What is not always true in such cases, but is usually true of Rorty, is that when he has run different questions together each of them turns out to have its own interest.

'It is impossible to step outside our skins – the traditions, linguistic and other, within which we do our thinking and self-criticism – and compare ourselves with something absolute.' That is one of Rorty's central theses. Or, rather, it is several theses. The least contentious is that we cannot think about the world without describing it in some way: the world cannot present itself uncategorized. Moreover, there is no way in which the world simply describes itself, or presents itself in terms that could not them- selves be the subject of inquiry, reflection and alternative proposals. Those claims, in themselves, are not too upsetting. They still allow us to think that there is an independent world that we are trying to describe, and that what it is actually like can control the success of our descriptions.

Rorty's pragmatist, however, reaches much more drastic conclusions than this, and claims (so it seems) that all we can ever do is compare one description with another. He denies that 'deep down beneath all the texts, there is something which is not just one more text but that to which various texts are trying to be "adequate"'. He does not think that we can say anything substantial about the purposes served by our descriptions, against which we might test them. Moreover, in addition to this, Rorty has a further, historicist thesis, according to which the categories that any human group uses are a function of its time, and are essentially formed through historically localized tradition. The historicist thesis plays a large part both in *The Mirror of Nature* and in the present essays.

If one says that any human thought is inescapably immersed in the traditions of its period, what counts as 'a period' is an important question; and, in particular, what tradition performs this basic function for us. Rorty is not very definite about this. In *The Mirror of Nature* sometimes it is the period of 'Western man' or 'modern Western man'. In the present book the relevant item, at least once, is 'human thought since 1600'. The question particularly presses, because Rorty is so insistent that we cannot, in philosophy, simply be talking about human beings, as opposed to human beings at a given time. In the course of a perceptive discussion of Thomas Nagel and Stanley Cavell, both philosophers who (in different terms) hope to recover from the tradition deep philosophical questions that relate to human experience as such, Rorty precisely contrasts the approach of taking some philosophical problem and asking, as they might, 'What does it show us about *being human*?' and asking, on the other hand, 'What does the persistence of such problems show us about *being twentieth-century Europeans*?' (original emphases).

The historicist ideas do provide one fairly natural way of interpreting Rorty's main thesis, but they do not merely follow from it, even in its most radical form. Basically, he accepts the historicist outlook because he believes that the history of philosophy has itself led us to it. He thinks that Dewey, Quine, Wittgenstein, Heidegger and Derrida are the true descendants in their various styles of Hegel and the nineteenth-century philosophers who reacted against the Kantian claim that philosophy could discover 'the a priori structure of any possible inquiry'. As he interprets them, they have led us to see that there is not much more to be said about the ways in which we describe the world than that they are the ways that suit us, now. Of course philosophy, traditionally, has tried to say more than that. It has tried to overcome what it has seen as deep and persistent problems about the relation of our thought and action to the world. For Rorty these writers have, accordingly, led us to a point at which traditional philosophy should end.

Sometimes Rorty takes a slightly different turn in his insistence on historical self-consciousness and in his rejection of general groundings for his or any other method. That we should see philosophy and other intellectual activities in the way he commends is not a lesson of where we have come to in history – something that we should rationally conclude from it – but simply a product of that history. We are where we now are, and that is how we, now, go on.

Rorty is not a relativist. He has as crisp a view as any positivist in agreeing, for instance, that it was a good thing that the world that was based on religious conceptions and authority has passed, and he cheerfully describes a certain attitude as 'merely a relic of pre-Galilean anthropomorphism'. But is he really in a position to dismiss relativism and the problems associated with it, as he does in one essay? The sort of dialectic in which Rorty's self-conscious historicism places him is one in which everyone can try to undercut everyone else by asking others whether they have allowed for the ways by which their own consciousness has evolved the very thesis they are advancing. Self-consciousness and reflective awareness, when made into *the* distinctive attitude of a sophisticated philosophy, make it revolve ever faster; the owl of Minerva, robbed by later scepticism of Hegel's flight plan to the transcendental standpoint, notoriously finds itself flying in ever-decreasing circles.

Rorty's procedures, in these respects, are an odd mixture. Sometimes he seems quite knowing about the status of his own thoughts (though he is not as quick on the turn as the French writers, such as Derrida, whom he most admires, or as the poststructuralist critics are, who need these reflexes to keep alive). At other times, he seems to forget altogether about one requirement of self-consciousness, and like the old philosophies he is attempting to escape, naïvely treats his own discourse as standing quite outside the general philosophical situation he is describing. He thus neglects the question whether one could accept his account of various intellectual activities, and still continue to practice them.

Some of the nastier problems of this sort arise with his treatment of the natural and biological sciences. Rorty's characteristic tone about science is that there is nothing in the least special or particularly interesting about it.

> Pragmatism . . . does not erect Science as an idol to fill the place once held by God. It views science as one genre of literature – or, put the other way around, literature and the arts as inquiries on the same footing as scientific inquiries. . . . Physics is a way of trying to cope with various bits of the universe; ethics is a matter of trying to cope with other bits.

In a similar vein he says, in an article called 'Method, Social Science, and Social Hope', that it simply turned out that the Galilean picture of the universe worked better than, say, an Aristotelian picture, but that there is no 'epistemological moral' to be drawn from this. In particular, he argues, it is a confusion to think that the success of physics since Galileo is somehow connected with the fact that it regards the universe as 'infinite and cold and comfortless', and it is a mistake to look for any scientific method that explains scientific success. Indeed, the question 'What makes science so successful?' is for him a bad question. He applauds T. S. Kuhn's notion of Galilean science 'as exemplifying the power of new vocabularies rather than offering the secret of scientific success.'

In the essay just referred to, and to a lesser degree in *The Mirror of Nature*, Rorty runs together two questions. One is whether the success of science invites or permits any interesting description of what the success of science *consists of*. The other question is whether, from its previous success, we can derive any general methods to secure its future success. The questions are distinct. Karl Popper, for instance, who, like Rorty, thinks that there is not much to be said about the second question beyond banal recipes of rational procedure, also believes, unlike Rorty, that there is something to be said about the objective progress of science in finding out what the world is really like.

It is harder than Rorty supposes to throw away conceptions of the *aim* of science such as Popper's, and it is harder in more than one way. It is harder, first of all, because it is not clear what Rorty wants us to put in their place. Science 'copes', 'is successful', its vocabularies have 'power'; but they have power or success in doing what? In generating predictions, Rorty is sometimes rash enough to say, and that means better predictions. Here we find we are being taken on an old-fashioned philosophical ride. Doesn't 'better' mean, for instance, 'true'? On Rorty's view there is no point in getting off at that stop: 'Truth is simply a compliment paid to sentences seen to be paying their way.' But what is it that we see when we see that they are paying their way?

This is a very old subject of debate, and it is still going on in orthodox analytical philosophy. Rorty's pragmatist does not want to win that debate or to continue it, but rather to opt out of the whole thing, to change the subject. Some analytical philosophers will say that he *can't* do that. But Rorty is surely right in saying that much philosophical achievement has consisted simply in changing the subject, and if the pragmatist changes this subject, he changes it.

To me the weakness of Rorty's position lies in something else, that he sees all this as a matter simply for *philosophy*; he sees changing the subject as making a move within, or out of, philosophy. This seriously neglects the extent to which the descriptions that he dislikes come from within science itself. Science itself moves the boundaries of explanation and of what is explained, just as it moves the boundary of what counts as observation. It was always a mistake for philosophers to contrast in any absolute way the 'observable' and the 'theoretical' in science, since theory creates and constitutes new forms of observation. Scientific theory explains, moreover, how such an elaborately constructed image as an electron micrograph can be the record of an observation.

The sharp distinction between theory and observation was a mistake made by Rorty's enemies, the positivists, who celebrated science for its respect for brute facts. But such criticisms of the positivists turn against Rorty himself, because they are an example of something which, it seems, he should regard as impossible, namely of science explaining the reliability of its own observations. Similarly science can often explain the truth of its conjectures. Advances in scientific theory quite often, in fact, involve explaining why some predictions of previous theories were true, while others failed. Not all scientific advance does that – no recipe fits all scientific advance – but it is one important phenomenon that gives substance to the idea of objective scientific advance.

More generally, it is an important feature of modern science, not mentioned by Rorty, that it makes some contribution to explaining how science itself is possible, and how creatures that have the origins and characteristics it says we have can understand a world that has the properties it says the world has. To say that such achievements as evolutionary biology and the findings of the neurological sciences, for example, are trivial, and that any old theory could do what they do, is simply a mistake (though it is true that limitless numbers of theories could deal with the same questions trivially). These ideas contribute, *from within scientific reflection itself*, to an image of the objects of science which Rorty says we should not have; they contribute, that is, to a conception of the world as it is, independently of our enquiries. That conception may be an illusion, but if it is, it is not the product of a simple philosophical error to be explained in a line or two of reference to Kant and his successors; and, above all, it is not simply a product of philosophy.

Correspondingly, it is not just a question of philosophy whether it is hard to give up that conception of the world. The other sense in which it will prove hard to give up is one in which it will be hard to give it up even if it is an illusion. It will be hard to give up for those working in science.

There is an important contrast here, which Rorty seems not to see, between scientific enquiry on the one hand and Rorty's interesting ideas about the future of philosophy. In a revealing passage he says that 'pragmatism denies the possibility of getting beyond the ... notion of "seeing how things hang together" – which, for the bookish intellectual of recent times, means seeing how all the various vocabularies of all the various epochs and cultures hand together.' That may be a programme for the successor of philosophy, or for the literary studies from which he does not want that successor to be distinct, but it is certainly no programme for science. The sense that one is not locked in a world of books, that one is confronting 'the world', that the work is made hard or easy by what is actually there – these are part of the driving force, the essential conscious-ness of science; and even if Rorty's descriptions of what science really is are true, they are not going to be accepted into that consciousness without altering it in important ways – almost certainly for the worse, so far as the progress of science is concerned.

But if that is so, then a dreadful problem confronts the pragmatist: whether his ideas can be, in their own terms, 'true' at all. For the pragmatist to say that his formulations are true presumably means simply that they work out: and what reasons have we to think that the pragmatists' sentences about science will work out better in the practice of scientists than scientists' sentences do? The point here is not that scientists have self-revealing knowledge of what they are up to, but merely that the scientists' sentences help to keep them going – and that, for the pragmatist, is all that can matter.

Indeed, there is a question whether the pragmatist can even appropr-iately *say* many of the things that Rorty says. Here there is a problem that was seen more clearly by Wittgenstein than by any of the other philosophers whom Rorty admires, certainly more clearly than by Rorty himself. If it is impossible to provide grounds for, or get beyond, what, at a very general level, we naturally say; and if philosophy, as traditionally understood, tried to go beyond that, and so should now end; why should it not *simply* end, so that all we should say is what anyway we naturally say? In *The Mirror of Nature* there are passages to the effect that we have merely found it overwhelmingly 'convenient' to say that physics describes a world which is already there, rather than, for instance, that the world changes in relation to our descriptions. But if that is overwhelmingly convenient, and the only consideration can be what is convenient, then what everyone should be saying is simply: physics describes a world that is already there. So why does Rorty go on telling us *not* to say that?

Here the Rortian pragmatist, like the follower of Wittgenstein, is likely to say something to the effect that without the startling reminders he provides one may be misled, and succumb to false images of our situation. Misled by what? The answer often is – by philosophy, or by similarly irresponsible kinds of discourse. Wittgenstein often gives this answer (though he also gives the materials for some better ones): it is what underlies his famous remark that philosophy occurs 'when language goes on holiday', a remark which, one might say, is, like some others of his, deeply shallow. In fact, the 'misleading' impressions are encouraged not just by philosophy but by such activities as pursuing physics. So unless science itself is revealed as an unnatural or holiday activity, it is part of our nature, and not simply a product of philosophy, that we should be 'misled'.

But then there is a real problem of what content is left, on the pragmatist's assumptions, to saying that we are *misled* at all, and of what basis he can have for saying it, unless he tries to reoccupy the kind of transcendental standpoint, outside human speech and activity, that is precisely what he wants us to renounce.

There is, then, more than one question about how to read Rorty's descriptions of scientific activity, if we accept his view of what such descriptions can be. There is a different set of problems about the self-understanding, and the future, of philosophy. The problems are different, in particular, because Rorty expects science to continue – its 'discoveries form the basis of modern scientific civilization. We can hardly be too grateful for them.' But philosophy should come to an end; or rather, as he often puts it, 'Philosophy' should, where the upper case stands for philosophy as a distinct *Fach* or professional undertaking. There will be room for a kind of post-Philosophical philosophy, a kind of cultural criticism, for which there is no very special expertise. Occasionally Rorty's speculations about the future of this activity strike a Marxian-utopian note; the non-professional inheritor of Philosophy will be a new Renaissance polymath doing literary criticism in the morning and history in the afternoon, and doing them in a spirit of Nietzschean gaiety.

Yet here again there is a problem about how this activity is supposed to co-exist with a consciousness of its own nature. It is hard to see how these new forms of intellectual life can thrive for long, when they are at the same time so professedly second-order, derivative and parasitic on the activities of those in the past who have taken themselves to be doing Philosophy in its own right. 'Philosophers could be seen as people who work with the history of philosophy and the contemporary effects of those ideas called "philosophic" upon the rest of culture.' The reference to the history of philosophy, and the quotes around 'philosophic', immediately reveal the inherited identity that backs up this image. Even the Nietzschean gaiety relates to the use of these figures of the past; it is with approval, I think, that he says of Derrida (one of those who recognize where we really are) that he 'does not want to comprehend Hegel's book; he wants to play with Hegel'.

I doubt, in fact, whether Rorty has extracted from the ruins, as he sees it, of Philosophy any activity that will sustain a post-Philosophical culture of the kind that he sketches. It is not very realistic to suppose that we could for long sustain much of a culture, or indeed keep away boredom, by playfully abusing the texts of writers who believed in an activity which we now know to be hopeless.

Rorty's views, however, affect more than the future of philosophy considered as a distinct activity. They raise important questions about the significance for culture in general of certain intellectual ideals – above all, a certain image of truthfulness – which philosophy, in some of its styles, particularly cultivates.

One of Rorty's aims is to overcome the division between scientific and literary culture; he refers surprisingly often to the late Lord Snow, associating with him various distinctions that are considerably subtler than any that occurred to Snow himself. At the same time, he wants to overcome the divide between two kinds of contemporary philosophy, broadly called 'analytical' and 'Continental'. I have already said that so far as the future of culture is concerned, the first of these aims is not going to be realized in Rorty's terms, since the business of engaging in scientific research, and the intellectual motivations that people have for doing so, are so totally unlike making comparisons within a web of texts that even if (in some sense that Rorty still needs to explain) that is what science *really* is, the activity will, so long as it flourishes, reject that description of itself.

But that was a point about describing the aims of science, not of adopting a specific methodology, and even if science successfully continues with the conception of itself as discovering what is really there – if, that is to say, science continues – this leaves open most questions about its connections with any wider cultural or social conceptions of rationality. Here the other divide, between the two kinds of philosophy, comes into the picture. There is something in what Rorty says when he claims that analytical philosophy and Continental philosophy have been the public-relations agencies of science and of literature respectively.

There is something in it, though much is left out. Positivism apart, analytical philosophy has not been committed to the supremacy of science, or to validating science's laudatory images of itself, and all of this Rorty himself explains very well, both here and in *The Mirror of Nature*. But it is certainly true that the discourse of analytical philosophy, its argumentative procedures, are more continuous with those of scientists. It seems to its practitioners more responsible, more consequential, less open to arbitrariness, whimsicality and rhetoric than other styles of philosophy, and I suspect that it seems so to scientists as well, in so far as it does not seem to them, along with most other philosophy, merely pointless.

If Rorty is right, there is nothing to these contrasts at all, and analytical philosophy's claim to greater intellectual virtue of a kind that has some general cultural significance, is simply baseless. It merely mistakes articulateness for clarity of perception and argumentativeness for rationality. It derives no prestige from its relation to science, both because there is no methodology that it can share with science, and because science isn't in any case what this philosophy generally thinks science is. Its characteristic neglect of the imagination is not a contribution to objectivity but a self-inflicted limitation. If analytic philosophy is like anything else at all, it most resembles the activities of lawyers under an adversarial system, and its admired skills are mainly the forensic skills of courtroom debate.

'Forensic' might be thought at least minimally a compliment, but the complimentary element is missing. Granted a legal system, forensic practices can be thought to assist justice. But without any analogous system of rules, without any accepted standards of argument and evidence, the forensic practices of philosophy will be left, for Rorty, only with the worst aspects of the adversarial system. Thus analytical philosophy is not more rationally organized than any other sort of philosophy; it merely employs a different kind of rhetoric, and uses different methods to bully opponents.

Rorty has made a vigorous and entirely serious challenge, which raises a question more important than merely how to do philosophy. That question can never in the end be that important, and Rorty himself criticizes some philosophers he admires, such as Heidegger, for overrating the significance of philosophy itself for civilization. But the value of philosophical styles of argument go beyond the value of philosophy, because of the virtues that they try to express. No one has to believe that the questions of philosophy are the most important questions there are, or that philosophy can discover what mankind should be doing. But analytical philosophy does hold that it offers a very abstract example of certain virtues of civilized thought: because it gives reasons and sets out arguments in a way that can be explicitly followed and considered; and because it makes questions clearer and sorts out what is muddled.

On this view, analytical philosophy asserts important freedoms, both to pursue the argument and, in its more imaginative reaches, to develop alternative pictures of the world and of human life. It is both a creative activity and an activity pursued under constraints – constraints experienced as, among others, those of rational consistency. Its experience of those constraints, and the terms in which it approves those who most imaginatively work within them, is one where its spirit overlaps with the sciences. Both in this philosophy and in the sciences, the ideal is the old Socratic ideal that mere rhetoric and the power of words will not prevail.

This is the image of philosophy and its virtues that Rorty radically criticizes. He seems to me, however, very unradical and excessively optimistic in his picture of an intellectual community that has got rid of this image. Certain 'conversational constraints' (of roughly Habermas's kind; he does not say much about them) will keep things together as much as anything ever does, and we shall just have to do whatever we can to sustain traditions of open-mindedness and receptiveness to new considerations. He does not want us to get too excited or unnerved by, for instance, Foucault's vision of discourse as a network of power relations. '"Power" and "culture"', he writes, 'are equipollent indications of the social forces which make us more than animals – and which, when the bad guys take over, can turn us into something worse and more miserable than animals.' *When the bad guys take over*: there are at least four different ways of intelligibly stressing the words in that phrase, and each of them expresses an equally shallow way of thinking about what happens to a society when rational civility collapses.

No more than in *The Mirror of Nature* does Rorty give many indications of how discourse should go on when freed of the illusions of truth and objectivity. In the general cultural context, he is just as optimistically neglectful as he was in the case of science about the effects of everyone's coming to believe what he has to say – effects which the pragmatist, least of all, can afford to neglect. But that still does not mean that he is wrong, except possibly by his own standards of what it is to be wrong, and his challenge to the standing of what analytical philosophy calls clarity and rationality remains one to be taken seriously.

His kind of questioning has great force in a field that he himself does not take up, that of moral philosophy. Analytical moral philosophy has now revived the activity of theorizing about what is right and wrong rather than merely analyzing ethical terms. What this activity urgently requires, and has never yet managed to provide, is some coherent understanding of the relations of such theory to practice, where this includes the relations of the theorists to the rest of society. In the work of such philosophers as Peter Singer, it seems merely to be assumed that the virtues of an intellectual theory, such as economy and simplicity, translate into a desirable rationality of social practice. That represents a Platonic rationalism of the most suspect kind. There is no advance guarantee of ways in which humane and just social practices may relate to philosophical theory of any sort. That is just one application of the question that Rorty rightly presses, of the relations between the discursive virtues of analytical philosophy on the one hand, and desirable forms of social rationality on the other.

These essays along with *The Mirror of Nature* should encourage philosophers, and not only philosophers, to ask and pursue that question. There are lessons to be learnt from the new and unexpected forms in which Rorty puts the question. There is also something to be learnt from the weak parts of his account. The two major weak points are the inadequacy (certainly the pragmatic inadequacy) of his account of science, and the very weak indications that he gives of the nature of a post-Philosophical culture. Perhaps this double weakness expresses a strength in the traditional idea that philosophy and science can share a conception of truthfulness that is not merely an application of the will to power.

An account of the relation of science to culture should still start, it seems to me, from that impression which so powerfully affects its practitioners, and which is so dismissively treated by Rorty: that science offers one of the most effective ways in which we can be led out of the web of texts, the archive of discourse in which Rorty finds himself imprisoned along with the 'bookish intellectuals of recent times'. In his optimistic dealings with Foucault, Rorty quotes the dreadful sentence 'Man is in the process of perishing as the being of language continues to shine ever brighter upon our horizon.' I suspect that unless we keep the sense (cherished but misinterpreted by empiricism) that science finds ways out of the cell of words, and if we do not recover the sense that pursuing science is one of our essential experiences of being constrained by the truth, we shall find that the brightness of language on the horizon turns out to be that of the fire in which the supremely bookish hero of Canetti's *Auto-da-Fé* immolated himself in his library.

NOTES

This essay is reprinted with permission from *The New York Review of Books*. Copyright ©
1983 Nyrer, Inc.

Part II

Mirrors, Mind and Truth

3

Descartes, Rorty and The Mind–Body Fiction

Jennifer Hornsby

Philosophers, having invented the mind, discovered some mind–body problems; then, relatively recently, they created the philosophy of mind. If we could gain the proper perspective, of historical contingency, on the mind's invention, then we should no longer feel that we needed solutions to mind–body problems. We should settle for materialism, but not the sort of philosophical materialism that has been fashioned in opposition to Cartesian dualism.

This is the message I read in the first two chapters of *Philosophy and the Mirror of Nature*.[1] As I have expressed it, in broadest outline, I find it congenial: I agree with Rorty that many of those who have fought against Cartesian dualism have failed to realize that the battles have always taken place on territory of the enemies' making. But I believe that something different from what Rorty insists on will be involved in liberating ourselves from the oppressive forces of traditional conceptions of mind. In this paper I shall try to bring out the manner in which the historical picture in Part I of Rorty's book seems to me to be partial. Lacking Rorty's command of the history, I cannot even try to present a complete picture myself. But I shall say some things about Descartes in order to make a suggestion about what I think is kept hidden by Rorty.

I

Rorty thinks that issues about materialism versus dualism would take care of themselves if only we could free ourselves from habitual ways of viewing the putative problems of the philosophy of mind. But he endorses a version of materialism himself – materialism without identities, as he calls it. It is supported partly by way of a thought-experiment about the

Antipodeans, a race of creatures, very much like us, discovered on a distant planet in the twenty-first century, who got on quite as well as us, but who were fortunate enough never to have invented the mind, or to have participated in the '"idea" idea'. Thanks to technological progress, they could label their neurological states. And they found themselves indifferent whether they reported (for instance) 'It appears to be red and rectangular' or 'It makes neuronic bundle G-14 quiver'. The Antipodeans are meant to show us (Terrans) that we should be *materialists*, because the mental can be renounced without loss; and that we should be materialists *without identities*, because, the mental having been thus renounced, we see that there should never have been any need to assert that mental things are identical with physical things.

Some people have suspected that Rorty is not quite the wholesale revolutionary that he presents himself as being. Suspicions arise from two quarters. First, Rorty's new doctrine seems uncomfortably close to his own earlier one, which it was natural to classify as eliminative materialism; and eliminative materialism was put together as a solution to the very problem that Rorty wants to show us we do not have to solve. So it can seem that Rorty's position is unduly revisionary for his own purposes. Second, Rorty's new version of materialism seems sometimes to be addressed only to such putatively problematic items as sensations, and to say nothing on what philosophers of mind would subsume under intentionality. So it can seem that Rorty's position is unduly narrow for his own purposes. I think that the first of these suspicions, on probing, will seem to be the reverse of the truth, but that the second, in the end, is much harder to remove.

To allay the first suspicion quickly for the time being, it may be enough to point out that eliminative materialism was always a revolutionary position (even if it has sometimes seemed like just one more in a catalogue of anti-dualist positions). Rorty wants to distance himself from older style eliminative materialists who acknowledge some more than historically given problem about the mental; and it may appear that he has not succeeded in doing so, if at his destination he has no disagreement with the eliminativists. But even if Rorty's difference from the eliminativists were only one of starting-point, we should not forget that eliminativists were always ready and willing to abolish the mind. (I shall return to this.)

The other suspicion was that Rorty's own position as arrived at in part I of the *Mirror of Nature* covers too little of what we have come to think of as mind. The suspicion is created in the first instance by Rorty's emphasis on *raw feels*. When he comes to say anything positive in the place of what is said by philosophers of mind, his only actual example of a putative mental attribute is 'having a sensation of *pain*'. And when he imagines his readers worrying about his Antipodeans (about whether they really have everything that we've got), their worries extend only to the existence or otherwise of *phenomenal* items in the Antipodean case. At first blush it may seem entirely appropriate that Rorty should put the emphasis where he does. After all, he believes that philosophers who have worried about mind–body problems have suffered both from the tendency to think of the intentional in a phenomenal way, and from regarding indubitability (which may strike us as more characteristic of the phenomenal than the intentional) as *the* characteristic of mentality quite generally. So it isn't surprising that Rorty should think that mind–body problems are laid to rest when the phenomenal has been disposed of. If Rorty's own version of materialism does not seem to be addressed to intentionality, and to limit its scope to the more sensational items, this may only be because it is Rorty's view that the whole of our misconception of mind can be located in the phenomenal realm.

This can all be said. But it may still leave us wondering about the intentional. If we are concerned about whether the Antipodeans can be assimilated to us, should all of our questions really revolve around how things might feel for them – rather than around what things are like for them (in a sense much broader than how they feel)? In fact Rorty somewhat distracts our attention from intentionality as a feature of Antipodean states. We are told that the Antipodeans 'built bombs and houses, wrote poems and computer programs'. And we know that the Antipodeans have sudden thoughts and make inferences, because such things occur in Rorty's examples. But in all their actually described dealings (not left to our imagination), they are static: nothing is spelled out in any detail about their interactions with the world beyond their lips, or about their interactions with one another.

The last decade of Anglo-American philosophy has seen an enormous amount of work devoted to the propositional attitude states and to representation. Rorty will tell us that historical accidents determine philosophical agenda from time to time, so that there isn't much to be made of the fact that philosophers in the present decade have been obsessed with 'content' where philosophers of the previous two decades had been obsessed with 'raw feels'. Nevertheless, the recent work on intentionality has certainly developed inside the very subject – philosophy of mind – which Rorty is concerned to undermine. And Rorty must acknowledge that if the mind is a fiction, then, for better or worse, its authors and perpetrators have decided what features in it.

So what of the fiction's perpetrators? Rorty thinks that the myths of dualist thinking have survived for three centuries, and still pervade philosophy. According to him, even contemporary *materialists* show themselves as guilty of being under the myth's influence – in their wish to assert identities. But if we want to see manifestations of the distinctive ways of thinking owed to the invention of the mind, then the kind of philosopher we should look to is the *neo-dualist* of Rorty's book. The neo-dualists presumably (given their name) are those in whom the invented mind is at its most recognizable.

Yet when we look to Rorty's summing up of neo-dualism, it seems to be a doctrine with a fragile basis on which nothing much is built: 'contemporary philosophers, having updated Descartes, can be dualists without their dualism making the slighest difference to any human interest or concern, without interfering with science or lending any support to religion'.[2] Of course Rorty's thinking that dualism can so easily be dispensed with is all of a piece with his view that the mind might never have been invented. But it is mysterious why philosophers should cling so tenaciously to their invention if dualist thinking can be abandoned with so little loss. Can there really be so little to the Cartesian legacy?

At two points Rorty is more explicit about what neo-dualists actually believe.

1   According to Rorty, neo-dualists endorse a conceptual dualism along the same lines as that which is required by Descartes' substantial division of mind from body.[3] In this variety of neo-dualism, ontological significance is accorded to a certain conceptual division. Let's call it conceptual neo-dualism.

2   A little later, neo-dualists are characterized as placing weight on two ways in which phenomena may be known about or understood.[4] Their variety of neo-dualism accords ontological significance to a certain epistemic distinction. Let's call it epistemic neo-dualism.

In the following section, I shall discuss Descartes' views with these two varieties of neo-dualism in mind. I shall suggest that it is not very likely that Rorty's conceptual neo-dualism is something that Descartes has left us with. Epistemic neo-dualism, though, which Rorty dismisses very rapidly, and which he does not connect with Descartes' thought, can be related to a Cartesian way of thinking. I believe that if we can see the relative unimportance dialectically of Descartes' dualism of substance as such, and the relative importance dialectically of views held by Descartes about how the world must be understood, then we may begin to be clearer about some of the feelings about Rorty's position that I have expressed. In particular, we may appreciate the true nature of its radicalism; we may see why intentionality is not quite as incidental to mind as (I have maintained) it appeared to be in Part I of the *Mirror of Nature*; and we may understand how it can seem that in Rorty's view the mind is both very hard and very easy to be rid of. In the final section, I shall try to make some of this out.

II

One reason why Descartes merits the title of dualist is that if he had been asked 'How many sorts of substance are there in the natural world?', he would have answered 'Two'. He thought that there are minds, whose essential nature is cogitative, and that there are bodies, whose essential nature is to be extended (or to occupy space in the world). One contradicts Descartes, and is a monist and not a dualist, then, if one says that there is only one sort of substance in the natural world. So in order to be a materialist, in one sense of that term at least, it is enough to deny that there are mental substances distinct from material substances – to deny that there are souls (or spirits or minds).

But Rorty's conceptual neo-dualists rely not on a distinction between soul and body, but a distinction between mental and physical *properties* of people. How are the two sorts of dualism related? Are the mental properties simply the properties that substance dualists thought of as properties of minds and the physical properties those of bodies?

In fact it is hard to know what should be included in a representative list of mental properties. But suppose that our aim is to capture out intuitions about this (and Rorty admits we have such intuitions wherever they have come from), but that we do not aim for anything distinctively Cartesian about our list (though Rorty thinks our intuitions lead us *willy-nilly* to draw lines in a roughly Cartesian way). Then we should presumably want to include among the mental properties at least those properties expressed by most of the following predicates:

is trying to hit the target
is intentionally annoying Mary
is aware of the blackboard
has a headache
knows that grass is green
believes that whales eat people
is behaving cheerfully
is arrogant

It seems evident that all such properties are properties of people, who are things that have height and weight and move around in space, and thus are equally bearers of physical properties. And in the case of at least some of these mental properties, we can form no conception of what it would be to ascribe them to things of any other sort: we have no idea of what it would be for, say, 'is behaving cheerfully' to apply except to something readily visible as it were. If the idea of possession of a mental life was meant to lead to the postulation of a substance leading that life, then the idea of

possession of a mental life could not plausibly be equated with possession
of properties that we feel inclined to put on a list of mental properties. The
answer to our question, then seems to be *No*: the neo-dualists' conceptual
distinction does not connect straightforwardly with Descartes' distinction
of substances.

In fact, and not surprisingly, Descartes would not have wanted to say
that a person's posssessing the properties in our list was a matter simply of
a soul's having certain attributes. A Cartesian soul is a *res cogitans*, and,
even though 'cogitare' has to be interpreted more broadly than 'think', not
every property which is intuitively a mental one is a *cogitative* one in a
sense that Descartes would have intended. Much of what we regard as
mental is not to be accounted for in the Cartesian scheme simply by saying
how things are with a soul. Descartes recognized a class of sensational
properties, for instance 'which arise from the union and, as it were, are an
intermixture of mind and body'.[5] Sensations include pain, hunger and
thirst, and sense perception. A person's seeing something is a composite
fact, made up from a figure's being printed on her senses, from an image
of the figure's being imprinted on her pineal gland, and from the mind's
attending to what is imprinted on the gland. Again a person's doing
something intentionally is a matter both of there being a volition (which is
a species of cogitation) and of there being some bodily movement.
Presumably Descartes needs to be able to tell some such story about any
property that we regard as intuitively mental – a story about how a
person's possessing that property can consist in the possession of attributes by each of his two sorts of substance taken separately. In *The
Passions of the Soul*, Descartes had much to say of a detailed sort under this
head. But in spite of his furnishing detail, Descartes resorted to evasively
vague suggestions in painting the general picture of how minds and bodies
conspire to produce people with properties such as those in our list: he
often alludes to the 'apparent intermingling of the mind with the body'.

There are then too many properties which we naturally conceive as
mental but which on Descartes' own admission cannot be assigned either
to a *res cogitans* or a *res extensa* for it to be plausible that Cartesian dualism
is the substantial counterpart of a distinction we may now naturally make
between mental and non-mental attributes of people. And of course we
know in any case that Descartes himself wasn't led to introduce his soul in
the *Meditations* because of some difference in two sorts of properties that
he possessed. When he announced 'Sum res cogitans', he was not at a
stage in his project where he was entitled to believe in the existence of
things having physical properties. He tells us that he had considered,
before engaging in his doubt, that he was nourished, that he walked, and
so on; but when he looked upon his own nature, these attributes were not
in the picture. 'It is very certain that the knowledge of my existence taken

in its precise significance does not depend on things whose existence is not yet known to me.'[6] The soul of the *Meditations* is not arrived at by way of thoughts about mental/physical difference as such.

Evidently Descartes ought eventually to make up his mind about how things turn out when physical things are acknowledged: he ought to be able to say whther he is his soul or whether he is the union of his soul and his body. In fact he settles for speaking sometimes of 'myself inasmuch as I am only a thinking thing' and sometimes of 'myself in my entirety inasmuch as I am formed of body and soul'.[7] It is as if we have to believe that Descartes is one thing inasmuch as he engages in the project of doubt, and a complex of two things inasmuch as he sits in his study while he does so. A soul conceived in the Cartesian way, then, so far from lining up with Rorty's neo-dualists' dualism between the mental and non-mental properties (by providing a bearer for the mental ones), actually gives rise to a problem about 'mind' and 'body' – a problem about what persons are, about what in the world bears what sorts of properties.

This is itself a Cartesian problem of course. My point has been that we do not automatically involve ourselves in it by making a distinction between mental and physical properties. In fact this problem is not much discussed nowadays. *Substance* dualism would seem to be thought to have been left behind. Nowadays questions about mental and physical things usually concern not substances (people, souls, people's bodies), but the states and events in which people participate. The identity theories that Rorty dismisses as superfluous make such claims as that every mental event or state is the same as some physical event or state. If we want to see connections between these materialists and Cartesian ways of thinking, then we need now to appreciate that there was another route leading Descartes to his dualism – other than that which he followed in the *Meditations*.

We might begin here with a distinction between two sorts of ontological question: macro-questions (about people) and micro-questions (about events and states).[8] Present-day concerns, which lead to identity theories, are, it seems, concerns with micro-questions. And Descartes, whose views engender various macro-questions, did not even introduce the 'micro-entities'. Even so, there may be a point in using a micro/macro distinction in thinking about Descartes. For Descartes did concern himself with questions at the micro level, if not the explicitly ontological micro-questions of today's identity theorists; he thought that interaction between mind and body had to be dealt with from the perspective of someone looking at the inside of a human being close up. present-day materialists speak of mental states and events in the brain: Descartes describes the soul's interaction with the body physiologically. He uses the same sorts of terms in treating of the mechanisms of blood circulation and digestion, as he uses in describing, for instance, voluntary agency, where the soul determines 'the subtle fluid styled the animal spirits, that passes from the heart through the brain towards the muscles ... to perform definite motions'.[9]

In order to see micro-questions as provoked by a problem of mind and body, we have to recognize a different sort of perplexity from that which led Descartes to say 'Sum res cogitans'. Non-mental properties of people, which are properties also of things that do not have mental lives, may be regarded as properties that characterize a world of nature that can be conceived independently of the fact of its containing things with mental lives. They are Physical properties. (Descartes sometimes capitalizes the 'P' of 'Physical' as thus introduced,[10] and I shall follow him in doing so.) The question then may be how the mental facts fit into a Physical world. Can mental facts be viewed as constituting the same natural realm as is characterized by those who study the Physical world and generalize about its workings? Descartes' answer was 'No'. He was sure that mental phenomena were not any part of what it is the scientist's task to study, because scientists are concerned with an extended substance which has its own essence precluding the features of thinking beings.

What is interesting now to see is the extent to which Descartes' general scientific enterprise lends support to his introspectively given conception of a mental substance – the extent to which his mechanism is at the service of his dualism. Margaret Wilson had argued that 'a *reason* for his dualism may be found in Descartes' commitment to mechanistic explanation in physics, together with the perfectly creditable belief that human intelligence could never be accounted for on the available mechanistic models'.[11] Descartes claimed that no mere machine could use language. And he thought that our aptitude to respond rationally in very various circumstances also could not be accounted for mechanistically: 'it is morally impossible that there should be sufficient diversity in any machine to allow it to act in all the events of life in the same way as our reason causes us to act'. He concludes that 'The rational soul ... could not be in any way derived from the power of matter.'[12]

At one point Descartes even explains his dualism as the upshot of a correct understanding of the Physical world. In the *Replies*, he writes that he has to confess that, despite the fact that his arguments for the real distinction of soul and body in the *Meditations* fully conform to his own most exacting standards, none the less he found himself 'not wholly persuaded'. But when he 'proceeded farther', and 'paused in the consideration of Physical things', he observed that:

> nothing at all belongs to the nature of essence of body, except that it is a thing with length, breadth and depth, admitting of various shapes and various motions. Its shapes and motions are only modes, which no power

could make to exist apart from it; and on the other hand . . . colour odours, savours and the rest of such things, are merely sensations existing in my thought, and differing no less from bodies than pain differs from the shape and motion of the instrument which inflicts it.

Thus a demanding conception of the Physical leads Descartes to refer to minds 'rather than to bodies' aspects of things which, before reflection on the essence of body, he says he had supposed to be corporeal.[13]

The particular treatment of the secondary qualities – of 'colours, odours, savours and the rest of such things' – makes the line of thought here more explicit. The scholastics, whose view of the secondary qualities prevailed at the time that Descartes wrote, held that when someone perceived, say, a yellow book, there was something in her mind resembling the yellowness of the book. Descartes not only rejected the resemblance doctrine, he gave a particular account of what it is about the book which makes for its being yellow. The book's yellowness is to be identified with a specific power to set the nerves in motion in certain ways;[14] the phenomenal quality yellowness is located in the mind's reading of what is delivered by the nerves from the organs to the glands. Here it can appear that Descartes was under pressure to think of what is external to the subject of experience in terms that apply whether or not there are any minds: we can say that yellowness is (in so far as it is a property of external objects) by allusion to the nervous system, but without any allusion to experience itself. It is as if everything that has to be said about anything that is yellow must be said without assuming the existence of anything except Physical bodies. There being no place in the world of matter for the book's appearing yellow, Descartes can then accommodate it only in something whose existence is independent of the existence of matter – the soul, which 'does not perceive excepting in as far as it is in the brain'. The only things in Physical reality that the mind is directly in touch with are the mechanical perturbations of the pineal gland.

It seems then that a thesis about the self-standing character of the Physical world as a subject of study serves for Descartes, just like the *Meditations*' thesis about the self-standing character of the mind, as a way of arriving at a view of the mental and Physical as autonomous realms. As Descartes said (speaking now of human bodies, rather than of bodies in the external world at large), 'considering the body in itself, we perceive nothing in it demanding union with the soul, and nothing in the soul obliging it to be united to the body.'[15] What has become clear is the extent to which the two doctrines are, though reciprocal, independently supported in Descartes. Each can equally be seen as underlying his idea that all mental–physical transactions are located at a place where mind and matter meet.

III

If the quick categorization at the start of the previous section does everything necessary to say what constitutes the properly *dualist* element in Descartes' philosophy, then it helps to show how very little it might take to make some materialist position attractive. There is something right about Rorty's thought that once the seventeenth-century notion of substance is abandoned, dualism ought to seem easy to dismiss. The philosophers of today who call themselves materialists have indeed dismissed it. Why in that case should Cartesianism about the mind seem to Rorty to be so persistent?

No immediate answer to this question is given by considering the conceptual neo-dualism of Rorty's opponents. For we saw that a distinction between what are and what aren't mental properties can be dissociated from any specifically Cartesian conception of the attributes of a *res cogitans*. Until more is said about a dualism of concepts – so long as it remains the intuitive one we looked at – there is nothing to place it in a tradition in which Descartes is a central figure.

Nor does the egocentric pathway of the *Meditations* appear to have much of a following in contemporary discussions of materialism versus dualism. The egocentrically arrived at conception of a soul is a conception of a subject of thought, where a thought is an object of introspective awareness or 'internal cognition'. It is the putative self that in modern writings features under such descriptions as 'ultimate private objects apparently lacking logical connections to anything else'.[16] Each person is meant to have a grasp of what her self is through reflection on what she can mean by 'I', just as Descartes is meant to discover his essential nature while making no assumptions except for those that pure introspection reveals as indubitable. Of course the *Meditations* conception of a soul or self has recurred often enough in the philosophy of the last three centuries that it is not to be dismissed out of hand. But it seems right nevertheless to dismiss the suggestion that it is Rorty's target when he speaks of neo-dualism. If present-day opponents of materialism persist in Descartes' errors, their fault is not to rehearse the arguments of the *Meditations*.

Selves arguably do recur in contemporary discussions – in discussions of personal identity. And it is curious, I think, the extent to which the literature on personal identity and the nature of persons and the literature on the mind–body question and materialism have come to be separated in our tradition. The separation is roughly that (spoken of earlier) between macro- and micro-questions. Recognizing the separation, and having seen an apparent overlap of Descartes' concerns with the concerns of those who address micro-questions, we should look for a different connection between Descartes and the neo-dualists of Rorty's book.

This is where Rorty's epistemic neo-dualists seem relevant. Their distinction between mental and physical is not introduced by way of intuitions about what constitutes mental vocabulary nor by way of what characterizes the soul. Rorty does not elaborate on their position; but from his gestures towards it, we can extract for them a recognizable and distinctive conception of the mental as a putatively problematic category: it is a conception of the features of a subject of experience that she is recognized as having when she is made sense of as a subject of experience. These features, the neo-dualists may suggest, could not be perceptible from the perspective of a student of matter, because recognizable only from a particular point of view.[17] And here epistemic neo-dualists seem to be at one with Descartes in his thesis of the impossibility of accommodating the rational soul in a world of mechanistically explicable things.

Two obvious differences between Descartes and those whom Rorty calls neo-dualists should be acknowledged. First, Descartes' views about the essence of the Physical as mind-excluding are not based straightforwardly in any obviously *epistemic* distinction.[18] Second, Descartes relied for those views on a specifically mechanistic idea of the Physical world, and on his (historically inevitable) ignorance of what machines are capable of. But there need be no very exact parallels between Descartes and the epistemic neo-dualists for us to see that no Cartesian ontological doctrine needs to be grounded in the initially epistemic distinction of the neo-dualists. For if we take Descartes at his word when he says that he had found reasons for his dualism 'in the consideration of Physical things', then we may accept that there is a thesis which is a candidate for neo-dualist assent and which is extricable from substantial dualism proper. What the neo-dualists' reflections on two modes of understanding leads them to can be summed up suggestively enough and without specifically epistemological or ontological overtones, as the irreducibility of the mental. Might not an irreducibility thesis be what Descartes expressed in saying that 'the rational soul ... could not be in any way derived from the power of matter'? (The reference to the rational soul seems eliminable: Descartes' thought at this point might be captured if one replaced 'the rational soul' with 'features of people, who are rational beings'.)

Here Descartes was denying that a material thing could have the character of a rational one (as opposed to his more familiar denial that a *res cogitans* could have a material character). If epistemic neo-dualists find problems in modern materialism parallel to those which at this stage Descartes would have thought to threaten any alternative to his dualism, then features of rational beings have to be seen now as problematic *relative* to what they are putatively irreducible to. A problem arises (neo-dualists may say) when it is supposed that concepts used for understanding the

Physical world are apt for understanding the subjects of experience as such. Perhaps Rorty's difficulties about characterizing the mental, about finding any coherent target for his remarks, derive from his thinking that he has to find a category of things which are problematic in their own right as it were, rather than a category of things which it is problematic to accommodate with other things – with items studied by science, or with bare extended and mechanical things, or with Physical things (depending on what exactly the mental is said to be irreducible to). Perhaps also we may be able to give a more revealing answer than Rorty's own to his question 'Why do we tend to lump the intentional and the phenomenal together as the mental?'[19]: they will be brought together by a good characterization of the mental as irreducible.

If Descartes bequeathed us a problem, then it seems possible now that we should want to fault him for his conception of the world in which minds had to operate as much as for his conception of mind. When this possibility is realized, the affinities of Descartes with modern materialists come to the fore. Modern materialists, like Descartes, work with an assumption about the natural world within, or on, which the mind operates. For Descartes, there are two autonomous realms; some of the items from each are 'made to be united' to one another, and they interact at points where mind and matter meet. For the modern materialists, there are the things whose identity with physical things needs asserting, and there are the unproblematically physical, external things; and the two meet up at the place where the central nervous system joins the visible body. For both Descartes and the materialists, location of mental phenomena is then achieved by slotting the mind in (as it were), and in such a way that its interactions with the Physical are intelligible in the terms in which the Physical was understood before the slotting-in. What is special about Descartes' position is that the nature of what is slotted in is different from that of what it is slotted in to.[20] But it is not only what is special to Descartes about which the neo-dualist complains. In either case, a neo-dualist will question the suggested accommodation of the mind: the modern materialist purports to have done what the irreducibility thesis showed to be impossible; Descartes has recognized the impossibility, but drawn the wrong conclusion and ensured that the mind itself is not any part of the natural world.[21] In both cases, something that the neo-dualist objects to is the equation of the natural world with a Physical world.

If this is right, then the radical character of Rorty's own position need not be thought to result from his having freed himself from all Cartesian ways of thinking. It may result from his sharing with Descartes and the materialists the assumption to which the neo-dualist objects. For Rorty, the metaphor of *slotting-in* is evidently inappropriate. But we might think of Rorty's refusal to endorse an identity theory as his own way of retaining

the picture which in the presence of the assumption that mental phenomena were problematic led to the claim that they were simply to be
slotted in among Physical phenomena: for Rorty, though, mental phenomena have been precluded from the picture before a question about
their location can arise.

This diagnosis of Rorty's view might seem to fit ill with his claims that
his version of materialism need make no appeal to the powers of science.
But my idea is that there is no need for such an appeal on Rorty's part
because the powers of science have been *presupposed*.

In order to see how and where 'the powers of science' enter the debate,
it will be useful now to distinguish between two kinds of eliminative
materialism; they might be called the vanishing kind and the banishing
kind. According to the first, science is to be put to work to uncover
materialist truths. Once the powers of science have been put to practical
effect, and mental/physical identities established, we shall see that the
mental was dispensable: it vanishes from the scene – or anyway it could
vanish once the scientists have done their work. The powers of science
come into the second sort of eliminative materialism not only in their
practical, truth-uncovering capacity, but also at a higher-order level, to
show us what sort of thing can be true. Proponents acknowledge that the
mental/physical identities that their metaphysics seem to demand might
not be forthcoming, and their reaction is to say so much the worse for the
mental: if its concepts are not such as to provide the sort of understanding
that science provides, then the mental must be banished from serious
enquiry. These eliminative materialists suppose that a great deal of what
we think about one another, which we express in everyday mental
concepts, will, when not vindicated by science, be shown to be false.[22]

Rorty may now be seen as combining the optimism of the materialists
who think that the mental can be made to vanish, with the ruthlessness of
the materialists who think that the mental ought to be banished. A certain
style of investigation such as his Antipodean neurophysiologists are
supposed to have undertaken, is, Rorty assumes, always suitable for
gaining understanding. In assuming this, he sides with the banishers. But
unlike the banishers (and perhaps because, unlike them, he does not make
his assumption explicit), Rorty does not consider the possibility that
confining investigation to the scientific mode could result in the rebuttal of
any common wisdom. In not envisaging his assumption as possibly
threatening, Rorty is like the vanishers, who simply place their faith in
scientific investigation, as destined to free us from needing to use mental
concepts.

Rorty's own claims that he does not need to appeal to science's powers
are supported by such remarks as this: 'Science's failure to figure out how
the brain works will cause no [real] danger to science's "unity."' 'Even if

neurons turn out to "swerve" – to be buffeted by forces as yet unknown to science – Descartes would not be vindicated'.[23] Rorty speaks here as if his opponent had already conceded that the mind would have to be slotted in (i.e. to where the brain is); the opponent then is worried that Rorty himself has put unwarranted trust in present science. But the danger that a neo-dualist opponent may see is different. It is not that Rorty has taken science to be the best bet (as the vanishers indeed do); rather, in taking it for granted that the Antipodeans' mode of understanding once applied to the brain is adequate to the whole of human understanding, Rorty has rendered unthinkable the possibility of any other mode.

The state of present science is not to the point in any case. Even materialists who would wish to make explicit appeal to science's powers will allow that science might show us that the world (or the neurons therein) works in ways that we have not yet imagined. And although it may be natural to think of Rorty's presupposition in terms specifically of science, this is not necessary. The 'powers of science' can allude to a kind of finding which scientists make. It is a kind of finding which the neo-dualists will insist on contrasting with our finding one another intelligible as fellow subjects of experience. But one does not need actually to believe in the neo-dualists' irreducibility thesis in order to appreciate some contrast between Physical explanations of Physical things (not necessarily physicists' explanations[24]) and rational explanations of people's experiences, states and doings. Conceptions of the Physical vary no doubt: Descartes' was more mechanistic than anyone's is today; Rorty's is more pluralist than most; and Rorty is less willing than Descartes was to judge what an accurate conception might be. But Descartes and Rorty evidently believe in a Physical realm which might be characterized by thinking of scientists as, *de facto*, the specialists in it – a realm on which a certain perspective is appropriate.

The vanishing kind of eliminative materialist would have us believe that from our usual perspective, the mental need not come into view. (This is what science was to demonstrate.) The banishing kind of eliminative materialist would have us believe that we are in error if we take a perspective from which the mental does come into view. (This is what metaphysical reflection is supposed to persuade us of.) Rorty's radicalism consists in his belief that we were always in error if we had supposed the mental had come into view.

The reluctance of almost everyone to be as radical as Rorty is registered in our thoughts about his Antipodeans. I mentioned earlier that Rorty's descriptions of them didn't speak to certain particular points of interest we may have about them. But now it seems that Rorty's account is not filled in at just the crucial points. When the Antipodeans use their own neurological counterpart of what we regard as mental vocabulary, they are envisaged as making reports of their own states, but never as shedding light or gaining understanding: there are examples where one or other of them avows his or her own state of mind to another, but none where anyone otherwise comes to know about the states of mind of another.

Rorty assures us that 'no predictive or explanatory or descriptive power would be lost if we had spoken Antipodean all our lives'. Of course this seems right when we are also assured about how much of what we do the Antipodeans also do. And if our doubts about the Antipodean had extended only to what we think of as phenomenal features, then the assurances about the Antipodeans' likeness to us might have made the doubts seem out of place. (There is always the view that we should never have expected any explanation of the phenomenal.) But if we had wanted to be sure that the Antipodeans make sense of one another as subjects of experience, then in order to be convinced of what Rorty says about the explanatory power of Antipodean, we should need to be told how their ways of attributing beliefs to one another (as we should put it) are connected with their modes of describing the world that they experience and have beliefs about. The Antipodeans can use 'F-11' to report their being struck by the thought that elephants don't occur on this continent. It is hard then to see why they should not also use the vocabulary of 'Fs' and '11s' from the neurological language when they want to *state* something about elephants. If even the semantic properties of their states of mind are neurophysiologically formulable, why should they not restrict themselves entirely to a neurophysiological vocabulary? But the idea that everything is sayable in terms of how things are in our heads seems preposterous: it precludes us from thinking that the external world is something on which we have a point of view.

That the world is something of which we can have a point of view is of course a Cartesian thesis in epistemology. It would take another paper to discuss whether this is a thesis to which either Rorty or Descartes is really committed.[25] But the apparent affinity between Rorty and Descartes at this point seems real to me – and to result from what I have been suggesting is a shared assumption of the two philosophers – that if we are to find a place for mind, it has to be a place for mind in the world conceived independently of mind. The consequence both for Descartes and for Rorty, though they would put the emphasis very differently, is that there is no place for mind in the natural world.

Where does this leave neo-dualists?

Well, they cannot now be seen as holding a monopoly on the Cartesian legacy in philosophy of mind. And if they 'lump together the intentional and the phenomenal', this need not be because 'Descartes used the notion of the "incorrigibly known" to bridge the gap between them'.[26] The neo-dualists in fact share with Descartes one, but only one, of the premises (the irreducibility thesis), in one, but only one, of his arguments for his dualism (the argument from the Physical). And the premise which they deny (which equates the natural and the Physical) is affirmed not only by Descartes but by Rorty. No doubt Rorty will continue to think that neo-dualism is pernicious; but perhaps he need no longer think of it as an inheritance of substantial dualism, nor as simultaneously pernicious and quite without consequence.

In Rorty's book the neo-dualist is an embarrassed figure – wanting to accept what Strawson and Wittgenstein have said about persons but to resist modern materialism.[27] But there need be no embarrassment about this, if one allows oneself to reject the assumption that I have suggested is at work in Descartes and (behind the scenes) in Rorty. Resistance to a Cartesian view of mind need not be resistance to the whole idea of the phenomenon of mind, but only to a conception of the mental informed by a particular view of what the natural world can contain.

NOTES

1 Richard Rorty, *Philosophy and the Mirror of Nature* (Princeton University Press, Princeton, 1979). I confine attention to the first two chapters. (If my view of Rorty's thought as presented here has been influenced by other of Rorty's writings, then these are his earlier writings in the philosophy of mind rather than later chapters in the book.)

2 Ibid., p. 68.

3 Ibid., p. 17, and see also p. 65.

4 Ibid., pp. 28–9.

5 René Descartes, *Sixth Set of Replies*, in *The Philosophical Works of Descartes*, tr. Elizabeth Haldane and G. R. T. Ross (Cambridge University Press, Cambridge, 1967), vol. 2, p. 251 (hereafter HR). For more on this, see John Cottingham on Cartesian 'Trialism', in *Descartes* (Basil Blackwell, Oxford, 1986), pp. 127–32.

6 Meditation II, HR, II, p. 151.

7 Meditation VI, HR, II, p. 196.

8 See the beginning of Bernard Williams, 'Are Persons Bodies?', reprinted in his *Problems of the Self* (Cambridge University Press, Cambridge, 1973) for this distinction. The distinction is useful when discussing writings about so-called 'Cartesian dualism'. But the distinction is arguably quite foreign to the thought of Descartes himself.

9 *Passions of the Soul*, Article XI, HR, I, p. 336.

10 E.g. in *Reply to the Sixth Set of Objections*, HR, I, p. 253.

11 See Margaret Wilson, *Descartes* (Routledge & Kegan Paul, London, 1978), pp. 183–4. I try in what follows to push further in one respect her view that much which now goes by the name of 'Cartesian dualism' is not attributable to Descartes: I suggest that some of what deserves to go by that name is attributable to modern materialists.

12 *Discourse on the Method*, HR, I, pp. 116–17.

13 *Reply to the Sixth Set of Objections*, HR, II, pp. 253–4.

14 *The Principles of Philosophy*, Part IV, Principle CXCVIII, HR, I. p. 296.

15 Letter to Regius, December 1641, in *Descartes' Philosophical Letters*, tr. and ed. Anthony Kenny (Clarendon Press, Oxford, 1970), p. 122 (hereafter K).

16 Thomas Nagel, *The View from Nowhere* (Cambridge University Press, Cambridge, 1985), pp. 32–3.

17 I am deliberately not much more explicit than Rorty is about the tenets of neo-dualism: the aim is only to make room for a position which is (1) coherent, (2) consistent with Rorty's few positive characterizations of it and (3) plausibly actually held by some present-day philosophers. I assume that Thomas Nagel and Donald Davidson (for rather different reasons) would both count as having seen virtues in epistemic neo-dualism; and it would be hard to define the position with greater explicitness or in greater detail without losing one of them. (As may be clear, I should also like neo-dualism to be true – if infelicitously named.)

18 This is not to suggest that we can have a clear idea of what counts as a 'purely epistemic' thesis in this area. (Is Davidson's thesis that there are no psychophysical laws epistemic, for instance?)

19 Rorty, *Mirror of Nature*, p. 68.

20 The affinity between Descartes and the modern materialists at this point is highlighted when Descartes responds to the objection that the soul is not the sort of thing to influence matter: he says 'if "corporeal" is taken to mean anything that can in anyway affect a body, then mind too must be called corporeal in this sense' (Letter to Hyperaspites, August 1641, K, p. 112). And the hylomorphism of Descartes (well brought out by Paul Hoffman, 'The Unity of Descartes' Man', *Philosophical Review*, XCV, 1986) may not interfere with this point of resemblance to the materialists: it can be the soul *as motive power* that plays for Descartes the role that the central nervous system plays for the materialists.

21 It may seem tendentious to represent Descartes as committed so straightforwardly to a non-natural view of mind. But for the idea that nature is something strictly external to perceivers, see e.g. *Principles*, Part IV, CXCIX, HR, I, p. 296.

22 A representative of 'banishing' eliminative materialism would be Paul Churchland. I take 'vanishing' eliminative materialism to be a view less recently propounded; and I agree with Rorty (*Mirror of Nature*, pp. 117–19) that it is not a more plausible version of reductive materialism, but rather, as it were, another way of putting certain reductive materialist beliefs.

23 Rorty, *Mirror of Nature*, p. 124.

24 Definitely *not* all physicists' explanations, in Rorty's view: this is to allow for what in the next sentence I call the pluralism in Rorty's conception of the Physical.

25 And it would also require taking account of Parts 2 and 3 of the *Mirror of Nature* (see n. 1 above). I confess to wondering whether I do Rorty an injustice by treating his Part I in isolation. But not only have I found it difficult to bring the Parts together, also I have wanted to see how *Descartes* in particular relates to present thinking about the mind (and Descartes looms large only in Rorty's Part I).

26 Rorty, *Mirror of Nature*, p. 68.

27 Ibid., p. 27.

4

Mirrors and Veils, Thoughts and Things:
The Epistemological Problematic

John W. Yolton

Richard Rorty tells us that 'the Sellarsian claim that "all awareness is a linguistic affair"' is his starting-point.[1] I had suggested in my review of *Philosophy and the Mirror of Nature* that in the *Treatise*, Hume was engaged in the careful inventory and description of mental phenomena and their interconnections.[2] Rorty claimed that 'sheer' or 'pure' description is not possible and that to the extent that Hume did try to describe mental phenomena, that was 'the bad Newtonian side of Hume'.[3] The bad side of Hume was, Rorty added, Hume trying to ape the sciences, as indeed Hume said he was doing in the introduction to the *Treatise* and in the subtitle. The sciences for Rorty are, I guess, just other languages, other voices in the conversation of mankind.

Rorty based his critique of what he calls the 'epistemological problematic' upon the assumption that Descartes and Locke used the term 'idea' to designate a special object located in 'an inner arena with its inner observer'.[4] This notion of ideas as mental objects posed 'the problem of the veil of ideas' standing between perceivers and the external, physical world. The epistemological problematic became, 'how can we acquire knowledge of the world behind the veil?' If ideas are representative of that world, the world may be mirrored in the inner arena, but the problematic would then be how to discover whether the images on the mirror correctly reflect the external world.

When Rorty wrote *Philosophy and the Mirror of Nature*, he recognized that I had 'suggested that the usual story (common to, e.g., Etienne Gilson and J. H. Randall) about the emergence of epistemological scepticism out of a theory of representative perception created by Descartes and Locke may be too simple-minded'.[5] Since the publication of that book, I have presented some of the details of the way of ideas tradition which supports, I believe, the view that there are many strands in the writers on perception from Descartes to Reid that indicate they were attempting to articulate a form of direct realism, and that the dominant view about ideas was not that they were proxy, inner objects preventing direct access to the physical world.[6] Even if the story I have traced of the way of ideas is accepted, even if I am correct in holding that Descartes and Locke did not hold to a veil or mirror theory, this reading will do little to oppose Rorty's own thesis about description. From his point of view we can no more look at or consult the outer world than we can the inner world. What we can do is form languages which have some function, but never the function of description.[7] What my reading of the way of ideas tradition would do if true, would be, as Rorty says, to force him to 'look further along in history for the emergence of what is now thought of as the epistemological problematic created by Descartes'.[8]

What I want to do in this paper is to present certain considerations about Descartes and Locke which free them from the stereotypes of mirror and veil, of an indirect representative theory of perception, and of the mind as an inner arena where 'the intellect *inspects* entities modelled on retinal images'.[9]

I

There are numerous passages where Descartes speaks of the 'close and profound union of our mind with the body';[10] of the body in which the mind is 'immersed';[11] of the way in which he is 'very closely joined and, as it were, intermingled with' the body, so that 'I and the body form a unit';[12] that the mind is 'substantially united with the body';[13] even, that mind and body are 'incomplete substances when they are referred to a human being which together they make up'.[14] The usual talk of 'Cartesian dualism' needs to be tempered by some recognition of this intimate union which constitutes humans. Many passages in the *Principles*, the *Passions*, and the correspondence deal with the specific ways in which mind and body influence each other. Two vocabularies appear in his discussions of the action of body and the motions of nerves on mind. Causal language is used to describe the action of motion on nerves and muscles (normal physical action), but in some passages 'cause' is also used to characterize the action of motion on the mind. Article 21 of the *Passions* distinguishes perceptions that are caused by the body by means of the nerves from other perceptions (imaginings) which are not actions but passions of the soul. These latter are still the result of physiology, errant animal spirits. Article 27 defines passions generally as 'those perceptions, sensations or emotions of the soul which we refer particularly to it, and which are caused, maintained, and strengthened by some movement of the spirits'. Article

23 says that 'The perceptions we refer to things outside us, namely to the objects of our senses, are caused by these objects, at least when our judgements are not false'. Article 35 is somewhat ambiguous, but the language there may also be causal: the two images from the eyes form one image on the pineal gland 'which acts directly upon the soul and makes it see the shape of the animal'. The French says, 'agissant immediatement contre l'âme', and then uses the term 'make' instead of 'cause', 'lui fait voir la figure de cet animal'.

The *Treatise on Man* also speaks of specific physiological events *causing* the sensations of red, white and pain, although this same passage has certain features of objects (their figure) providing the *occasion* for the soul to feel or sense (*sentir*) motion, size, distance, colour, sound and so on.[15] The phrase, 'give occasion for the soul to sense', is the second language used by Descartes to characterize the action of body on mind. Hall uniformly ignores the distinction between 'cause' and 'occasion', translating both as 'cause'. A later passage in this work speaks of ideas being caused by physiological motion, but the term 'idea' here probably means 'brain impression'.[16] In this same paragraph, Descartes speaks of the motion of animal spirits giving the occasion to the soul to sense or feel the arm turning toward an object.[17] Earlier in this treatise, the particles of the gastric fluids are said to give occasion to the soul to conceive the idea of thirst.[18] Much earlier, following the passage about God joining or uniting the rational soul to the machine of the body, the stretched nerves are said to *cause* motion in the brain but that motion 'donnera occasion à l'âme' to have the feeling of pain, and a certain motion in the brain 'donnera occasion à l'âme de sentir une certaine volupté corporelle', i.e. 'tingling'.[19] The phrase, 'donnera occasion à l'âme', occurs in the next paragraph also. Two paragraphs later, the fibres of nerves are said to 'lui feront sentir toutes les autres qualités', not making it entirely clear whether 'make' means 'cause' or 'occasion'.

It would be useful to search systematically through Descartes' writings for other occurrences of the two vocabularies of cause and occasion, in order to see whether there are other passages where he uses the latter for the action of physical motion on the soul. There *are* a few places where he suggests another non-causal relation between physical motion and mind. There is also the important distinction drawn in the *Meditations* between formal and objective reality, a distinction which is, I think, related to the language of cause and occasion, even perhaps parallel with it.

Formal to formal causation is exemplified by normal physical processes and events. If there is also mental causation for Descartes, one idea or thought giving rise to others, this would be formal to formal:[20] causation within the same category, between substances of the same kind, or between the modes of one substance. While the soul seems to be able to act directly on the pineal gland to cause it to move in specific directions, the influence from body to soul is, as we have seen, not always described in causal language. The language of *occasion* may be a forerunner to the psychophysical parallelism of Leibniz or the occasionalism of Malebranche, but I suspect it reflects Descartes' attempt to find a non-causal relation (a non-causal interaction) between bodies (or physical motion) and the soul.

Meditation III makes it clear that the formal reality of ideas is due to the mind alone: it is the mind or soul which forms ideas. Some of these ideas also have a dependence on formal realities other than the mind, for example, the idea of God, the ideas of physical objects. 'But my hearing a noise, as I do now, or seeing the sun, or feeling the fire, comes from things which are located outside me, or so I have hitherto judged'.[21] Descartes makes it clear that he accepts the scholastic maxim which says an effect cannot have more reality or perfection than its cause. This maxim applies to ideas, both with respect to their formal reality and to their objective reality. The latter is both epistemic and ontic. Its epistemic reality is the representative or information-bearing feature of ideas. The *idea* of heat or of a stone, he explains, 'cannot exist in me unless it is put there by some cause which contains at least as much reality as I conceive to be in the heat or in the stone'.[22] In general, the objective reality of ideas must be derived from 'some cause which contains at least as much formal reality as there is objective reality in the idea'.[23]

In these passages which explain the doctrine of objective reality, Descartes uses the language of cause: both the formal and the objective reality of ideas have causes.[24] He does not tell us how the soul or mind is the cause of the formal reality of ideas (he does not give us, as Locke did later, an account of the formation of specific ideas), but it is clear that even in the case of adventitious ideas, the soul or mind is still the formal cause. The posssibility of Descartes himself being also the cause of some aspects of the objective reality of 'my ideas of corporeal things' is explicitly suggested. For example, the properties of being a substance, of having duration and number could easily have been borrowed from Descartes as a thinking thing, since they are his properties, part of his formal reality. Even the properties of extension, shape, position and movement may derive from Descartes in the sense that they may be 'contained in me eminently'.[25] The one idea whose objective reality could not have come from Descartes is the idea of God. With that idea, the objective reality, the properties it contains epistemically, are greater than any properties possessed by finite minds.

The ontic aspect of objective reality becomes evident in Descartes' discussion of the idea of God in Meditation III, but even more forcefully in his replies to Caterus (the first set of objections). There, he explains that

' "objective being" simply means being in the intellect in the way in which objects are normally there'.[26] Descartes' use of the doctrine of objective reality does not place the object in the mind *formally*, but in some sense the object's reality *is* present to the mind. It may turn out that the ontic feature collapses into the epistemic feature of objective reality, but what we are hearing in Descartes' use of this doctrine is a clear echo of the scholastic doctrine of the form of objects existing in the mind. The intent is the same for Descartes and the scholastics: to find a way of protecting direct realism while recognizing the difference between cognitive and physical reality.[27] Reverberations of the doctrine can be heard in a number of successors to Descartes in France and England, even into the eighteenth century.

Besides the non-causal language of 'give occasion to the soul', there is another non-causal but interactive relation briefly mentioned in Meditation VI and somewhat elaborated in *Le Monde, ou Traité de la lumière*. In the latter work, Descartes suggests that just as words make us conceive of things which the words do not resemble (a conventional signification relation), so nature could have instituted certain natural signs which trigger specific sensations and ideas. The physical motion of light particles *signifies* the ideas we have of light. Motion becomes, on this suggestion, a natural sign for the mind: motion in my body does not cause but it signifies my sensations. Motions in the brain are said to represent objects in Section 13 of the *Passions*. It may be that Descartes thought of the formula, 'give occasion to the soul', as a signification relation of this sort. When movements of a certain kind occur in the nerves and brain, we have specific sensations. The motion enables the mind to know, but knowing is not reading off properties of the world from our sensations or ideas. The representative function of ideas is not a sign function: ideas are not signs of things, they are the interpretations of, or cognitive responses to, physical motion. The reaction to these signs is cognitive, not physiological, but it does work in tandem with the physical and physiological reactions.

This significant relation is somewhat obscure in Descartes' brief use of it, but it does receive some further analysis in a few writers after Descartes, for example, Joseph Glanvill, Ralph Cudworth and Charles Bonnet.[28] They all talk of motion in the brain being a 'species of natural signs of ideas which they excite'. Very little attention has been paid to this curious doctrine. I suspect it must be present in other writers as well, but so far I have not discovered other occurrences of it.[29] What is important about this doctrine is the indication it gives of Descartes' effort to preserve an interaction between body and mind which is not causal, or which is more than causal.[30] The two languages that he also employs reinforce this suggestion: he recognized the causal relation between physical objects and our body, but he also recognized that that causal relation is inadequate for cognition. For the latter, a different, non-causal but still interactive relation is needed.

So far I have called attention to (1) the unity of mind and body in humans; (2) the two vocabularies for talking about the action of body on mind; (3) the distinction between formal and objective reality of ideas (the latter being an attempt to capture the reality of objects in the mind and also requiring a relation different from the formal-to-formal relation); and (4) the curious notion of motions in the brain serving as signs to the mind of objects whose reality the ideas capture, those ideas being the mind's reaction to motion-signs. Each of these components reflects Descartes' attempt not to isolate the perceiver in the immaterial substance, cut off from the material substance of the perceiver's body and the objects impinging upon it. In humans, these two substances make an intimate union. Ideas are still modes of mind, but in their representative role they capture the reality of objects that cause reactions in the body; that reality is caught by the cognitive reactions to natural signs in nerves and brain. There are two reactions operating in perception: the causal, physiological reaction and the signification reaction. To those who think the difference between causal and significatory reactions distances the mind from objects, isolating the mind among its ideas, the alternative needs to be recognized: it would be the elimination of the significatory reaction – that is, the elimination of awareness, of cognition.

II

I have said very little about the nature of ideas for Descartes. The cluster of features (1) through (4) indicates the various attempts he made to make cognitive relations with objects direct. Ideas for Descartes *were* modes of mind (a feature later rejected by Berkeley), but the origin of adventitious ideas is dual: the mind and physical objects (at least, motion caused by those objects). Physical motion affects the body causally and it also affects the mind semantically or cognitively. The product of the causal action of motion is certain brain states. The product of the significatory action is cognition. Cognition requires a content, to perceive is to perceive some object, to be aware of some content. The object itself cannot be present to the mind formally (a possibility raised and rejected by Malebranche) but it *is* present objectively. I suppose it would be possible for this dual interaction to lead to the formation of special inspectable entities, ideas, which veil the world of objects. The significatory interaction might end with proxy objects.

Even if Cartesian ideas are not proxy *objects* but cognitive *contents* of awareness, the meanings signified by physical motion in nerves and brain, do they not block our view of the objects whose meanings they are? To accede to this tempting suggestion would be similar to saying words and phrases in a language hide their referents. We might conclude from these considerations that we are left with words and ideas, not with the objects which they are used to talk about or which they represent. The alternative would be to have the things themselves in hand or in view, rather than words or ideas. But we can no more talk or write with objects than we can know or be aware of objects directly. The word 'directly' here would mean 'without being aware', just as writing or speaking with objects would be not to write or to speak. The difficulty with the Swiftian notion of carrying a bag of objects as a medium of discourse is not the weight but the inability of objects to form a language. To replace ideas as cognitive contents with objects would similarly result in the loss of perceptual awareness. Words and ideas belong to the domain of meaning and cognition. Just as sounds without *conventional* rules which transform them into meaningful words would not constitute a language, so, Descartes is suggesting, physical and physiological motions without a *natural* significatory relation would not constitute perceptual awareness.

Rorty's response to these sorts of remarks is to say that the very notion of relating language or thought to a world supposed to be different in kind is precisely what got us into the epistemological problematic: the notion that we can use thought (ideas) to know a world of objects, or that we can use a language to describe that world, is misdirected and misconceived. Whether we accept Rorty's 'edifying' injunction to 'drop the notion of correspondence for sentences as well as for thoughts', and consider sentences and ideas as connected with other sentences and other ideas rather than with the world, we should recognize that the seventeenth-century notion of representation and correspondence was not based upon the notion of glassy essence, mirrors and veils, or inspectable entities.[31]

The textual evidence for appreciating that Descartes' ideas are not inspectable, proxy objects may not be decisive, but once we cease to approach the texts with this stereotype, it becomes easier to understand what ideas were for Descartes. I do not know what texts Rorty would cite to support his claim that 'in the Cartesian model, the intellect *inspects* entities modelled on retinal images'.[32] Descartes denied Gassendi's charge that ideas were images; the denial of resemblance between natural signs and their causes would also seem to rule out an image interpretation of ideas. To say that 'it is *representations* which are in the mind'[33] misleads because the 'in' suggests that the mind contains ideas in a way analogous to space containing objects. To 'exist in the mind' in this tradition, as Arnauld, Locke and Berkeley made quite clear, meant 'to be understood'. Arnauld is, I think, one of Descartes' best expositors. In his *Des vraies et des fausses idées* (1683), he explained that to be objectively in the mind is simply to be conceived (Def. 5). Arnauld also explains that the representative function is a property of the act of perceiving (to have an idea and to perceive are, he says, the same). Moreover, the representativeness of our perceptions is unlike the way a picture represents its original. To be conceived, to be objectively in the mind, is to represent (Def. 8). I am suggesting that this representative relation is similar to the way words stand for things.

III

Locke picked up some of the features of Arnauld's interpretation, insisting as Arnauld did that 'having ideas and perceptions' are the same thing,[34] and repeating Arnauld's definition 5: 'For if these words (*to be in the understanding*) have any propriety, they signify to be understood'.[35] Arnauld and Locke wrote against Malebranche, the one writer who *did* treat ideas as objects, special objects placed in our minds by God on specific occasions, when sense organs were causally activated by physical motions. The information carried by these special objects was limited mainly to geometrical properties, for example extension and shape, but Malebranche was never very detailed on what these ideas do for us in perception. What is important for us to understand is that both Arnauld and Locke considered their accounts of ideas to differ from that of Malebranche, both in terms of the information-content and the status of ideas. To have an idea for them was not to have a special object (proxy or not) replacing the physical object in the perceptual environment. Having an idea was, Locke told Malebranche, the same as having a sensation or having his soul modified.[36] Throughout his tract on Malebranche's doctrine of ideas, Locke discounts the object-nature of ideas. Locke also admits that he does not know how 'the alteration is made in our souls', although he does say in this same passage that 'the ideas of figure and colour' are had 'by the operation of exterior objects on our senses'.[37] In other passages, Locke is more cautious, saying (using Malebranche's language), that 'God has made our souls so, and so united them to our bodies, that, upon certain motions made in our bodies by external objects, the soul should have such and such perceptions or ideas.'[38]

The occasionalist sound of this last passage is at variance with Locke's usual account of the origin of ideas. He accepted the corpuscularian theory whereby tiny, insensible particles caused changes in sense organs and nerves. He used this same causal language for the production of sense ideas in the understanding or mind.[39] It is powers in bodies that produce ideas in us,[40] the causation of such ideas is by impulse.[41] In later passages, Locke is concerned to deny that we can discover any *necessary* connection between 'the bulk, figure, and motion of several Bodies about us' and the sensations or ideas they produce in us.[42] This causal connection has, he suggests, been the result of 'the arbitrary Will and good Pleasure of the Wise Architect', the word 'arbitrary' indicating that this is not a *natural* relation.[43] A remark in the next chapter of this same book appears to make the causation of bodies on minds natural: simple ideas 'must necessarily be the product of Things operating on the mind in a natural way', but the next clause indicates that this action is the result of 'the Wisdom and Will of our Maker' who has 'ordained and adapted' bodily motion to ideas or perceptions.[44]

Whether natural or conventional, ideas, perceptions or sensations (all more or less synonymous terms) will not arise in the mind merely by impressions made on sense organs, nerves and brain. These impressions must 'reach' the mind, they must be 'taken notice of' by the mind.[45] 'A sufficient impulse there may be on the organ of Hearing; but not reaching the observation of the Mind, there follows no perception'.[46] The observation or notice of the mind is also necessary for the causation of an idea. Locke is rather silent on what this process of noticing is, but he at least has included some action of the mind in idea-causation. That action is not described, as Descartes did, as a response to signs, but it *is* a suggestion of more than physical causation in the genesis of sense ideas.

Locke recognized that for Malebranche, 'it is *ideas*, not *things*, that are present to the mind', the reason being that 'the soul cannot perceive things at a distance, or remote from it'.[47] The notion of being 'present to the mind', and the principle of 'no cognition at a distance', were generally accepted from Descartes' time to late in the eighteenth century. Both are found in Locke's *Essay*. The strongest statement of what is present to the mind is found near the end of the *Essay*: 'For, since the things the mind contemplates are none of them, besides itself, present to the understanding, it is necessary that something else, as a sign or representation of the thing it considers, should be present to it: and these are *ideas*'.[48] In discussing types of qualities in the *Essay*, Locke remarks that 'external objects be not united to our minds when they produce *ideas* in it'.[49] It is these ideas in the mind which are described as the *immediate* objects of the mind, the mind having 'no other immediate object but its own *ideas*'.[50]

What is the force of the word 'immediate'? Rorty seems to suggest that Locke uses this term in association with *incorrigibility*: 'Immediacy as the mark of the mental (with the criterion of immediacy being incorrigibility) became an unquestioned presupposition in philosophy because of such passages as these'.[51] Rorty had just cited *Essay* 1.1.8, where Locke explains that he uses the word 'idea' to 'stand for whatsoever is the Object of the Understanding when a Man thinks'. Locke goes on to say, although Rorty does not quote this clarifying clause, that he has used the term 'to

express whatever is meant by *Phantasm, Notion, Species*', a clear reference
to various doctrines found in his contemporaries and predecessors. For the
term 'immediate', Rorty does not go to the *Essay*, but to what he refers to
as the 'Second Letter to the Bishop of Worcester'. He does not give a page
reference, so I am not sure just what work of Locke's he is citing. There is
no work with that title; there is a work often called 'Mr Locke's Second
Reply', that is *Mr Locke's Reply to the Right Reverend the Lord Bishop of
Worcester's Answer to His Second Letter*. There, Locke explains that what
he means by 'idea' is 'the immediate object of the mind in thinking'.[52]
There is no indication here or elsewhere that by 'immediate' Locke means
'incorrigible'.

It is clearly a word designed to catch the sense of 'present to the mind',
as well as the rejection of cognition at a distance. The alternative to *ideas* or
perceptions being united or present with the mind was the one Malebranche
suggested, *external objects* united or present with the mind. This alternative was clearly seen as absurd, although in his attack, Arnauld suggested
that Malebranche showed a more than passing interest in it. Aristotle and
certain scholastics had a metaphysic which enabled them to have the
object present to the mind: the form of the object could exist in matter and
mind. Descartes' objective reality concept was his version of that scholastic notion, a concept designed to avoid any third entity between perceiver
and the world. Locke was firmly in this same tradition. Well read in the
Cartesians, reading the exchanges between Arnauld and Malebranche
while in the final stages of writing the *Essay*, Locke joined Arnauld in
rejecting the indirectness of Malebranche's special entities. Both Arnauld
and Locke agreed with Malebranche and most of the writers on perception
at that time, that perceptual knowledge cannot be direct, if directness
requires the cognitive content (ideas) to be replaced by the objects
themselves.

The notion of the literal presence in the mind of physical objects strikes
us, as it did Arnauld, as bizarre, but it was the only alternative then to
ideas being the medium of awareness. We can find this yearning for the
assimilation of the object with the mind (or the absorption of ourselves
into the world) in many later and even recent writers.[53] There is a notion
found in some recent cognitive psychologists that representation means
indirectness. Arnauld showed us that representation is quite compatible
with realism, even with *direct* realism.[54]

IV

Rorty's ascription of incorrigibility to Locke's use of 'immediate' goes
along with the bugbear of *foundationalism* which he also finds in Locke and

Descartes. The Descartes of the *Meditations* lends some weight to this charge, with its stress on certainty and clear and distinct ideas. But the certainty of knowledge found in the *cogito* is not found elsewhere. Nor is the certainty of God's existence, which is derived from the metaphysical doctrine of objective reality and the principle that the cause must have as much reality as its effect, applied to our knowledge of body. The 'proof' for the existence of body elaborated in Meditation VI rests on a number of assumptions and premises, the result being far from either the certainty of 'I exist' or of 'God exists'. That 'proof' for body does not involve the inspection of entities in an inner arena, although it *is* a reflective exercise laying out various possibilities and probabilities, arriving slowly at the conclusion that bodies exist even though they may not be as they seem. I do not see that any of the three main truths in the *Meditations* – I exist, God exists, bodies exist – are reached by the inspection of entities, certainly not modelled on retinal images. These truths are the result of careful analysis of ideas and, in the case of the *cogito*, the activity of trying to doubt that I exist. There really is no account in the *Meditations* of our perception of bodies, no analysis of our knowledge of physical objects, of scientific knowledge. When Descartes wanted to discover the nature of some object, event or activity, such as light, vision, or the mechanism of the body, he resorted to observation and experiment – at least, to what he took to be observation, as with the examination of the eyes of bulls. He of course also relied heavily upon existing theory and views about the nerves, the propagation of light, the circulation of the blood. The various assertions in the *Passions* and the treatises on man, light and rainbows were not based upon the inspection of entities 'modelled on retinal images'.[55]

Even more so than Descartes, Locke was writing with scientists in mind (in Locke's case, the members of the Royal Society). He was himself in close relations with the leading chemist, Boyle, and the leading medical doctor, Sydenham. In both these areas, he and they employed careful observation of phenomena and symptoms. I do not know whether Rorty wants to say that the diagnosis and cure of diseases is a 'linguistic affair', that Sydenham and Locke were mistaken in thinking they could describe symptoms uninfluenced by language, but what they did not claim for their diagnoses was incorrigibility. These medical men did not look to their own inner states in order to diagnose illness: they watched carefully the symptoms and signs as they developed. Rorty refers to something called 'Lockean empiricism', without explaining what he takes that label to mean, but with it, he is confident that 'foundationalist epistemology emerged as the paradigm of philosophy'.[56] The 'philosophy' Locke knew was 'natural philosophy', that is science. What his account of the origin, extent and limits of knowledge did was urge us to be careful observers, make detailed natural histories of symptoms and phenomena, so that we might discover better the workings of nature. Only an experimental knowledge of nature was possible, never, he insisted, a demonstrative science, a science of certainty or incorrigibility.

Just as Rorty characterized Hume's efforts to construct a descriptive science of man as Hume's 'bad Newtonian side', so he charges Locke's similar efforts at discovering and describing the workings of the mind as 'confusedly thinking that an analogue of Newton's particle mechanics for "inner space" would somehow be "of great advantage in directing our Thoughts in the search of other Things", and would somehow let us "see, what Objects our Understandings were, or were not fitted to deal with"'.[57] Rorty goes on to say that 'This project of learning more about what we could know and how we might know it better by studying how our mind worked was eventually to be christened "epistemology".' I would have thought the science of man with Hume and the study of the workings of the mind with Locke were psychology, not epistemology. To develop a psychology at this time required the construction of a proper vocabulary for describing human emotions, perceptual awareness, and acts of judgement. There were many books published in the seventeenth and eighteenth centuries which were psychological treatises (they often carried the word 'soul' in their titles). The problem they faced was in part a linguistic one. Often such works borrowed from the language of physics and optics. The latter was closely linked with the interest in perceptual acquaintance. Metaphors of mirrors, of camera obscura, of blank tablets were frequently employed. A few writers may have become lost in these metaphors, but most were aware that they *were* metaphors, used in lieu of an existing psychological vocabulary. Rorty cites T. H. Green's charge that Locke and Hume confused propositions (the elements of knowledge for Green) with physiological conditions.[58] The use of the term 'impression' convinced Green (and Rorty?) that Locke took a metaphor for a fact. Rorty even suggests that Locke confused physical with cognitive impression when Locke talks of 'imprinting' of truths in *Essay* 1.2.5. Rorty does not tell his reader that this passage is one of Locke's chapters attacking innate ideas and truths. Locke's point there is that to have a truth or principle in the mind but not be aware of it is absurd. Rorty seems to have confused Locke's perceptual use of the metaphor of a blank tablet with his rejection of the doctrine of innate, imprinted truths. That Locke was fully aware that the blank tablet was a metaphor, I have no doubt.[59]

V

Rorty actually has Locke addressing the question 'How can I escape from behind the veil of ideas?'. Locke's answer, we are told is, 'Make the same use of your certainty about how things appear to your senses as Plato made of the axioms of geometry – use them as premises to infer everything else'[60] I do not recognize Locke in this characterization. What Locke was asking was, 'How can we escape the appeals to authority, the confusion of words for things?' Locke's answer to this question (a question which he *did* address) was clear, it is repeated many times in the *Essay*: make careful observations, compile histories of phenomena, do not be misled by language, study things not words. Rorty, of course, does not agree with Locke that we can escape the confusion of language and get at the things themselves, but it was just that programme which motivated Locke and the Royal Society. Locke and others at that time even believed it possible, though difficult, to separate thought from language. We do not have to agree with this extreme thesis in order to appreciate the scientific (i.e. observational) programme Locke supported: not only a careful science of nature but also a careful science of human nature. If, as Rorty believes, even this programme is misconceived because all awareness is a linguistic affair, we should not foist on Locke or Descartes doctrines and dilemmas that are not found in their writings. The mystery of the so-called 'veil of ideas' is not, 'how can we escape from the veil', but, 'who invented (and for what reason) this label to throw over the writings of Descartes and Locke'?

If this metaphor of a veil of ideas involves holding that (1) ideas are special objects, (2) we can only be aware of ideas, (3) ideas are modelled on retinal images and (4) these ideas inhabit an inner space, I do not think the majority of writers in the way of ideas tradition (and certainly neither Descartes nor Locke) held to, or were committed to, this metaphor. Subsequent readers of these writers have let themselves be beguiled into believing these writers were speaking literally. Ideas in this tradition were not images in a mirror or on the retina to be examined by some glassy eye in the hopes of discovering what the world beyond the mirror is like. Ideas, perceptions or thoughts (three terms often used interchangeably by these writers) were considered to be the cognitive counterpart, response to, or translation of physical stimuli. To be aware of, to think about things, these writers believed we needed to have ideas or thoughts about those things. Not mirrors and veils, but thoughts and things were what interested them.

NOTES

I would like to thank Emily Grosholz, Catherine Wilson and Luca Bonatti for their helpful comments on an earlier draft of this paper.

1   Richard Rorty, 'Reply to Professor Yolton', *Philosophical Books*, 22 (July 1981), p. 134.
2   John W. Yolton, 'Phenomenology and Pragmatism', *Philosophical Books*, 22 (July 1981), p. 132.

3 Rorty's 'Reply', p. 135.
4 Richard Rorty, *Philosophy and the Mirror of Nature* (Princeton University Press, Princeton, 1979), p. 50,
5 Ibid., p. 49n.
6 John W. Yolton, *Perceptual Acquaintance from Descartes to Reid* (University of Minnesota Press, Minneapolis; Basil Blackwell, Oxford, 1984), and 'Representation and Realism: Some Reflections on the Way of Ideas', *Mind*, 96 (July 1987), pp. 318–30.
7 I am not sure how much Rorty objects to claims for 'sheer' or 'pure' description, and how much he rejects all claims for description independent of the influence of language.
8 Rorty, *Mirror of Nature*, p. 50n.
9 Ibid., p. 45.
10 René Descartes, *Principles of Philosophy*, Part I, Art. 48, in *The Philosophical Writings of Descartes*, tr. J. Cottingham, R. Stoothoff and D. Murdoch (Cambridge University Press, Cambridge, 1984). Quotations in English from Descartes' writings are taken from this edition.
The most recent translations use 'mind' rather than 'soul' for the French 'âme'. It may not make any difference for our purposes. Many writers in the seventeenth and eighteenth centuries used 'âme' and 'esprit' interchangeably.
11 Descartes, *Principles*, Part I, Art. 71.
12 Descartes, *Meditations on First Philosophy*, VI (tr. Cottingham) in *The Philosophical Writings of Descartes*, vol. 2, p. 56. Cf. *Principles*, Part I, Arts 60, 73; Part II, Art. 2; Part IV, Art. 190.
13 Descartes, *Replies to Fourth Set of Objections*, p. 160.
14 Ibid., p. 157.
15 References to English translations of the treatise are to the edition by Thomas Steele Hall (Cambridge, Mass.: Harvard University Press, 1972). The reference here is found on pp. 85–6. Future references will be indicated as Hall. For the original French, see the Adam and Tannery edition of Descartes' *Oeuvres* (Vrin, Paris, 1974), vol. 11, p. 176. Subsequently abbreviated as AT.
16 Hall, p. 94; AT, vol. 11, p. 182.
17 Hall, p. 92; AT, vol. 11, p. 181.
18 Hall, p. 70; AT, vol. 11, p. 164
19 Hall, pp. 37, 38; AT, vol. 11, p. 144. The translation by Stoothoff in the new Cambridge edition honours the 'occasion' language (vol. I, p. 103). Only a small selection of the *Treatise* has been included in this edition.
20 Meditation III says: 'and although one idea may perhaps originate from another', p. 29.
21 Ibid., p. 26.
22 Ibid., p. 28.
23 Ibid., pp. 28–9.
24 See his replies to Caterus (*The First Set of Objections*), where he also insists that the objective feature of ideas must have a cause.
25 Meditation III, p. 31.
26 *Replies to the First Set of Objections*, p. 74.
27 For the evidence and arguments supporting this claim, see Yolton, *Perceptual Acquaintance*, pp. 6–10, 32–4, and also Brian O'Neil's *Epistemological Direct Realism in Descartes' Philosophy* (University of New Mexico Press, Albuquerque, 1974).
28 See Joseph Glanvill, *Essays on Several Important Subjects in Philosophy and Religion* (1675) and *The Vanity of Dogmatizing* (1661); Ralph Cudworth, *A Treatise Concerning Eternal and Immutable Morality* (1731); and Charles Bonnet, *Essai analytique sur les facultés de l'ame* (1760) and *Essai de psychologie* (1754).
29 For the details of this notion, and the general account of perception in Descartes, see my

Perceptual Acquaintance, ch. 1. I also refer there to two brief discussions of Descartes' natural sign doctrine by Rodis-Lewis and Louis Marin (pp. 26–7). For a more recent discussion, see Rodis-Lewis, *Descartes, Texts et débats* (Libraire générale française, Paris, 1984), pp. 465–7, 514–15.

30 This non-causal interaction relation (both the *occasion* and the *significatory* interaction) applies only in the direction of body to mind. The mind seems able to cause or make the pineal gland move and hence affect the body's physiology.

31 See Rorty, *Mirror of Nature*, pp. 371–2. Cf. p. 368, where he says of 'the great edifying, peripheral, thinkers', Dewey, Wittgenstein and Heidegger, that 'They hammer away at the holistic point that words take their meanings from other words rather than by virtue of their representative character, and the corollary that vocabularies acquire their privileges from the men who use them rather than from their transparency to the real.'

32 Ibid., p. 45.

33 Ibid.

34 *Essay*, 2.1.9.

35 Ibid., 1.2.5. Cf. Arnauld's definition 4: 'Je dis qu'un objet est présent à notre esprit, quand notre esprit l'apperçoit et le connoit.' The detailed presentation of Arnauld and Locke on these points can be found in my *Perceptual Acquaintance*, chs 3 and 5. The echoes in Berkeley can be found in two passages. *Principles*, section 49, says that qualities (a term used interchangeably with ideas) 'are in the mind only as they are perceived by it, that is, not by way of mode or attribute, but only by way of "idea"'. In the third *Dialogue*, Philonous says that ideas exist in the mind 'not by way of mode or property, but as a thing perceived in that which perceives it'. Both passages, but especially the second, carry strong echoes of Descartes' notion of the objective reality of ideas.

36 See John Locke, *An Examination of P. Malebranche's Opinion of Seeing All Things in God*, in *Works* (1823), vol. 9, s. 47.

37 Ibid., s 30; Cf. s. 15.

38 Ibid., s. 8.

39 Locke, *Essay*, 2.8.2, 7.

40 Ibid., 2.8.8.

41 Ibid., 2.6.11.

42 Ibid., 4.3.28.

43 Ibid., 4.3.29. What was and was not a natural relation was a question of great importance at that time. Were gravity natural to bodies, that would, it was thought, give active powers to what was generally (though not always by Locke) viewed as passive and inert. Locke's suggestion that God could add thought to suitably organized matter would be another instance of an *arbitrary*, not a *natural*, feature of bodies.

44 Ibid., 4.4.4.

45 Ibid., 2.9.3.

46 Ibid., 2.9.4.

47 Locke, *Malebranche's Opinion*, s. 30.

48 Locke, *Essay*, 4.21.4.

49 Ibid., 2.8.12.

50 Ibid., 4.1.1; cf. 4.4.3.

51 Rorty, *Mirror of Nature*, p. 48n.

52 In *Works* (1823), vol. 4, p. 233.

53 For a reference to the use of this notion, though not always favourably, by Nelson Goodman, David Hamlyn and Nicholas Rescher, see John W. Yolton, 'Pragmatism Revisited: An Examination of Professor Rescher's Conceptual Idealism', *Idealistic Studies*, September 1976, pp. 224–8. See also Yolton, 'How is Knowledge of the World Possible?', in *The Philosophy of Nicholas Rescher*, ed. E. Sosa (Reidel, Dordrecht, 1979).

For an interesting discussion of 'direct presence to the mind', see J. Cook-Wilson, *Statement and Inference* (Oxford University Press, Oxford, 1926), vol. 1, pp. 60–6. Cook-Wilson brings out the error of concluding from 'the *real* object is not directly present to consciousness', that 'we are not conscious of the "real"' (p. 62).

54 For some discussion of this point, see Yolton, 'Representation and Realism'.
55 Rorty, *Mirror of Nature*, p. 45.
56 Ibid., p. 59.
57 Ibid., p. 137.
58 Ibid., p. 143. See Green's Introduction to the Green and Grose edition of Hume's *A Treatise of Human Nature* (Longmans, Green & Co., London, 1898), p. 11. The Introduction has been separately reproduced in T. H. Green, *Hume and Locke* (Thomas Y. Crowell, 1968), p. 11.
59 Cf. Rorty, *Mirror of Nature*, p. 146: 'The notion of an "immaterial tablet" splits the difference between simple physiological fact and speculative metaphor, and any philosophy which uses it will be torn both ways.' He goes on to make a strange claim: 'Since Locke views himself as an up-to-date scientist he would love to cash the "tablet" metaphor in physiological terms.' I can find no justification whatsoever for such a claim. Locke, like most writers at that time, accepted that physiological processes underlie or accompany psychological awareness. There are even physiological explanations in the *Essay* of psychological phenomena. Perhaps this strange remark by Rorty results from his rejection of psychology as a science.
60 Rorty, *Mirror of Nature*, p. 160.

5

Veritable Reflections

Gerald Vision

The chief *aperçu* about truth in *Philosophy and the Mirror of Nature* (hereafter *PMN*) is implicit in the deplored image of The Mirror of Nature. For Rorty truth is not a kind of conformity to (/mirroring of) the way things are, but merely whatever we are entitled to believe at the time. Chatting non-metaphysically, Rorty allows, as we might put it, that 'true utterances state the way things are': he is careful to preserve ordinary modes of speech. But very little probing reveals that this formula is the merest platitude or a form of self-congratulation. Were we to claim anything as a *basis* for saying that truths state the way the world is, that basis would be caught up in the same circle of our current views (/our best science) that we introduced it to validate. Thus the conformity of our truths to reality is ultimately empty; and to assert it serves no function beyond reaffirmation of the truths themselves or stylistic variation.

The orthodoxy being denounced broadly fits the classical Correspondence Theory of Truth (hereafter, Correspondence). I have set myself the task of examining Rorty's case against it. I conclude that his attack fails. There are other familiar objections to Correspondence against which we shall not here defend it, but at least Rorty's distinctive reasons for rejecting it leave it unscathed.

We shall not be able to cover all the sources of Rorty's dissatisfaction. This is largely because he is contending, *inter alia*, that Correspondence is an integral part of a more extensive philosophical outlook that virtually the whole of *PMN* is devoted to repudiating. And I see no way to address that larger issue without a tome at least the size of *PMN*. Nevertheless, despite considerable difficulties of interpretation, it seems that his case is occasionally built from smaller bits of argument about this or that aspect of the philosophical tradition. For purposes of this paper we may take the bits that seem most directly relevant to truth to form his case against

Correspondence. Given the nature of the argument of *PMN* just described, we shall also naturally confront the question, in various guises, whether the defence of Correspondence requires other elements of the grander outlook.

The Correspondence Theory of Truth

Rorty and others write allusively about Correspondence. But the view is too central to our sort of dispute to be left so shadowy. We cannot here launch into a detailed exposition of Correspondence; but perhaps we can say enough to bring into clearer focus just what it is Rorty must propose that we give up.

In its most general form Correspondence holds that truth-bearers (e.g. statements or beliefs) are *made (/constituted) true by* particular somethings in the world. Their truth consists in their discriminating those somethings. A something may be, on different versions, a fact, state of affairs, situation, set of objects, sequence of members of a domain, or a piece of spatio-temporal real estate. Differences between kinds of truth-bearers and kinds of worldly somethings are emphasized by Correspondence's numerous votaries. But they are less important for our purposes than the following matters of detail.

First, above all Correspondence concerns the constitution or make-up of truth: truth's mechanisms, as it were. As such, *it need not be*, on some understanding of these accounts, a theory about the meaning of 'truth' (/'is true'), an explanation of truth, what it is to say that something is true, how one goes about establishing that something is true, the circumstances in which 'true' is used, or even the necessary and sufficient conditions for a bearer's being true. Of course, any account of these things may also be an account of what truth consists in, and then the accounts will coincide. But there are also understandings of each of the distinguished items on which they provide something additional to or different from what it is that makes a bearer true.

Second, the truth-constituter cannot be *essentially* cognition-dependent. Nothing in the characterization of truth itself can require that the state of affairs, and so on, be conceptual, require our cognitive contribution, impose a human viewpoint or categories, or the like. Of course, my true statement may be about someone's thought, and then the state of affairs making it true will be a mind-dependent something: say, that someone has a certain thought. Strictly, it is conceivable that all truth-constituters happen to be like this. But it cannot be part of the position that truth-constituters are so: the cognition-dependence of the truth-constituter can flow from the nature of the particular subject-matter or

from an unrelated version of idealism and the nature of the world, but
cannot flow from any articles of Correspondence itself. Truth, then, is not
per se epistemologized.

Third, the quasi-causal vocabulary to which we are reduced in describing truth-constituters is too crude to avert all potential misunderstanding.
Here we encounter a problem first scouted by Aristotle,[1] that our causal
vocabulary is not finely-grained enough. For example, I want to say that
that this woman is wielding an axe is the reason for or cause of ($\alpha\check{\iota}\tau\iota\text{o}\nu$) the
truth of 'This woman is wielding an axe.' But that she was given the wrong
dosage of medicine may also be the reason for the truth of that sentence
since it is the cause of her madness. Thus, we want to distinguish the state
of affairs that constitutes the bearer's truth from those which merely
brought about its truth. The closest analogy to this relation I can think of
would be the way fragments glued together constitute a coffee mug. But
the sense of 'constitution' we need may be *sui generis*, and any analogies no
more than vague signposts.

To say, as we have, that Correspondence is the view that truth is
constituted by a relation between a truth-bearer and something in a
not-essentially-mind-dependent world may be too sketchy for some. But it
is not vacuous. It distinguishes the view from others that hold, say, that
truth consists in the bearer's logical and/or evidential relations to other
truth-bearers (Coherence), or in the bearer's lending itself to further
satisfactory experiences (Pragmatism), or in 'what is good in the way of
belief'[2] or in 'what we will believe if we keep inquiring by our present
lights'.[3] Thus the view outlined here is substantial enough, just by virtue
of its popular contrasts, for us to describe a genuine philosophical
controversy.

Correspondence and cognition

The second point above deserves further comment. The absence of a
connection between Correspondence and mind-dependence is the basis for
the puzzlingly frequent charge that Correspondence leads to scepticism, or
at least that it leads to a transcendent notion of truth while departing from
whatever commonsense one we may have. But all that the refusal to write
into the notion of truth the cognition-dependence of the truth-constituter
does is to prohibit an advance *guarantee* that cognizers will have accessible
to them the world that would make an utterance true. This supplies no
argument that we are not in fact cognizant of such a world. In fact,
Correspondence is compatible with virtually any other potential refutation
of scepticism, so long as that refutation is not founded just in the concept
of truth.

Rorty praises pragmatists for offering a useful notion of truth, and scolds realists for not doing so. He writes of pragmatists that they provide 'something continuous with commonsense instead of something which *might be* as remote from commonsense as the Mind of God' (my emphasis).[4] However, *might be* isn't tantamount to *is* or even to *likely*. And since Rorty is elsewhere not keen about philosophical assurances, it is mildly incongruous that he is here so laudatory about a conception just for implying the usual antirealist assurance of cognitive accessibility. If, as he says, 'nothing can refute the sceptic',[5] and for this reason scepticism isn't an issue we need concern ourselves with, it is difficult to see why Correspondence shouldn't be as good an account of commonsense practice as is the pragmatic identification of truth with 'warranted assertibility'. Moreover, regarding commonsense commonsensically – rather than in the manner of philosophers who appropriate it against transcendental notions – advance guarantees against failure are seldom available for implements, such as ovens, pens and clocks, which work quite well in spite of that. Though the comparison will not sit well with some, I must confess that I cannot see why the demand for a guarantee that truth interact as promised with epistemic notions should be any more reasonable than one of the aforementioned devices. Indeed, scepticism aside, it might be said that Correspondence fits our practice better than pragmatism, since it escapes the latter's difficulty of distinguishing truth from the epistemic notions. That aside, the difficulty remains of making sense of Rorty's combining the view that scepticism cannot be refuted with his preference for a view of truth just for its ability to do what (he also says) cannot be done.

Elsewhere, working from a similar set of assumptions, Rorty supposes that the Davidsonian–Stroudian principle, roughly, that we could not find intelligible a community of beliefs that are mostly false or mostly different from ours, rules out our discovering any cognition-independent conception of truth.[6] The principle cited is central to his reworking of the Davidsonian claim that conceptual schemes radically distinct from ours are unintelligible. (This is a comment only upon *Rorty's understanding* of Davidson's argument.) The hallmark of Rorty's realist conception of truth is a sharp distinction between the way things are and the way they appear. And he exposes the view as maintaining that 'for all we know, [reality might] prove to contain none of the things we have always thought we were talking about'.[7] This remark lends itself to several questions, but here I only wish to mention one seriously misleading implication. Realism or Correspondence is not, as such, the view that things *could be* other than they appear, or the view that our ultimate theories might turn out false. That is rather a widely supposed consequence. Realism itself would be a view about *what* accounts for each truth, even ones that we may now hold. The Correspondence theorist need only claim that our grasping of truth-constituters does not make them mind-dependent. (He need not even claim this much, but we can allow the overstatement for simplicity.) This may make the realist un-Kantian, but it is a realist view all the same.

Starting-points

Rorty's conclusions are generally extracted from expositions of those of others – the sorts of thinkers he calls 'heroes of this book'.[8] We might summarize his views on truth as follows. In so far as we have a usable conception of truth, it is nothing over-and-above what enquiry allows. He suggests, rather casually, that 'truth' can be indifferently glossed as 'what we will believe if we keep inquiring by our present lights' or 'what it is better for us to believe' or 'what can be defended against all comers' or 'warranted assertibility'; though he also seems to think it is of no moment whether these are taken as elucidations of truth or substitutes for it.[9] The crucial point is that there is nothing – not the external world, not a realm of noumena, not the Forms – with which to ground our current practice; thus truth can be no firmer than our best lights. He allows a further, attenuated, notion of truth, which he calls Platonic and transcendent. I shall also call it 'unglossable'. On it we are careful to note that no gloss – via epistemic, scientific or, generally, inquisitive, notions – can be accurate. The fact that we can make sense of the remark 'warranted assertible (/"justified"/"reasonable"), but not true' is important here. It is unclear whether Rorty takes the sensibleness of the remark to be a distinctive trait of the transcendent notion, but it certainly accounts for its unglossability. It is not, according to him, our 'workaday' or 'homely and shopworn' notion of truth, since on it it is conceivable that the truth-constituter turn out to be very different from what our best ideas on the subject reveal. Thus, it is vulnerable to the sceptical challenge. Correspondence, of course, is designed for unglossable truth.

We have seen, in the last section, some of the flaws with these conclusions. Here I want to concentrate on another problem, namely the way in which Rorty arrogates to himself ground rules that virtually assure him victory. They do not tell against Correspondence unless one is first committed to Rorty's view. Thus, even if one is convinced, with Rorty, that there are no mutually acceptable starting-points, he does not provide the kind of persuasive retelling of philosophical theory which he claims to be using to make his case.[10]

Rorty begins with a conception of truth that is already epistemologized. His first important sallies into the topic in *PMN* begin by coupling 'knowledge and truth'[11] as if a single treatment will suffice for both. Moreover, when treating the Correspondence notion of 'representation', he tackles it in terms not of truth but of the paradigmatically epistemic notion of knowledge. Not only does Rorty write of the problem of trying to 'bridge the gap' between knowledge and its subject[12] – adding that the choice of a solution is a choice between different notions of *truth* – but he regularly talks of 'the relation of knowledge to reality',[13] and of different assertions counting as knowledge which are required, on some accounts, 'not only to cohere with other assertions ... but to "correspond" to something'.[14] None of this need be in itself wrongheaded, but notice that the kinds of word–world relations standardly discussed first about truth are in Rorty's exposition raised first about knowledge; on top of which, knowledge and truth are combined in a single stroke of pen as if there were no significant differences between them. It is scarcely cause for astonishment that Rorty is unable to discover, in his later treatment, any useful concept of truth other than an epistemologized one (which, given our recent characterization, is incompatible with Correspondence).

Indeed, even when he is discussing knowledge exclusively, Rorty engages in commentary, baffling though it may be, to preordain that any 'representational' notion of truth will be burdened with excessive epistemological baggage. He says of 'knowledge ... conceived of as accurate representation' that the accuracy of representation element 'requires a theory of privileged representations, ones which are automatically and intrinsically accurate'.[15] I haven't any reliable basis for surmising what 'automatic' or 'intrinsic' accuracy might convey here. (What would it be for something to be *extrinsically* accurate?) But from the remainder of his exposition, I would venture that when Rorty writes of a representation being 'privileged' he has in mind a variety of assurance of infallibility traditionally assumed to be implicit in knowledge. But, if I am right – and if I'm not, I don't have even a vague idea of what Rorty means – it is very difficult to see how any of this gets introduced just through the idea that knowledge involves accurate *representation*. Of the conceptions of knowledge that amount to something like assured infallibility, some are representational and some are not. And of the conceptions of knowledge that reject an assurance of infallibility as a condition, once again some are representational and some are not. Thus we have yet another confusion of issues. When this is added to the conflation of knowledge with truth, we are left with the daunting task not only of elucidating the correspondence relation for truth, but of showing how the truths in question are instances of knowledge, and thus how we are entitled to assume that anyone has an assurance of infallibility for them. *Pace* Rorty I have been maintaining that the question of what constitutes the truth of an utterance is not dependent on first answering how we can know (much less with infallibility) of any utterance that it is true.

Problems proliferate. When Rorty comes to discuss the philosophy of language in chapter 6 of *PMN*, the chapter which supplies most of the text for this sermon, he divides the philosophy of language (I shall henceforth call it 'semantics') into the 'pure' and the 'impure'. Pure semantics for Rorty can have no ontological implications; its only concern being the logical and quasi-logical relations between a set of semantically significant notions. Impure semantics purports to have ontological consequences, but only, according to Rorty, because it smuggles in epistemological theses which already have been exploded (according to the author) through the adoption of epistemological behaviourism. Thus we see in the end that ontology can be nothing but a branch of epistemology. If there are no epistemological theses, there are no ontological ones.[16] Of course, Correspondence does not by itself demonstrate the existence of a mind-independent world. But it provides at least one barrier to arguments against such a world, and thus is occasionally accorded the status of an ontological thesis. What here prohibits such ontological theses? Only, it appears, Rorty's undefended juggling of philosophical classifications, which he uses to close off any route to ontological significance other than those running through a certain selective group of epistemological concerns.

Is this a criticism of Rorty's position? He concedes, indeed insists, that there are no perfectly objective, neutral or mutually agreeable starting-points. That each view will appear circular to the other side is just a consequence of Kuhnian incommensurability applied to philosophy. But even if that is so, we still want to distinguish between the old-fashioned variety of question-begging and the unavoidable kind; and the sort uncovered here seems to fall into the former category. (Rorty himself complains about a question-begging ploy he ascribes to realism.[17]) In some generous sense Rorty does seem to want his 'reading [of] the history of philosophy' *to show* that Correspondence is an ill-fated view; and to misdescribe the view from the outset can scarcely accomplish that. He has also claimed elsewhere that the standard philosophical view sees Correspondence 'interlocked' with the Platonic notion of *reason*,[18] and presumably with other epistemic notions such as justifications and evidence that would go along with reason. Let us grant for the sake of argument that all these notions are parts of a pattern constituting what might be called the traditional outlook. But to assume on nothing more than the basis of the metaphor of 'interlocking' that, say, Correspondence and a certain view of knowledge are interdependent notions, rather than, say, otherwise non-implicational contributions to this single outlook, would be to distort rather than report the view.

That aside, Rorty certainly seems to believe that the dispute between his brand of antirealism and the traditional outlook is relevantly mooted by one side or the other providing a persuasive, tendentious overview of the philosophical debates. In those terms, I do not see why anyone conversant with the subject should suppose that a remotely plausible retelling could assume at the outset that truth is thoroughly epistemologized.

What good is a theory of truth?

Whatever its virtues, Correspondence *is not* a very helpful criterion of truth. That is, it neither supplements nor supplants whatever other tests we have for justified belief. Rorty hints that we could only connect an ahistorical truth theory to our practice, for him a requirement of admissibility, if it supplied a method of verification or justified our past practice. He claims that a truth theory failing to pass his tests (namely, a theory of transcendent truth) has the disqualifying fault of 'float[ing] free of all questions of justification'.[19] We shall return shortly to question the plausibility of this requirement. But first notice that the realist notion of truth, Correspondence, does not 'float free' of questions of justification: though no doubt its connections would not be of a kind of which Rorty approves. Justification, as an epistemic notion, belongs to a group of concepts I shall entitle 'the evidentiary family'. Members of the family are, in Alvin Goldman's useful phrase 'truth-linked'.[20] On the realist conception, individual justifications and their standards are evaluated by the strength of their propensity to deliver truth. There may be other tests to which systems of justification are also subject (e.g. speed, avoidance of error), and the requisite strength of the propensity for truth may vary with context; but it is an indispensable part here of the realist outlook that being justified is a worthless property of beliefs if having it does not improve the chances of its subject being true.

Nothing in the truth-link requires that we have access to a proposition's truth other than the means we have for justifying it. The 'truths' by which the standard is tested are only things we *think* true. The connection is a conceptual one, assured only through thought-experiment. But it would be irrelevant to object to the truth-link by appealing, as Rorty so often does elsewhere, to our sociocentric predicament; to the fact that we have access to no better beliefs than the ones we are justified in believing.[21] For the truth-link is *no more* conceptual and *no less* legitimate than, say, the view that our only useful conception of truth is as what is warrantedly assertible.

If realism is correct, truth functions as a regulator of evidence. There are further details of this regulatory function worth mentioning – especially its role with respect to defeasible evidence – but we haven't the space for a discussion of them here. However, we should note that the possible combination 'warranted assertible (/justified) but not true' is unproblematic for the realist. That this remark makes sense immediately raises suspicions about any proposal for epistemologized truth. I am not implying that antirealists cannot account for the remark; but only that it is a challenge or problem for epistemologized truth, while it creates no difficulties for realism.

Nevertheless, a Rortyian might find the truth-link pointless because it only marks a connection between several *concepts*. This line might continue, using one of Rorty's favourite analogies, that to be told that justification must increase the chances of truth is as empty as being told that good action conforms to The Moral Law or The Form of The Good. However, this would be to miss an important consequence of the view. For it makes it impossible to fashion the notion of truth out of any notion from the evidentiary family. Truth cannot both regulate and be merely supervenient upon these other notions. Thus the realist point cannot be shrugged off concessively. If it is correct, it is futile to claim that it is pointless. For far from being innocuous, it is incompatible with the direction of conceptual priority presupposed in schemes of epistemologized truth.

We are, of course, only considering the case in which 'truth' and, say, 'warrented assertibility' are both preserved. The question is how they must interact if we are to have both. Another antirealist view might replace 'truth' by 'warranted assertibility'. This openly revisionist policy does not fall prey to the foregoing difficulty. But if one seeks to preserve a notion of truth, one cannot divide it from the place recognized above by realism without severing too much of what is central to its ordinary signification.

Rorty seeks to avoid this consequence, but without success. For example, he uses what he takes to be Sellars's notion of the relativity of truth to conceptual framework to argue that the antirealist might accommodate the remark by 'interpret[ing] "warranted assertible in our conceptual framework but not true" as an implicit reference to another, perhaps not yet invented, conceptual framework in which the statement in question would not be warranted assertible'.[22] But who could want to make that remark? Although conceptual frameworks may not be as plentiful as possible worlds, with a bit of imagination – and mindful that the proviso that the relevant conceptual framework doesn't even have to be invented yet – it would appear that this remark is applicable to virtually *every* (contingent) truth. For we might imagine almost any truth as an untruth on some conceptual framework or other. (Consider, for example, a theory that enthroned Descartes' evil deceiver.) Our test remark is not tantamount, as Rorty would have it, to 'can be imagined to be false (/untrue)', as a bit of reflection makes obvious, but rather is a musing upon the slack between our two notions. Rorty's gloss fails to capture that. Speaking again about the conceptual framework in which Rorty says the statement would not be true, he would no doubt also hold that neither could the statement be warrantedly assertible there. And, he would similarly add, that in that framework if it were warrantedly assertible it would have been true. Thus Rorty's envisaged circumstance might as well have been displaying the sensibleness of the remark 'warranted assertible but not warranted assertible'. The preservation of the expression 'true' does not play any role here; does not preserve enough of the features mentioned earlier in the section to deliver anything but a familiar name. Better to foreswear all such subterfuge.

But perhaps this misses what Rorty takes as the main question: 'What would we lose if we have no ahistorical theory-independent notion of truth?'[23] The question is rhetorical, or at least taken as an unmet challenge for Correspondence. Rorty puts it slightly differently in a number of other places: as what there is to be gained from such a theory of truth, or in the form of another rhetorical question, 'What do we need the notion of truth, as opposed to justification, for?'[24] The basic thrust of the queries might be summed up in the demand that a philosophical theory of truth have some sort of utility.

How are we to deal with this requirement? My first impulse is to say with J. S. Mill that 'the truth of an opinion is part of its utility';[25] indeed, that it is all the utility a philosophical opinion needs. If Rorty could establish, as he attempts with his analogy involving The Idea of The Good, that the doctrine we are proposing is vacuous or empty in a stronger way, that would be fatal. But given that the view is incompatible with various things about truth that Rorty himself wants to hold, it is difficult to see how he will be able to show this. Moreover, I do not see how we are to remove the crucial vagaries of the requirement (encapsulated, in our summary, in the term 'utility'). As I mentioned earlier, Rorty suggests two 'uses' that might legitimate an ahistorical notion of truth, namely providing a criterion of truth (/a theory of justification) and justifying past (scientific) practice. Both would indeed be desirable traits for any theory of truth to have. But as candidates for *necessary* conditions, they seem to be non-starters. Perhaps they are merely intended as specimens from which we are to generate a larger class of such virtues. But I confess that I haven't any clue about how to construct the larger class from them. I would claim on behalf of Correspondence that it has the 'utility' of laying bare the mechanism by means of which truth works. But I don't know if this is a suitable candidate for the class of utilization virtues enshrined in the requirement. My own view is that the utility requirement leads nowhere. As for Rorty, he seems to require nothing less than a conception of truth that would be epistemic in just the way that a criterion for justifying beliefs would be so. But we have seen that without further argument this is not a requirement we have any reason to countenance.

Reference

Although Rorty makes sundry and desultory comments directly about truth, he suggests in *PMN* and elsewhere that the realist outlook, of which Correspondence is merely a centrepiece, is motivated by the causal/historical account of reference. That account provides the word–world relations to 'preserve' Correspondence.[26] If it were correct, it would vindicate what he calls the 'impure' ('hybrid' might be a more appropriate title) philosophy of language. But, according to Rorty, the view rests on a confusion of senses of 'refer'. His summary in *PMN* is sketchy in critical places; and I shall fill it out, as he recommends, with his fuller treatment of the matter in 'Realism and Reference' (hereafter RR).[27] However, there are serious stumbling blocks to accepting Rorty's argument. Let us first sketch his view and then examine its drawbacks.

Rorty distinguishes three kinds of reference, only the first and third of which are central to our concerns. *Reference₁* or *talking about* is 'a commonsensical notion'. It is 'a purely "intentional" relation which can hold between an expression and a non-existent object'.[28] On it 'you refer to whatever you think you're referring to'.[29] *Reference₃* is 'a factual relation which holds between an expression and some other portion of reality whether anybody knows it holds or not'.[30] It is a technical philosophical notion, and as the recent passage implies, it satisfies the inference pattern 'The term X (or language-user P) refers to A, A is identical with B, therefore X ($/P$) refers to B.' For completeness, *reference₂* is an intermediate notion, which allows us to correct (what we take to be) misguided efforts of a user to refer, say, to outdated theoretical entities or to non-existents. Operating with reference₂ we may expect to hear remarks such as, 'When the Greeks spoke of Zeus' thunderbolts they were *really* referring to electrical discharges.' On reference₃ the Greeks would have failed to refer, while on *talking about* they would have referred to Zeus' thunderbolts.

We shall have more to say about these distinctions. But to complete Rorty's argument, we must first clarify his views about the two major competing accounts of reference. They are:

1 *The causal theory* – associated with Kripke, Donnellan and Putnam – in which reference is secured by the instance of the expression appearing on a chain of usage properly linked, causally or historically, to the right referent.

2 *The descriptivist theory* – associated with Frege, Russell, Strawson and Searle – in which reference is secured by (our intention to use) a term being backed (/abbreviated/defined) by a set of descriptions (/beliefs/identity criteria), a sufficient number of which accurately and uniquely identify the referent.

As the alternative formulations indicate, there are significant intra-theoretical differences amongst the advocates in each camp. Nevertheless, there is enough similarity to distinguish broadly between those who think of reference as grounded in the right sort of 'contact' with the referent, causal theorists, and those who believe it can be brought off by the possession of accurate information or recognitional abilities, descriptivist theorists.

At various places Rorty writes that (1) is physicalistic, non-intentional, and demands the truth of what we may call 'the axiom of existence'.

(AE) 'Whatever is referred to must exist'[31]

We can, however, easily 'talk about' fictional (=non-existent) figures since *talking about* is a function of a speaker's intentions. But Rorty contends that there is no genuine issue between (1) and (2) that is to the point. For example, we cannot use the phrase 'really talking about', reference$_2$, to turn reference$_1$ into reference$_3$ because 'really talking about' just places the speaker's knowledge into a context of greater knowledge, and 'really talking about' fictional figures is consistent with that.[32] What to do about putative references to non-existents is not answered by a discovery but by a decision. On our common understanding, reference$_1$, there is no problem. Our intuitions are clear here: (AE) is simply false. On a conception of reference, such as the causal theory, which attempts to secure an existent referent, the question is merely what decision to take about the referential- or truth-value of sentences whose putative referent is non-existent. But in neither case has the causal theory of reference achieved what epistemology couldn't, namely to guarantee that our references do not go astray in ways that would subvert our truths.

There is much unclarity here. To begin with, it is unclear what this has to do with anyone's account of *truth*. In addition, Rorty seems to assume that a realist would have to abjure fictional truths, at least if he wanted a robust version of Correspondence. But this simply ignores a series of complicated issues that have been ventilated recently. Should the realist want to maintain that there are truths about non-existents, a host of possibilities is open; for example, reduction of such statements to those of another type, an appeal to the basis of 'fictional fact' in something non-fictional (e.g. an event involving an author), the acceptance of fictional facts (and this needn't be vacuous or *ad hoc* if combined with the second strategy) or a contextualist notion of truth.[33] I am not suggesting that any of these will work, but only that they are not to be precluded *ab initio*, and Rorty simply ignores the potential for incorporating them into Correspondence.

Of course, Rorty would reply to the second, and perhaps the first, of these misgivings that if we allow reference to, and thereby truth about, non-existents, we will forfeit the only basis for an 'interesting' employment of Correspondence. For the point, according to him, of having a theory of reference$_3$ is to show why our current attempts to refer are not doomed to the same fate as those undertaken during the heyday of (now) outdated scientific theories, and why past science has been an approximation to our present practice. Only by guaranteeing that we are now referring to what (from a larger perspective) exists can we accomplish this. But this rejoinder leads me to two further criticisms.

First, once again Rorty assumes that the issue must be over an epistemic criterion. In doing so he not only mangles a number of the texts he is commenting on – his views perhaps fit an earlier incarnation of Putnam, but scarcely resemble Kriple or Donnellan – but turns what was basically a dispute over concrete singular terms such as proper names, and only peripherally over natural kind and theoretical terms, into one whose focus and critical test is its handling of theoretical terms.

Second, even if we grant his epistemological *parti pris*, he has mislocated the problem. The issue is not focally over *non-existent* (would-be) referents and *fictional* (would-be) facts, but over *mistaken* referents and facts. Conceding that there is no such element as phlogiston, still the fatal flaw in its theory is that phlogiston was used to give mistaken explanations. The only cause we had to suppose phlogiston existed was that it explained, say, combustion; thus, once we forswore such explanations, we abandoned the belief that phlogiston exists. But even supposing we had a theory of reference that allowed us to continue saying phlogiston existed, if our scientific theories evolved otherwise similarly, we would still not be referring to phlogiston when we referred to the cause of combustion. Sherlock Holmes, on the other hand, may not exist, but there is no more reason why anyone attempting to refer to him should be mistaken or confused than there is for someone trying to refer to Arthur Conan Doyle. Allowing reference to the non-existent has no tendency to force upon us reference to the mistaken or confused, and so introducing the question of (AE) into these proceedings is just a red herring. The significance of this emerges when we examine the alleged role of (AE) in distinguishing Rorty's senses of 'refer'.

Nevertheless, two questions about Rorty's discussion of reference remain. The first is, 'Given the distinctions between kinds of reference, is Rorty entitled to use it as he has?' The second is, 'Are the distinctions genuine ones (=sufficient to support his specific criticisms)?' I shall deal with the first question in the remainder of this section and with the second in the next.

The *epistemological behaviourism* our author believes disposes of all forms of realism is, for him, a form of holism.[34] The latter implies that there are no conceptual truths or semantic facts from which to proceed; for we cannot draw, in a principled way, a distinction between a language-user's semantic component for a term X and her deeply-felt but contingent beliefs about Xs. This is the nerve of Rorty's attack on textbook epistemology, not its window dressing. By the time we arrive at realism's last stand, its impure theory of reference, Rorty has used repeated applications of his epistemological behaviourist weapon to exhaust the remainder of what he takes to be realism's total wherewithal for redeeming the view. Thus it comes as no small surprise when Rorty delivers, in chapter 6 of *PMN*, and in RR, a standard philosophical attack on this theory of reference based upon an alleged confusion among its proponents between *senses* or *meanings* of 'reference'. Though he writes indifferently of the word 'reference' and the notion reference, the distinction between defining traits of the senses is unmistakable. He writes of 'the equivocity of "refer"',[35] the confusion of different notions,[36] what *defines* a notion of reference,[37] and senses of 'refer'.[38] And it couldn't be said that these sorts of distinctions (as opposed to others) are inessential to his purposes. He requires that there be a confusion between at least two somethings. If not senses, two whats? Moreover, it must involve a confusion between items that have certain tenets, such as (AE), belonging to them *by definition*. Only this assumption could explain contentions such as the following: 'Reference$_1$ is fully opaque: if one is talking in the nineteenth century about genes, one is not talking about bits of DNA molecules, even if the twentieth discovers that that is what genes are.'[39] To the natural rejoinder that older biologists *were* talking about bits of DNA molecules though they didn't know it, can Rorty reply in any way other than by pointing out that this is prohibited by the meaning of 'reference$_1$' (/'talking about')? Here it looks as if he is helping himself to the crucial step his epistemological behaviourism denies modern neo-Kantian philosophy. Applying his usual method to his own case, we might ask Rorty how he can distinguish between what is merely unquestionably true about reference and what belongs to the meanings of the term. If that challenge is not fatal to Rorty's line of reasoning, it is difficult to see why others shouldn't be allowed to draw a distinction between what is necessarily true, true by definition, and what is only a deep-seated belief.

Are there distinct senses of 'refer'?

But let us press the issue beyond this *ad hominem*. To do that we shall accept the usual, albeit informal, ground rules for distinguishing senses of terms or for individuating notions. Some of the differences Rorty cites are like scope distinctions, though there may be no intensional verbs, modalities or negative particles in a particular relevant sentence upon which to hang a scope differentiation. But, as the characterization of reference$_3$ as satisfying an inference pattern indicates, the referents of reference$_3$ are open to free substitution while those of reference$_1$ are not. 'Talking about' fails on this score for two conspicuous reasons: (1) a language user or her words cannot refer to x without her knowing that she is referring to x (under just that characterization), and (2) she or her words can refer to a non-existent. However, upon closer inspection it seems to me that (1) is not true of any conception of 'taking about' that can be culled from our practice (and the extent to which it embodies an insight about *intentions* is as applicable to reference$_3$), and the situation with regard to (2) is similar for reference$_1$ and reference$_3$. To see both points, let us begin with Rorty's way of characterizing the differences.

Putting (2), reference$_1$ to non-existents, on the back burner for the moment, recall that Rorty characterizes 'talking about' as a truly 'intentional' notion, one on which 'you refer to whatever you think you're referring to'[40] and on which 'We are talking about whatever most of our beliefs are true of'.[41] Let us ask whether there is any notion of 'talking about' in which *if* a speaker believes he is talking about x, he is talking about x. I think not, and the culprit is incurable confusion; what I prefer to call referential inscrutability. Of course, the most notorious reason philosophers have tended to give for reference failure, even when writing in what they take to be a non-technical vein, has been the non-existence of the referent (e.g. the present King of France, Piltdown man, caloric). But each of these cases also has been marked by referential confusion, by the attempt to refer to something that couldn't fulfil the most rudimentary ends for the attempt. Referential inscrutability is more basic than mere falsity of utterance; it is more like confusion undermining an intention. The problem in the cases exemplified is not primarily the non-existence of the would-be referents, but that in the contexts of utterance assumed in those cases, non-existence was emblematic of dissolution of speaker intention. If the present King of France, Piltdown man or caloric did not exist, the speaker would be unable to pick out some other thing, existent or not, about which she wanted to say just what she originally purported to say. This is not the situation with established fictional 'referents'. To take a simple sort of case, suppose someone asks 'How can Francis Bacon have

had time to paint so many canvasses and write all those philosophy books?'
Now this *needn't* turn out to be an instance of inscrutability: the speaker
may, when apprised of her confusion, want to have spoken primarily of
the man born in 1561 rather than the contemporary artist. But there also is
the case of present interest in which the speaker will have been so
thoroughly confused that upon englightenment she could not sincerely say
which of the two she was inquiring about. And here the fact that she
believed she was referring to *x*, read opaquely, does not assure us that there
is a sense of 'talking about' in which she was talking about *x*. 'Divided
back up descriptions' is not the only sort of case leading to referential
inscrutability, but it is the easiest to describe. Thus there is no sense of
'refer' which can be defined in terms of a guarantee of referential
intentions.

Perhaps we can distinguish reference₁ and reference₃ by stressing the
intentionality of the former. The problem here is that genuine theories of
reference that have something satisfying what Rorty calls 'reference₃' as
their product are not as non-intentional as Rorty (or some of their
proponents) seem to think. Consider, for example, a typical causal theory,
which Rorty takes as a model for reference₃. Even if a particular use of a
name gets it reference by being on a certain (causal) chain of communication, the user must have *intended* to use the name that way. As Kripke
points out,[42] I can intend to use the name 'Darwin' for my pet tortoise
rather than the author of *On the Origin of Species*. My intention is the
ticket that puts my name-use on one causal line rather than another. And
this can be as physicalist as one chooses. Rorty's contrast of intentional
with physicalistic theories is a mismatch. Intentions may be needed for all
reference; and whether this is incompatible with physicalism will depend
on how intentions are to be understood.

We now come to Rorty's *pis aller*: he could use (AE) as a condition of
reference₃ but not of reference ₁. But then is reference₁ just reference₃
without (AE)? If that is the only difference, it is difficult to see what basis
there is for a distinction of sense, much less for calling one ordinary and
the other technical, especially if successful references in each are brought
off by the same mechanism. Now it seems preferable to view this as a
dispute over whether to attach a certain condition to a single kind of
reference. But there is a deeper problem with Rorty's contention. *If*, when
he says that (AE) is part of the *meaning* of 'reference₃', or that it attaches to
it *by definition*, he means that this is a matter of stipulation, and there are
no considerations pro or con other than those for the advisability of a
stipulation, he seems to me gravely mistaken. There is a snare in these
discussions, in which Rorty gets caught and I would like to avoid, of
writing as if we could deal with groups of philosophers *en bloc*. But I
would aver that not even the major causal and descriptivist theorists agree

amongst themselves on reasons for including (AE). Most accept (AE), but from my own experience most also believe there are reasons, of a conceptual sort, for doing so. The reasons may range from the alleged paradoxicality of non-existent referents to the adoption of a certain kind of discourse (usually scientific) as the model for all discourse. The motives are seldom as overtly epistemological as Rorty seems to believe. But both among descriptivists and causal theorists, there have been a minority of dissenters, who have accepted the broad outlines of one or another of these views, but have rejected (AE). A striking feature of disputes generated by this dissent is that the dissenters have not been treated by the main body of theorists as having simply committed a solecism, erring because they were badly informed about the rules of the game. Where rejected, their views have been rejected for apparently typical philosophical considerations, such as the problems encountered by the interaction of referential position and quantifiability.[43]

This points up a broader moral. Rorty writes as if all we have to know about reference$_3$ is that it is a *technical* notion, cooked up by philosophers for the sake of their systems. And he points to the adoption of (AE) as a reason for saying that they simply impose upon the view they want any additional requirements, not sanctioned by our ordinary notion, for their purposes. But that account would be unfaithful to actual practice. The various notions of reference developed in philosophy may be regimented and quasi-technical; but they grow out of efforts to elucidate the pre-reflective speech data reportable by at least some occurrences of our 'talking about' idiom. Philosophers may then reshape a notion that they don't believe wholly coherent; but the product must still be responsive to the ordinary data. It is never so transcendent or rarefied that it can ignore with impunity a regular or non-paradoxical class of relevant data from H. M. English. This does not mean that the data are always conclusive; they may be traded off against considerations of system. But it is erroneous to suppose that when either descriptivists or causal theorists are discussing reference they are not treating something which they take to be continuous with the ordinary phenomenon of linguistically picking out or focusing upon something to say something further about.

It may still be unclear how these animadversions on reference bear on Correspondence. Just as Rorty couples truth with knowledge in his earlier remarks, he links truth with reference in his discussion of referential semantics. Results concerning the effortlessness of referring$_1$ to non-existents are assumed to raise havoc with Correspondence. My educated guess is that he has in mind the popular *semantic principle* that a statement made with sentence S is true *if* the thing referred to by the use of S's subject term has the property ascribed or denied to it in S's predicate expression. ('Only if' is omitted because not all true statements are made with subject-predicate sentences.) It is important to note that virtually all the problems for Correspondence Rorty envisages as arising out of reference, and in particular out of reference to the fictional, depend on an adoption of this principle or one very much like it. Only through such a principle can we make intelligible the link between concerns over reference and the issue of the truth of the larger utterance containing the reference.

Two questions remain. Should we accept the principle? Should Rorty accept it? The first is too big an item to tackle here, so I shall just mention a consideration that seems to bear upon any decision. Unquestionably, reference's apparent contribution to truth has generated much of its current philosophical interest. But if we do not *begin with* a requirement that reference must make a systematic and formalizable contribution to the truth of any utterance in which it occurs, it is unclear that we will *arrive at* one. That is, if our concern is simply to unearth the workings by means of which we manage, with singular terms, to link our uses of them to the world, it is not beyond controversy that successful reference then makes the truth of an utterance a function of the attachment of the predicated property to the referent. If we assume that the referent exists – that is, adopt (AE) as a condition of reference – the contributory role of reference to truth will be less complicated. But even here it is not indisputable, as is illustrated by Donnellan's claims about the referential uses of mistaken descriptions.[44] Whether it is worth regimenting reference to gain the advantage of a uniform contribution to the truth of whole utterances is something I here leave to others to decide.

But, as for our second question, it is difficult to see what basis Rorty can give for requiring this principle. The need for reference and truth to work in such close harmony is motivated by just the same sort of quasi-technical considerations that Rorty supposes led to the confection of reference$_3$; and, so far as I can tell, there is very little to motivate the principle merely through a consideration of 'talking about'. Thus Rorty's introduction of reference into such matters, and his way of making the connection, provide us with yet another enigma. Why should he feel compelled to adopt the principle that makes his observations about reference relevant to truth?

Senses of 'True'

Even were we to grant Rorty's rejections of Correspondence and its tradition, it is not easy to discover what he believes entitles him to his preferred conception, in which truth can be indifferently glossed by various of its operational tests. One potential argument might be Rorty's recurrent appeals to our sociocentric predicament; to the fact that we can never grasp truths that elude actual enquiry. Despite a number of scattered references to this predicament as a justification for adopting his glossable truth, it involves (at least) two confusions. First, it confuses truth with truth*s*. It is not the nature of truth that gets labelled warrantedly assertible, but the things we consider true. Second, and more important, it seems to rest on an exotic form of the notorious Berkeleyan confusion between *the fact that we are conceiving something* and *what we are conceiving*.[45] That whatever we call true is conceivable (/justified by our best lights/warranted) doesn't show that being conceivable (etc.) is part of what we are affirming when we call it true. But this appeal, though it may contribute in subterranean ways to his conclusions, does not appear to be the mainstay of Rorty's thinking. Rather, he seems to argue that his view triumphs by default. He distinguishes two notions of truth, and accepts the one we have described because the other is unsuitable. The other in this case is of course what we have called 'unglossable truth'. Let us trace the reasoning in a bit more detail.

We begin with Davidson's attack on the notion of *a conceptual scheme*. A conceptual scheme alternative to ours would ultimately come down to a language in which the community having it held beliefs (expressible in the sentences of that language) which were largely true but not translatable into our language. This is unintelligible, on Rorty's understanding of Davidson, because if we can recognize that these people have a conceptual scheme at all, we must be able to translate their language into our own. But, *ex hypothesi*, our translations will be incorrect, though their differences with our source's actual beliefs will not show up anywhere in our experience.[46] Rorty compares this with Max Black's treatment of the inverted spectrum problem in which 'we can "divide through" the difference for all purposes of communications'.[47] As Rorty acknowledges, this looks at first like verificationism pure and simple. But he denies that it is verificationism, and he introduces his distinction of senses of 'true' to support the denial. According to him, it is merely escaping from the transcendent sense. He writes, 'To suggest that Davidson is verificationist and relativist in saying that most of our beliefs are true or that any language can be translated into English *is just to say* that he is not using the "Platonic" notions of Truth and Goodness and Reality which "realists" need to make their realism dramatic and controversial' (my emphasis).[48] Taken literally this is patently implausible. Surely, to say of anyone that he is a verificationist is not to say that he is not using a Platonic notion; rather, it is to comment on the notion he *is using*. However exemplary his motives in acquiring it, if the notion of truth he is using amounts to no more than the operational tests for it, it is verificationist. Of course, we have not shown here that this is a fault. Rorty presumably believes it is, for he is eager to deny the charge. But he doesn't say what more specifically is wrong with verificationism, so we cannot proceed further with that issue here. At all events, if verificationism is a charge worth escaping, Rorty's defence is cold consolation.

But if Rorty is correct, and his notion of truth as warranted assertibility is not verificationist, he is still in grave trouble – namely, in danger of not having said anything. Presumably, from everything Rorty has said, he *is not claiming* that if someone seriously proposed '*x* is warranted assertible' as a traditional analysis of '*x* is true' that this wouldn't be a form of vericationism. That is, it is not that the predicate 'warranted assertible' (and the other suggested glosses for 'is true') is (are) insufficiently operational to make this count as a verificationist analysis. The claim is rather that Rorty is not offering an *analysis* of truth (/'true'). But this immediately leads us to query just how we are to take his many claims of identity between truth and his preferred notions. It is not simply that the philosophical life has corrupted us to accept an abbreviated menu of possible interpretations. On the most generous construal imaginable, what could Rorty mean when he writes of 'James's *definition* of "the true"',[49] of 'the pragmatists (having) *identified* truth with . . .',[50] of 'truth *as* "what is good for us to believe"'[51] or of our '*simply identifying* truth with warranted assertibility'?[52] In each of these cases we have either a matter of the identity of truth with something operational or, stronger yet, a question of the definition of 'true'. But if these aren't genuine identities, what else is there for them to be?

There is a way to repair the situation by taking a more relaxed construal of Rorty's claims. This involves him in strict misstatement, but perhaps it minimizes it to an acceptable degree. On this interpretation, in the apparent 'identity' statements, Rorty is not saying that this is what truth *is*, but is claiming only, say, that we will be inclined to predicate 'is true' of things when we also regard them as warrantedly assertible (/good for us to believe/defensible against all comers/. . .). These remarks do not tell us what truth *is*, but – so the account may continue – they are all we have; for there is nothing any more philosophical to discover about truth. Frankly I don't know how warmly Rorty would receive this suggested interpretation. As I have said, it does make his identity claims strict misstatements, though they are perhaps forgivable ones for a writer who isn't dismayed by the model of philosophy as a kind of kibitzing. But it has other drawbacks. What is (positively) disclosed about truth in these utterances, taken in the intended spirit, turns out to be at best platitudinous. Rorty should and probably will be agreeable thus far, since he does not believe that philosophy as such has anything insightful to contribute to the topic. But it throws the burden of his case wholly on the negative part of his argument, namely the view that traditional philosophy cannot disclose anything more enlightening about truth. And we have seen that his criticisms of Correspondence, which is what his defence reduces to on this interpretation, is laced with misconceptions about the nature of the view, unwarranted assumptions about requirements for any such theory and mistaken presuppositions about the kinds of other notions, views and connections with which the traditional concept of truth must be involved. Most importantly, we can dispense with Rorty's thesis about the nature of commonplace truth as contributing anything to his case.

However, what reasons has Rorty given us to hold that unglossable truth is not our homely and shopworn notion of truth? No better reasons are offered than those scouted earlier in this essay (see the section 'Correspondence and Cognition', p. 76). At one point he claims that no word served the purpose of transcendent truth before Pythagoreans, Orphics and Plato 'invented' idealism.[53] However, this historical claim stands in need of the same sort of defence as the one about two senses of truth.[54] If we discovered that unglossable truth was after all our workaday notion, we would have grounds for regarding what these ancient thinkers achieved not as the invention of a new notion, but as the articulation of an old one. The only genuine evidence Rorty provides is that on unglossable truth, the world *might be* different from our conception of it. That doesn't show that if (as is likely the case) it *is not* different, unglossable truth won't serve as our commonplace notion.

As for the remainder, Rorty writes, 'The trouble with Platonic notions is not that they are "wrong" but that there is not a great deal to be said about them – specifically, there is no way to "naturalize" them or otherwise connect them to the rest of inquiry, or culture, or life.'[55] If having enough to say about unglossable truth is connecting it to the rest of enquiry, then the truth-linked nature of notions from the evidentiary family should suffice. The alleged vacuity of unglossable truth as it occurs in Correspondence is, to repeat, more the confusion of a question about what it is for a belief (/statement) to be true with questions, say, about what it is *to say* a belief is true or about what 'is true' *means*. Beyond this, it is difficult to discover what reasonable demands lay implicit in Rorty's gnomic commentary on Platonic truth.

Epistemological behaviourism

This is Rorty's title for a method, introduced in chapter 4 of *PMN*, with which he attempts to dispose of a galaxy of traditional philosophical theories, all those founded on the analysis of a concept or the meaning of a word. Since Correspondence appears to fit into that very generous category, we cannot ignore this precursor to his more direct attacks.

The method itself is a pastiche, combining elements drawn from Rorty's understanding of Quine's approach to translational semantics and Sellars's assault on the given and epistemic privilege. The Quinean contribution consists in showing, on Rorty's use of it, that there is no language/fact distinction, which Rorty then takes as saying that there are no distinctively semantic or conceptual facts. If correct, this would entail that there are no isolable kinds of information that would provide an account of the concept of truth. As we said earlier, Rorty, takes this to be nothing more than holism. But, as Quine notes, we must be careful not to make this hinge on differences between sentences and theories. For if we take it to imply, say, that no isolated sentence has meaning save in light of its theory, we run up against the fact that we can rewrite any theory as a long sentence.

Although the matter is much broader than we can adequately probe, we should note here – because of its bearing on our main issue – that the explanation of the Quinean contribution will not support Rorty's claims against conceptual truths. Quine doesn't reject semantic facts, indeed his method is a means for uncovering them.[56] But, more importantly, the aspects of the method admired by Rorty don't seem to warrant the morals he needs to draw from them. Our author writes:

> Quine asks how an anthropologist is to discriminate the sentences to which natives invariably and wholeheartedly assent into contingent empirical platitudes on the one hand and necessary conceptual truths on the other. We can . . . simply ask 'How do our peers know which of our assertions to take our word for and which to look for further confirmation of?' It would seem enough for the natives to know which sentences are unquestionably true, without knowing which are true 'by virtue of language'.[57]

This almost exhausts Rorty's explanation of Quine's contribution to epistemological behaviourism, and it suits Rorty's general approach well because it appears that nothing of philosophical importance, beyond utility, dictates an answer to his query. Even so, we must ask: does Quine's method abolish any distinction between necessary, conceptual truths and empirical platitudes, between linguistic and empirical fact? Before answering, we might first query just what Rorty takes for the relevant method. Apparently it is that of radical translation; but against that answer it must be noted that Rorty refuses to acknowledge Quine's account of indeterminacy which seems to be a consequence of radical translation.[58] However, let's set aside that worry and assume that, as the quoted passage suggests, Rorty's appeal *is* to the method of radical translation. Thus construed, the answer to the initial question is not as straightforward as Rorty seems to believe, and thereby not conducive to his polemical applications of it.

What is certain is that even if we restrict attention to whole sentences,

stimulus-synonymy is not tantamount to synonymy as ordinarily understood. It is perhaps a bit less explicit that for purposes of philosophical
practice Quine would reject the latter, for want of its responsiveness to
empirical evidence, in favour of the former. But let us grant that also.
Nevertheless, as Quine's specimen sentences 'Indian nickel' and 'Buffalo
nickel'[59] make abundantly clear, he does not think that this implies that
'means the same' cannot be distinguished from 'is empirically held to be
true on all occasions'. For although every stimulus that evokes 'Indian
nickel!' may in fact evoke 'Buffalo nickel!', the question of intrasubjective
stimulus-synonymy hinges upon whether every stimulation that *would*
evoke the one *would* evoke the other. For starters, it is not the use,
advisable or not, of a favoured philosophical doctrine of meaning, but *the
presence of the subjunctive* that distinguishes empirical platitudes from
conceptual truths. (Additional matters enter in more advanced cases.[60])
But the elimination of the subjunctive, or at least its eventual indisting-
uishability through analysis from the happenstance universal, is a much
more serious matter. I know of none of Rorty's heroic pragmatists who
could afford it; and I dare say that Rorty's own claims could not withstand
its elimination. Whatever the imprecise boundaries, the elimination would
take us beyond the exhilarating and liberating carefreeness of philosophical conversation into frivolously denouncing what we could not forgo in
practice.

But could the semantic data gathered by this method be identical with
the privileged information, institutionalized as linguistic intuition, upon
which traditional philosophy has relied? Without entering the list for or
against the Sellarsian critique of privileged representations, we can, and
should, distinguish what philosophers have said about matters such as
truth, knowledge, causation and so on from whatever estimates they may
have made of the quality and provenance of their information. Granting
for the sake of argument the limitations Quine and Sellars might place
upon such data, it does not seem that much of what Correspondence
theorists say about truth (or much about what Hume says about causation)
would be affected by rejecting the mentalism and claims to infallibility
that may have prevailed at the time.

I might mention another dubious feature of the way Rorty sets up
epistemological behaviourism. As a first step he enlists the joint efforts of
Quine and Sellars to defeat claims to epistemic *privacy*. The upshot is that
knowledge is *public*. He concludes that this is tantamount to 'Explaining
rationality and epistemic authority by reference to what society lets us
say'.[61] The last step is indeed questionable. The sense in which 'public'
contrasts with 'private' in epistemology is not a sense in which 'public' is
indistinguishable from 'social', and certainly not a sense in which it can be
transmuted into social authority. What is public just by not occurring in a

subjective mental domain may be personal rather than social. I am not maintaining that Rorty is unable to get from the sense in which knowledge is public (and thus encapsulated in a language that is a social product) to the view that our standards for rationality and justification are social artefacts. But I don't wish to excuse him from having to rely upon the (to my mind) dubious Whorfian and Kuhnian intermediary premises he is likely to invoke to argue the point.

Conclusion

Rorty's attitude towards traditional philosophical problems and their solutions is scupulously carefree. But it is not without a basis, and it is that basis I have tried to dig out of its literary trappings to examine at closer quarters. But, as I have occasionally noted along the way, there are also tactical ploys that we must guard against. Rorty concedes that there are no neutral starting-points and no discussions of an antagonist's doctrines that won't look question-begging on his opponent's account of them. But we should not allow such concessions to beguile us into accepting grotesque distortions or question-begging adequacy conditions for traditional truth theory. He contends, with some plausibility, that Correspondence is a central element in a larger traditional outlook that includes sundry Platonic and neo-Kantian elements. But we should not allow him to raise objections to Correspondence by way of treating knowledge, reason, justification, reference or of any elements other than truth that go to form that outlook. For his claim does not show that Correspondence is so interlocked with the remainder of the picture that it cannot stand if one modifies or abandons its other elements. Rorty also declares that the posing of problems and proffered solutions he is rejecting arose from a Cartesian–Lockean conception of an epistemological project that would obliterate the sceptic and certify classical physics. But we must not overlook insinuations of the genetic fallacy, as when he applies those standards of success to all and every subsequent effort, up to the present time, of epistemologists, philosophers of language and formal semanticists. Finally, Rorty bifurcates philosophical vocabulary – into abstract and commonplace senses of terms – to avoid taking to heart what other philosophers have claimed are unsettling implications of our ordinary uses of such terms. We have canvassed a few of these attempts, for 'reference' and 'truth'. But there are a number of less conspicuous applications of the same step. We should be more circumspect than Rorty seems to have been about the warrant for such a convenient and effortless method for dismissing out of hand virtually all philosophical difficulties and results.

Alertness to these ploys, I suggest, makes Rorty's claims about what he

has accomplished look much less persuasive. For example, in one of the
last summaries of his philosophical method he reiterates that there is no
way 'to *argue* the issue' between those who share his view of philosophy
and those he calls Kantians, but 'all we can do is to show how the other
side looks from our own point of view.... That is, all we can do is be
hermenutic about the opposition – trying to show how the odd or
paradoxical or offensive things they say hang together with the rest of what
they want to say, and how what they say looks when put in our own
alternative idiom.'[62] But on those terms, epistemologizing truth from the
outset is not the unavoidable difference of bias that *looks* question-begging
to the other side – it *is* question-begging. And, if our earlier argument is
correct, Rorty hasn't shown how Correspondence 'hangs together' with
the rest of the classical outlook, he has assumed that it does. Thus, by
paying heed to the sorts of executive devices mentioned above, we can
more easily detect the yawning chasm between Rorty's sober reflections on
method and his practice.

These instances constitute only a small sample of the larger strategies
Rorty uses to make his case. The fact that he deploys very many of these
global manoeuvres – and does so with considerable learning and narrative
skill – may make our attempt in this essay to pin him down to specific
arguments that are disputable in isolation seem woefully inadequate.
Nevertheless, I hope we have made a start at identifying some of the basic
misconceptions and faulty notions on which his censure of Correspondence rests. Once those are cleared away, we can begin afresh the task of
making Correspondence look not only unblemished, but attractive.

NOTES

1 Aristotle, *Categories*, 14b9–14b23.
2 William James, quoted in Richard Rorty. *Philosophy and the Mirror of Nature* (Princeton
   University Press, Princeton, 1979), p. 162. (Hereafter, *PMN*.)
3 *PMN*, p. 308.
4 *PMN*, p. 308.
5 *PMN*, p. 294.
6 Richard Rorty, 'The World Well Lost' (hereafter, WWL), in *Consequences of Pragmatism* (hereafter, *CP*) (University of Minnesota Press, Minneapolis, 1982), p. 14.
7 *CP*, p. 14.
8 *PMN*, p. 288.
9 *PMN*, p. 280.
10 For example, Richard Rorty, 'Pragmatism, Relativism, and Irrationalism' (hereafter,
   PRI), in *CP*, p. 174.
11 *PMN*, for example pp. 176, 178.
12 *PMN*, p. 176.
13 *PMN*, p. 178.
14 *PMN*, p. 179.

15 *PMN*, p. 170; cf. pp. 318–19.
16 Cf. *PMN*, p. 179 and note.
17 *CP*, p. xxx.
18 PRI, p. 172.
19 *PMN*, p. 281.
20 Alvin Goldman, *Epistemology and Cognition* (Harvard University Press, Cambridge, Mass., 1986), p. 69.
21 This is Russell's egocentric predicament extended to a community of cognizers. Rorty frequently reminds us of this circumstance to dampen our ambitions. For example, to rebut the charge of idealism he remarks, 'we do not know how to find a way of describing an enduring matrix of past and future inquiry into nature except in our own terms . . . To say [this] is, when disjoined from scary rhetoric about "losing touch with the world," just a way of saying that our present views about nature are our only guide in talking about the relation between nature and words' (*PMN*, p. 276).
22 *PMN*, p. 289.
23 *PMN*, p. 281.
24 *PMN*, p. 282.
25 John Stuart Mill, *On Liberty*, ed. David Spitz (W. W. Norton, New York, 1975), p. 23.
26 *CP*, p. xxiii.
27 Richard Rorty, 'Realism and Reference', *The Monist*, 59/3 (1976), pp. 321–40. (Hereafter, RR.)
28 *PMN*, p. 289.
29 RR, p. 324.
30 *PMN*, p. 289.
31 John R. Searle, *Speech Acts* (Cambridge University Press, Cambridge, 1979), p. 177; see Richard Rorty, 'Is There a Problem about Fictional Discourse?' (hereafter, FD), in *CP*, pp. 127 ff.
32 *PMN*, p. 292.
33 Rorty does seem to take note of some of these options in FD, originally delivered as a lecture in the same year in which *PMN* was published. But he does not seem to see them as options for realism, or to give them as much mileage as the realist might get from them. The fact that fictions have *real*, not fictional, causes may serve as a basis for tracing references to fictional characters to appropriate termini.
34 *PMN*, p. 170.
35 *PMN*, p. 289.
36 *PMN*, p. 290.
37 *PMN*, p. 292.
38 RR, p. 324.
39 RR, p. 325.
40 RR, p. 324.
41 *PMN*, p. 289.
42 Saul A. Kripke, *Naming and Necessity* (Harvard University Press, Cambridge, Mass., 1980), p. 96.
43 I am not suggesting Rorty is mistaken in dumping (AE) – see Vision, 'Reference and the Ghost of Parmenides', *Non-Existence and Predication, Grazer Philosophische Studien*, vol. 25/26, ed. by Rudolf Haller (1985/1986) – but only that he has misunderstood the place it has had for both its supporters and detractors.
44 K. Donnellan, 'Reference and Definite Descriptions', *The Philosophical Review*, 75 (1966), pp. 298–302.
45 See, for example, Bernard Williams, 'Imagination and the Self', *Studies in the Philosophy of Thought and Action*, ed. P. F. Strawson (Oxford University Press, Oxford, 1968), pp.

192–4; Thomas Nagel, *The View from Nowhere* (Oxford University Press, Oxford, 1986), pp. 92–3.

46 Although, in light of his subsequent discussion of incommensurability it is difficult to see what limitations Rorty takes this restriction to convey. He points out, correctly it seems, that the Davidsonian argument does not imply that translational equivalents into our own language will be available; but adds puzzlingly 'even "in principle"'. What then does that imply? Rorty claims only 'that we cannot make sense of the claim that there are more than temporary impediments to our know-how' (*PMN*, p. 355n). What could this mean other than that the 'conceptual scheme' must be learnable? And this is something we already know, since we have assumed that its holders have acquired it.

47 *PMN*, p. 305.

48 *PMN*, pp. 310–11.

49 PRI, p. 162.

50 *PMN*, p. 308.

51 *PMN*, p. 176.

52 FD, p. 136.

53 *PMN*, pp. 306–7.

54 In certain passages (e.g. *Symposium*, 202A), Plato gives every indication that his readership understands unglossable truth without the aid of his specialized views on the subject. On the other hand, early evidence for Rorty's 'workaday' sense is not easy to come by. Though all such evidence could be 'explained away', if Rorty's claim is counted as genuinely historical, the evidence must be taken seriously and not 'reinterpreted' without adequate independent motivation. So far as I can determine, such evidence seems to tell against Rorty's conjecture about the origins of unglossable truth.

55 *PMN*, p. 173.

56 See, for example, W. V. Quine, 'Reply to William P. Alston', in *The Philosophy of W. V. Quine*, ed. Lewis Hahn and Paul Schilpp (Open Court Press, Illinois, 1986), p. 73; Quine, 'Indeterminacy of Translation Again', *The Journal of Philosophy*, 84/1 (1987), p. 9.

57 *PMN*, p. 173.

58 See, for example, ibid., pp. 194–5.

59 W. V. Quine, *Word and Object* (MIT Press, Cambridge, Mass., 1960), p. 50 (cf. p. 69).

60 Ibid., pp. 59–60.

61 *PMN*, p. 174.

62 *PMN*, pp. 364–5.

6

Pragmatism and Choosing to Believe

Jane Heal

In *Philosophy and the Mirror of Nature*[1] Richard Rorty provides a panorama of the development and current state of philosophy. In the richness of the picture two major themes are clearly emphasized. One of them is an attack upon a way of conceiving of knowledge, truth and philosophy, the idea which Rorty summarizes with the image of the mind as the mirror of nature. The other which emerges late in the book and is pursued also in some of the papers in *Consequences of Pragmatism*[2] is the recommendation of an alternative stance, Pragmatism, and of a future culture and role for philosophy which Rorty thinks might spring from the adoption of that stance.

In this chapter the major claim I want to make is that sympathy with the first and negative theme does not provide the support which Rorty supposes for the second and positive recommendation. Abandonment of the mirroring idea which Rorty so persuasively urges on us, does not leave us where he thinks it does, and the way of life which he proposes is not, when we think it through, one of which we can make any sense. Rorty believes that Wittgenstein, among others, had an outlook similar to his own. Another and interrelated claim I wish to make is that this is not an entirely accurate reading of Wittgenstein, and that by reflecting on differences between Rorty's view and Wittgenstein's we can see how there might be possibilities other than the ones Rorty discusses. The thread which I shall pursue through this tangled web of ideas starts from consideration of the question whether we can in any sense choose what to think. Rorty's version of Pragmatism presupposes that it does. But my two themes, put together in a nutshell, are that it has thus become an unacceptable and nonsensical *empirical* sort of Pragmatism where it should have remained *transcendental*.[3] But before we embark on that we need to sketch a little more fully both Rorty's negative and positive theses.

There is difficulty right at the start in being sure that we have done justice to Rorty in attributing to him certain 'claims' for which he 'offers arguments'. He would see himself as doing (at least in part) what he calls 'edifying' rather than 'systematic' philosophy – that is, as offering remarks which encourage us 'to break the crust of convention',[4] to abandon certain traditional pictures of ourselves and the disputes that go with them, to conceive of ourselves as free to invent and move on to new and exciting forms of discourse. There are, according to him, no (agreed) forms of argument by which one can persuade people to think of themselves one way rather than another; the activities by which these changes of self-image are accomplished (activities which Rorty calls 'conversation') are more like poetry and literature than like doing mathematics and science (activities which do sometimes proceed by agreed rules of argument and are by Rorty called 'inquiry').

But since it is an implication of my claims that these contrasts are exaggerated by Rorty and that what he calls 'conversation' is more like 'inquiry' than he allows, I shall not scruple to represent him as proceeding in the customary fashion by offering claims and defending them with argument. Indeed, it is one indication of some strain in his position that it is extraordinarily difficult *not* to treat him as so proceeding. And I do not think that the difficulty stems merely from my adherence to an outmoded conception of discussion.

So what is the view of ourselves and knowledge that Rorty challenges? No thumbnail sketch can do justice to the richness of insights in his account, but here are some of the salient points. The central target is the idea that there is, out there, and totally independent of us, a reality, Nature, and that it is our business (or at least a very important part of our business) to gain Knowledge – that is, a more and more accurate and complete view of what Nature is like in herself. How on this conception can we attain this knowledge and know that we have attained it? We can do so only if certain of our representations of the world are 'privileged' – are seen to be for one reason or another guaranteed as reliable; candidates for this role are, on the one hand, analytic or conceptual truths and, on the other, the basic givens of sense experience; these provide firm points of anchorage, thoughts in the having of which Nature forces upon us apprehension of her essential features; given these we can proceed in an orderly manner to fill in more and more details of the picture. The central element of philosophy is, on this conception, epistemology. Epistemology's aim is to pinpoint and defend the privileged representations and to show which intellectual enterprises are and which are not proceeding in the licensed ways. Rorty shows, most persuasively, how a great variety of philosophical positions, dualism, scientific materialism, transcendental idealism, positivism, can be seen as attempts to work out within this broad framework some detailed account of the Mirror and its functioning.

But suppose, however, that there are no privileged representations? This, Rorty says, is what a number of philosophical discussions (Nietzsche, Heidegger, Sellars, Quine, Wittgenstein, Kuhn) have made overwhelmingly plausible. One response is to retain the ideal of Mirroring Nature, to be beset with sceptical doubts because of the lack of firm anchorage points, and to seek for reassurance in such things as causal theories of reference. But this Rorty points out, is a vain enterprise. Rather we should recognize that the idea of Truth as mirroring or correspondence is a historical creation of a particular philosophical tradition, one which has not led to particularly interesting results and which we should now abandon.

In favour of what? Rorty is at pains to deny that subjectivism, idealism or relativism is what now emerges. These are views which say (absurdly) that we create the world by our thinking, or that all that exists are our ideas, or that we each have our own reality. Rorty's view of such philosophical positions is that they, in one way and another, traffic in the suspect mirroring notion. They are, as it were, heretical or atheistical movements which take for granted the importance of questions about God. But what we should do, according to Rorty, is let this whole set of concerns drift away and adopt instead the pragmatic stance. Here we move to consider the positive side of Rorty's conception.

Epistemology, says Rorty, is the form that philosophical reflection takes when the idea of mirroring, its articulation and defence, is our main concern. Hermeneutics is his name for the discipline which he commends to us as the successor, what philosophers will concern themselves with once the mirroring notion has lost its grip. Hermeneutics is the study of various different ways of looking at and approaching the world, together with the attempt to interpret one way to another and to see what they or their derivatives and combinations have to offer. The hermeneutic philosopher is a pragmatist in that he sees different kinds of discourse (scientific, literary, moral) as so many different kinds of linguistic strategy that we have evolved for coping with the world and living our lives. Some of these linguistic practices are pursued by agreed rules and result in the delivery of agreed verdicts which are labelled 'objective' and 'true'. But there is no more to 'objectivity' than this resulting from an agreed procedure, in particular there is no link with the discarded idea of Truth. The pragmatist sees it as sometimes advantageous to have agreed procedures and verdicts. But he thinks that philosophers have tended to be obsessed with such agreement and have desired to strait-jacket themselves with privileged representations and rules of thought; they have been absurdly frightened of disagreement, inconclusiveness or mutual misunderstanding, seeing in every irresoluble dispute and every argument with incommensurable premises a threat of loss of contact with Reality. Rorty's pragmatist thinks that the more language-games the merrier and that we should assess any proposed new way of looking at things by asking not 'Does this mirror Reality?' but 'How should we live if we adopted this? Would it be an improvement on our present ways?' The pragmatist does not suppose that there can be rules for answering this question. He recognizes that the clashes between world-views are exactly of the type that involve incommensurable concepts.[5] But we can at least hope that the proponents will enter into some sort of dialogue; and it is the philosopher's business to be the promoter of and participator in (but not the adjudicator or referee of) the ensuing conversation.

This, then, is a brief account of the position Rorty recommends. What are we to make of it? The problem I wish to raise is this: it seems central to the pragmatist stance as sketched that acquiring beliefs, theories or views can be regarded as a matter of *choice*. Rorty writes very explicitly at one point: 'When the contemplative mind . . . takes large views its activity is more like deciding what to *do* than deciding that a representation is accurate.'[6] But are our beliefs things that we can in any sense choose? I shall suggest that they are not.

It might seem that we face importantly different questions in asking whether we can choose particular humdrum beliefs and whether we can choose whole world-views. Perhaps we can choose the latter but not the former? This is indeed a distinction that Rorty seems to suggest in the remark quoted above and its neighbouring discussion. But it is not unequivocally clear that he is making the distinction. Perhaps he is saying rather that the choice-determined nature of belief shows up most clearly in the case of large views. The idea that there is a real distinction to be drawn in respect of choosability between particular small beliefs and large views is not in any case a limitation on his pragmatism that he can consistently accept, given his frequent insistence on holism and his denial of the possibility of drawing a sharp distinction between individual beliefs, theories and conceptual schemes. Let us note also that acceptance of the criteria of judgement we use in routine cases are, for Rorty's pragmatist, just 'temporary resting places constructed for specific Utilitarian ends'.[7] If this were so, then we could see why there might be a phenomenological difference between routine judgement and choice of world-view – in one case I just carry out an existing policy without reflection or hesitation while in the other I debate the policy itself. But this picture does nothing to undermine the idea that activity and choice are involved in the routine case as much as in the non-routine one. I act and choose when I, without reflection, drive my car on the left as much as when I vote new road legislation in Parliament.

So finally to the question: can a person choose his or her beliefs? There is already in the field a powerful argument, proposed by B. A. O. Williams against the idea that beliefs are subject to the will.[8] However this is not one which will serve our turn in discussion of Rorty, since it proceeds from the premise that in acquiring beliefs (or doing things which we think will result in acquisition of beliefs) we aim at acquiring true ones – that is, ones which accurately represent some reality independent of us. Williams's plausible claim is that a state of myself which I could knowingly and consciously produce at will could not be taken by me to be one in which I accurately represent an independent world; I can only do that by having my state determined by the world and not by myself. But since Rorty's view is that the idea of 'independent reality' on which Williams's argument trades is itself unfortunate and due for the philosophical chop, he is not going to be moved by these considerations. We need, then, to try another tack.

How do we distinguish in general between those aspects of our lives in which we are active and those in which we are passive? There is one conception of the difference between activity and passivity which is perennially tempting. This view of action ties it to what we might call 'arbitrary plumping'. When we deliberate on what to do, very often we find that there is no course for which there are conclusive reasons. Perhaps this comes about because the options available offer chances of realizing important but incommensurable goods. More prosaically, even in cases where there is no problem of determining an ultimate or even a middle-distance goal, there may still fail to be conclusive reason for any one action because there are several equally adequate means to the end.

The temptation, then, is to identify choice or activity precisely as that which determines the outcome when reason, but not conclusive reason, can be given. Those who think this way will very probably put an extra stage between even conclusive reason and action – the stage where the self without reason decides to act on reason. This is how such a view accommodates *akrasia*, seeing it not as a mysterious irrationality but rather as the natural fall-back position, failing intervention of the active self. Such a move is necessary if the view is to accommodate the commonsense idea that action on conclusive reason is just as much action as action on inconclusive reason. This outlook thus stresses a causal and hence a predictive gap between having reasons and the occurrence of what those reasons rationalize.

From this perspective the 'passivity' of belief is seen in the fact that there is, in the case of judgement, supposedly no such gap and no such arbitrary plumping. Belief seems to conform itself directly to perceived strength of evidence. Of course there are cases of cognitive *akrasia* – but they seem to have this difference from volitional *akrasia* that they cannot come to full consciousness and still persist. And it is clear that for the unproblematic cases of arbitrary plumping among a range of actions, there is no parallel on the cognitive side. If I have conclusive reason to do X or Y but no reason for choosing between them, I must pick one or the other. But if I have conclusive evidence that p or q but no further information, I cannot, knowingly, just move on to have one or the other belief.

As many discussions of free will have made familiar, this linkage of activity with arbitrariness is arguably a distortion and a muddle. But it must be allowed that we cannot easily conjure away those features of ourselves and the world which make it necessary to initiate action on less than conclusive reasons. If we try to remove in imagination the incommensurability of goods, we end up with monomania and impoverishment.[9]

What would the world have to be like for the second source of inconclusiveness to disappear? Suppose I have conclusive reason to eat something now. I am hungry, my life is worth continuing for me and there are no penalties attached to eating, no more pressing concerns to be attended to. Moreover, I am in my kitchen at home with various usual resources around me. In order to get from this general assessment of the situation to the moment when my hands are actually opening the tin of baked beans, I have to decide to eat the beans rather than the bread and cheese or scrambled eggs. I must think to myself what is available and fix on one dish rather than another. At a certain detailed level of decision, however, such further options will not present themselves and decisions are not required. If I decide on picking up the tin-opener, I do not then have to consider which trajectory my arm shall move through nor how my fingers shall grasp the object; something else sorts that out for me.

The distinction at which I have gestured is not a sharp one. There is no fixed cut-off point between descriptions of decisions which will generate need for further thought and those which will not. Matters may well vary from person to person and context to context. Moreover, what exactly we mean by 'further thought' is not an entirely clear-cut matter. But it would be a strange existence in which nothing like the distinction could be drawn. It would be for us always to find ourselves going through some behaviour appropriate to a decision as soon as that decision had been taken, irrespective of the level of generality of the decision. I decide to improve my fitness and, lo and behold, I am jogging on my way to the running track (rather than the swimming pool or the gymnasium) without any further bother. In these barely imaginable circumstances our awareness of the long and by no means reliable causal chains which link our bodily movements to their eventual outcomes would all be telescoped into nothing. We lose grip on the idea that there is a world of things and people whose properties and interconnections require investigation before we can anticipate the effect of our interventions on them. As things are, the insides of our bodies and their workings are largely opaque to us. No sooner do I decide to move my arm than there I am moving it. How? I do not know. The envisaged situation is one in which this feature of my bodily behaviour has enormously extended itself outwards. (It already does so a little beyond where we might expect, as witnessed by the well-known tying-the-bow-tie phenomenon.) But in describing a person to whom this has happened I seem to have described someone who does not possess the concepts in terms of which our goals are specified and who lacks our distinction between him or herself and the world.

The upshot, then, of the considerations of these last three paragraphs is that we cannot get some quick refutation of the 'arbitrary plumping' theory of the activity/passivity distinction by suggesting that action on conclusive reason could be the norm, suggesting in other words that it is a trivial feature of our world that the model seems to fit it in a good number of cases. But nevertheless, reflection on cases where there are conclusive reasons to act, and where the addition to the scene of some (arbitrary) decision to act on the reasons seems quite uncalled for, will suggest another account of the matter which, once enunciated, is considerably more persuasive. It is just this: that I am active when the explanation of why things are as they are is (at least in part) that I thought their being that way would be good. My view of how things *ought* to be has an explanatory role in making intelligible why they *are* that way. I am passive, on the other hand, inasmuch as the explanation of why things are a certain way does not lie in my thoughts about their advantageousness but elsewhere.

From this perspective the question 'Am I active in judging, in coming to have the beliefs that I do?' comes out as the question whether the explanation of my believing something is (ever or always) that I conceived it a good thing to have that belief. And the view I want to defend is that the explanation cannot in general be of this form.

It might be thought that the claim I am offering is another version of Anscombe's remarks about 'direction of fit'.[10] But this is not so. My point is quite independent of, although compatible with, Anscombe's. Her remarks are addressed to the question of what the difference is between a belief and an intention, given that both involve representation of a certain state of the world. Her view is, roughly speaking, that a state is a belief if, on its failing to match the world, the fault lies in it, while a state is an intention if failure to match implies a fault in the world. One could well agree with some version of this while still holding that coming to have a belief is an event explicable in the active sense. Consider for example drawing a plan. I can draw one intending it as an accurate representation of an existing building or as a blueprint from which a building is to be constructed. The Anscombian account may throw light on an important difference between the role and use of the two drawings. But in either case the production of the drawing is an active matter; my placing of the lines is explicable by my conception of the desirability of their being placed thus and so. Now, if we construe 'matching the world' in some correspondence-theory sense, then the Anscombian characterization of belief would link up with Williams's argument (mentioned earlier) to the non-choosability of belief. But as we remarked before, that is not a line which we can employ against Rorty.

So to return to the main question, suppose I have some belief that p, can this ever or in general be explained by referring to my awareness that having that belief was a good thing?

There is clearly an absurdity in the idea generated by pursuing the plan drawing model, the idea that I arrive at my beliefs by comparing candidate judgements with the world and putting myself in that cognitive state which I see to have the desirable property of matching the world. This requires me to have access to the world, that is get some beliefs about it, before I fix on my beliefs. But might I not choose my beliefs in the light of their having the desirable property of coherence with my existing belief set (which perhaps I take to be the best and only available clue to the correspondence with reality which I seek) or in the light of other pleasant features such as enabling me to live a satisfactory life? (Perhaps I think that enabling me to live a satisfactory life is all that 'truth' could amount to.) What, if anything, is wrong with these versions of the idea that beliefs are chosen?

It seems that I can on certain occasions choose my beliefs in something like these ways – indeed that it would be perfectly right and proper to do so. Suppose you are on trial charged with murder. I know that you are innocent but can prove this to others only by swearing to an alibi in court. I know that I shall not be able to do this convincingly (pass lie-detector tests and so forth) unless I come myself to believe in the alibi. But at the moment I do not believe in it. So I undertake to make myself believe (by hypnosis, neurosurgery or what not) that you were dining with me on a particular evening.

This is certainly a strange case. And in order to make clear that it is a case of *choice* of belief, I have had to build into the story unusual routes of belief formation. One might object that it is patently obvious that I do not in everyday cases go via these roundabout causal routes. So if beliefs were in general to be chosen, they would have to be determinable at will, directly, without use of roundabout routes. And, one would add, clearly they are not.

But this is too rapid. Consider this parallel. Our bodily movements are (by and large) determined directly at will. But there are cases (e.g. thrusting my hand into the fire), where I may find the movement pretty hard to do, and where, if I am determined on doing it, I may have to go by roundabout routes. Our pragmatist can similarly respond that why I cannot at this instant just make myself believe that I could fly if I stepped out of the window is that I am aware of the overwhelming advantageousness of not so believing and cannot bring myself to abandon these benefits.

The opponent of the overall pragmatist position need not deny that one can sometimes choose ones beliefs (the trial and alibi case) nor that there are wilfulness and self-deception. Nor need he deny that there are such things as setting oneself to behave as if so and so (Do I accept this undergraduate's story about why he did not produce his essay on time? Well at least I shall treat him as if I did) and that the line between this kind of case and others may not be clear-cut. The question is, however, whether we can make sense of the idea that there is a place for the idea of choosing in *every* case of belief formation, whether the *routine* explanation of a person's acquiring a belief should be in terms of his or her favourable attitude to that belief.

Having done my best to defend the pragmatist view against some objections and to make it as palatable as possible, I want now to suggest that it is nevertheless not defensible or in the limit fully intelligible. Let us consider first deliberation which is obviously practical and hence where considerations of advantage do come in. There are two questions which I might pose to myself and which we need to distinguish:

(1) What shall I do?
(2) What shall I intend?

These are different questions, and different considerations are relevant to answering them. There may, for example, be advantages in having an intention (it enables me to behave convincingly *vis-à-vis* others, for example) which have nothing to do with the advantageousness of the intended action. One might argue that there was an asymmetry here – that advantages in intending were not necessarily advantages in action while disadvantages in intending would necessarily count somewhat against the intended action. For example, if I know that resolving on a certain course of action will make me extremely tense and perhaps ill, is this not itself a reason against that course of action? It may seem to be so, given the fact that the course of action cannot be undertaken without advance formation of the stressful intention. But we should ask whether this is contingent or necessary. If the latter, then what we are labelling 'intention' might better be seen as part of the action itself and be called 'planning'; if the former, then what the agent has most reason to do is to try and get the benefits of the action without the disadvantages of the intention – for example, by postponing thought about the matter until the last moment or temporarily obliterating knowledge of his purpose with a convenient amnesia pill. This is the reverse of the case where he wants the advantages of the intention without the action and has to fool himself into forgetting his decision to renege or his knowledge that the project cannot come off.

The upshot, then, is that we can hold questions (1) and (2) apart and claim that considerations that bear on the one do not *ipso facto* bear on the other. There is another reason also for maintaining this separation; namely, that if we suppose that question (2) really is a deep version of question (1), then we are embarked on an infinite regress. Question (2) itself is a practical question. Hence, on the given supposition, it has the deep form 'What shall I intend to intend?' and so on.

One further observation on the pair: question (1) does not explicitly invoke the concept of intention. It is not a question about intention. Yet asking and answering it will result in the formation of intention – hence, perhaps, part of the temptation to confuse it with (2). To put the moral in general terms one can be in a certain state (and know that one is) and be in it for certain reasons, without the concept of that state entering into the content of the reasons. In the case in hand, the reasons are reasons *for acting*. Yet, of course, what they rationalize and explain is the intention. (This is an observation that one can assent to whatever ones view of a reason – whether one thinks of it as a circumstance, the apprehension of that circumstance or the content of that apprehension.)

Let us turn now to the belief side of deliberation, where there should be, if the non-pragmatist is right, at least some questions which are *not* practical. Here we have an analogous pair:

(3)   What is so?
(4)   What shall I believe?

But (4) is, on one natural interpretation at least (i.e. where it is not taken as asking for a prediction) a practical question. It is equivalent to 'What shall I get myself to believe?' What the pragmatist, one who sees us as choosing all our beliefs, is trying to do is to get us to see (4) as providing the underlying form of (3) – to get us to suppose that (4) is the only question we can ever really ask. But our examination of (1) and (2) should make us resistant to this move. If I ask (3), certain considerations are relevant and they may be quite different from those needed for answering (4). In marshalling what is relevant for (3), I need not think of belief at all.

Our language, whether for deeper or more trivial reasons, is liable to mislead us here. We do naturally speak of 'reasons for believing' as we speak of 'reasons for intending'. And usually we mean by these phrases considerations bearing on questions (3) and (1). But we can also speak even more naturally in the latter case of 'reasons for acting' – and this alternative locution inoculates us to some extent against the temptation to confuse (1) with (2), in that we are aware that 'reasons for intending' usually are reasons for acting. But we do not speak naturally of 'reasons for things being thus and so' (or if we do, we move into a different space of practical enquiry). Hence, once we are embarked on this 'reasons' style of talk we are perhaps more likely to fall into the muddle of assimilating (3) to (4) and of seeing (4) rather than (3) as the pair to (1) on the 'theoretical' side.

But we do have a concept – namely that of evidence – which will do the job for us.[11] And using this terminology I can put the central point thus: my awareness of evidence that things are thus and so is what (usually) explains my believing that they are thus and so. If I have asked question (3) and not (4), then considerations which amount to evidence are what I seek and what, once found, will explain my answer. No awareness of considerations about the advantageousness of belief will figure in the explanation. Hence acquisition of the belief is not to be ascribed to me as an action.

Could it be, however, that we *ought* to ask (4) rather than (3)? Is there some imaginable way of going on in which all we ever posed to ourselves were practical questions? The pragmatists would perhaps acknowledge the difference between (3) and (4) but suppose that asking (3) rather than (4) went together with the suspect idea of Mirroring Nature and was thus to be eschewed. But the idea that we can abandon (3) in favour of (4) is absurd. Our notion of action is of something which operates under certain constraints which we do not place there but, in some sense, find. The question of what those constraints are, questions of form (3), must then present themselves to any creature who is also asking questions (1), (2) and (4) in any manner comprehensible to us. And the posing of questions of form (3) presupposes that the questioner *may* find an answer *given* to him. Of course, he may not find such an answer, evidence may not be forthcoming. Perhaps he will realize that he does not know what evidence he wants and that he does not understand his own question; perhaps he will come to think that it was the wrong question to ask. But in all these cases other questions of form (3) will be askable and they will in turn be posed on the assumption that an answer to them will not be *chosen* but will, so to speak, impose itself. We cannot get away from the idea of *finding* things to be so, *having it borne in on us* that they are and the like.

We need now to spell out the implications of this conclusion for Rorty's view that we, or at least the philosophers among us, should see ourselves as the pragmatist suggests, namely as in a position to choose between views of the world in the light of the excitingness and usefulness of the descriptions of ourselves that they allow us to give. Can we see our acceptance of the criteria and standards of evidence we employ as 'temporary resting places constructed for specific utilitarian ends'?

Rorty's account of objectivity is that talk of the 'objective' is a label we attach to types of talk where the rules for what we should say are (temporarily and for utilitarian ends) agreed. So any particular judgement is an action undertaken in the light of awareness of its advantageous feature of conformity with the rule, and the rule itself is adopted in awareness of its advantageousness as a policy. If I say that I *must* say or judge such and such, I mean only that, as I see things, there are overwhelming practical reasons for the choice. But overwhelming reasons in the light of what? In the light of the facts, we surely want to respond. And we cannot, on pain of infinite regress, explain this in turn in terms of there being overwhelming practical reasons to accept that these are the facts. Thus Rorty has mislocated and misdescribed the notions of 'objectivity' and of 'fact'. It is not our having temporarily agreed criteria constructed for utilitarian ends which grounds the notions but our (unavoidable) practice of asking questions of form (3) and our justified expectation of having answers given to us – answers our acceptance of which we rightly explain to ourselves and others in the light of reasons which are not practical at all. Our reasons are ones which show us *what is so*, not what we have reason to *say* or *think* is so.

Does this mean that I wish to reinstate the idea of the Mirror of Nature? Not at all! We should not construe the ineluctability of certain judgements as Nature's own conception of herself being printed on our *tabula rasa*. I agree with Rorty that Nature has no conception of herself; we bring to her the concepts we use and they are concepts we have because our interests and way of life are as they are. This Wittgensteinian point could be put another way: to say that a creature has merely 'an interest in the truth' is not enough of a determinate interest to make intelligible why it should slice the Universe in one way rather than another and it gives no clue as to what concepts it will employ; yet the Mirror of Nature idea presupposes that it does. So if we want to understand why we have the concepts we do (to make them intelligible to ourselves, to 'justify' our having them in some sense), then we must look at how the whole pattern of our lives fits together – how making these kinds of judgements in this sort of way is bound up with our caring about the kinds of things we care about and doing the kinds of things we find worth doing. To repeat the phrase used above, we have our concepts *because* we have our interests – no interests, no concepts. But this is not to be heard as saying that we choose or devise our concepts in the light of knowledge of our interests. That way of reading things presupposes that we can conceptualize our interests before we have any concepts, which is absurd.[12]

Let us consider some further points of contrast between Rorty's outlook and the Wittgensteinian one sketched above. It is often remarked that in any debate, whether theoretical or practical, some things must be taken for granted. Those of a pragmatist persuasion suppose that this can be accommodated by saying that we choose to hold certain things fixed. But another way of putting the earlier points about the form of question (3) and about objectivity is that this response will not do. It will do in certain cases. We know what it is to say 'We don't know for certain that so and so, but let's assume it. And now . . .' But this pragmatic move is intelligible to us as a contrast with cases where we do know what is so and where we hold firmly to some conception of things because we see that they really are like that.

Thus the question 'Why do certain things stand firm for me?' cannot be answered by saying 'I *hold* them firm'. But neither must we retreat again to the idea that they stand firm because they are imposed upon us by Nature. The Wittgensteinian wants us to avoid both responses by finessing the question. He will ask us to reflect on how our concepts, judgements, interests and practices all fit together in an intelligible way, and he will invite us to make what we can (i.e. not much) of the idea of carrying on in radically different ways. He will say 'Look' and 'My spade is turned' and 'Justification comes to an end'.

An upshot of these kinds of reflection, if the process works, may be the sense of liberation that Rorty tries to induce, liberation in particular from temptation to the gloomy view that science has shown the world to be really nothing but atoms and the void, and all human concerns (except finding out more truths of science) to be precariously sustained on an unreliable web of ignorance, blind feeling and illusion. But the Wittgensteinian thinks that we can avoid paying the price which Rorty thinks we must pay for this – the price, that is, of saying such things as that 'our criteria are temporary resting places' and thus disabling ourselves from making those blunt assertions of fact that we wish to make. Certainly, to repeat, it is only because I have the concerns I do (with my life, with others' lives, with children, food, music, happiness, pain, justice, etc.) that I approach the world as I do. But to say that judgements are bound up with, interdependent with, concerns and projects is not to *subordinate* the notion of judgement and fact to that of project. What is illuminated, shown to be bound up with projects, are real, honest-to-God claims that things are so. If the Wittgensteinian outlook can be made coherent, nothing is shown to be the upshot of applying some temporarily adopted set of rules. Inasmuch as my interests and projects stand firm (these things really do matter, these plans are worth pursuing), the facts stand firm too. It may be that Rorty's sense that we have to make some choice in order to keep the fact from, as it were, dissolving or sliding about, is connected with his only partial repudiation of the fact/value distinction. Does he perhaps think that in the realm of mattering and being important, at some level it all comes down to reasonless choice?

Both Rorty and Wittgenstein recommend the abandonment of certain questions – but they are different questions, and the abandonment is imagined to come about in different ways. The Wittgensteinian thinks that we should not press the question 'Why do some things stand firm for me? Is it that they are forced on me or that I choose to hold to them?' He thinks that if, with as much intellectual honesty and sensitivity we can muster, we lay ourselves open to his considerations, we shall *see* that the question is not to be pressed. This will be the upshot of reasoning – although there may be all kinds of difficulties in expressing the reasoning or the insight it produces, and the outcome is perhaps not to be represented as the adoption of some kind of theory. Rorty thinks that we should *choose* not to press the question 'Is there a Truth about Nature which all our best theories might have got wrong?' because we grasp that pursuing it has got us nowhere. And he thinks that we can answer the question about things standing firm for us by talking of our choice.

Unless we can find a third way through, a way of finessing the question of why we hold so firmly to certain opinions, we shall fail to walk the tightrope between 'mirroring realism' on the one hand and some form of idealism on the other. Protest he never so much, Rorty has wobbled and fallen off on the idealist side. The experienced Wittgensteinian can keep up the balancing act for much longer. I have not attempted to show here that it can be kept up for ever, but only that the alternatives Rorty considers do not exhaust the field.

NOTES

1   Richard Rorty, *Philosophy and the Mirror of Nature* (Blackwell, Oxford, 1980). (Hereafter *PMN*.)
2   Richard Rorty, *Consequences of Pragmatism* (Harvester Press, Brighton, 1982). (Hereafter *CP*.)
3   B. A. O. Williams, *Ethics and the Limits of Philosophy* (Fontana, London, 1985), p. 217, n. 4.
4   *PMN*, p. 379.
5   *PMN*, p. 311.
6   *CP*, p. 163.
7   *CP*, p. xli.
8   B. A. O. Williams, *Problems of the Self* (Cambridge University Press, Cambridge, 1973), pp. 148 ff.
9   See, for example, M. Nussbaum, *The Fragility of Goodness* (Cambridge University Press, Cambridge, 1986), esp. Ch. 4.
10   G. E. M. Anscombe, *Intention* (Blackwell, Oxford, 1957), pp. 56 ff.
11   I owe this point to Hugh Mellor.
12   *CP*, p. xix, shows Rorty well aware of this but not, it seems to me, drawing the right moral.

Part III

Knowledge and Language

7

Let Me Accentuate the Positive

W. V. Quine

One of the quiet pleasures that a philosophical writer is sometimes vouchsafed is that of reading a colleague's favourable and faithful account of one's views. When, on the other hand, the account is favourable but mistaken, it is with some regret that one undertakes to set the colleague straight; for the colleague might no longer favour one's views if he saw them aright. However, let truth prevail, come what may.

In ascribing to me the 'claim that there is no "matter of fact" involved in attributions of meaning to utterances, beliefs to people, and aspirations to cultures',[1] Rorty overstates my negativity. How words and sentences are used, in what circumstances and in what relations to one another, is very much a matter of fact, and moreover I cheerfully call its study a study of meaning. My reservations concern rather the ascription of a distinctive meaning or cognitive content to each separate sentence, as something shared by the sentence and its correct translations. I hold that two conflicting manuals of translation can do equal justice to the semantic facts, while distributing the meaning load differently sentence by sentence. The manuals can be counted on to agree over sentences whose affirmation is pretty regularly linked to concurrent sensory stimulation, but they may diverge over others.

When we turn to attributions of belief, I see factuality as grading off from case to case. Some beliefs can be ascribed even to dumb animals, in the light of behaviour. Some beliefs can even be measured, in human subjects, by laying bets and offering odds. But the grammar of the general belief idiom, 'x believes that p', outruns the idiom's factuality. The idiom counts as grammatical no matter what declarative sentence we put for 'p', but for some sentences there is nothing factual about holding the belief: nothing but pious lip-service.

Partly because the grammar of the belief idiom outruns its factuality, the idiom is not acceptable as an idiom of an austere scientific language. It is this exclusion, evidently, that leads Rorty to suppose that I find no matter of fact in attributions of belief.[2] I often do, and I would want to see it conveyed in scientifically more acceptable idioms.

As for attributions of aspirations to cultures, I see factuality as threatened, again, only in the obvious way: by vagueness or dimness of criteria.

Rorty writes that the 'author of "Two Dogmas of Empiricism" *should* have said that concepts and meanings are harmless if posited to give explanations of our behavior'.[3] Not quite. They are often harmful in giving the illusion of explanation of our behaviour.

Rorty raises again Chomsky's old point that my indeterminacy of translation is just a case of the more general under-determination of science by observation.[4] My answer, as usual, is that even the adoption of a full theory of nature, from among the under-determined options, still leaves translation indeterminate.

Rorty levels again Putnam's charge of essentialism:[5] that I gratuitously reckon some guidelines as intrinsic to translation and others as mere supplementary canons for choosing among equally correct manuals of translation. Boorse urged much the same point.[6] No, I favour no such invidious distinction; my thesis merely comes to this: two complete manuals of translation can conflict with each other without conflicting with any speaker's verbal behaviour or propensities. One of the manuals may still be better than the other in various ways.

Rorty mentions my 'holistic claim that there is no "first philosophy"'.[7] No, it is a naturalistic claim.

'Why', Rorty asks, 'do "believes in . . ." and "translates as . . ." owe more to the necessities of practice than "is the same electron as . . ." and "is the same set as . . ."?'[8] Theoretical terms for hypothetical entities are a mainstay of science, and I agree that mentalistic terms bear consideration in that capacity along with 'electron' and the rest. Theoretical terms stand or fall according to how well they serve theory. The trouble with mentalistic terms is their want of theoretical promise and not their conflict with a prior dogma.

For that matter, reservations are in order even regarding electrons and other elementary particles. In the Einstein–Bose statistic and again in quantum mechanics, there are resons for saying that 'is the same electron as . . .' does *not* in general make sense. There are reasons for settling rather for point events, a sequence of which may sometimes conveniently be called an electron but with no assurance of making sense of its identity through thick and thin. Thus 'electron' fares, after all, rather like 'x believes that p' above: factuality succumbs to vagueness after a point.

Rorty ascribes five tenets to me, numbered 1 to 5.[9] I disown:

(2) There is no special epistemological status which any sentence has apart from its role in the maintaining of that 'field of force' which is human knowledge and whose aim is coping with sensory indications.

I deny that the sole or main aim of knowledge is coping with sensory input, though this was perhaps its prehistoric survival value. For us a major aim of knowledge is satisfaction of intellectual curiosity. Prediction, or the anticipation of sensory stimulation, is rather where *confirmation* lies. My further departure from (2) is on the score of observation sentences, which do have the 'special epistemological status' of being keyed directly to sensory stimulation and thus linking theory with outer reality.

I can substantially agree with Rorty when he writes 'that the world *can* be completely described in a truth-functional language, while simultaneously granting that pieces of it can also be described in an intentional one'.[10]

NOTES

1 *PMN*, p. 192.
2 Cf. *PMN*, p. 193.
3 *PMN*, p. 194.
4 *PMN*, p. 195.
5 H. Putnam, 'The Refutation of Conventionalism', Nous 8 (1974), pp. 25–40.
6 C. Boorse, 'The Origins of the Indeterminacy Thesis', *The Journal of Philosophy*, vol. LXXII, No. 13 (1975), pp. 369–87.
7 *PMN*, p. 199.
8 *PMN*, p. 201.
9 *PMN*, p. 202.
10 *PMN*, p. 204.

A Coherence Theory of Truth and Knowledge

Donald Davidson

In this paper I defend what may as well be called a coherence theory of truth and knowledge. The theory I defend is not in competition with a correspondence theory, but depends for its defence on an argument that purports to show that coherence yields correspondence.

The importance of the theme is obvious. If coherence is a test of truth, there is a direct connection with epistemology, for we have reason to believe many of our beliefs cohere with many others, and in that case we have reason to believe many of our beliefs are true. When the beliefs are true, then the primary conditions for knowledge would seem to be satisfied.

Someone might try to defend a coherence theory of truth without defending a coherence theory of knowledge, perhaps on the ground that the holder of a coherent set of beliefs might lack a reason to believe his beliefs coherent. This is not likely, but it may be that someone, though he has true beliefs, and good reasons for holding them, does not appreciate the relevance of reason to belief. Such a one may best be viewed as having knowledge he does not know he has: he thinks he is a sceptic. In a word, he is a philosopher.

Setting aside aberrant cases, what brings truth and knowledge together is meaning. If meanings are given by objective truth conditions there is a question how we can know that the conditions are satisfied, for this would appear to require a confrontation between what we believe and reality; and the idea of such a confrontation is absurd. But if coherence is a test of truth, then coherence is a test for judging that objective truth conditions are satisfied, and we no longer need to explain meaning on the basis of possible confrontation. My slogan is: correspondence without confrontation. Given a correct epistemology, we can be realists in all departments. We can accept objective truth conditions as the key to meaning, a realist view of truth, and we can insist that knowledge is of an objective world independent of our thought or language.

Since there is not, as far as I know, a theory that deserves to be called 'the' coherence theory, let me characterize the sort of view I want to defend. It is obvious that not every consistent set of interpreted sentences contains only true sentences, since one such set might contain just the consistent sentence *S* and another just the negation of *S*. And adding more sentences, while maintaining consistency, will not help. We can imagine endless state-descriptions – maximal consistent descriptions – which do not describe our world.

My coherence theory concerns beliefs, or sentences held true by someone who understands them. I do not want to say, at this point, that every possible coherent set of beliefs is true (or contains mostly true beliefs). I shy away from this because it is so unclear what is possible. At one extreme, it might be held that the range of possible maximal sets of beliefs is as wide as the range of possible maximal sets of sentences, and then there would be no point to insisting that a defensible coherence theory concerns beliefs and not propositions or sentences. But there are other ways of conceiving what it is possible to believe which would justify saying not only that all actual coherent belief systems are largely correct but that all possible ones are also. The difference between the two notions of what it is possible to believe depends on what we suppose about the nature of belief, its interpretation, its causes, its holders and its patterns. Beliefs for me are states of people with intentions, desires, sense organs; they are states that are caused by, and cause, events inside and outside the bodies of the entertainers. But even given all these constraints, there are many things people do believe, and many more that they could. For all such cases, the coherence theory applies.

Of course some beliefs are false. Much of the point of the concept of belief is the potential gap it introduces between what is held to be true and what is true. So mere coherence, no matter how strongly coherence is plausibly defined, can not guarantee that what is believed is so. All that a coherence theory can maintain is that most of the beliefs in a coherent total set of beliefs are true.

This way of stating the position can at best be taken as a hint, since there is probably no useful way to count beliefs, and so no clear meaning to the idea that most of a person's beliefs are true. A somewhat better way to put the point is to say there is a presumption in favour of the truth of a belief that coheres with a significant mass of belief. Every belief in a coherent total set of beliefs is justified in the light of this presumption, much as every intentional action taken by a rational agent (one whose choices, beliefs and desires cohere in the sense of Bayesian decision theory) is justified. So to repeat, if knowledge is justified true belief, then it would seem that all the true beliefs of a consistent believer constitute knowledge. This conclusion, though too vague and hasty to be right, contains an important core of truth, as I shall argue. Meanwhile I merely note the many problems asking for treatment: what exactly does coherence demand? How much of inductive practice should be included, how much of the true theory (if there is one) of evidential support must be in there? Since no person has a completely consistent body of convictions, coherence with *which* beliefs creates a presumption of truth? Some of these problems will be put in better perspective as I go along.

It should be clear that I do not hope to define truth in terms of coherence and belief. Truth is beautifully transparent compared to belief and coherence, and I take it as primitive. Truth, as applied to utterances of sentences, shows the disquotational feature enshrined in Tarski's Convention T, and that is enough to fix its domain of application. Relative to a language or a speaker, of course, so there is more to truth than Convention T; there is whatever carries over from language to language or speaker to speaker. What Convention T, and the trite sentences it declares true, like '"Grass is green", spoken by an English speaker, is true if and only if grass is green', reveal is that the truth of an utterance depends on just two things: what the words as spoken mean, and how the world is arranged. There is no further relativism to a conceptual scheme, a way of viewing things, a perspective. Two interpreters, as unlike in culture, language and point of view as you please, can disagree over whether an utterance is true, but only if they differ on how things are in the world they share, or what the utterance means.

I think we can draw two conclusions from these simple reflections. First, truth is correspondence with the way things are. (There is no straightforward and non-misleading way to state this; to get things right, a detour is necessary through the concept of satisfaction in terms of which truth is characterized.[1]) So if a coherence theory of truth is acceptable, it must be consistent with a correspondence theory. Second, a theory of knowledge that allows that we can know the truth must be a non-relativized, non-internal form of realism. So if a coherence theory of knowledge is acceptable, it must be consistent with such a form of realism. My form of realism seems to be neither Hilary Putnam's internal realism nor his metaphysical realism.[2] It is not internal realism because internal realism makes truth relative to a scheme, and this is an idea I do not think is intelligible.[3] A major reason, in fact, for accepting a coherence theory is the unintelligibility of the dualism of a conceptual scheme and a 'world' waiting to be coped with. But my realism is certainly not Putnam's metaphysical realism, for *it* is characterized by being 'radically non-epistemic', which implies that all our best researched and established thoughts and theories may be false. I think the independence of belief and truth requires only that *each* of our beliefs may be false. But of course a coherence theory cannot allow that all of them can be wrong.

But why not? Perhaps it is obvious that the coherence of a belief with a substantial body of belief enhances its chance of being true, provided there is reason to suppose the body of belief is true, or largely so. But how can coherence alone supply grounds for belief? Perhaps the best we can do to justify one belief is to appeal to other beliefs. But then the coutcome would seem to be that we must accept philosophical scepticism, no matter how unshaken in practice our beliefs remain.

This is scepticism in one of its traditional garbs. It asks: why couldn't all my beliefs hang together and yet be comprehensively false about the actual world? Mere recognition of the fact that it is absurd or worse to try to *confront* our beliefs, one by one, or as a whole, with what they are about does not answer the question nor show the question unintelligible. In short, even a mild coherence theory like mine must provide a sceptic with a reason for supposing coherent beliefs are true. The partisan of a coherence theory can't allow assurance to come from outside the system of belief, while nothing inside can produce support except as it can be shown to rest, finally or at once, on something independently trustworthy.

It is natural to distinguish coherence theories from others by reference to the question whether or not justification can or must come to an end. But this does not define the positions, it merely suggests a form the argument may take. For there are coherence theorists who hold that some beliefs can serve as the basis for the rest, while it would be possible to maintain that coherence is not enough, although giving reasons never comes to an end. What distinguishes a coherence theory is simply the claim that nothing can count as a reason for holding a belief except another belief. Its partisan rejects as unintelligible the request for a ground or source of justification of another ilk. As Rorty has put it, 'nothing counts as justification unless by reference to what we already accept, and there is no way to get outside our beliefs and our language so as to find some test other than coherence.'[4] About this I am, as you see, in agreement with Rorty. Where we differ, if we do, is on whether there remains a question how, given that we cannot 'get outside our beliefs and our language so as to find some test other than coherence', we nevertheless can have knowledge of, and talk about, an objective public world which is not of our own making. I think this question does remain, while I suspect that Rorty doesn't think so. If this is his view, then he must think I am making a mistake in trying to answer the question. Nevertheless, here goes.

It will promote matters at this point to review very hastily some of the reasons for abandoning the search for a basis for knowledge outside the scope of our beliefs. By 'basis' here I mean specifically an epistemological basis, a source of justification.

The attempts worth taking seriously attempt to ground belief in one way or another on the testimony of the senses: sensation, perception, the given, experience, sense data, the passing show. All such theories must explain at least these two things: what, exactly, is the relation between sensation and belief that allows the first to justify the second? and, why should we believe our sensations are reliable, that is, why should we trust our senses?

The simplest idea is to identify certain beliefs with sensations. Thus Hume seems not to have distinguished between perceiving a green spot and perceiving that a spot is green. (An ambiguity in the word 'idea' was a great help here.) Other philosophers noted Hume's confusion, but tried to attain the same results by reducing the gap between perception and judgement to zero by attempting to formulate judgements that do not go beyond stating that the perception or sensation or presentation exists (whatever that may mean). Such theories do not justify beliefs on the basis of sensations, but try to justify certain beliefs by claiming that they have exactly the same epistemic content as a sensation. There are two difficulties with such a view: first, if the basic beliefs do not exceed in content the corresponding sensation they cannot support any inference to an objective world; and second, there are no such beliefs.

A more plausible line is to claim that we cannot be wrong about how things appear to us to be. If we believe we have a sensation, we do; this is held to be an analytic truth, or a fact about how language is used.

It is difficult to explain this supposed connection between sensations and some beliefs in a way that does not invite scepticism about other minds, and in the absence of an adequate explanation, there should be a doubt about the implications of the connection for justification. But in any case, it is unclear how, on this line, sensations justify the belief in those sensations. The point is rather that such beliefs require no justification, for the existence of the belief entails the existence of the sensation, and so the existence of the belief entails its own truth. Unless something further is added, we are back to another form of coherence theory.

Emphasis on sensation or perception in matters epistemological springs from the obvious thought: sensations are what connect the world and our beliefs, and they are candidates for justifiers because we often are aware of them. The trouble we have been running into is that the justification seems to depend on the awareness, which is just another belief.

Let us try a bolder tack. Suppose we say that sensations themselves, verbalized or not, justify certain beliefs that go beyond what is given in sensation. So, under certain conditions, having the sensation of seeing a green light flashing may justify the belief that a green light is flashing. The problem is to see how the sensation justifies the belief. Of course, if someone has the sensation of seeing a green light flashing, it is likely, under certain circumstances, that a green light is flashing. *We* can say this, since we know of his sensation, but *he* can't say it, since we are supposing he is justified without having to depend on believing he has the sensation. Suppose he believed he didn't have the sensation. Would the sensation still justify him in the belief in an objective flashing green light?

The relation between a sensation and a belief cannot be logical, since sensations are not beliefs or other propositional attitudes. What then is the relation? The answer is, I think, obvious: the relation is causal. Sensations cause some beliefs and in *this* sense are the basis or ground of those beliefs. But a causal explanation of a belief does not show how or why the belief is justified.

The difficulty of transmuting a cause into a reason plagues the anti-coherentist again if he tries to answer our second question: what justifies the belief that our senses do not systematically deceive us? For even if sensations justify belief in sensation, we do not yet see how they justify belief in external events and objects.

Quine tells us that science tells us that 'our only source of information about the external world is through the impact of light rays and molecules upon our sensory surfaces.'[5] What worries me is how to read the words 'source' and 'information'. Certainly it is true that events and objects in the external world cause us to believe things about the external world, and much, if not all, of the causality takes a route through the sense organs. The notion of information, however, applies in a non-metaphorical way only to the engendered beliefs. So 'source' has to be read simply as 'cause' and 'information' as 'true belief' or 'knowledge'. Justification of beliefs caused by our senses is not yet in sight.[6]

The approach to the problem of justification we have been tracing must be wrong. We have been trying to see it this way: a person has all his beliefs about the world – that is, all his beliefs. How can he tell if they are true, or apt to be true? Only, we have been assuming, by connecting his beliefs to the world, confronting certain of his beliefs with the deliverances of the senses one by one, or perhaps confronting the totality of his beliefs with the tribunal of experience. No such confrontation makes sense, for of course we can't get outside our skins to find out what is causing the internal happenings of which we are aware. Introducing intermediate steps or entities into the causal chain, like sensations or observations, serves only to make the epistemological problem more obvious. For if the intermediaries are merely causes, they don't justify the beliefs they cause, while if they deliver information, they may be lying. The moral is obvious. Since we can't swear intermediaries to truthfulness, we should allow no intermediaries between our beliefs and their objects in the world. Of course there are causal intermediaries. What we must guard against are epistemic intermediaries.

There are common views of language that encourage bad epistemology. This is no accident, of course, since theories of meaning are connected with epistemology through attempts to answer the question how one determines that a sentence is true. If knowing the meaning of a sentence (knowing how to give a correct interpretation of it) involves, or is, knowing how it could be recognized to be true, then the theory of meaning raises the same question we have been struggling with, for giving the meaning of a sentence will demand that we specify what would justify asserting it. Here the coherentist will hold that there is no use looking for a source of justification outside of other sentences held true, while the foundationalist will seek to anchor at least some words or sentences to non-verbal rocks. This view is held, I think, both by Quine and by Michael Dummett.

Dummett and Quine differ, to be sure. In particular, they disagree about holism, the claim that the truth of our sentences must be tested together rather than one by one. And they disagree also, and consequently, about whether there is a useful distinction between analytic and synthetic sentences, and about whether a satisfactory theory of meaning can allow the sort of indeterminacy Quine argues for. (On all these points, I am Quine's faithful student.)

But what concerns me here is that Quine and Dummett agree on a basic principle, which is that whatever there is to meaning must be traced back somehow to experience, the given, or patterns of sensory stimulation, something intermediate between belief and the usual objects our beliefs are about. Once we take this step, we open the door to scepticism, for we must then allow that a very great many – perhaps most – of the sentences we hold to be true may in fact be false. It is ironical. Trying to make meaning accessible has made truth inaccessible. When meaning goes epistemological in this way, truth and meaning are necessarily divorced. One can, of course, arrange a shotgun wedding by redefining truth as what we are justified in asserting. But this does not marry the original mates.

Take Quine's proposal that whatever there is to the meaning (information value) of an observation sentence is determined by the patterns of sensory stimulation that would cause a speaker to assent to or dissent from the sentence. This is a marvellously ingenious way of capturing what is appealing about verificationist theories without having to talk of meanings, sense-data, or sensations; for the first time it made plausible the idea that one could, and should, do what I call the theory of meaning without need of what Quine calls meanings. But Quine's proposal, like other forms of verificationism, makes for scepticism. For clearly a person's sensory stimulations could be just as they are and yet the world outside very different. (Remember the brain in the vat.)

Quine's way of doing without meanings is subtle and complicated. He ties the meanings of some sentences directly to patterns of stimulation (which also constitute the evidence, Quine thinks, for assenting to the sentence), but the meanings of further sentences are determined by how they are conditioned to the original, or observation sentences. The facts of such conditioning do not permit a sharp division between sentences held true by virtue of meaning and sentences held true on the basis of observation. Quine made this point by showing that if one way of interpreting a speaker's utterances was satisfactory, so were many others. This doctrine of the indeterminacy of translation, as Quine called it, should be viewed as neither mysterious nor threatening. It is no more mysterious than the fact that temperature can be measured in Centigrade or Fahrenheit (or any linear transformation of those numbers). And it is not threatening because the very procedure that demonstrates the degree of indeterminacy at the same time demonstrates that what is determinate is all we need.

In my view, erasing the line between the analytic and synthetic saved philosophy of language as a serious subject by showing how it could be pursued without what there cannot be: determinate meanings. I now suggest also giving up the distinction between observation sentences and the rest. For the distinction between sentences belief in whose truth is justified by sensations and sentences belief in whose truth is justified only by appeal to other sentences held true is as anathema to the coherentist as the distinction between beliefs justified by sensations and beliefs justified only by appeal to further beliefs. Accordingly, I suggest we give up the idea that meaning or knowledge is grounded on something that counts as an ultimate source of evidence. No doubt meaning and knowledge depend on experience, and experience ultimately on sensation. But this is the 'depend' of causality, not of evidence or justification.

I have now stated my problem as well as I can. The search for an empirical foundation for meaning or knowledge leads to scepticism, while a coherence theory seems at a loss to provide any reason for a believer to believe that his beliefs, if coherent, are true. We are caught between a false answer to the sceptic, and no answer.

The dilemma is not a true one. What is needed to answer the sceptic is to show that someone with a (more or less) coherent set of beliefs has a reason to suppose his beliefs are not mistaken in the main. What we have shown is that it is absurd to look for a justifying ground for the totality of beliefs, something outside this totality which we can use to test or compare with our beliefs. The answer to our problem must then be to find a *reason* for supposing most of our beliefs are true that is not a form of *evidence*.

My argument has two parts. First I urge that a correct understanding of the speech, beliefs, desires, intentions and other propositional attitudes of a person leads to the conclusion that most of a person's beliefs must be true, and so there is a legitimate presumption that any one of them, if it coheres with most of the rest, is true. Then I go on to claim that anyone with thoughts, and so in particular anyone who wonders whether he has any reason to suppose he is generally right about the nature of his environment, must know what a belief is, and how in general beliefs are to be detected and interpreted. These being perfectly general facts we cannot fail to use when we communicate with others, or when we try to communicate with others, or even when we merely think we are communicating with others, there is a pretty strong sense in which we can be said to know that there is a presumption in favour of the overall truthfulness of anyone's beliefs, including our own. So it is bootless for someone to ask for some *further* reassurance; that can only add to his stock of beliefs. All that is needed is that he recognize that belief is in its nature veridical.

Belief can be seen to be veridical by considering what determines the existence and contents of a belief. Belief, like the other so-called propositional attitudes, is supervenient on facts of various sorts, behavioural, neurophysiological, biological and physical. The reason for pointing this out is not to encourage definitional or nomological reduction of psychological phenomena to something more basic, and certainly not to suggest epistemological priorities. The point is rather understanding. We gain one kind of insight into the nature of the propositional attitudes when we relate them systematically to one another and to phenomena on other levels. Since the propositional attitudes are deeply interlocked, we cannot learn the nature of one by first winning understanding of another. As interpreters, we work our way into the whole system, depending much on the pattern of interrelationships.

Take for example the interdependence of belief and meaning. What a sentence means depends partly on the external circumstances that cause it to win some degree of conviction; and partly on the relations, grammatical, logical or less, that the sentence has to other sentences held true with varying degrees of conviction. Since these relations are themselves translated directly into beliefs, it is easy to see how meaning depends on belief. Belief, however, depends equally on meaning, for the only access to the fine structure and individuation of beliefs is through the sentences speakers and interpreters of speakers use to express and describe beliefs. If we want to illuminate the nature of meaning and belief, therefore, we need to start with something that assumes neither. Quine's suggestion, which I shall essentially follow, is to take *prompted assent* as basic, the causal relation between assenting to a sentence and the cause of such assent. This is a fair place to start the project of identifying beliefs and meanings, since a speaker's assent to a sentence depends both on what he means by the sentence and on what he believes about the world. Yet it is possible to know that a speaker assents to a sentence without knowing either what the sentence, as spoken by him, means, or what belief is expressed by it. Equally obvious is the fact that once an interpretation has been given for a sentence assented to, a belief has been attributed. If correct theories of interpretation are not unique (do not lead to uniquely correct interpretations), the same will go for attributions of belief, of course, as tied to acquiescence in particular sentences.

A speaker who wishes his words to be understood cannot systematically deceive his would-be interpreters about when he assents to sentences – that is, holds them true. As a matter of principle, then, meaning, and by its connection with meaning, belief also, are open to public determination. I shall take advantage of this fact in what follows and adopt the stance of a radical interpreter when asking about the nature of belief. What a fully informed interpreter could learn about what a speaker means is all there is to learn; the same goes for what the speaker believes.[7]

The interpreter's problem is that what he is assumed to know – the causes of assents to sentences of a speaker – is, as we have seen, the product of two things he is assumed not to know, meaning and belief. If he knew the meanings he would know the beliefs, and if he knew the beliefs expressed by sentences assented to, he would know the meanings. But how can he learn both at once, since each depends on the other?

The general lines of the solution, like the problem itself, are owed to Quine. I will, however, introduce some changes into Quine's solution, as I have into the statement of the problem. The changes are directly relevant to the issue of epistemological scepticism.

I see the aim of radical interpretation (which is much, but not entirely, like Quine's radical translation) as being to produce a Tarski-style characterization of truth for the speaker's language, and a theory of his beliefs. (The second follows from the first plus the presupposed knowledge of sentences held true.) This adds little to Quine's programme of translation, since translation of the speaker's language into one's own plus a theory of truth for one's own language add up to a theory of truth for the speaker. But the shift to the semantic notion of truth from the syntactic notion of translation puts the formal restrictions of a theory of truth in the foreground, and emphasizes one aspect of the close relation between truth and meaning.

The principle of charity plays a crucial role in Quine's method, and an even more crucial role in my variant. In either case, the principle directs the interpreter to translate or interpret so as to read some of his own standards of truth into the pattern of sentences held true by the speaker. The point of the principle is to make the speaker intelligible, since too great deviations from consistency and correctness leave no common ground on which to judge either conformity or difference. From a formal point of view, the principle of charity helps solve the problem of the interaction of meaning and belief by restraining the degrees of freedom allowed belief while determining how to interpret words.

We have no choice, Quine has urged, but to read our own logic into the thoughts of a speaker; Quine says this for the sentential calculus, and I would add the same for first-order quantification theory. This leads directly to the identification of the logical constants, as well as to assigning a logical form to all sentences.

Something like charity operates in the interpretation of those sentences whose causes of assent come and go with time and place: when the interpreter finds a sentence of the speaker the speaker assents to regularly under conditions he recognizes, he takes those conditions to be the truth conditions of the speaker's sentence. This is only roughly right, as we shall see in a moment. Sentences and predicates less directly geared to easily detected goings-on can, in Quine's cannon, be interpreted at will, given only the constraints of interconnections with sentences conditioned directly to the world. Here I would extend the principle of charity to favour interpretations that as far as possible preserve truth: I think it makes for mutual understanding, and hence for better interpretation, to interpret what the speaker accepts as true when we can. In this matter, I have less choice than Quine, because I do not see how to draw the line between observation sentences and theoretical sentences at the start. There are several reasons for this, but the one most relevant to the present topic is that this distinction is ultimately based on an epistemological considera- tion of a sort I have renounced: observation sentences are directly based on something like sensation – patterns of sensory stimulation – and this is an idea I have been urging leads to scepticism. Without the direct tie to sensation or stimulation, the distinction between observation sentences and others can't be drawn on epistemologically significant grounds. The distinction between sentences whose causes to assent come and go with observable circumstances and those a speaker clings to through change remains however, and offers the possibility of interpreting the words and sentences beyond the logical.

The details are not here to the point. What should be clear is that if the account I have given of how belief and meaning are related and understood by an interpreter is correct, then most of the sentences a speaker holds to be true – especially the ones he holds to most stubbornly, the ones most central to the system of his beliefs – most of these sentences *are* true, at least in the opinion of the interpreter. For the only, and therefore unimpeachable, method available to the interpreter automatically puts the speaker's beliefs in accord with the standards of logic of the interpreter, and hence credits the speaker with plain truths of logic. Needless to say there are degrees of logical and other consistency, and perfect consistency is not to be expected. What needs emphasis is only the methodological necessity for finding consistency enough.

Nor, from the interpreter's point of view, is there any way he can discover the speaker to be largely wrong about the world. For he interprets sentences held true (which is not to be distinguished from attributing beliefs) according to the events and objects in the outside world that cause the sentence to be held true.

What I take to be the important aspect of this approach is apt to be missed because the approach reverses our natural way of thinking of communication derived from situations in which understanding has already been secured. Once understanding has been secured we are able, often, to learn what a person believes quite independently of what caused him to believe it. This may lead us to the crucial, indeed fatal, conclusion that we can in general fix what someone means independently of what he believes and independently of what caused the belief. But if I am right, we can't in general first identify beliefs and meanings and then ask what caused them. The causality plays an indispensable role in determining the content of what we say and believe. This is a fact we can be led to recognize by taking up, as we have, the interpreter's point of view.

It is an artifact of the interpreter's correct interpretation of a person's speech and attitudes that there is a large degree of truth and consistency in the thought and speech of an agent. But this is truth and consistency by the interpreter's standards. Why couldn't it happen that speaker and interpreter understand one another on the basis of shared but erroneous beliefs? This can, and no doubt often does, happen. But it cannot be the rule. For imagine for a moment an interpreter who is omniscient about the world, and about what does and would cause a speaker to assent to any sentence in his (potentially unlimited) repertoire. The omniscient interpreter, using the same method as the fallible interpreter, finds the fallible speaker largely consistent and correct. By his own standards, of course, but since these are objectively correct, the fallible speaker is seen to be largely correct and consistent by objective standards. We may also, if we want, let the omniscient interpreter turn his attention to the fallible interpreter of the fallible speaker. It turns out that the fallible interpreter can be wrong about some things, but not in general; and so he cannot share universal error with the agent he is interpreting. Once we agree to the general method of interpretation I have sketched, it becomes impossible correctly to hold that anyone could be mostly wrong about how things are.

There is, as I noted above, a key difference between the method of radical interpretation I am now recommending, and Quine's method of radical translation. The difference lies in the nature of the choice of causes that govern interpretation. Quine makes interpretation depend on patterns of sensory stimulation, while I make it depend on the external events and objects the sentence is interpreted as being about. Thus Quine's notion of meaning is tied to sensory criteria, something he thinks that can be treated also as evidence. This leads Quine to give epistemic significance to the distinction between observation sentences and others, since observation sentences are supposed, by their direct conditioning to the senses, to have a kind of extra-linguistic justification. This is the view against which I argued in the first part of my paper, urging that sensory stimulations are indeed part of the causal chain that leads to belief, but cannot, without confusion, be considered to be evidence, or a source of justification, for the stimulated beliefs.

What stands in the way of global scepticism of the senses is in my view the fact that we must, in the plainest and methodologically most basic cases, take the objects of a belief to be the causes of that belief. And what we, as interpreters, must take them to be is what they in fact are. Communication begins where causes converge: your utterance means what mine does if belief in its truth is systematically caused by the same events and objects.[8]

The difficulties in the way of this view are obvious, but I think they can be overcome. The method applies directly, at best, only to occasion sentences – the sentences assent to which is caused systematically by common changes in the world. Further sentences are interpreted by their conditioning to occasion sentences, and the appearance in them of words that appear also in occasion sentences. Among occasion sentences, some will vary in the credence they command not only in the face of environmental change, but also in the face of change of credence awarded related sentences. Criteria can be developed on this basis to distinguish degrees of observationality on internal grounds, without appeal to the concept of a basis for belief outside the circle of beliefs.

Related to these problems, and easier still to grasp, is the problem of error. For even in the simplest cases it is clear that the same cause (a rabbit scampers by) may engender different beliefs in speaker and observer, and so encourage assent to sentences which cannot bear the same interpretation. It is no doubt this fact that made Quine turn from rabbits to patterns of stimulation as the key to interpretation. Just as a matter of statistics, I'm not sure how much better one approach is than the other. Is the relative frequency with which identical patterns of stimulation will touch off assent to 'Gavagai' and 'Rabbit' greater than the relative frequency with which a rabbit touches off the same two responses in speaker and interpreter? Not an easy question to test in a convincing way. But let the imagined results speak for Quine's method. Then I must say, what I must say in any case, the problem of error cannot be met sentence by sentence, even at the simplest level. The best we can do is cope with error holistically, that is, we interpret so as to make an agent as intelligible as possible, given his actions, his utterances and his place in the world. About some things we will find him wrong, as the necessary cost of finding him elsewhere right. As a rough approximation, finding him right means identifying the causes with the objects of his beliefs, giving special weight to the simplest cases, and countenancing error where it can be best explained.

Suppose I am right that an interpreter must so interpret as to make a speaker or agent largely correct about the world. How does this help the person himself who wonders what reason he has to think his beliefs are mostly true? How can he learn about the causal relations between the real world and his beliefs that lead the interpreter to interpret him as being on the right track?

The answer is contained in the question. In order to doubt or wonder about the provenance of his beliefs an agent must know what belief is. This brings with it the concept of objective truth, for the notion of a belief is the notion of a state that may or may not jibe with reality. But beliefs are also identified, directly and indirectly, by their causes. What an omniscient interpreter knows a fallible interpreter gets right enough if he understands a speaker, and this is just the complicated causal truth that makes us the believers we are, and fixes the contents of our beliefs. The agent has only to reflect on what a belief is to appreciate that most of his basic beliefs are true, and among his beliefs, those most securely held and that cohere with the main body of his beliefs are the most apt to be true. The question, how do I know my beliefs are generally true? thus answers itself, simply because beliefs are by nature generally true. Rephrased or expanded, the question becomes, how can I tell whether my beliefs, which are by their nature generally true, are generally true?

All beliefs are justified in this sense: they are supported by numerous other beliefs (otherwise they wouldn't be the beliefs they are), and have a presumption in favour of their truth. The presumption increases the larger and more significant the body of beliefs with which a belief coheres, and there being no such thing as an isolated belief, there is no belief without a presumption in its favour. In this respect, interpreter and interpreted differ. From the interpreter's point of view, methodology enforces a general presumption of truth for the body of beliefs as a whole, but the interpreter does not need to presume each particular belief of someone else is true. The general presumption applied to others does not make them globally right, as I have emphasized, but provides the background against which to accuse them of error. But from each person's own vantage point, there must be a graded presumption in favour of each of his own beliefs.

We cannot, alas, draw the picturesque and pleasant conclusion that all true beliefs constitute knowledge. For though all of a believer's beliefs are to some extent justified to him, some may not be justified enough, or in the right way, to constitute knowledge. The general presumption in favour of the truth of belief serves to rescue us from a standard form of scepticism by showing why it is impossible for all our beliefs to be false together. This leaves almost untouched the task of specifying the conditions of knowledge. I have not been concerned with the canons of evidential support (if such there be), but to show that all that counts as evidence or justification for a belief must come from the same totality of belief to which it belongs.

AFTERTHOUGHTS, 1987

The paper printed here was written for a colloquium organized by Richard Rorty for a Hegel Congress at Stuttgart in 1981. W. V. Quine and Hilary Putnam were the other participants in the colloquium. Our contributions were published in *Kant oder Hegel?*[9] After Stuttgart the four of us had a more leisurely exchange on the same topics at the University of Heidelberg. When the Pacific Division of the American Philosophical Association met in March of 1983, Rorty read a paper titled 'Pragmatism, Davidson, and Truth'. It was in part a comment on 'A Coherence Theory of Truth and Knowledge'. I replied. Rorty subsequently published his paper with revisions in *Truth and Interpretation: Perspectives on the Philosophy of Donald Davidson*.[10] This note continues the conversation.

A few ageing *philosophes*, which may include Quine, Putnam and Dummett, and certainly includes me, are still puzzling over the nature of truth and its connections or lack of connections with meaning and epistemology. Rorty thinks we should stop worrying; he believes philosophy has seen through or outgrown the puzzles and should turn to less heavy and more interesting matters. He is particularly impatient with me for not conceding that the old game is up because he finds in my work useful support for his enlightened stance; underneath my 'out-dated rhetoric' he detects the outlines of a largely correct attitude.

In his paper, both early and late, Rorty urges two things: that my view of truth amounts to a rejection of both coherence and correspondence theories and should properly be classed as belonging to the pragmatist tradition, and that I should not pretend that I am answering the sceptic when I am really telling him to get lost. I pretty much concur with him on both points.

In our 1983 discussion I agreed to stop calling my position either a coherence or a correspondence theory if he would give up the pragmatist theory of truth. He has done his part; he now explicitly rejects both James and Peirce on truth. I am glad to hold to my side of the bargain. If it had not already been published, I would now change the title of 'A Coherence Theory', and I would not describe the project as showing how 'coherence yields correspondence'. On internal evidence alone, as Rorty points out, my view cannot be called a correspondence theory. As long ago as 1969 I argued that nothing can usefully and intelligibly be said to correspond to a sentence;[11] and I repeated this in 'A Coherence Theory'. I thought then that the fact that in characterizing truth for a language it is necessary to put words into relation with objects was enough to give some grip for the idea of correspondence; but this now seems to me a mistake. The mistake is in a way only a misnomer, but terminological infelicities have a way of breeding conceptual confusion, and so it is here. Correspondence theories have always been conceived as providing an *explanation* or *analysis* of truth, and this a Tarski-style theory of truth certainly does not do. I would also now reject the point generally made against correspondence theories that there is no way we could ever tell whether our sentences or beliefs correspond to reality. This criticism is at best misleading, since no one has ever explained in what such a correspondence could consist; and, worse, it is predicated on the false assumption that truth is transparently epistemic.

I also regret having called my view a 'coherence theory'. My emphasis on coherence was probably just a way of making a negative point, that 'all that counts as evidence or justification for a belief must come from the same totality of belief to which it belongs.' Of course this negative claim has typically led those philosophers who held it to conclude that reality and truth are constructs of thought; but it does not lead me to this conclusion, and for this reason if no other I ought not to have called my view a coherence theory. There is also a less weighty reason for not stressing coherence. Coherence is nothing but consistency. It is certainly in favour of a set of beliefs that they be consistent, but there is no chance that a person's beliefs will not tend to be self-consistent, since beliefs are individuated in part by their logical properties; what is not largely consistent with many other beliefs cannot be identified as a belief. The main thrust of 'A Coherence Theory' has little to do with consistency; the important thesis for which I argue is that belief is intrinsically veridical. This is the ground on which I maintain that while truth is not an epistemic concept, neither is it wholly severed from belief (as it is in different ways by both correspondence and coherence theories).

My emphasis on coherence was misplaced; calling my view a 'theory' was a plain blunder. In his paper Rorty stressed a minimalist attitude towards truth that he correctly thought we shared. It could be put this way: truth is as clear and basic a concept as we have. Tarski has given us an idea of how to *apply* the general concept (or try to apply it) to particular languages on the assumption that we already understand it; but of course he didn't show how to define it in general (he proved, rather, that this couldn't be done). Any further attempt to explain, define, analyse or explicate the concept will be empty or wrong: correspondence theories, coherence theories, pragmatist theories, theories that identify truth with warranted assertability (perhaps under 'ideal' or 'optimum' conditions), theories that ask truth to explain the success of science or serve as the ultimate outcome of science or the conversations of some elite, all such theories either add nothing to our understanding of truth or have obvious counter-examples. Why on earth should we expect to be able to reduce truth to something clearer or more fundamental? After all, the only concept Plato succeeded in defining was mud (dirt and water). Putnam's comparison of various attempts to characterize truth with the attempts to define 'good' in naturalistic terms seems to me, as it does to Rorty, apt. It also seems to apply to Putnam's identification of truth with idealized warranted assertability.[12] (*Realism and Reason*, Cambridge, 1983, p. xvii.)

A theory of truth for a speaker, or group of speakers, while not a definition of the general concept of truth, does give a firm sense of what the concept is good for; it allows us to say, in a compact and clear way, what someone who understands that speaker, or those speakers, knows. Such a theory also invites the question how an interpreter could confirm its truth – a question which without the theory could not be articulated. The answer will, as I try to show in 'A Coherence Theory', bring out essential relations among the concepts of meaning, truth and belief. If I am right, each of these concepts requires the others, but none is subordinate to, much less definable in terms of, the others. Truth emerges not as wholly detached from belief (as a correspondence theory would make it) nor as dependent on human methods and powers of discovery (as epistemic theories of truth would make it). What saves truth from being 'radically non-epistemic' (in Putnam's words) is not that truth is epistemic but that belief, through its ties with meaning, is intrinsically veridical.

Finally, how about Rorty's admonition to stop trying to answer the sceptic, and tell him to get lost? A short response would be that the sceptic has been told this again and again over the millennia and never seems to listen; like the philosopher he is, he wants an argument. To spell this out a bit: there is perhaps the suggestion in Rorty's 'Pragmatism, Davidson, and Truth' that a 'naturalistic' approach to the problems of meaning and the propositional attitudes will automatically leave the sceptic no room for manoeuvre. This thought, whether or not it is Rorty's, is wrong. Quine's naturalized epistemology, because it is based on the empiricist premise that what we mean and what we think is conceptually (and not merely causally) founded on the testimony of the senses, is open to standard sceptical attack. I was much concerned in 'A Coherence Theory' to argue for an alternative approach to meaning and knowledge, and to show that if this alternative were right, scepticism could not get off the ground. I agree with Rorty to this extent; I did not set out to 'refute' the sceptic, but to give a sketch of what I think to be a correct account of the foundations of linguistic communication and its implications for truth, belief and knowledge. If one grants the correctness of this account, one *can* tell the sceptic to get lost.

Where Rorty and I differ, if we do, is in the importance we attach to the arguments that lead to the sceptic's undoing, and in the interest we find in the consequences for knowledge, belief, truth and meaning. Rorty wants to dwell on where the arguments have led: to a position which allows us to dismiss the sceptic's doubts, and so to abandon the attempt to provide a general justification for knowledge claims – a justification that is neither possible nor needed. Rorty sees the history of Western philosophy as a confused and victorless battle between unintelligible scepticism and lame attempts to answer it. Epistemology from Descartes to Quine seems to me just one complex, and by no means unilluminating, chapter in the philosophical enterprise. If that chapter is coming to a close, it will be through recourse to modes of analysis and adherence to standards of clarity that have always distinguished the best philosophy, and will, with luck and enterprise, continue to do so.

NOTES

1 See my 'True to the Facts', *The Journal of Philosophy*, Vol. 66 (1969), pp. 216–34.
2 Hilary Putnam, *Meaning and the Moral Sciences* (Routledge & Kegan Paul, London, 1978), p. 125.
3 See my 'On the Very Idea of a Conceptual Scheme', in *Proceedings and Addresses of the American Philosophical Association* (1974), pp. 5–20.
4 Richard Rorty, *Philosophy and the Mirror of Nature* (Princeton University Press, Princeton, 1979), p. 178.
5 W. V. Quine, 'The Nature of Natural Knowledge', in *Mind and Language*, ed. S. Guttenplan (Clarendon Press, Oxford, 1975), p. 68.
6 Many other passages in Quine suggest that Quine hopes to assimilate sensory causes to evidence. In *Word and Object* (MIT Press, Cambridge, Mass., 1960), p. 22, he writes that 'surface irritations . . . exhaust our clues to an external world.' In *Ontological Relativity* (Columbia University Press, New York, 1969), p. 75, we find that 'The stimulation of his sensory receptors is all the evidence anybody has had to go on, ultimately, in arriving at his picture of the world.' On the same page: 'Two cardinal tenets of empiricism remain unassailable. . . . One is that whatever evidence there *is* for science *is* sensory evidence. The other . . . is that all inculcation of meanings of words, must rest ultimately on sensory evidence.' In *The Roots of Reference* (Open Court Publishing, 1974), pp. 37–8, Quine says 'observations' are basic 'both in the support of theory and in the learning of language', and then goes on, 'What are observations? They are visual, auditory, tactual, olfactory. They are sensory, evidently, and thus subjective. . . . Should we say then that the observation is not the sensation. . . .? No . . .' Quine goes on to abandon talk of observations for talk of observation sentences. But of course observation sentences, unlike observations, cannot play the role of evidence unless we have reason to believe they are true.
7 I now think it is essential, in doing radical interpretation, to include the desires of the speaker from the start, so that the springs of action and intention, namely both belief and desire, are related to meaning. But in the present talk it is not necessary to introduce this further factor.
8 It is clear that the causal theory of meaning has little in common with the causal theories of reference of Kripke and Putnam. Those theories look to causal relations between

names and objects of which speakers may well be ignorant. The chance of systematic error is thus increased. My causal theory does the reverse by connecting the cause of a belief with its object.

9 Dieter Henrich (ed.), *Kant oder Hegel?* (Kett-Cotta, 1983).

10 Ernest LePore (ed.), *Truth and Interpretation: Perspectives on the Philosophy of Donald Davidson* (Blackwell, Oxford, 1986).

11 Donald Davidson, 'True to the Facts', reprinted in *Inquiries into Truth and Interpretation* (Oxford University Press, Oxford, 1984).

12 Hilary Putnam, *Realism and Reason* (Cambridge University Press, Cambridge, 1983), p. xviii.

9

Deep Epistemology without Foundations (in Language)

Alan R. Malachowski

In the *Critique of Pure Reason*, Kant famously complains that 'it still remains a scandal to philosophy and to human reason in general that the existence of things outside us . . . must be accepted on *faith*, and that if anyone thinks good to doubt their existence, we are unable to counter his doubts by any satisfactory proof'.[1] Kant is complaining largely, of course, about the Cartesian legacy of epistemological scepticism. A legacy which arguably still has Russell saying in 1923, 'If you are willing to believe that nothing exists except what you directly experience, no other person can prove you wrong, and probably no valid arguments against your view exists'.[2] But then, in 1927, in *Being and Time*, Heidegger dramatically redescribes the situation: 'The "scandal of philosophy" is not that this proof has yet to be accepted but that *such proofs are expected and attempted again and again*'[3] – a pronouncement which has not been treated lightly by those who now rank Heidegger alongside Wittgenstein as one of the great critics of the Cartesian legacy for our age.[4]

Descartes, Kant, Russell, Heidegger are class acts to follow. But this does not deter Richard Rorty, whose *Philosophy and the Mirror of Nature* (hereafter, *PMN*) issues a bold challenge to entrenched epistemological conceptions of philosophy. Indeed, one perceptive commentator (presumably neglecting Heidegger) maintains that Rorty offers 'perhaps the most fundamental and challenging contribution to metaphilosophy since Kant created philosophy as we know it'.[5]

In *PMN*, Rorty tries to dismantle the 'Cartesian framework' of modern philosophical thinking. He suggests some far more flexible 'constraints', and – siding with Heidegger against the Kant–Russell outlook – makes it clear that the 'redescription' should cover epistemology in general. The *real* 'scandal' is that, for too long, philosophers have been preoccupied with 'theories of knowledge' and the like. This verdict merits some reflection. Rorty is not just popularizing the views of Heidegger, nor is he simply providing an eloquent outlet for the kind of hostility towards traditional epistemology which has been in the air since the time of Hegel and Nietzsche. No, Rorty should be given credit for putting his own slant on things. The rich sources for some of his main ideas may create the flavouring, but the brew is his own.

In the following response to Rorty, I want to throw a little weight behind two claims which take the sting out of his negative view of epistemology. The first claim is that in his attack on 'epistemology-centred philosophy', Rorty tends to underestimate both epistemology and the problems it confronts. And, the second is that in advocating a post-epistemological form of philosophy, Rorty is inclined to exaggerate the creative autonomy of language. These errors of judgement seem to me to be essential to Rorty's scheme of things. Without them, it is easier to see why we still need epistemology, and why the epistemology we need cannot be grounded in the kind of 'literary performances' of language that Rorty finds so enchanting.

The first parts of my discussion focus on some fairly narrow points concerning difficulties in characterizing Rorty's position. Then I deal with some flaws in his conception of epistemology, querying the associated argumentation. Finally, I broaden things out to consider epistemological shortcomings in Rorty's vision of philosophy as a quasi-literary enterprise. I round-off with a brief comment on the role of post-Rortyan theories of knowledge.

Epistemology-centred philosophy: does Rorty have a position?

One of Rorty's main aims in *PMN* is stated boldly at the outset when he tells us he wants to 'undermine the reader's confidence in "Knowledge" as something about which there ought to be a "theory" and which has "foundations"'.[6] There is scope here for more than one reading, but a plausible working interpretation suggests that Rorty needs to show at least that:

(1) it is unwise to crave for a *theory* of knowledge and
(2) it is unwise to think of knowledge as something which has (or needs) *foundations*.

We can safely assume that in the face of a demonstration of (1) and (2), confidence in the corresponding conceptions of knowledge *should* drain away. But Rorty's further aim in threatening the reader's confidence seems to be more positive:

(3)   to make his own favoured pragmatic/hermeneutic conception of philosophy more attractive, to make *that* something we can have confidence in (albeit, confidence of a different order[7]).

When pursuing these aims of undermining, and then rebuilding, confidence, Rorty says a number of very insightful things about how epistemology came to play a central role in modern Western philosophy, and about the consequences of this. But , in the present response, I want to challenge (1) to (3) as interwoven elements of a substantive position on epistemology. I will argue three things: (a) that Rorty tends to conflate (1) and (2); (b) that he fails to establish either (1) or (2); and (c) that Rorty's anti-epistemological contentions generally do nothing for his picture of what philosophy should really be like (so he does not deserve to achieve (3)).

My principal concern in staking out (a) to (c) is not to fasten hard on some *particular* failing on Rorty's part which, when rectified, might salvage, or even strengthen, his position (it is not that 'Rorty might have liberated us from epistemology if only he had . . .'), but rather to challenge his whole approach, and to show that epistemology, itself, has the kind of interesting depth which: (i) requires that it be approached speculatively by way of theoretical procedures (even if not necessarily by way of *theories of foundations* in Rorty's derided sense of 'foundations'), and (ii) cannot be catered for within the sort of philosophy Rorty would have us prefer. The discussion of (ii) leads on to some considerations involving Rorty's view of language.

Since Rorty urges us to move 'beyond' the concerns of traditional epistemologists, is it fair to start out on the assumption that the views he expresses in *PMN* add up to a 'substantive position on epistemology'? This is a tricky question. Not least because, in practice, Rorty is somewhat equivocal about the power of reason and arguments, and does not make it clear, either, whether the 'problems of knowledge' somehow get *resolved* in the 'move beyond epistemology', or simply left behind as dusty relics on the shelf of history (along with other ideas that 'didn't work out'). We need to locate an argument, or something like one, if we are to define a 'position', and we need to find a connection with the 'problems of knowledge' if we are to characterize that position as a 'position on epistemology'. Rorty's nimble dialectical dancing does not make this an easy task, but here goes.

On the one hand, Rorty wants to downplay the role of reason-based discourse: as a matter of fact such discourse does not, and in important cases (as a matter of principle, as it were) *cannot*, underwrite our various social practices (call those connected with knowledge 'our ways of knowing'). What we *do* has to sign its own guarantees (pragmatism) and then read its own writing (hermeneutics). On the other hand, Rorty continues to give reasons for his own views, and points out fallacious steps in the reasoning of his opponents. Now, of course, Rorty is too sophisticated to leave himself open to the charge of 'self-contradiction'[8]: his use of piecemeal argumentation is perfectly compatible with his desire to diminish the *global* role of reason. But, a residual worry, even for sympathetic readers, is to gauge the weight he is putting on certain lines of argument.

This problem becomes acute in Rorty's treatment of *foundationalism* in epistemology ('knowledge' is one of the 'important cases' just alluded to). According to Rorty, reason cannot *justify*, or in any other strong sense 'legitimate', our established ways of knowing. And the 'reason' for this is that there can be no *foundational principles*; there is nothing upon which reason can build the appropriate theoretical edifice (to press this point home, Rorty harnesses Quine's attack on the analytic/synthetic distinction and Sellar's attack on the 'given' in experience[9]). The difficulty for those readers who feel uneasy about Rorty's eventual conclusions, is to figure out whether he intends them to depend *entirely* on their associated arguments.

To be blunt, the dilemma is as follows. Does Rorty want to say that certain considerations which tell against the notion of 'foundations' in matters epistemological *entail* his pessimistic conclusions concerning the prospects for any fruitful continuation of the line of traditional 'theories of knowledge' (so that if we were able to show that his reasoning was incorrect (and/or his premises questionable), we should also be able to undermine *his* confidence, at least to the extent of showing that, by his own lights, his conclusions are not warranted), *or* is Rorty deliberately using methods of argumentation in another way – strategically in (what is for some of *us*) a weaker, heuristic, or even just 'cosmetic', manner; as *one means* of making his conclusions 'look good' (so that any attempt to uncover flaws in his argument could not have a decisive outcome on the confidence front: if we were successful, he might simply switch the means of garnishing his preferred conclusions)?

The quick way with this dilemma (the long way merits attention, but would take at least another chapter[10]) is to remain confident in those familiar techniques of philosophical analysis which assign priority to details of argumentation (in short, to refuse to see it as a dilemma!). For, to have confidence in these techniques, is to regard substantive conclusions as depending more or less entirely on their embedding argument(s) – and not to waste much time worrying whether some *other* context might be invoked to enhance such conclusions once we have ventured to unravel, and then perhaps discard, their attendant reasoning. At worst this approach (call it, for its arrogance, the 'no-contest approach') will smoke out transrational contexts, giving us a better view of the way they are supposed to work.

So much for landing Rorty with a *position* by taking his use of reasoning and argument completely seriously, what makes this position a real live 'substantive position on epistemology'?

Rorty *does* make it clear that in advertising 'Hermeneutics', he is not preparing the ground for a 'successor' to epistemology: '"Hermeneutics" is not the name for a discipline, nor for a method of achieving the sort of results which epistemology failed to achieve'.[11] Thus it looks as if our question about the fate of epistemological problems has a definite answer: they *do* get left on the shelf. And, it also looks as if Rorty's talk of a move beyond epistemology should not be construed as talk of any attempt to make 'the next move *within* epistemology' (Rorty's idea is not to show how we can carry on playing roughly the same game under reformed rules and a change in nomenclature). Nevertheless, in advocating a radical shift away from epistemology, Rorty can be seen to be subscribing to a distinct set of views *on* the nature, and value, of that area of philosophical endeavour and the problems it typically confronts (when we go back to brush the dust off the relics on the shelf, their gleam should no longer mesmerize us into trying to *theorize* about them). And, it is in this sense of presenting grounds for changing our view of a subject (rather than simply 'changing the subject') that Rorty can be interpreted as holding a substantive position.

How do (1) to (3) hang together as elements of this position? Well, from (1) and (2), Rorty appears to think it follows that:

(4) it is unwise to want an epistemology-centred philosophy (or, stronger, even any special epistemological precinct within philosophy).

In addition, he writes as if a further implication here is that the wise thing for philosophers to do is to pursue the aim expressed in (3); namely, to make the idea of a *post-epistemological* philosophy look more appealing. The 'position' we can attribute to Rorty then, is that the considerations in *PMN* which tell in favour of (1) and (2) render normal epistemology both profitless and optional, and make (3) virtually a mandatory aim. It is this position that I wish to challenge.

Theories and foundations: some lack of stability in Rorty's position

Although, as I have already intimated, Rorty should not be expected to deliver a 'new epistemological framework' which yields 'better results' with regard to the 'old problems of knowledge', his *evaluative* position on the nature of epistemology ought to be substantial enough, in appearance at least, for us to leave these problems behind us with a clear conscience. Indeed, his views need a good deal of stability if they are to serve as the kind of springboard many will require to make the leap forward into post-epistemological philosophy. Unfortunately, when we put pressure on his arguments and assumptions, Rorty's position rapidly becomes unstable. It has too many potential weak spots to serve such a purpose.

The first notable cause for concern is his apparent assumption that what tells against the notion of 'foundations', tells against the notion of 'theory' in general. Rorty envisages theories of knowledge as *would-be comprehensive accounts of representations*, where the crucial theoretical operations are those which are supposed to enable us to distinguish between 'good representations' (knowledge) and 'bad representations' (anything less than knowledge purporting to be knowledge) both within, and as between, different cultures. He countenances three main possibilities for the construction of a criterion of 'good representation':

Proper causal origins
Correct relation to objects so represented.
Appropriate connection with other representations.

Rorty takes the first two possibilities to be essentially *foundational possibilities* which can be fairly easily ruled out. And he co-opts the third as a *bona fide* atheoretical possibility, as something we need do no more than chat about amongst ourselves in the normal run of things.

By adroit use of well-known objections,[12] Rorty encourages us to abandon the foundational options. Where thinkers such as Locke *do* rely on the 'causal criterion', he reminds us, they tend to confuse 'causal explanation' with 'justification'. To give an account of where a representation 'comes from' (in the sense of causal origins), is not thereby to furnish any *justification* regarding an interpretation of its content unless we are already in possession of an independent account as to why representations which satisfy certain causal requirements must, under that interpretation of their content, also manifest appropriately reliable information. As for the 'correct relation', here Rorty simply invokes a generalized version of the classic 'veil of perception' problem. Ultimately, we cannot put ourselves in a position to judge whether our representations stand in a correct (e.g. mirroring) relation to the world because 'there is no way to get outside our beliefs and our language so as to find some test other than coherence'.[13]

The 'weak spot' is that even if we accept such pre-emptory foreclosures on the foundational options, we cannot automatically draw any grand gloomy conclusions about the prospects of *theoretical* work in epistemology as a whole. To support such conclusions, Rorty needs to show that 'theories of knowledge' can *only* turn up in the shape of 'would-be comprehensive accounts of representations', and that such accounts *must* be based on (*per impossible*) 'special theories of *privileged* representations'. And, even then, Rorty still needs to explain how the 'appropriate connection' criterion can be cashed out *sub-theoretically* (why, for instance, is there no need for a theory of 'special connections'?). Without strengthening along these lines, Rorty's expressed position provides no incentive to accept (1).

Furthermore, we might object to Rorty's dismissive treatment of the foundational options in the first place. On the causal front, there have been significant developments which Rorty ignores. We can let Alvin Goldman, one of the leading lights, speak for us on this score:

> The putative dichotomy between reasons and causes has been challenged in recent years by causal theorists of knowing, and Rorty is silent about this challenge. Why can't one hold that whether a belief constitutes knowledge partly depends on how it is caused, or causally sustained? Admittedly, justifiedness is an 'evaluative', or 'epistemic', notion. So it cannot be *defined* in purely non-epistemic terms. But if we seek not so much a *definition* of 'justified' as a specification of non-epistemic facts on which epistemic status 'supervenes' – why shouldn't these non-epistemic facts include causal ones?[14]

With regard to the 'generalized veil' problem, here again there are possibilities Rorty overlooks. Some time before the publication of *PMN*, both Chisholm and Pollock, for instance, attempted to show how certain 'basic propositions' concerning a person's sensory experience can, under some specifiable conditions, *justify* certain other, non-basic, propositions.[15] Irrespective of whether the resulting accounts of knowledge turned out to be entirely satisfactory, it would be stretching things too far to insist that the kind of appeal they make to 'basic propositions' *necessarily* involves an infringement of the general constraint on 'stepping outside language'.

Rorty's view that the problems of the 'given' and the 'veil' force the conclusion that nothing outside language can be a ground for knowledge, is relatively coarse-grained. As such it is not sufficient to rule out *any* appeal to extra-linguistic justification. Some theorists have considered specific instances of unconceptualized sensory awareness to be natural candidates here. Furthermore, features of Rorty's own approach would seem to lend credence to the sort of fine-grained realism which they wrap around this move. For, as Triplett has pointed out,[16] Rorty does not deny the existence of 'non-propositional awareness' *per se*. Rorty's main contention is rather that the *connection* between such awareness and propositional knowledge is, at best, *weakly causal*: 'the former is an insufficient and unnecessary causal condition for the latter'.[17] Since he warns against

confusing causal considerations with matters of *justification*, this contention cannot innocently serve as a premise in his argument against the
possibility of foundationalists trading fairly on a notion of sensory
awareness. In addition, Rorty's emphasis on the *social* nature of justification fits in neatly with the idea of 'intersubjectively verifiable testimony'
which is sometimes given an important role in less orthodox foundationalist theories. Such theories are not created to meet obsessive demands for
'metaphysical underpinning'; and they recognize the importance of social
practices and other contextual factors. To 'testify', a person needs to
satisfy requirements for epistemic competence. Rorty appears to endorse
the Rylean point that 'if we are not content to take "he sees it" as sufficient
justification for the man's knowing that there is a dog before him, then we
shall not be able to take anything else as a justification either',[18] and in any
case, if he were to deny that a combination of 'competence' and
'awareness' could be cited as *justification* for propositions like 'I am in pain'
or 'This thing is blue', this would leave little room for any *social* account of
knowledge which both matched our practices and preserved our useful
distinctions between reasonably held beliefs and wishful thinking.
Perhaps Rorty is prepared to foresake descriptive accuracy in pursuit of
something 'new' to say, but he appears to want to avoid the slippery slope
to anarchic relativism.

The foundationalist approaches I have been alluding to are likely to
assume that 'in looking for justification of ordinary propositions, it
appears both natural and reasonable to point to a subject's sensory
experience'.[19] Rorty's point about the causal connection here being 'weak'
does not render such an assumption absurd. Nevertheless, large problems
remain: how can the local justification of certain 'ordinary propositions'
support a case for *basic propositions* in the traditional foundationalist's
mould? How can we give a detailed explanation of the *justificatory transition*
from the realm of the non-propositional to the propositional? And so on.
But nothing Rorty says in *PMN* shows that a foundational solution to
some of the key problems of knowledge is *impossible*. Causal, 'modest
foundational' and even traditional foundational, options are still open.
PMN provides no strong incentive for accepting (2).

To recap: Rorty does not demonstrate the impossibility of 'theories' or
'foundations'. And, he fails to consider some of the more recent ventures
in those directions. In this sense, he underestimates epistemology.

Deep epistemology: its varieties and its depth

Suppose we accept that, in principle, there *are* opportunities for 'theories'
and/or 'foundations', is epistemology worth taking seriously in the light of

such opportunities? When Rorty suggests that the quest here is unwise, is he offering an incentive which differs radically from the one we were expecting? Does he mean to make us realize that even if we *were* to find what we were looking for in terms of theoretical results about knowledge, we would not be substantially better off? That we have more to gain than to lose by simply dropping epistemology altogether? And, if this is Rorty's main concern, is he right? Are the benefits of epistemological studies always likely to be ephemeral? Can post-epistemological philosophy cater for the sort of things we need to say about knowledge?

Although it has raised a number of different questions which counter the drift of these speculations, one of the regrettable features of traditional epistemology has been a tendency to gloss over both the variety and the depth of the problems connected with knowledge. Perhaps this was necessary in the early stages – perhaps the blinkered search for a single, all-embracing account was necessary then to wet the intellectual appetite for more selective, more refined, and 'deeper' approaches. At any rate, in focusing on the alleged failings of traditional approaches, Rorty, too, has glossed over variety and depth. Thus it is not surprising that he appears to attach little value to epistemological goals. His lack of attention to 'variety' leads him to ignore the potential for certain worthwhile, 'limited', results. And, in steering clear of the 'depths', he misses much of what is important in studying our 'ways of knowing'.

The existence of 'variety' becomes apparent as soon as we take the trouble to separate out some of the strands of metaphysics, scepticism, psychology, pragmatism and social anthropology (not to mention natural science, history, politics and religion) which have been woven together in traditional approaches to knowledge. Thinkers ranging from Foucault to the sociologists of knowledge,[20] have begun this task already; though, unfortunately, their work is all too often taken to support Rorty's view that epistemology is simply a dead-end, when a much better conclusion here is simply that epistemology now has the chance to enter a new phase. Old avenues have not been completely blocked off, but new ones are opening up, along with all sorts of side-streets which might lead to interesting places. And, even if it has to be conceded that orthodox approaches have presupposed, and yet failed to bridge, a 'metaphysical gap' between language and reality,[21] if it is thus felt that such approaches are bound to raise the boring spectre of Cartesian scepticism, this does not mean that the route is blocked for moves towards limited, naturalistic, accounts of knowledge which do not seek to build such a bridge or put such a demon to rest. Rorty should be sympathetic towards attempts to distinguish the *metaphysics* of epistemology (which thrives on deep questions like 'How is knowledge *possible*?) from various descriptive accounts of the ways in which we come to know things. The trouble is that he debunks the metaphysical side of knowing, and then – despite nodding approvingly in the direction of the descriptive varieties of epistemology – fails to explore the social nature of (say) justification in any detail, almost as if his distaste from 'grand theories' has put him off *all* theorizing about knowledge. Yet nothing in his professed line of argument shows that theoretical epistemology cannot go pluralistic,[22] that investigations in distinct areas of epistemological interest cannot yield useful results in each case. One suspects that, in their fervour, the bees in Rorty's bonnet have stung his own pragmatic instincts into submission.

It would take far too long to catalogue the diversity I have in mind, but some of the issues definitely call out for an initial division between 'descriptive problems' (concerning the things which are taken to constitute knowledge in particular communities, the grass-roots mechanics of knowledge acquisition, and so on[23]) and 'normative, or evaluative, problems' (concerning the efficacy of the social practices depicted in the descriptive accounts: are they reliable on their own terms? Do they meet implicit constraints? Are there circumstances which would defeat them – and do they stand in need of modification accordingly?). Such a move is surely worth making even on Rorty's view that the community is the only genuine 'source of epistemic authority', for, as Brodsky puts it, 'if social agreement plays a large part in determining truth it does not follow that no critical standard of a non-algorithmic kind can be formulated to assess the grounds of such an agreement'.[24] In writing as if all theorizing about knowledge can be thrown out with crude notions of 'foundations' and 'correspondence', Rorty does not allow for *any* separation of issues, not even one along these lines.

Let us grant that different avenues might be worth exploring, what *philosophical* significance does this have? I hinted that a new, fruitful diversity is imminent. Rorty would presumably disagreee. He would no doubt argue that we should block off the route to metaphysics at once (for that could lead to nothing of value), and then hive off what remains to disciplines which are more suited to the specific subject-matters involved than philosophy is – a sort of intellectual privatization programme. This would leave little of special interest to philosophers *qua* philosophers. But such a swift sale of assets would fail to do justice to the depth of the problems concerned in the study of knowledge.

Here we must be careful. Rorty is surely right to mock the imperialistic sounding pretensions of some traditional epistemologists.[25] And to make 'depth' about knowledge the preserve of philosophers sounds suspiciously like imperialism.

Nevertheless, there are non-imperialistic reasons why only philosophers are likely to be able (or to want) to tackle certain important questions about knowledge. Such questions persist even when the grand ambitions of 'would-be comprehensive theories of representations' have been abandoned in favour of multifarious, modest approaches. The reasons for keeping philosophers in the knowledge business, even at branch level, do not, in fact, reflect adversely on other thinkers. Take the hardest case: Rorty's bugbear of metaphysical questions about knowledge.[26] It may well be that questions of deep metaphysical motivation will have scant practical influence on the ways in which distinct epistemological issues are best settled outside of philosophy. Thus the theorist who is working on (say) an empirical account of certain aspects of human cognition is probably going to want to (and have to) ignore the question as to whether we might really be 'brains in a vat'.[27] However, *pace* Rorty, this kind of question has its importance, even for that kind of investigation. It can, *inter alia*, be pressed to test the presuppositions of empirical approaches to cognition, it can help us decide whether there is, after all, some deep metaphysical motivation at work, and it can test such motivation. To a large extent, this kind of questioning can be done behind the practitioners back, without embroiling her in what might turn out to be diversionary issues.

The example seems to play itself into Rorty's hands. He can simply point out the irony of our admission that the issues might turn out to be 'diversionary' as far as the practitioner is concerned. When will we learn the pragmatists' lesson that it is the *practical pay-off* that counts? That the ways of the practitioner are the *ways to follow*, that nothing is to be gained by holding back in hope of prior theoretical justification? These are worthy sentiments. But they obscure the point. A degree of 'standing-back' to examine abstract possibilities is desirable. This is something the practitioners of philosophy have recognized and characteristically re-lished. Despite my remarks about a lack of 'variety', the questions they consider about knowledge have always exhibited more diversity than Rorty admits: What is knowledge? What is the meaning of 'knowledge'? How is the concept of 'knowledge' connected with other concepts such as 'belief', 'truth' and 'evidence'? How is knowledge related to virtue, freedom, well-being, desire and so on? Are there things which in principle cannot be known? . . . the list goes on. To insist that no single theory is likely to provide the answers to all such questions (for a long time the ambition for such a theory probably prevented further 'diversification' within epistemology) is reasonable, but it is not reasonable to insist, without grounds stronger than those Rorty lays claim to in *PMN*, that *no* such questions are worth pursuing in the deep theoretical manner of philosophers. When Rorty assumes that other thinkers can take on the responsibilities here, he is selling philosophy short. He ignores the 'commitment to thoroughness, consistency, and integrity – to following the argument where it leads – to looking for the ways in which one's views on one matter make trouble for one's views on another' which is 'part not just of the self-image but of the reality of what is special to philosophy'.[28]

The literary end of epistemology?

Rorty seems to think that after 'privatization', the philosophical remains of the study of knowledge will be safe in the hands of those who bother to dig out the classic texts of Descartes, Locke, Kant and company (making what they will of them) and those who continue to practise literary and conversational arts. But epistemology is not the kind of subject which belongs in the archives. Nor is it the kind of subject which we can pursue by telling any old story. Let me reiterate some of the constraints on the story, and then conclude by saying why it is far from ready for the archives.

In my preliminary remarks, I used the phrase 'literary performances of language'. Here, I was alluding to the sort of Heideggerian 'language-speaks-for-itself' view[29] which looks as if it might have to come as part of the whole package in Rorty's conception of the self (recall that, for Rorty, the self is a 'web' without, as Martin Hollis nicely puts it, 'an active weaver'[30]). If we agree that stories about knowledge should, minimally, conform (empirically) with our social practices (if they are to be 'realistic') and explore the appropriate conceptual issues (if they are to have 'depth'), then there is no good reason to think that 'literary performances' are going to deliver the goods (the chances seem equivalent to those of the proverbial monkey on the typewriter). To retort, as Rorty might, that from a certain perspective all complex uses of language dissolve into 'contingency' (and here one might remember the 'deconstructions' of Rorty's hero Derrida) is to invite a reply in turn to the effect that this seems to either reintroduce 'the subject' (otherwise who is doing the 'seeing') or resurrect 'commensurability' (it has to be shown that claims pertaining to the level at which the alleged all-encompassing contingency makes its appearance can engage with an understanding which is 'closer to the scene' – Rorty does not appear to have made a case for this brand of commensurability.[31] If Rorty simply repudiates the quasi-Heideggerian, 'literary performance' view altogether, bringing 'the subject' back into the picture completely to take charge of the story as 'author', 'poet' or whatever, then again there are no grounds for optimism. Rorty belittles the epistemological achievements of philosophers. But they have obtained results. These results are not to be found in novels, poems or plays. Literature has dealt well with the connections between knowledge and virtue. On other epistemological issues it has tended to mimic traditional philosophers, muddy the waters or simply pass over in silence. Rorty is prepared to abandon epistemology because of a dearth of results: by parity of reasoning, he should not expect us to turn to literature for direct compensation.[32]

I have tried to show how Rorty underestimates the philosophical approach to knowledge. Like Charles Taylor,[33] I find that Rorty does this mainly because he is inclined to take a narrow, traditional, view of epistemology. One good reason why epistemology does not belong in the archives is that its central questions, even those conceived long ago, remain challenging.[34] A further good reason is that new questions, of greater diversity and equal challenge, are pressing on the heels of these questions. Rorty has not demonstrated that a 'grand traditional resolution' of all such questions is impossible or undesirable, but he has put considerable pressure on the means by which (and on the usual reasons why) theorists have sought such a resolution. Unfortunately his brush strokes are too broad, and they blot out the potential space for fresh developments. Rorty's picture does not let him recognize that epistemology is still a live option. His brief remarks on the social nature of justification do not satisfy the legitimate need for an empirically accurate account of our ways of knowing. Moreover, as we have stressed, he ignores the depth and diversity of epistemological issues which have been generated by the tradition he deplores. In societies where knowledge is intertwined with power, economics, politics, religion, race, gender and ideology, we need to become more self-conscious, more sophisticated and more theoretical about what it is to know. Post-Rortyan epistemologies can take some important steps towards raising our consciousness in this respect. And, if they do so, they will be all the more effective for having confronted Rorty's concerted, and elegant, attempts to divert intellectual resources into other channels.

<h2 style="text-align:center">NOTES</h2>

1 I. Kant, *Critique of Pure Reason*, tr. N. Kemp, Smith (Macmillan, London, 1978), Preface to Second Edition, p. 34 (Bx1).
2 B. Russell, 'On Vagueness', *Australasian Journal of Psychology and Philosophy*, 1 (1923), pp. 84–92.
3 M. Heidegger, *Being and Time*, tr. J. Macquarrie and E. Robinson (Basil Blackwell, Oxford, 1962), p. 249. As Dorothea Frede points out, 'Heidegger does not suggest that we should simply forget the old controversies.... He explicitly criticizes what he regards as the fundamental *mistakes* of the realists and anti-realists (in his case the idealists) in *Being and Time*' (see ibid., pp. 244–73); 'Beyond Realism and Anti-Realism: Rorty on Heidegger and Davidson', *Review of Metaphysics*, 40/4 (1987), p. 739. For further discussion see also Frede's 'Heidegger and the Scandal of Philosophy', in *Human Nature and Natural Knowledge*, ed. Donagan, Perovich and Wedin (Reidel, Dordrecht, 1986), pp. 129–51.
4 See, for example, J. Richardson, *Existential Epistemology* (Oxford University Press, Oxford, 1986), and C. Guignon, *Heidegger and the Problem of Knowledge* (Hackett, Indianapolis, 1983).
5 C. Murphy, 'Critical Discussion of Rorty (*PMN*)', *Australasian Journal of Philosophy*, 59 (1981), p. 345.
6 *PMN*, p. 7.

7   Rorty wants his readers to take a more 'relaxed' stance; the 'confidence' is supposed to be the kind which comes from seeing the futility of traditional worries about 'theories' and 'foundations'.

8   Rorty might be unperturbed by any such charges, perhaps sharing (the later) Wittgenstein's view that philosophers tend to make too much fuss about 'contradictions'.

9   Much of Rorty's discussion of Quine is actually critical. I guess he assumes the reader will be familiar enough with Quine's doctrines to see how he supposes that they undercut foundationalism. For Quine's response to some of Rorty's views on him, see 'Let Me Accentuate the Positive', chapter 7 of the present volume.

10 Rorty is sensitive to the issues here, and his views on the respective roles of reason and rhetoric in intellectual upheavals deserve serious attention. In particular, his views that 'causes of' (rather than 'reasons for') change should be the goal in the current historical situation threatens our whole approach to his work in this response. It is primarily because I am still thinking about how to engage with this view, that I do not consider its viability in the main text (on the line I take there, reasons would still be required to motivate the search for such 'causes' (and, indeed, to identify them).

11 *PMN*, p. 315.

12 And not so well-known; see, for instance, Rorty's interesting discussion of Kant's 'confusion between predication and synthesis' (*PMN*, pp. 148–55).

13 *PMN*, p. 178.

14 A. I. Goldman, 'Review of Rorty (*PMN*)', *Philosophical Review*, 90 (1981), p. 426. See also his 'A Causal Theory of Knowing', reprinted in *Essays on Knowledge and Justification*, ed. G. S. Pappas and M. S. Swain (Cornell University Press, Ithaca, 1978).

15 R. M. Chisholm, *Theory of Knowledge*, 2nd edn (Prentice-Hall, Englewood Cliffs, NJ, 1977), and J. L. Pollock, *Knowledge and Justification* (Princeton University Press, Princeton, 1974). One of the best cases for foundationalism I have seen is presented by Paul Moser in his excellent study *Empirical Justification* (Reidel, Dordrecht, 1985). Moser also puts forward trenchant objections to 'contextualism' which seem to demonstrate the 'insufficiency' of the kind of 'conversational' model of knowledge Rorty envisages (see pp. 53–6 for a summary). And for an argument that Rorty's position can, itself, be seen as *foundational*, see E. Sosa's 'Nature Unmirrored: Epistemology Naturalised', *Synthese*, 55 (1983), pp. 49–72. Pollock later rejected classical foundationalism, but not for Rortyan reasons: see J. L. Pollock, 'A Plethora of Epistemological Theories', in *Justification and Knowledge*, ed. G. S. Pappas (Reidel, Dordrecht, 1979). For an update on Chicholm's views, see his *Foundations of Knowing* (Harvester, Brighton, 1982).

16 T. Triplett, 'Rorty's Critique of Foundationalism', *Philosophical Studies*, 52 (1987), pp. 115–29. This paper reinforced my initial suspicions about Rorty's handling of foundationalism, and influenced this part of my discussion considerably.

17 *PMN*, p. 174.

18 Ibid., pp. 231–2.

19 Triplett, 'Rorty's Critique', p. 125. I am inclined to say that if one expects too much of foundationalism in the sense of expecting it to slot in neatly with a *general* theory which mops up *all* the problems of knowledge, then the complexity of the conditions attached to 'non-propositional awareness' will seem counterintuitive. But that, if one recognizes there are many *different* epistemological questions, requiring different approaches, and different answers, one can tolerate a good deal of 'artificiality' in *this* area (because one can see it primarily as an area in which the chief concern is to block a 'regress of justification' which threatens under certain plausible theoretical assumptions – with other questions being set aside). Moser (*Empirical Justification*) is clearer than most on what is *specifically* at stake for foundationalism. Michael Williams, in an otherwise

even-handed attack on foundationalism, ignores the possibility of 'limited' approaches –
like Rorty, he seems to think it is 'all or nothing' as far as the foundationalist is
concerned; see M. Williams, *Groundless Belief* (Basil Blackwell, Oxford, 1977).

20 M. Foucault, *Power/Knowledge*, ed. C. Gordon (Harvester, Brighton, 1980); D. Bloor,
Wittgenstein: A Social Theory of Knwoedge (Macmillan, London, 1983); and B. Barnes
and D. Bloor, 'Relativism, Rationalism and the Sociology of Knowledge', in *Rationality
and Relativism*, ed. M. Hollis and S. Lukes (Basil Blackwell, Oxford, 1982). For Rorty's
own, somewhat ambivalent view of Foucault on knowledge, see 'Foucault and
Epistemology', in *Foucault: A Critical Reader*, ed. D. C. Hoy (Basil Blackwell, Oxford,
1986). For a response, see T. E. Wartenberg, 'Foucault's Archaeological Method: A
Response to Hacking and Rorty', *The Philosophical Forum*, 15/4 (1984). Wartenberg
makes some interesting points about how Rorty's narrow conception of epistemology
leads him to miscast Kant 'as a conservative Cartesian, working with a single model of
what constituted genuine knowledge' (pp. 352–3).

21 For an insightful discussion of this 'gap', and of the standard philosophical reactions to
it, see T. Nagel, *The View from Nowhere* (Oxford University Press, Oxford, 1986), esp.
pp. 69–71.

22 Cf. A. Edel, 'Philosophical analyses that are pluralistic or that insist on a contextual
approach are none the less philosophical though usually less pretentious' ('A Missing
Dimension in Rorty's Use of Pragmatism', *Transactions of Charles S. Peirce Society*, 21/1,
1985, p. 31).

23 Cf. D. Papineau, 'We can perfectly well direct epistemological attention to, say, the
social processes by which information gets transmitted from one person to another, or
the social processes by which beliefs become part of the established consensus in a
community' (*Reality and Representation*, Basil Blackwell, Oxford, 1987, p. xviii).

24 'Rorty's Interpretation of Pragmatism', Transactions of Charles S. Peirce Society, Vol.
XVIII No. 4 (1982), p. 329.

25 Cf. M. Foucault: 'There is always something ludicrous in philosophical discourse when
it tries, from outside, to dictate to others, to tell them where their truth is and how to
find it' (*The Use of Pleasure, Volume 2: The History of Sexuality*, Penguin, Harmondsworth, 1987, p. 9).

26 For an argument to the effect that the philosophical treatment of knowledge cannot be
exhausted by empirical considerations alone, that it has to touch on metaphysical issues
of modality, see George Bealer's 'The Boundary Between Philosophy and Cognitive
Science', *Journal of Philosophy*, 84/10 (1987). The papers by Goldman and Churchland
(*Journal of Philosophy*, same issue) that Bealer is commenting on here, exemplify the
'imminent diversity' I allude to in the main text. I see Bealer as keeping metaphysical
issues on the agenda rather than as asserting any kind of hegemony of the 'circumscribed
rationalism' he refers to. Given more space, I could have made a case for the value of
sceptical questions as well (the Cartesian demon need not be that boring!); for, as Pollock
persuasively argues (in his *Contemporary Theories of Knowledge*, Hutchinson, London,
1987, ch. 1), a typical sceptical argument can be seen as putting pressure on its own
premises rather than proving its conclusion, and since, in a good argument, the premises
will embody things we believe about knowledge, the sceptical ploy can be used to test
our presuppositions about what it is to know something.

27 For a brief, rather heavy-handed, discussion of morality, epistemology and 'vat-life', see
Alan Malachowski, 'Metaphysical Realist Semantics: Some Moral Desiderata', *Philo-
sophia*, 16/2 (1986), pp. 167–74.

28 J. Bennett, 'Wisdom and Analytical Philosophy', *Analyse and Kritik*, October 1982,
p. 98. Bennett goes on to question Rorty's 'suggestion that analytical philosophers
belong on the left-hand side of a sophist/sage antithesis'.

29 Cf. J. J. Kocklemans, *On the Truth of Being: Reflections on Heidegger's Later Philosophy*
    (Indiana University Press, Bloomington, 1984): in Heidegger's later thought, 'Language
    is no longer just a tool, but it itself speaks, and man's speaking is merely a response to its
    speaking, a response which presupposes that *Dasein* must learn to hear and listen to
    what the language of Being has to say' (p. 147). And see especially Heidegger's
    'Language', in *Poetry, Language, Thought*, tr. A. Hofstadter, with its refrain: 'Language
    speaks'. Of course the interpretation of Heidegger's view of language need not be as
    simplistic as I imply, but my purpose is not to show that Rorty must be wrong if he
    wants to turn epistemology over to language itself – for *it* to somehow do the work in
    Heideggerian fashion (whatever, in the end, that amounts to). My point is rather that
    Rorty owes us an explanation as to how literary language is to carry the burden of
    accounting for knowledge. And, that without such an explanation, the simple-minded
    objection I raise will perhaps seem compelling to the reader who is not already
    predisposed to accept the 'priority of literature to philosophy'.
30 'The Poetics of Personhood', chapter 15 of this volume.
31 Compare the shuttling back and forth between levels in discussions of (say) scepticism or
    objectivity – where an important part of the project is to try to integrate these levels,
    subsume one under another, or simply find a way of living with the tensions between
    them. Perhaps Rorty's account of 'contingency' would have been more fruitful if he had
    been more inclined to hang on to the perspective from which things seem to be
    non-arbitrarily ordered by 'reason', 'laws of nature', 'progress' and so on.
32 The relationship between literature and philosophy has been a subject of much
    interesting debate in recent years, and Rorty has provoked his share of it. Rorty's
    'solution' to the 'demarcation' dispute is to obliterate virtually everything on the
    philosophy side of the fence, and then extend literature accordingly (although at times
    he writes as if the boundaries of literature *already* extend far enough to take in
    philosophy, and on other occasions he implies that philosophy is needed as a 'foil', as
    something for more liberated disciplines to react against; see M. Fischer, 'Redefining
    Philosophy as Literature: Richard Rorty's "Defence" of Literary Culture', chapter 14
    of this volume. Here it looks as if Rorty is the one who should 'relax': there is no need to
    get 'heavy' about the boundaries between literature and philosophy, they can stay as
    fluid as the exchange of ideas, themes and techniques between the two disciplines will
    allow in practice. And there is no need, either, to deny that deep within their own
    territories these disciplines are vastly different (in ways which entail no 'hierarchical'
    conclusions about their relative merits). For a good case study, consider the great
    differences between Samuel Beckett's treatment of 'solipsistic consciousness' in such
    works as *Company* (Calder, London, 1980) and *ILL Seen ILL Said* (Calder, London,
    1982), and P. F. Strawson's treatment of the conditions for a 'non-solipsistic conscious-
    ness' in the second chapter of *Individuals* (Methuen, London, 1959) (in connection with
    the latter, see also Evans's brilliant commentary 'Things without the Mind' in Z. Van
    Straaten, *Philosophical Subjects*, Clarendon, Oxford, 1980, pp. 76–116). Strawson and
    Evans illustrate the 'theoretical depth' I spoke of earlier. They operate with logical, and
    conceptual, constraints which do not concern Beckett; but, this does not mean that
    Beckett's imaginative explorations are any less 'rigorous' on their own terms. One could,
    incidentally, read Beckett as portraying not so much the tragicomedy of human
    existence as, more ironically, the tragicomedy of living out Cartesian assumptions.
33 'Rorty in the Epistemological Tradition', chapter 16 of this volume.
34 For an elegant revival of some of the classic questions, see Nagel, *The View from
    Nowhere*. See also his, even more incisive, *What Does It All Mean?* (Oxford University
    Press, New York, 1987), where he shows how little of the historical background needs to
    be filled in before such questions begin to exert a grip on us. Of course, this, in itself,

could be an important historical consideration which would require unpacking in a Rortyan approach to the same questions. Although I may not have indicated as much in the present paper, it seems to me that there should be more efforts to integrate the Nagelian and Rortyan approaches to the central questions of philosophy; the tendency to regard them as mutually exclusive is creating a stifling atmosphere.

10

Rorty's Talk-About

David Houghton

It would have been disappointing if Richard Rorty's splendidly iconoclastic work *Philosophy and the Mirror of Nature* had not taken the 'theory of reference' as one of its targets. For few matters in recent academic philosophy have been treated with such respect and devotion, and few can be more tempting to the fearless shaker of pedestals.

Under the influence of Frege the view became dominant that reference is determined by sense, where this was taken to mean that, in order to be referred to, an object had to satisfy certain conditions or criteria which could be grasped by the mind if not spelt out in words. On this view, definite descriptions like 'the discoverer of the jet engine' were taken as model cases to which all other referring expressions had to be assimilated. However, it is an approach which can seem counter-intuitive, particularly when applied to proper names, and a new theory has since come to the fore which holds that the reference of names at least is determined by causal, historical or factual relationships between them and their objects and not by the application of associated criteria. On Kripke's causal theory of names, the reference of a proper name is given by a history of use traceable back to the initial bestowal of the name upon an object, and on an account put forward by Kripke and Putnam, the correct application of a natural kind term like 'tiger' or 'gold' depends upon the scientifically discoverable nature of paradigm instances, not upon an appeal to some ready-made list of specifications.

In Rorty's eyes, concern with these issues is a pointless obsession, the last vestiges of a misguided Cartesian quest to 'underwrite science' and 'block scepticism' by seeking *a priori* guarantees that knowledge and the accurate representation of reality is attainable. It is part of an incoherent project to try to step outside language and prove that it hooks onto the world. Rorty recognizes that most practitioners in the field will disown the motivation he attributes to them, and will claim that what they are doing is trying to explain the workings of language from the inside, from within a received account of what the world is like. The theory of reference, they will say, is part of an ultimately empirical theory of language. Rorty is deeply suspicious of this reply, continually expressing his surprise that these particular matters should have received so much attention if it were true. However, he also sees the need to counter it, and so sets out to show that, even on this more modest job-description, the theory of reference has nothing of value to offer.

In part, he is following here the work of Davidson and others who argue that an empirical theory of meaning must proceed holistically and not through establishing prior links between individual expressions and items in the world. Nothing general and substantial either can be said or needs to be said about the relationship between referring expressions, like names, and what they refer to.[1] But Rorty has points of his own to add. The philosopher's notion of reference, he claims, is a purely technical one, shaped by interests which ordinary speakers do not share. Familiar meanings of the verb 'to refer' are quite distinct from this specialized one, and it is only as the result of a confusion between them that philosophers have been able to claim any intuitive basis for their particular theories of reference. Moreover, says Rorty, we can make do quite adequately with these familiar non-technical notions in answering all the questions that arise concerning what others are, or were, talking about. These are questions which call for individual judgement to answer and not for some general semantic theory. Is the philosopher's concept of reference a pointless one then? Not quite. There are issues in logic, concerning identity and necessity for example, where it can be usefully employed, but there is nothing here to justify its being given a central place in philosophy.

As it unfolds, the story Rorty tells has all the plot of an old morality tale. A dazzling new creature appears upon the scene. Some credit it with miraculous powers, seeing it as the answer to their ancestors' prayers. Others, more cautious souls, secretly nurture these same hopes but are content to remark upon more mundane purposes to which the creature can usefully be put. But all agree that it is a momentous thing and all are fascinated by it. Then comes exposure, denunciation and the fall from grace. First, the recognition dawns that ancestral dreams are best buried with the ancestors. Then even the creature's more modest pretensions are challenged. Are these lesser tasks tasks that need doing at all? Or are they not tasks which, so far as they can be done, are already well done by homely less regarded, beasts? Is the creature itself not a hybrid, bred from these same old retainers, and does it not, cuckoo-like, take sustenance from them by posing as one of their number? Yet no one is beyond redemption, and the creature is spared the ultimate humiliation of being caged for ever as a horrible lesson to all. Instead, the tale ends with its being led away to some distant cloister, or remote underground workshop, where, reformed, it will live an ascetic life, pursuing honest if rather abstruse duties, never again to catch the public eye and bewitch the gullible. It is an engaging tale, but is it credible?

Reference and scepticism

Does the theory of reference really seek to provide guarantees that 'we are getting the world right'? It is not easy to reconcile Rorty's various comments on this point. On the one hand, he seems to be saying that all theories of reference, all accounts of how words are connected to things, be they Fregean or Kripkean, conceptualist or causal, are motivated by a desire to refute the sceptic. 'Debates about theories of reference get their . . . philosophical interest from hints that they might somehow answer [the question of how to refute the sceptic]'.[2] On the other hand, it is this motivation to which he appeals to explain the growth of opposition to conceptualist, or descriptivist, theories and the development of causal ones. 'The idea is that if the world reaches up and hooks language in factual (e.g. causal) relationships, then we shall always be "in touch with the world", whereas in the old Fregean view we are in danger of losing the world, or may never have hooked onto it in the first place'.[3]

Nevertheless, he is clearly saying that, with the emergence of causal theories, if not before, the subject of reference has become enmeshed in a sceptical problematic. But is this plausible? The issue with scepticism is, after all, about knowledge, and if it were a consequence of the causal view that our words were bound to hook onto something, it would not follow that what we said about it was true, and so it could not follow that we were in the possession of knowledge. On the contrary, it seems to be a consequence of causal theories – many take it to be an objectionable consequence – that all of our claims could turn out to be false, taken literally as claims about the stated referent, whereas on descriptivist theories some of our claims, if not most of them, would have to be true in order for them to be claims about anything. Far from attempting to close the sceptic down, the causal approach appears to give him a field day. It is true that, in Rorty's book, opening the door to scepticism is as reprehensible as trying to block it, but if justice is to be done, even the guilty must be convicted on the right charge.

Does the new theory of reference imply that our words are bound to refer? It is evident that it does not. There is no truck with the idea of infallible naming such as one encounters in Russell's theory of logically proper names. It is accepted that the history of a name may end in what Donnellan calls a 'block', and that there may be nothing to which the name was given in an initial act of dubbing. An account of proper names like Kripke's which takes the reference of a name to be grounded in some such performance as that of baptizing an infant, is an unlikely stratagem for putting the wind up the malignant demon and an end to hyperbolical doubt. Nor does the indexical theory of natural kind terms offer guaranteed reference. If 'paradigms' for the term exist, there is no certainty that they exemplify a natural kind or that they exemplify one and the same kind.

Most of this is rather blurred in Rorty's exposition by his caricature of these theories as attempts to substitute purely factual or natural relationships between words and things in place of intentional or conventional ones. They are theories according to which 'there are word–world relationships which hold independently of any choice of conventions, conceptual schemes, identifying descriptions, or other "subjective" factors, and are themselves physical relationships'.[4] He then goes on to say that 'the very idea that we could have a theory which would find representations which stood in "natural" rather than merely conventional relations to the objects represented is so odd that only something like Heidegger's view of the West as obsessed by the "metaphysics of presence" can account for it'.[5] But, one protests, the idea is indeed so odd, so very odd, that a better explanation of what is going on, certainly a more charitable one, would be that this is not what these authors intend at all, and that Rorty is simply misreading them. The notion of an intention has a crucial place in Kripke's account of proper names – the intention to preserve reference – and it makes perfect sense to treat this account, not as an attempt to do away with convention (Nomos) in favour of nature (Physis), but as an attempt precisely to explain what the conventions governing the reference of proper names are, an explanation which is opposed to that given by the descriptivist theories of Frege, Searle and others. Likewise, Putnam's indexical theory of natural-kind terms is not to be understood as saying that these words have indexical meanings without our having any say in the matter, as if these things were just forced upon us. If the application of a natural-kind term is determined by the underlying nature of paradigm cases, 'that can only be because it is now a feature of the socially accepted use of that word that its application be determined in that way'.[6] It is because this is how that 'language-game' is played.

But whatever their authors' intentions, we still have to consider what merits these theories have when read in less extravagant ways, and Rorty recognizes clearly enough that his location of causal theories of reference within an old sceptical problematic is not sufficient to show that they lose

all value and interest when divorced from it. He has to show that such
theories serve no useful purposes as attempts to explain the workings of
language from within our currently accepted theory of the world. It is to
this part of his discussion that I turn.

Concepts of reference

Much of the originality in Rorty's critique of the theory of reference stems
from his insistence that the philosopher's concept of reference is quite
different from familiar everyday notions of what it is to refer to or talk
about something, so different that it cannot be counted even as a technical
refinement, or theoretical elaboration, of some more familiar concept. The
philosopher's notion is one according to which you cannot refer to the
person at the bus stop unless there is, in point of fact, a person at the bus
stop to be referred to. On Rorty's account of matters, this marks a
difference from the commonsensical notion of talking about something
because on that notion, he holds, 'the criterion for what a statement is
"about" is just whatever its utterer . . . *thinks* he's talking about'.[7] Talking
about something, in this sense, implies nothing about the existence of
what is talked about. There is, Rorty goes on, a familiar notion which does
carry implications of existence. This is the notion of 'really' talking about
something. If I have mistaken a shadow near the bus stop for a
semi-recumbent human figure and comment that there must be something
amiss with the person at the bus stop, then what I am really talking about
is nothing more than a shadow. However, this notion again is distinct from
the philosopher's one, since in the case just described the philosopher will
want to say that I have not succeeded in referring to anything.

On Rorty's view of things, this makes the philosophical notion of
reference an artificial construct. Accordingly, it is not a concept about
which ordinary speakers can be said to have intuitions, and philosophical
theories of reference which appeal to ordinary speakers' intuitions are
guilty of imposture.[8] The intuitions, for example, to which Kripke
appeals in propounding his causal theory of the reference of proper names
are in fact, Rorty holds, intuitions which surround the non-philosophical
notion of really talking about something.[9] Not only are there no intuitive
data upon which a philosophical theory of reference can legitimately draw.
Worse still, the two commonplace notions of talking about and really
talking about are sufficient between them to say all we need to say in an
account of people's thoughts and utterances. We do not need the
philosopher's notion of reference, so it is claimed, in explaining the
workings of natural language and everyday discourse.

The certainty with which Rorty draws these lines of demarcation fits oddly with the relaxed stance he takes elsewhere on questions of conceptual identity and difference. But, that aside, is he right to say that these two notions he defines and identifies as familiar ones are sufficient for all reasonable intents and purposes in the analysis of discourse? On reflection, it is hard to see how they are. The apparatus he thinks we can make do with leaves a vacuum which the philosophy of language would have to create a concept to fill were one not already available. For, as Rorty admits, a speaker can be really talking about something, a shadow in the example just given, and yet what she says, and thinks, can be doomed to outright falsification or to being completely unassessable. If there is nobody there at the bus stop, then what I say will be automatically false, if indeed it is even capable of being judged either true or false. But what readier explanation can there be of this state of affairs than that, in some important sense, the speaker has failed to refer to anything? That is to say, in order to explain this outcome we shall need a concept of reference where intention does not guarantee success – thinking that you are referring does not mean that you are – and where success is a pre-requirement for a statement to qualify as true. This is what the philosophical notion of reference attempts to give us. It is not something provided by either of the other two concepts Rorty favours.

But the inadequacy of Rorty's preferred apparatus shows up just as clearly at the point where he thinks the philosophical notion is at its most counter-intuitive – in discourse about fictional characters. On the philosopher's notion, says Rorty, one cannot refer to what does not exist, whereas it is part of the commonsense idea of reference that one can refer to fictional characters. It merely fudges the issue to say that fictional characters exist in some sense or other. But if discourse about fiction shows the inadequacy of what he takes to be the philosopher's notion, it also shows the inadequacy of the concept he questionably identifies as the commonsense one. For surely there is no more sense in the idea that in order to refer to a fictional character, intention is enough, than there is in the idea that it is enough when it comes to referring to a historical person. Someone who believes that in the play Hamlet gets married is mistaken, and while he may think he refers to a character in the play in using the words 'Hamlet's wife', he fails to do so. We may wish to say that he is really talking about Ophelia, but again Rorty's apparatus lets us down, since, according to Rorty, really talking about something implies its existence. If so, there is no more possibility of really talking about Ophelia than of really talking about Hamlet's wife. We are left needing to make a distinction but deprived of the resources to do so.

Rorty takes it for granted that a causal theory of reference has nothing to offer in the case of reference to characters in fiction. But it is surprising how many of Kripke's observations can be carried out over here. If one can refer to Cicero knowing about him only that he was a famous Roman orator, so one can refer to Iago knowing only that he is a character in a Shakespearian play. And if a whole community of speakers can be in error about who a certain historical figure was, say, the real Thales, so it can be in error about the identity of particular literary characters. Going on misinformation supplied by some ancient commentator, we may believe falsely, say, that Archipelagos was a buffoon in one of Aristophanes' lost comedies, whereas he was really a character from a play by a rival comedian. The descriptivist theory of proper names falters just as much when the names are names of fictional characters as when they are names of historical characters, and Rorty is mistaken in claiming that if one wants a theory of reference which permits reference to fictional characters, 'the cluster-concept view will be one's choice'.[10]

However that may be, it is evident that in all cases we need a notion of reference in which successful reference is not guaranteed. And this is what the philosophical concept attacked by Rorty claims to provide, in spite of his repeated accusations that philosophers' interest in reference is really motivated by a search for guarantees. Rather than challenge this notion and try to make out that commonsense gets along with a purely intentional one, Rorty would have done better to confine his challenge to the principle that successful reference always requires the existence of what is referred to. The vacuous, purely intentional, notion could then have been dispensed with altogether. How, after all, can there be an intelligible concept of X-ing which makes X-ing and thinking one is X-ing one and the same thing? The 'philosophical' notion of reference, on the other hand, could have been seen as central, and to it appended a diagnostic or corrective notion of really talking about something, by which A is what one really talks about if it is as a result of mistaking A for B that one makes a reference, or putative reference, to B, or if it is A to which one would have had to refer in order to have said something which was literally true.

But to have taken this line would, of course, have been to abandon the attempt to isolate and marginalize the philosophical theory of reference, and Rorty's critique would have been less radical if he had taken it.

The suggestion of an alternative line here – to renounce pure intentionality but challenge the existential requirement – is not meant as an endorsement. There is much to be said for the widespread view that one can refer to fictional characters only in some extended sense, a view based on the thought that sentences like 'Hamlet was a bachelor' are implicitly intensional contexts with some such prefix as 'In the story/play . . .' being understood and waiting to be made explicit in the event of misunderstanding. Just as one can ask who or what, in real life, did so and so, one can also ask who or what, within the context of the story or play, did so and so, and this makes it natural here, because convenient, to talk of reference.

But it would be a misconstruction of what is going on to suppose that there must then be some underlying concept of reference, coherent and unproblematical, to which these cases are as central as any others. It may seem that there is something high-handed about not treating all examples in which it is conversationally natural to use the word 'refer' as equally genuine and significant cases of reference. Yet it is foolish to deny that precision has often to give way to ease of expression. In commenting casually on what another says, it would smack of pedantry to complain that he used a singular noun-phrase 'S' which lacks a reference. We should prefer to say, at the cost of apparent contradiction, that in talking of S, he was talking of nothing. And if that is so, then no account of reference, however latitudinarian, can remain coherent while attempting to embrace all the linguistic data, taken at face-value.

Perhaps it is not surprising then that Rorty should appear at times to be offering an alternative account of the notion that interests philosophers rather than trying to debunk the notion, an account which focuses on the idea of a 'language-game'.[11] He does not develop the approach sufficiently to make possible a proper comparison with existing theories. But one thing is clear. A distinction will have to be observed between thinking one has made a valid move in the game and actually making one, and so between thinking one has referred to something and actually referring. Hence, any concept of reference elucidated in this way will have to differ from the two non-technical concepts Rorty describes, and it is hard to see then how this approach to reference can avoid being subject to the same arguments he uses to discredit existing theories.

So the conceptual apparatus Rorty bids us make do with leaves something essential missing. The principle that nature abhors a vacuum has been used in the past to justify belief in some very strange creatures, but, I submit, the philosopher's notion of reference is no mermaid nor hippogryff.

Search for a general theory and consequences of failure

It is Rorty's contention that semantics cannot tell us anything about how words relate to the world, 'for there is nothing *general* to be said'.[12] And there is nothing general to be said because not even in the case of proper names, the model case for referential semantics, can we give an account which is both general and substantial, an account which says more than that a name 'N' stands for N. The search for a general decision-procedure to determine the reference of proper names is a hopeless one.[13]

I think that there are good grounds for scepticism about the possibility of a general account of name-reference, and I shall begin by saying why I think a causal theory on the lines laid down by Kripke is unlikely to succeed. Where I part company from Rorty and others is in the conclusions they draw from this rejection, in particular the conclusion that the reference of a name neither can be, nor has to be, determined in advance of establishing the meaning and truth-value of sentences containing the name.

According to Kripke, the reference of a name is determined by a chain of communication stretching back from current uses of the name to an original act of baptism in which something was first assigned the name. Later users who pick up the name intend to comply with earlier uses, so preserving the reference. Hence, the reference of the name is ultimately fixed by the identity of the thing upon which it was initially conferred.[14] Such a theory has the virtue of being able to account for certain intuitions with which descriptivist theories seem to be unable to cope, the intuitions that, for all we know, we may be quite mistaken about, for example who the real Thales and the real Godel were. We may be quite wrong, for example, in thinking that it was actually Godel who invented Godel's Theorem. Any theory which takes the reference of a name to be fixed by our beliefs, or salient beliefs, about the thing named would seem to rule these possibilities out – to its own detriment.

The problem, however, with Kripke's theory is that, if it were true, then we ought likewise to have no difficulty in supposing that we might be radically mistaken about which planet is the real Venus. And this is not so. It may be that earlier astronomers used the name 'Venus' differently, but this will be no more than a matter of etymological curiosity. It could not show that we are now guilty of a mistake in using the name to talk about the second planet, even if our use of the name to refer to a planet is causally connected to theirs. So why is there a difference? What facts explain the intuitions upon which Kripke's account draws, but also explain the absence of parallel intuitions in the case of other names?

They have, I believe, to do with the way in which names play a role in the existence and history of people, and some other things too, but not in the history of such things as planets and plants. A person has a name which he recognizes as his own and what that name is becomes as much a fact about him as is his birthplace and nationality, and is as important to his identity as they are. Not to have a name is to lack something which is essential to one's status as a person. Personal names, then, are not merely convenient devices we have for referring to people. We answer to our names, are addressed by them, sign documents by writing them, and use them in manifold ways, all of which, taken together, give them an important role in our lives. Certain things follow from this. It follows that there is nothing circular in saying that 'NN' refers to a person who is called 'NN', since 'called' here is not synonymous with 'is referred to as' or even with 'has in the past been referred to as'. It likewise follows that we do not need a separate convention governing the reference of each name. A general convention is available. Let us say that the name a person answers to, and so on, is his 'real' name. Then the general convention will be one which permits us to use a person's real name as a device for referring to him. In finding out what a person's real name is, we acquire, via this general convention, a means of referring to him. But to find out what a person's name is is not one and the same thing as finding out the name by which he is conventionally referred to. We do not have to find out the name by which people refer to him in order to find out what his name is. That may be manifested in all sorts of ways.

We can also see here how critics of the historical account of names, like Michael Dummett, are mistaken when they object to the account that it makes modern usage mysteriously subservient to past linguistic practice. 'In using words of a language, a speaker is responsible to the way that language is used now, to the presently agreed practices of the community; he cannot be held responsible to the way people spoke many centuries ago'.[15] But people continue to have 'real' names as they did in ancient times, and we sensibly continue the natural practice of using these names as referring devices. So if the reference of the name 'Thales' depends on historical fact about which we may be mistaken or unsure, this is a consequence of our own present conventions of language and not the result of blind subservience to ancient custom. It would simply be inconsistent with the practice of referring to our contemporaries by their real names if we did not refer to the ancients by theirs.

It is not only personal names to which these considerations apply. If my name is a fact about me, and part of my history, so the names of New York, Red Square, The Old Kent Road and Harrod's are facts about them, and resonant parts of their history. Were archaeologists of the future, in excavating New York and Washington, to get the names of these two cities mixed up, then, however, many historians were to follow them, perpetuation of the mistake would not eliminate it. This is not to say that persons and places cannot undergo changes of name. Of course they can. But name changes that occur within the living history of a person or within the working history of a place, changes which may indeed have their origin in some error, must not be confused with changes of belief, about who or what the name refers to, that occur, as the result of error, in the later writing of historical records. The legitimacy of changes of the first kind does not validate changes of the second kind. To suppose otherwise is to confuse the role of proper names in the history of persons and places with their role in historical discourse about persons and places. Historians use place names and personal names with the intention of being historically accurate and it is no more within their power to change the historical facts in the matter of who or what bore what name than it is to change any other historical facts.

These, then, I maintain, are the facts which explain our intuitions about the cases to which Kripke and others appeal in developing their causal-*cum*-historical theories of proper names. But, seen for what they are, these facts also expose the weaknesses of such theories. For it is only where a thing can be said to have a real name, a name which is part of its history and identity, that the original application, the baptism or whatever, can be supposed to have endowed the thing with a real name, and so only there will the original application be of sufficient significance to regulate later uses of the name as a referring expression. Where this cannot be said, as, for example, in the case of the planet Venus, the early history of the name has no binding force, and the correctness of current practice in using the name to talk about the second planet is not at the mercy of some previous nomenclature. The Kripkean theory is strong, then, on personal names and on proper names given to human artefacts like towns, roads, shops and brands of manufactured goods (consider how important a brand-name like 'Coca-Cola' is in differentiating a product). But it is weak on proper names used to refer to things in the natural world. It is also weak on those names which are used solely, or primarily, as devices for referring to people and places, for example code-names. It fails, then, as a comprehensive theory of proper names, or even as a general 'picture',[16] and these considerations explain why.

Second, these considerations call into question the need for the further element in the Kripkean theory, the idea of the chain of communication in which referential links are preserved between earlier and later users of the name. For so far as things may be said to have and bear names independently of those names' being used to refer to them, then a later user's access to the name of a thing does not depend on his being party to any such chain of communication. In exhuming a corpse, one may be able to determine the dead person's name without benefit of an epitaph saying 'Hic jacet . . .' or any other inscription in which the name occurs referentially. The dead person may be wearing some amulet which bears his name, or have about him some papers of identification or correspondence addressed to him. The name can be said to be used in each case, but not as a referring expression in the making of some statement. So far, then, as a person's name is an ascertainable fact about him, independent of his being referred to by that name, it is not clear why chains of communication, or causal links of any kind, should come into an account of the semantics of the name, any more than they should come into an account of the semantics of expressions which are not names. Of course, if knowledge itself involves a causal element, then when we come to find out what a person's name is, however we come to find it out, there is, as a result, bound to be a complex causal relationship of some kind which exists between the investigator and the bearer of the name. But how we know the meaning is one thing, what the meaning is is another.

Attempts have been made to produce non-descriptivist theories of names which avoid the weaknesses in Kripke's account. Evans, for example, proposes that a name refers to a particular thing within a community if users of the name can rely on its being common knowledge that the name is used with the intention of referring to that thing.[17] But, whatever cases this may seem to fit, it does not appear to apply to the historical kind of cases which inspired Kripke's account, or to apply to the way in which individuals themselves acquire personal names.

There is, then, good reason for being sceptical about the possibility of a theory of the reference of proper names which is both general and substantive. But what follows from this? Does it follow that to ask what entities in the world particular names refer to is not to ask sensible questions, as Rorty seems to hold? That there are no hard matters of fact here? Or that we do not need to ask such questions as a preliminary to asking what people have in mind when they use the names?[18] Rorty is quite right, in the passage cited, to say that in answering questions about what people have in mind we become involved in matters of 'expository or historiographical convenience', matters where no decision-procedure is available and where 'nothing but tact and imagination will do'.[19] But he is wrong if he thinks that this shows the question 'To what does the name "N" refer?' to be one which lacks any hard factual answer. To think it does is to fail to make a crucial distinction. Just as we can distinguish between what a word means and what a particular speaker means by it – he may be quite mistaken about what the word means – so, as Kripke observes, we can distinguish between semantic reference (the name's conventional reference) and speaker reference – what particular speakers have in mind in using it, or even what a whole community of speakers has in mind, since if what has been said above is correct, then a whole community of speakers may fail to use a name in accordance with their own recognized conventions of use.[20]

Now suppose that the Baconian hypothesis were true, that the famous plays were written by Sir Francis Bacon and that they had been falsely attributed to some Elizabethan actor by the name of William Shakespeare. It would still be the case that, for the most part, Shakespearian scholars had in mind the author of the plays, whoever he was, when they used the name 'Shakespeare' in their critical commentaries. It is not a consequence of the historical theory of names that if these plays have been falsely attributed, then centuries of critical comment have to be discarded on the grounds that the comments are literally false, even where it is a consequence of the theory that they are literally false. Here questions of speaker-reference arise, some of which may call for tact and imagination to answer. Kripke's distinction between semantic and speaker reference is expressly meant to allow for that. In certain cases – for example, in cases of biographical comment on 'Shakespeare' – Rorty is right to say that we should have a choice between treating them as false remarks about one person or as true remarks about another. In other cases, we may be at a loss what to say, however much tact and imagination we employ.

But none of this shows that there is no fact of the matter about the semantic reference of the name 'William Shakespeare', nor that that fact is totally irrelevant in answering these expository questions. On the contrary, since speakers in general will mean their words to be taken according to prevailing conventions, then, on an historical theory of names, Shakespearian scholars will turn out to have conflicting intentions if the Baconian hypothesis is correct, and it is precisely because they will that difficult questions of exposition arise, questions which may require us to weight these various intentions differently in different contexts. For unless the historical theory did apply here, it would be inexplicable why we should ever have the option of taking any of the speaker's remarks as being about someone other than the author of the play. To say that, if the Baconian hypothesis were true, some of these remarks would not be true of the author of the play (e.g. that he was born at Stratford) is no explanation. Even if most of our beliefs about *A* could not be false, some of them could be. The explanation, of course, is that, in the circumstances envisaged, it is this other person who was called 'Shakespeare', and if this is to be a real explanation, being called 'Shakespeare' here cannot mean being the person whom Shakespearian scholars have in mind. Rather, it means being the real owner of that name, and that, the historical theory tells us, is what constitutes being the correct semantic referent of the name.

So the question 'What is the semantic referent of "N"?' does make sense; is, or can be, one whose answer is a hard matter of fact; and while its answer does not itself 'determine' speaker-reference – Kripke would never have made the distinction between semantic and speaker-reference if he did not think they could sometimes diverge[21] – nevertheless, an answer is needed in tackling these difficult expository questions about speaker-reference.

Finally, the absence of a general non-trivial account of the reference of names does not mean that the reference of a name has to be, or can be, determined holistically – that is, by finding out what assignment of name to object will maximize the truth of utterances containing the name, or will maximize it subject to the proviso that the speakers have been 'exposed to the causal influence of that object, in ways suitable for the acquisition of information (or misinformation) about it'.[22] Whatever the merits of an holistic approach as a general strategy in interpreting a language, it will not produce accuracy of detail. For no interpretation can be accurate that does not take account of linguistic conventions which native speakers themselves recognize, and in the case of some names at least, the historical or causal theorists are right to maintain that operative conventions make it possible for speakers' claims about the objects named to be largely erroneous.

Pragmatism and holism

Whatever the semantic similarities between the two kinds of expression, defenders of an historical or causal theory of proper names are not committed to giving a similar account of natural kind terms. And if Rorty's arguments fail to dispose of the historical theory of names, it seems to me that he has a good case against an account of the application of natural-kind terms which takes it to be determined by the nature of those instances to which the terms were *originally* applied. We do not need this idea in order to explain the continuity of science, for, as Rorty observes, our ancestors were talking about the same world as we are, if not about the very same things. Nor is the continuity of science well explained by this idea. For modern science has no access to the internal constitution of rabbits and elm trees long since perished. If the application of natural-kind terms is determined by the nature of paradigms, the paradigms in question must be our paradigms, not irrecoverable ones from centuries past.

Still, this leaves intact the idea that it is the nature of paradigms that determines correct application, and it is puzzling why Rorty should be so dismissive of the idea. After all, he claims to be a pragmatist, and there seem to be good pragmatic reasons for having terms which function in this way. If it does not ensure continuity of reference with our ancestors, it does ensure that we are not talking at cross-purposes with one another even though we have no agreed observational criteria to rely on.[23] The reason Rorty rejects this 'indexical' theory of natural-kind terms, in spite of its pragmatic appeal, is, I suspect, because it conflicts with his holism, his belief that our utterances are about what most of them are true of. This is not to suggest that there is some irresolvable tension between pragmatism and holism, but it is to say that much work needs to be done to bring them into line, much still remains for old-fashioned epistemologists to do. On this point, as on many others, Rorty's attempts to dismiss systematic and constructive philosophy only serve to reveal that there is a place for it after all.

NOTES

1 D. Davidson, 'Reality without Reference', in *Reference, Truth and Reality*, ed. M. Platts (Routledge & Kegan Paul, London, 1980); J. McDowell, 'On the Sense and Reference of a Proper Name', in *Reference*, ed. Platts.

2 R. Rorty, *Philosophy and the Mirror of Nature* (Basil Blackwell, Oxford, 1980), pp. 293–4. (Hereafter *PMN*.)

3 *PMN*, p. 289.

4 R. Rorty, *The Consequences of Pragmatism* (Harvester, Brighton, 1982), p. 123. (Hereafter, *CP*.)

5 *CP*, p. 133.

6 M. Dummett, *Truth and Other Enigmas* (Duckworth, London, 1978), p. 429.

7 *CP*, p. 127; see also Rorty, 'Realism and Reference', *The Monist*, 59, July (1976), p. 324 (hereafter, RR), and *PMN*, p. 289.

8 RR, p. 329.

9 *PMN*, p. 290.

10 RR, p. 330.

11 *CP*, p. 127 ff.

12 *CP*, p. 127.

13 *PMN*, p. 293.

14 S. Kripke, 'Naming and Necessity', in *Semantics of Natural Language*, ed. G. Harman, and D. Davidson (Reidel, Dordrecht, 1972), p. 302.

15 Dummett, *Truth and Other Enigmas*, p. 430.

16 See Kripke, 'Naming and Necessity', p. 303.

17 G. Evans, 'The Causal Theory of Names', in *Naming, Necessity and Natural Kinds*, ed. S. Schwartz (Cornell University Press, Ithaca, 1977), p. 209.

18 *PMN*, p. 290.

19 *PMN*, p. 293.

20 S. Kripke, 'Speaker's Reference and Semantic Reference', in *Midwest Studies in Philosophy*, ed. P. French et al. (University of Minnesota Press, Minneapolis, 1977), vol. 2.

21 Contra *PMN*, p. 290.

22 McDowell, 'On the Sense and Reference', p. 162.

23 J. Mackie, *Problems from Locke* (Clarendon Press, Oxford, 1976), p. 97.

11

Fact and Fiction

Michael Clark

'The question of whether to treat language as a picture or a game,' says Rorty, 'is brought to a head by debates about "truth in fiction" because the whole problematic of realism vs. idealism, or of "representationalism" vs. "pragmatism", can be crystallized in the question: what, if anything, turns on the difference between being "really there" and being "made up"?'[1] His aim is to assimilate fictional truth to factual: in neither case does language mirror the world. 'Holmes lived in Baker Street' and 'Henry James was born in America' are both true in the same sense, since both are warranted assertions. It is just that they are warranted in different ways. All we need is the ordinary notion of *talking about*, for we can talk about Holmes just as we can talk about James, whereas the notion of *reference* is 'a pointless . . . philosopher's invention'.[2]

Realism about fictional individuals: Parsons and Lewis

In his attempt to establish these large claims Rorty examines several different accounts of discourse both within and about fiction. I shall begin with the view he considers last, a Meinongian theory due to Terence Parsons, who has worked out a detailed semantics for sentences about non-existent objects, treating fictional individuals as incomplete objects which are indeterminate with respect to many of their properties.[3] These objects are collections of 'nuclear' properties somewhat like universals: properties like existence are distinguished as 'extranuclear' in order to exclude such paradoxical objects as existent golden mountains that don't actually exist.

Rorty objects that a given fictional character could be any one of a number of incomplete objects, since the author need not know all about it.

This is a fair point, because there will typically be some uncertainty about what background is to be incorporated into the story, for in reading the Holmes stories, for example, we draw on our knowledge of Victorian England and assumptions about the author's knowledge and intentions. And there is often a possibility of different interpretations: was Hamlet mad or just a moral coward?

It is no doubt counter-intuitive to treat these alternatives as a matter of the *identity* of the fictional object. But the position is worse than that. Parsons's fictional objects are congeries of properties, and so two such objects will be the same if and only if their properties are the same. Change a single property and you have a different object. Make an indeterminate property determinate and you have a different object. As Conan Doyle wrote more and more about Holmes and thereby made more properties determinate, the reference of 'Holmes' would have kept changing. It would have been impossible to write a new novel about the same character.

Even so, Parsons's account fits discourse about fiction better than discourse within it. For the Holmes novels are surely not stories about a detective with indeterminate properties, someone who at a given moment lacks a precise, determinate height and weight, for example. True, we are offered a distinction between two types of incompleteness. Suppose that the novels have nothing to say about whether Holmes weighed twelve stones or not. Then Parsons will say that it is indeterminate whether Holmes weighed twelve stones but that he had the property of weighing-twelve-stones-or-not-weighing-twelve-stones. If he had lacked even the latter property he would have been 'radically incomplete'. But Holmes is a man of flesh and blood, and men have determinate weights, they are not incomplete even in the weaker sense (if this is genuinely distinguishable from radical incompleteness).[4]

Parsons's is not the only realist account to be offered recently: David Lewis, whom Rorty does not discuss, treats fictional individuals as objects in other possible worlds. What is it, he asks, for 'Holmes was a detective' to be true in the fiction of Conan Doyle? As a first shot Lewis considers saying that it is true in those possible worlds in which the plots are enacted. He rejects this partly because of the problem of determining what exactly is to count as the plot; but he is also concerned with another difficulty. It is in principle possible that the plots might, by enormous coincidence and without the knowledge of the author, be enacted in our own world. Yet we should not then want to say that the novels were about a real Holmes.

So Lewis focuses on those worlds where the story is recounted not as fiction but as known fact, and where 'Sherlock Holmes' accordingly functions as an ordinary, non-fictional proper name: I shall call these 'the

H-worlds'. If we are to take into account the background which we read into the story, claims Lewis, the truths of the Holmes stories are 'what would be true if those stories were told as known fact'. This, presumably, has the effect of picking out that subset of H-worlds in which the background obtains. Thus he offers, as the first of two alternative analyses:

> *A sentence of the form 'In the fiction* f, φ' *is non-vacuously true iff some world where* f *is told as known fact and* φ *is true differs less from our actual world, on balance, than does any world where* f *is told as known fact and* φ *is not true.*[5]

(I shall disregard his second analysis, since my remarks apply equally to both.)

Lewis thinks that there is a pragmatic paradox if the author says, for example, that none were left to tell the tale. But this is no genuine paradox, since the author is engaging here in a non-delusive pretence. He does not seek to convince his audience that he no longer exists. However, it would be an irresolvable paradox if Lewis's account were right, for there is no possible world in which a story-teller knows he no longer exists.

It is true that there are some fictions which are not presented as if known by the story-teller, as when a narrator pretends to be offering a translation, or to be uncertain of all the details. In such cases Lewis is prepared to replace the clause 'where *f* is told as known fact' with an appropriate variant like 'where *f* is presented as a translation' or 'where *f* is told as known in essentials'. But there *are* cases where the story-teller says none were left to tell the tale, and whether these stories are presented as known fact, or simply as true, a paradox arises on Lewis's account.

And what about (conceptually) impossible stories? (In his classic paper on imaginary objects Gilbert Ryle was surely over-influenced by Wittgenstein's *Tractatus* when he ruled these out.[6]) As a young child at school I once had to write a story about a day in the life of a (personified) penny. In the brothel scene in *Ulysses* a shoe and a fan make speeches. At first, however, Lewis maintains that everything is true in an impossible fiction, though he suggests, reasonably enough, that we should accommodate minor unwitting inconsistencies, like the discrepancies in Hamlet's age or over Dr Watson's first name,[7] by revising the plot. These cases, however, are not the problematic ones. In a later postscript he proposes that inconsistent fictions be partitioned into consistent fragments:[8] what is true in the whole fiction will be what is true in at least one of the fragments. But how do you divide a story about a personified penny into consistent fragments? The conceptual impossibility of a penny's thinking and acting like a person cannot plausibly be handled in this way. Nor, surely, can it be dismissed as one of those hardest of cases that Lewis thinks are intended to 'defy our efforts to figure out what's true in the story'.[9]

On this last matter Parsons's account is superior to Lewis's, for his semantics countenance such objects as round squares, though not squares which are not square. It can therefore cope better with impossible fictions, apart from those which are formally inconsistent.

It is not inconceivable that one or other of these accounts could be patched to avoid the difficulties, nor is it unthinkable that an alternative realist account might be found. But, fundamentally, all accounts of this sort are unsatisfactory, because they fail to explain what fiction is and how fictional names get their sense. In particular they ignore the role of pretence in the creation of fiction.[10] Instead, we find ourselves grappling with spurious questions about the identities of incomplete objects or of acts of story-telling across possible worlds. Rorty is right to reject such accounts (though he is unlikely to endorse this basic objection in full). This leaves us, he thinks, with only two alternatives: a language-game approach, which will 'separate semantics from epistemology so drastically that semantics will have no interesting distinctions to make between truth about fact and about fiction' and a physicalist approach, that will 'bring semantics together with a realistic epistemology of "picturing" which, in the manner of Donnellan, will disallow truth about fiction altogether.'[11]

Searle and the language-game approach

For John Searle, the difference between fiction and non-fictional discourse is not a matter of meaning, since the same illocutionary acts that occur in the latter can occur in the former.[12] Searle's point is particularly evident in the case of plays and films, which typically contain questions, commands, requests, exclamations and optatives as well as plain assertions. As he points out, if fictional meaning differed from non-fictional, we should have to learn new meanings for our words before we could understand a fictional work. Fiction is a matter of *pretending* to perform illocutionary acts.

Two senses of 'pretend' are distinguished, deceptive and non-deceptive. (To avoid multiplying senses beyond necessity it would be better to distinguish two types of pretence rather than two senses of the word.) His account employs only the second, which seems unnecessarily restrictive, for although novels, plays and films are typically presented *as* fiction, the myths about Santa Claus that parents tell their children, like the more insidious stories that authoritarian governments feed to their subjects, are genuinely intended to deceive.

Searle's main conclusion is that 'telling stories really is a separate language game; to be played it requires a separate set of conventions, though these conventions are not meaning rules; and the language game is not on all fours with illocutionary language games, but is parasitic on them.'[13]

As Rorty reminds us, it is axiomatic for Searle that whatever is referred to must exist. So in story-telling we do not refer but merely pretend to do so, thereby pretending that certain individuals and objects exist, and perhaps also, or alternatively, pretending that certain things happen to real individuals and objects. But when we stand outside the story and talk about its make-believe characters, what are we referring to then? Searle's answer is that we are referring to fictional characters:

> By pretending to refer to (and recount the adventures of) a person [Iris] Murdoch creates a fictional character. Notice that she does not really refer to a fictional character, because there was no such antecedently existing character; rather, by pretending to refer to a person she creates a fictional person. Now once that fictional character has been created, we who are standing outside the fictional story can really refer to a fictional person. Notice that in the passage about Sherlock Holmes above I really referred to a fictional character (i.e. my utterance satisfies the rules of reference). I did not *pretend* to refer to a real Sherlock Holmes; I *really referred* to a fictional Sherlock Holmes.[14]

This seems akin to the view that Russell was understandably so severe about:

> To say that unicorns have an existence in heraldry, or in literature, or in imagination, is a most pitiful and paltry evasion. . . . Similarly, to maintain that Hamlet, for example, exists in his own world, just as truly as (say) Napoleon existed in the ordinary world, is to say something deliberately confusing, or else confused to a degree which is scarcely credible.[15]

Conan Doyle's novels were about an amateur sleuth, but there existed no amateur sleuth they were about, nor any surrogate, like a character. It does not matter whether we limit existence to spatio-temporal objects or whether, like Frege, we are more Platonic, and admit sets, numbers, colours, concepts and the like into our ontology. We do not have to share in full that nominalistic 'sense of reality' that Russell appealed to when he wrote the words quoted above.[16] Whether or not numbers exist, Sherlock Holmes does not: never did and never will. How then can we use his name outside the story?

Sometimes we can be seen as continuing the pretence. Retelling stories, as Charles Lamb does in his *Tales from Shakespeare*, and summarizing stories, still involve make-believe. So does reading or hearing or seeing them. We can even say this of some discussions of the plot. (Will the hero escape? Was Hamlet really mad?) Some discourse about fiction can be seen, then, as keeping up the pretence of the original. *Pace* Gareth Evans,[17] this is not plausible for other talk about fiction, for example discussions of the author's craft and comparisons between characters in different works. (The one use sometimes merges into the other, so that at the borderline we may construe the sentences in either way.)

The following critical extract, chosen more or less at random, will serve as illustration. It includes no proper names except as part of a film title, so that preconceptions about such names need not cloud our judgement.

> The cinema has so long taught us to look for meaningful trifles that one is apt to misinterpret, to forget that like the novel the screen can describe as well as narrate. There is a scene early in *Angel Heart* when the detective searches a dark tumbled house. How much of what we see is description and how much hinted narrative? The litter in the room: how much of it is pertinent to the narrative and how much a decoration to add realism or deepen anxiety? The vase which he picks up belongs, as we learn finally, to narrative. But the ventilators swinging and reversing: should one count their movement as significant apart from its contribution to tension? It doesn't matter; one will know as the story unfolds.[18]

Russell and Ryle regarded such sentences as synonymous with sentences about sentences/pictures, and so on, just because they are checkable by reference to them.[19] But, if you try to find some finite conjunction of statements about sentences in books and the like which is logically equivalent to 'Hamlet was the eponymous anti-hero of Shakespeare's great tragedy' (say), you will appreciate the error of this claim. (Cf. Rorty's comparison with material-object and sense-datum statements.[20])

Nevertheless, the sentences are intelligible only against the background of the story-telling. It is perfectly idiomatic English to say we are referring to a fictional character, but in that benign sense Searle's rules of reference do not have to be satisfied: what we refer to, in this sense, need not exist, any more than the objects of my desires or fears. Except in this benign sense we should refuse to answer the question what or whom we are referring to. Nothing is lost by this refusal, since we can still explain the conditions under which talk about fictions is meaningful and how it has become so.

Because Rorty is aiming to show that there is really no problem about fictional discourse, he cannot afford to admit that he is endorsing any of the accounts he examines. But in the end it is difficult to find any salient feature of Searle's account that he rejects. Even the existence axiom which Rorty is concerned to undermine becomes so diluted as to be innocuous from his point of view. Indeed, Rorty goes on to maintain that insistence on preserving the existence axiom undiluted is explicable only in terms of a *Tractatus* picture theory.[21] But language-games are played in the spatio-temporal world. There is no unique way in which language latches on to the world, not because it floats free from it but because in using language we latch on to the world in many different ways. It is possible to accept the essentials of Searle's language-game approach without diluting the existence axiom.

Negative existential statements

We have moved on from discussing fictional discourse to considering discourse about fiction. The most problematic sentences here are those which ascribe what Parsons called 'extranuclear' properties, sentences like 'Holmes is fictional' and 'Santa Claus does not exist'.

We do not have to satisfy ourselves that there was no detective answering to the description of Holmes in the novels in order to know that Holmes was a fictional character. The point was made above in explaining the motivation behind David Lewis's analysis. If we are talking about the Holmes of those novels, then Holmes did not exist. This creates a difficulty for descriptivist accounts of ordinary proper names, whether, as in Russell, the names are regarded as abbreviations for descriptions, or whether, as in Searle, descriptions are more loosely connected with names. For on descriptivist accounts 'Holmes' will refer to a real man if any real man uniquely satisfies the relevant descriptions. The problem is avoided by what Keith Donnellan has called 'historical explanation' views.[22] On these views a proper name has a bearer only if those who introduced the name into the language were related in a certain way to that bearer, and their use of the name has been transmitted in an appropriate way to current users. Different names may have the same spelling, but there will be different histories associated with distinct uses of the word. Various accounts of the baptismal relation have been proposed. Many have regarded it is as a causal relation, mediated perhaps by perception. Alternatively, some sort of non-causal spatio-temporal relation has been regarded as sufficient. We need not choose between these proposals here.

Now, according to Donnellan no proposition is expressed by an utterance like 'Holmes does not exist' in which the name fails to refer, because the history of the relevant use of the name does not reach back to a baptism of the required sort. The history 'ends in a block'.[23] Indeed, *N does not exist* is true, he holds, if and only if the history ends in a block. This paradoxical separation of truth-conditions from meaning is the price that Donnellan must pay, claims Rorty, for adhering to the existence axiom, the principle that we can refer only to what exists. (Rorty assumes, I think rightly, that Donnellan is committed to the same view of utterances about fiction like 'Holmes was the hero of the Conan Doyle novels').

Without falling back on a descriptivist account or abandoning the existence axiom, we have at least two ways of avoiding the paradoxical

position that Donnellan reaches. One is to construe negative existentials
meta-linguistically: to say that Holmes didn't exist will be to say that the
name was vacuous, to say that Santa Claus doesn't exist will be to say that
'Santa Claus', and names like 'Father Christmas' and 'le père Noël' which
share its origin, are pseudo-designations.[24]

It seems anomalous, however, to treat proper names differently in the
sentences 'Holmes is the hero of Conan Doyle's novels' and 'Holmes did
not exist'. What if we say 'Holmes was the fictional detective hero of
Conan Doyle's novels'? Is the name 'Holmes' being used in two different
ways in this sentence? So a second account commends itself: treat fictional
names in negative existentials in the way I suggested for that other talk
about fiction which could not plausibly be construed as continuing the
pretence.

Gareth Evans claims that proper names in negative existentials have a
'conniving' use.[25] On this view, just as Conan Doyle pretends (non-
deceptively) to refer to a detective in his novels, and parents pretend
(deceptively) to refer to an old man who brings presents down the chimney
at Christmas, so the person who says 'Santa Claus doesn't exist' begins
with a pretended reference; but in the last case the speaker then falls out of
the pretence. Once again, this is too strained to be plausible. Further,
suppose one child denies the existence of Santa and another retorts that
Santa does exist. Clearly the second child need not be pretending to refer.
So we should need one type of account for the negative existential and
another for its contradictory. But the first child need not be pretending to
refer either: imagine that she still believes in Santa Claus but denies his
existence merely to tease her brother.

I suggested above that talk about fiction which cannot be regarded as
continuing the pretence was intelligible against the background of the
fiction, and that we did not need to ask about the reference of any proper
names used in such discourse. We can say the same of negative existentials
containing fictional names, provided we are prepared to countenance a
first-level existence predicate, one which is satisfied by everything.[26] If
not, we shall have to fall back on one of the other accounts.

Happily it is not necessary here to decide which, if any, of these views is
correct. In the first place, it is arguable that an historical account of proper
names is not really incompatible with pragmatism. Why should pragmatists not accept an historical account? They could accept that genuine
proper names can be introduced into the language only by those in a
certain causal, or perhaps spatio-temporal, relation to the bearers. They
will still recognize truths about spatio-temporal existence and causality:
true proper names will be recognized only where it is good to believe their
bearers exist and that their original users were related to them in the
favoured way. The relations will not be regarded as truly non-intentional,

in view of 'Putnam's simple but devastating point that non-intentional relations are as theory-relative as intentional relations':[27] our language will not mirror them but rather they will be our own constructions. Pragmatism will not discard such relations, it will simply presuppose a different account of them.

In the second place, whatever the correct account of them, the negative existential claims about fictional objects are true.

Consequences for pragmatism

This last point is one of three all too obvious but nevertheless significant truths that any discussion of fact and fiction has to recognize, and which makes it implausible to play down the distinction in the manner of Rorty:

(1)   Fictional objects, unlike real objects, do not exist.

The second is a consequence of the first:

(2)   Fictional objects are causally insulated from real objects: they cannot interact causally with them.

(2) follows from (1) because causal relations hold only between what exists.[28] A fictional character cannot kill a real one, although a story about a fictional character might so depress a reader that he committed suicide, or, losing concentration while driving, crashed his car and died. But in these cases what causes the death is not the fictional character, or any activity of that character, but reading the story: the character does not become a killer because of the story's fatal effect. Again, authors create fictional characters, and there is a sense in which they can kill them off, as Conan Doyle once killed off Holmes, but it doesn't follow that they are interacting causally with those characters. Of course, these things cannot be done without *some* causal interactions, but they are interactions with real objects, like pieces of paper, not with fictional ones. *Within* fiction the real and the fictional can interact causally as much as we like, but these are only pretended interactions. It is even doubtful whether we can genuinely fear or love fictional objects unless we are deluded into believing they are real, since it is arguable that you can fear or love only what you believe to exist.[29] This last claim has been much contested, but the very fact that it has been discussed so extensively reflects the contrast between fact and fiction.

The third point emerges from the consideration of impossible stories:

(3)   What happens in fiction, as opposed to what really happens, need not be physically, or even conceptually, possible.

There is indeed a problem about how we can understand what is not conceptually possible; and a story could be so nonsensical that it was genuinely unintelligible. But suppose we have a story about disembodied survival of death, or about time travel: there are those who would argue that one or both were conceptually impossible, but we do not have to determine whether they are wrong before deciding whether the tales are to count as genuine stories.

In order to avoid begging the question against Rorty, this third point of difference would need to be recast, since he follows Quine and Davidson in rejecting distinctions between the conceptual and the empirical. But even if Rorty is right to accept the relevant doctrines of Quine and Davidson – which I for one am not prepared to concede – there will be constraints, relative to our firmer and more fundamental beliefs, on what it is good for us to believe, constraints which do not apply to the fictions we create.

As for 'physical possibility' he will presumably regard this as a matter of what scientific theories it is good to accept within the prevailing culture. Now such theories need not entirely determine the empirical data we are entitled to accept. Even the best of our theories do not always fit all our data. When first propounded, Copernicus's theory fitted the available data less comprehensively than Ptolemy's. Nevertheless, there are limits to the extent to which acceptable theory can clash with our lower-level beliefs, and in any case we will seek to revise one or the other in the hope of making them match better.

Rorty claims that 'all we need is the commonsensical notion of "talking about", where the criterion for what a statement is "about" is just whatever its utterer "has in mind"'.[30] But this is simply to ignore the substantial and pervasive differences between the real and the fictional, a distinction we disregard at our peril. How could it be good to conflate fiction with fact? How could we get along in the world if we did? Our very survival would be threatened by any radical failure to distinguish the two. Indeed, wholesale confusion between the two is taken as a sign of madness.

It is difficult to conceive of any culture which survives for any appreciable time without making such a distinction. Suppose the pragmatist replies that of course he does not deny this, that he merely denies that there is an objective distinction according to which fact is reality or the world as opposed to the fiction which people make up, the world being given and fiction being created. If he is right, then this does not abolish the distinction: after all we still make it, and our welfare and very survival depend on making it. Even if the human race found itself in an horrendous situation in which survival was undesirable, where unmitigated misery and suffering were the only prospect and universal suicide the only reasonable course, it would be important that the prospect should be a genuine one, not a fiction we had embraced as the truth.

None of this is to deny that we can learn truths from fiction, that fiction has an important role to play in our learning about the world. It is not just in ethics that we can learn from fiction; we can gain historical, social and psychological insights, and the creative imagination of the novelist or film-maker is matched by that of the theoretical physicist. Fiction can help us make sense of our experience and show us what is possible. Even a conscientious juror, mindful of the need not to go beyond the evidence, may need to test that evidence for coherence and probative value by trying to amplify it fictionally, in the manner of a drama documentary. But he should not reach his verdict in the light of any old fictions. Not if he is to convict only in the absence of reasonable doubt – or even, for that matter, on the balance of probabilities.

Rorty does not deprive us of constraints but his are 'conversational' – the contraints local to our culture that must be recognized if we are to converse with our fellows. These cannot be laid down in advance or anticipated. There are no 'wholesale constraints derived from the nature of the objects, or of the mind, or of language, but only those retail constraints provided by the remarks of our fellow-inquirers'. Consequently, we never know when we have reached the truth or approached it more closely.[31] But now we have struck the fundamental paradox of pragmatism. If it is right, then how can we know, how can Rorty be so sure it is right? Applied to itself, his pragmatism is self-defeating. And by what divine right does it escape self-application?

Setting this paradox aside, Rorty's constraints still seem dangerously inadequate. When he is brought to consider what defence the pragmatist has against a totalitarian state which peddles fictions as 'objective truths' in Lenin's sense, he echoes Habermas by requiring conversation to be *undistorted*. For Rorty this is a matter of 'employing *our* criteria, where *we* are the people who have read and pondered Plato, Newton, Kant, Marx, Darwin, Freud, Dewey, etc.'[32] But, as he admits, this reply is circular, for how are we to determine which writings to include in the list, what disqualifies *Mein Kampf*? The answer has to be: the criteria of those who have read these works; and, presumably, who have drawn the right liberal and humane conclusions.

I conclude that Rorty has failed to show that there is no problem about fictional discourse. He has not shown that the dichotomy between fact and fiction should be abandoned. Physicalist views about proper names that have been appealed to in dealing with discourse about fiction are perhaps not as great a threat to his pragmatism as he imagines. In any case, a

182 *Fact and Fiction*

language-game approach to fiction does not rule them out. But our very need to respect the dichotomy is a major threat to his variety of pragmatism, and one he is all too aware of.

NOTES

1 Richard Rorty, 'Is There a Problem about Fictional Discourse?' in his *Consequences of Pragmatism* (Harvester, Brighton, 1982), p. 110. See also his paper 'Realism and Reference', *The Monist*, 59 (1976), and *Philosophy and the Mirror of Nature* (Basil Blackwell, Oxford, 1980), pp. 284–311.
2 Rorty, *Consequences of Pragmatism*, p. 127.
3 Terence Parsons, 'A Prolegomenon to Meinongian Semantics', *Journal of Philosophy*, 71 (1974); 'A Meinongian Analysis of Fictional Objects', *Grazer Philosophische Studien*, 1 (1974); *Nonexistent Objects* (Yale University Press, New Haven, Conn., and London, 1980).
4 Cf. David Lewis, 'Truth in Fiction' in his *Philosophical Papers* (Oxford, 1983), vol. 1, p. 262.
5 Ibid., p. 270.
6 Gibert Ryle, 'Imaginary Objects' in his *Collected Papers* (London, 1971), vol. 2, pp. 74–5.
7 Watson's first name is usually 'John' but in one novel it is 'James'.
8 David Lewis, Postscript B to 'Truth in Fiction', pp. 277–8.
9 Ibid., p. 277.
10 Cf. Gareth Evans, *The Varieties of Reference* (Oxford, 1982), p. 367.
11 Rorty, *Consequences of Pragmatism*, p. 127.
12 John R. Searle, 'The Logical Status of Fictional Discourse', in his *Expression and Meaning* (Cambridge University Press, Cambridge, 1979).
13 Ibid., p. 67.
14 Ibid., pp. 71–2.
15 Bertrand Russell, *Introduction to Mathematical Philosophy* (London, 1919), p. 169.
16 Ibid., p. 170.
17 Evans, *The Varieties of Reference*, ch. 10. Cf. also Kendall L. Walton, 'How Remote Are Fictional Worlds from the Real World?', *Journal of Aesthetics and Art Criticism*, 37 (1978–9).
18 Dilys Powell, film column in *Punch*, 7 October 1987.
19 Cf. Ryle, 'Imagining Objects', p. 70.
20 Rorty, *Consequences of Pragmatism*, p. 128.
21 Ibid., p. 129.
22 Keith S. Donnellan, 'Speaking of Nothing', *Philosophical Review*, 83 (1974).
23 Ibid., p. 25.
24 Ryle offered a confused mixture of descriptivist and meta-linguistic views: 'What or whom are *our* propositions about when we say "Mr Pickwick is an imaginary entity"? Clearly we are just saying that the quasi-designations in the propositions which profess to be about a Mr Pickwick are pseudo-designations. We are saying "there was no *such* person"; i.e., no one in fact had the name, qualities, chops and changes which someone would have had to have for Dickens' propositions to have been true or false of a person' (Ryle, 'Imaginary Objects', p. 70).
25 Evans, *The Varieties of Reference*, loc. cit.
26 Ibid., p. 348.

27   Rorty, *Mirror of Nature*, p. 299.
28   Cf. Walton, 'Fictional Worlds'.
29   Cf. Kendall Walton, 'Fearing Fictions', *Journal of Philosophy*, 75 (1978).
30   Rorty, *Consequences of Pragmatism*, p. 127.
31   Ibid., pp. 165–6.
32   Ibid., p. 173.

Part IV

At the Periphery

12

Philosophy and the Mirage of Hermeneutics

Jacek Holówka

A sense of malaise is a common feeling in philosophy. Time and again it seemed that philosophy had come to an end, or had been enclosed in the confinements of currently popular theories and patterns of thought. But no matter how helpless it may have appeared in this predicament, somehow it always managed to break out, to find a new bold point of view, to get rid of old paradigms, to invent a new vocabulary or simply step unto yet uncharted areas. Its new success was never certain, but neither was its demise.

Predictions about philosophy

Watching these shifts of focus and temporary setbacks, one is tempted to look for some moral behind the stumbling pace of philosophy – one is tempted to predict its further course. By doing so one engages in philosophy of history of philosophy – a subject which proposes to explain the limitations of all systems of philosophy by showing that they are 'historically determined' and thus cannot provide final answers to the questions they deal with. But a brief review of the history of philosophy will show that the historical embeddedness of theories explaining the faltering pace of philosophy is even more pronounced than the shortsightedness of philosophical theories themselves. There are more gaps and more incommensurability between, say, Augustin's *The City of God*, Hegel's *Lectures on the Philosophy of History*, Engel's *Ludwig Feuerbach and the End of Classical German Philosophy*, Jasper's *The Origin and Goal of History* and Rorty's *Philosophy and the Mirror of Nature* than there are between different versions of ethical theory or systems of logic. The names just quoted may seem too few and far between, and thus my sample too biased. It may be so, but the point I want to make is that the continuity that can be observed in the succession of theories of metaphysics, epistemology or moral philosophy – within, for example, British empiricism or German classical philosophy or in the entire history of European philosophy – will never be matched by the congeniality of views offered as historical explanation of the discontinuity in philosophy. In every selection, the authors of historical criticism of philosophy will tend to be few and far between.

I am saying this to make it be clear why I find Rorty's obituary for epistemology rather premature. Several similar forecasts have been made in the past and all proved wrong. Of course, Rorty is cautious. He is not trying to prove that epistemology must be replaced by hermeneutics. He does no more than express his hope that it will, that epistemology will fade away and hermeneutics become an attractive and edifying form of discourse instead. I find it hard to see, however, that there is much room between his 'instead' and my saying that one will replace another. However it may be, Rorty's claim (held with a serious reservation) that hermeneutics is a suitable successor subject to philosophy, as we have known it (the reservation being that strictly speaking the successor subject is not needed but it will be good if it comes around), can neither be supported by a wider view about the sense of history of philosophy (because there is no such sense, and the belief to the contrary lands us in philosophy of history of philosophy – in my opinion, an entirely dubious discipline), nor by the internal logic of the last view accepted (which on Rorty's interpretation was some form of Cartesianism and has led to a dead-end). I do not think that philosophy's end is anywhere so near or that having hermeneutics in the place of epistemology would make a lot of people happy, let alone wiser.

Rorty's treatment of hermeneutics is very interesting, however. Even though what he finds appealing in it is strikingly negative and virtually devoid of content. Hermeneutics is unsystematic, he says abnormal, makes unpredictable use of historical facts, provides proper cultural upbringing (my rendering of German *Bildun* which Rorty translates as *edification*) and inspires conversation on any subject that one may find conducive to one's internal enhancement, growth and mental maturity.[1] I have no quarrel with this description of hermeneutics, but I am surprised by the promptness with which Rorty abandons philosophy and by his hope that the field so vacated will not be filled by a new theory but rather by a new form of conversation. Even if epistemology were dead, I do not see how going through gestures of questioning and asserting, asking and being answered, elevating oneself and imbibing culture could satisfy anyone who wants to learn substantive truths. Shall sophistication be bought at such steep price, by depriving oneself of real interest in the world and the knowledge of one's own functioning?

But let us turn to the question of why Rorty believes that philosophy has come to an end. On the closing pages of *Philosophy and the Mirror of Nature* he offers what can be read as a summary of his book.[2] (The numbering of paragraphs is mine.)

we can assert all of the following:

[1] ... Some atoms-and-the-void account of micro-processes within individual human beings will permit the prediction of every sound or inscription which will ever be uttered. There are no ghosts.

[2] Nobody will be able to predict his own actions, thoughts, theories, poems, etc., before deciding upon them or inventing them. (This is ... a trivial consequence of what it means to 'decide' or 'invent'.) So no hope (or danger) exists that cognition of oneself as *en-soi* will cause one to cease to exist *pour-soi*.

[3] The complete set of laws which enable these predictions to be made (in atoms-and-the-void terms) ..., would not yet be the whole 'objective truth' about human beings. There would remain as many other distinct sets of such objective truths ... as there were incompatible vocabularies ... (all those vocabularies, within which we attribute beliefs and desires, virtues and beauty).

[4] Incommensurability entails irreducibility but not incompatibility, so the failure to 'reduce' these various vocabularies to that of 'bottom-level' atoms-and-the-void science casts no doubt upon their cognitive status.

[5] The assemblage, *per impossible*, of all these objective truths would still not necessarily be edifying. It might be a picture of a world without a sense, without a moral. ... Whether his knowledge of the world leaves him with a sense of what to do with or in the world is itself predictable, but whether it *should* is not.

[6] The fear of science, ... self-objectivation, of being turned by too much knowledge into a thing rather than a person, is the fear that all discourse will become normal discourse.

[7] But the dangers to abnormal discourse do not come from science or naturalistic philosophy. They come from the scarcity of food and from the secret police. ...

I am impressed by succinctness and aptness of [7], so I will not discuss it beyond noting that scarcity of food and the secret police are as inimical to normal discourse as they are to abnormal ones; and as for which kind of discourse may prove more helpful in getting rid of these nuisances, my guess is that normal discourse has better chances (I assume one may speak about chances even without having much hope).

A theory of no ghosts

In [1] Rorty says that there are no ghosts, but in [2] he says that when the ultimate, atoms-and-the-void theory is formulated it will give no agent a full list of all his future actions, but will leave it to him to 'decide' what he would do, as if, indeed, he were unpredictable and therefore a ghost, and in [3] Rorty says that even with this strong theory, man will see his objectives in other terms than those of the strong theory, as if, again, he were a ghost, and not an aggregate made up of atoms-and-the-void.

These not obviously well adjusted beliefs are supported by Rorty's deep-seated realism, I suspect. He must believe, if I understand him at all, that nothing else exists but atoms and the void. This is the simplest, and also fair, explanation for his attachment to '*wholehearted behaviourism, naturalism and physicalism.*'[3] These theories '*help us avoid the self-deception of thinking that we possess a deep, hidden, metaphysically significant nature which makes us "irreducibly" different from inkwells and atoms*'.[4] We may need to be helped out of that illusion only if in fact we are not different from inkwells and atoms, so this indicates that (his reservations about reductionism notwithstanding) Rorty believes that ultimately we are not much different from inkwells and atoms.

Unfortunately, this interpretation is incompatible with Rorty's claim that we should liberate ourselves from the common hope of reaching reality as it is. The world as such will never be given in our knowledge, argues Rorty. We must think of it in terms of '*reality-under-c-certain-description*'.[5] I think he is correct about that. But if so much is true, then behaviourism, naturalism and physicalism are no more than a method of mirroring the world within certain conventions of description, and are by no means objectively more trustworthy than any abnormal discourse. Perhaps Rorty wants it that way. He has a predilection for abnormal discourse (fortunately never practically betrayed in his book), and as things are today, he is not thereby doing injustice to behaviourism, naturalism and physicalism. These theories are not offered as parts of the all-encompassing, atoms-and-the-void theory. They are on the verge of abnormal discourse: have gaps and commit obvious simplifications, they do not reduce all human knowledge to the ultimate structure of the world, and are obviously helpless in predicting a great part of human behaviour.

The situation would be entirely different if we had the ultimate atoms-and-the-void theory that Rorty speaks about in [1]. This theory would be strongly compatible with any other correct description of the world. It would be so far-reaching and fine-tuned as to be able to '*predict every inscription and every sound that may be uttered.*' To meet this condition it would have to be (1) fully deterministic, (2) entirely explicit and (3) practically applicable. Such theory is conceivable at all only on the assumption that human beings (along with the rest of the world) are 100 per cent deterministic automata-machines without ghosts, so to speak. This theory would probably have to simulate the initial conditions of every machine in order to predict its behaviour. If it could do it successfully, however, its pronouncements would not be abnormal discourse or 'reality-under-a-certain-description'. They would constitute the ultimate knowledge which offers exhaustive explanations and predictions.

This is the first inconsistency in Rorty that I do not know how to cope with: you cannot have the atoms-and-the-void theory which explains everything and also say that you only have a reality-under-a-certain-description. Another inconsistency arises from the fact that when we finally have this strong theory which in principle predicts everybody's behaviour, it is unclear how anything can still be left for the agent to 'decide'. Maybe Rorty is only using 'decide' in a Pickwickian sense, as his scare quotes indicate, and means that it will seem to the agent that he makes his decisions when in fact his brain has already made them and their nature has been scientifically established by those who use the strong theory. If so, we must presume that the agent is not able to use the strong theory and that students of his behaviour know more about his future actions than he does himself.

One can imagine circumstances in which this could be true. The strong theory may be very complicated, or its application costly and time-consuming. The theory may require, for instance, that in order to predict someone's behaviour, that person must be monitored day and night for ten years by 100 specialists sitting at 100 consoles. This in itself would not necessarily defeat the theory, for technically speaking it could still provide desired predictions, but its practical applicability would be put to a severe test. For the purposes we have in mind the theory cannot simply assume that we already know the initial conditions, that we have the readings on 100 consoles and that we have observed a child for ten years. The theory must show how these data can be obtained, and it can be applied only after the data have been actually collected.

Let us suppose that these conditions have been satisfied, that we have the requisite observations of the child. Next we will have to face the problem how the child will respond to being told how it will behave. We can deal with a compulsively negative or a perfectly docile character, as well as various mixes of the two. Suppose that the child is moderately negative, and we know exactly his pattern of fighting back. On certain well-defined occasions the child reacts to a prediction about his behaviour by 'deciding' to act differently from the prediction. But we know the pattern that he uses to pick up a substitute behaviour after his initial intentions have been betrayed, so we can predict what he will do. In the simplest case, he may simply defer the act he intended by a certain time interval. Knowing that, we must keep our genuine predictions to ourselves lest we trigger his negative response. We must give him a false prediction to let him play out his pattern of negative response. We may know, for instance, that if we tell him nothing, he is going to have a glass of milk in a moment. We also know that if we tell him so, he will wait one hour before he drinks the milk. Now we tell him that he is going to drink it now, and tell everybody else that he will drink it in one hour. By giving him a false prediction we make sure that the true prediction comes true. We relate to his 'en-soi', to use Rorty's language, and leave his 'pour-soi' intact (as a pure illusion, of course, as we nimbly manipulate the boy leaving him with the feeling that he is still a sovereign, self-determining entity). It is important to see that we cannot help cheating the boy if we want to predict him. No amount of knowing his atoms and the void will help us in discovering what he will do eventually if his atoms and the void react to predictions. If they do, the boy cannot be studied as an isolated unit whose reactions can be predicted irrespective of what he is told, because he responds (albeit negatively) to what he is told. Thus we can reconcile [1] and [2] only at the price of manipulating the boy. We can let him decide only if we feed false predictions to him.

But now, [1] and [2] cannot be squared with [3] and [4]. [3] says that '*the complete set of laws which enable these predictions [. . .] would not yet be the whole "objective truth" about human beings*' and [4] adds that those 'other vocabularies' would have a legitimate 'cognitive status'. How is it possible? What else is there to be known about the boy but his atoms and the void? We cannot ask why he acts like he does, because this knowledge is in the atoms or it is not in him at all, as (on the strength of [1]), there are no ghosts. His thoughts (if we keep the terms) are fully identifiable by his behaviour, and we already possess all knowledge which can predict his behaviour. There is no further 'objective truth' about his behaviour beyond his behaviour. Objective truth is about facts, and we already know all future facts concerning the boy as far as they depend on him, so there is nothing else to be known. A lot can be said about the boy in a hermeneutical or other conversation, but this talk will not contain truths about the boy. If there are no ghosts, he is only his body and his behaviour, and we know his body and his behaviour perfectly.

Obviously we must choose between [1] and [2] versus [3] and [4]. Which will we have? I think we should keep [3] and [4]. The strong theory that Rorty speaks about in [1] cannot be produced. We will never have an atoms-and-the-void description of human behaviour, not because such knowledge is logically impossible, but because it is too vast and will never be practically available. It requires the entire knowledge that Laplace assumed for his Demon. In our example, which was already complicated, we assumed that the boy had a simple pattern of 'deciding', that is, changing his mind – he deferred his action for one hour. But what if he has a random mechanism, some sort of roulette, in his head? Suppose that when we tell him that he will have a glass of milk now, he spins the roulette, and after a few seconds picks a course of action on which his imagination has been somehow fixed. If we were able to predict this free play of imagination we would be able to predict the outcomes of all lotteries, dice throws, card games and random-number generators in computers. That would involve nothing short of knowing exactly what happens to billions of interrelated atoms, and I do not think that anyone has an idea how it could be done. That means that we will never have full objective knowledge about human beings in terms of atoms-and-the-void. This also eliminates the need for abnormal discourse (except for amusement). We will never come to the end of the normal discourse. It cannot be exhausted because we will never replicate the states of the atoms in the universe in a computer. If so, there is no reason to rid ourselves of ghosts; they can remain, not as mysterious, haunting spectres, but as theoretical constructs which can handle the job with which we charge the ego, the self, consciousness, thoughts, emotions, decisions, intentions and so on.

I think there is no escape from Putnam's argument[6] about the square peg and a round hole. It is practically impossible to prove using the atoms-and-the-void theory why a square peg will not go through a round hole. We would have to monitor the momentum of billions of particles and calculate probability distribution for their travel through space. This cannot be done, so we must use simple physics, which shows what it means to say that one object is bigger than another, and simple geometry, which explains why only objects smaller than a hole can go through that hole. This is not a happy solution, of course. We cannot be satisfied with simple physics and simple geometry. We quickly notice that their use is limited to everyday problems, and that they distort the picture of the world. The world, we like to think, does not consist of pegs and holes but of atoms and the void. So we form a picture of the world which is very different from the operational theories that we use.

Sometimes the crude, operational theories are misleading, as the theory of the glassy essence is; but we should think twice before we reject them. We cannot run for help to the atoms-and-the-void picture of the world on every occasion. It is not even a theory but a hypothesis that may never grow into a body of knowledge to be used to make explanations and predictions. A crude theory can only be replaced by a less crude but still operational theory. If something is wrong with the glassy essence, and of course something is, we should turn to psychoanalysis, clinical psychology, neurology, artificial intelligence studies, and so on, depending on what our problem is. The findings of these disciplines will not be commensurate, but that is not a serious problem as long as the findings are sound.

We can turn to philosophy to get a more unified picture of the situation, but then we should remember that we wanted a unified picture, and not new facts, new proofs and new theorems. Philosophy does not provide operational knowledge but explanations and insights, hypotheses and interpretations. It must not be crude or narrow-minded, but the problem of its literal truth should not even arise. Its purpose is to rearrange known truths rather than find new ones, to give them a consistent and unified interpretation. In this sense it already serves the function that Rorty reserves for hermeneutics.

Philosophy is wrong when it is either oversimplistic or relies on fallacies derived from falsifiable theories. So epistemology would be wrong if it were literally true that human beings are incapable of forming representations of the world around them or if epistemology could only be expressed through misleading metaphors. Rorty says that the latter is the case; the metaphor of the glassy essence is undoubtedly crude and cannot be taken at face value. But after all, it comes from Shakespeare rather than Descartes, and it can be easily substituted (it normally is) with a more abstract concept of representation (even if it means no more than '*an automatic and empty compliment which we pay to those beliefs which are successful in helping us to do what we want to do*').[7] This replacement is enough, as far as I can see, to save epistemology from the faults that Rorty finds with it, and enough to let us steer back towards the mainstream.

The moral agent and bad faith

To return to the mainstream is an act of bad faith, argues Rorty.

This attempt to answer questions of justification by discovering new objective truths, to answer the moral agent's request for justifications with descriptions of a privileged domain, is a philosopher's special form of bad faith – his special way of substituting pseudo-cognition for moral choice.

This means that moral choice should be separated from normal discourse. In [5] Rorty has said only that the atoms-and-the-void theory may be able to predict what a man intends to do, but it will not tell him what he *should* do. I take it that Rorty follows Hume and G. E. Moore here: the world as it is, implies nothing about the world as it should be. Of course it is true, especially if one sees the world as an aggregate of atoms and the void.

There is a serious difference, however, between what Rorty calls normal discourse and the atoms-and-the-void picture. To draw conclusions from the atoms-and-the-void theory would be bad faith because it would be cheating. The theory does not yet exist, and as a hypothesis it is inoperative at best. But why should we not draw moral conclusions from psychology and sociology; that is, from crude, perhaps, but operative versions of normal discourse? Rorty rejects all forms of normal science from the area of moral philosophy and philosophical psychology in [6]: '*The fear of science, . . . of self-objection, of being turned by too much knowledge into a thing rather than a person, is the fear that all discourse will become a normal discourse.*'[9]

This proposal is extremely radical: Rorty has removed from morality not only the dubious, all-encompassing, strongly deterministic hypothesis of human functioning in terms of the void and particles, but also every other form of normal discourse. Human beings have been left with their 'pour-soi' and exorcized entirely of their 'en-soi'. Rorty abrogated every naturalistic conception of the moral agent (*pace* his 'whole-hearted naturalism') when he dissected and rejected all conceptions of the mental faculty in man. For Rorty all philosophical symbolism of mental functioning was bogus. Mind, soul and reason were summarily rejected[10] along with the 'idea' idea,[11] theory of knowledge,[12] and privileged representations.[13] The moral agent was presented as 'a person rather than a thing' (cf. [6]), but a person was construed as a highly complicated biological organism with or (preferably) without the mind,[14] equipped with the ability to act 'pour-soi' (cf. [6]). The end result was rather strange: the moral agent was presented as a physical organism whose mental functions are not seriously considered but who is granted the ability of self-reflection. I would be afraid to entrust any moral decisions to such a creature, probably as much as Rorty would be afraid to leave them with creatures clumsily described as minds-and-bodies.

His book convinced me beyond any doubt that the mind-and-body symbolism is clumsy. I certainly cannot say that I know that I have a mind, reason, an intellect, a soul, consciousness, the self or a mental centre. But I am sure I have something like one of these in me, or even that I am it. Of course, the mind-stuff does not exist, but this is not to say that I am only a body capable of a function, a disposition, a tendency to react in a certain manner, that I am like a frog which catches flies.[15] I guess that frogs are thoughtless and have no inner sense of identity (here I may be right or wrong – remember the prince?), but I cannot believe that I am thoughtless, that my thoughts are not my private states, that they are not at the same time determined by my idiosyncrasies and by logic, by my emotions and by my memory, by the books I have read and by the plans I have made. I think that I am a complicated mental structure, and I do not believe that its existence can be challenged by pointing out that no one knows how to describe it without being clumsy, or by showing that I can give no physical proof of my mental existence.

It may be that no one has a good theory on how the mind functions, but there are several clumsy theories which describe it fairly well, say, parts of psychoanalysis or middle-class sociology. I am also ready to accept some unifying hypotheses, for example that my mind is no more than software. But then, my program, which I can call the self, has been running too long without any other program being used on the same hardware to warrant saying that I am only a body with a set of dispositions. Moreover, one can deduce so little about my software from my hardware that I do not see why the former should be considered a derivative of the latter. Of course, if we had the atoms-and-the-void theory, things might look different, but not before.

Furthermore, we must assume the existence of a mental structure if we want to ascribe moral faculties to an individual. This structure must be relatively permanent, capable of understanding arguments and willing to offer some. It must have a moral character or moral integrity, the power to predict the effects of its decisions and the ability to formulate intentions and make plans. All this may be housed in a frog, if you like, and may or may not be called the mind. But it cannot be simply identified as a living body with its tendencies, unless by tendencies one means what I am trying to describe here as a mental structure – but then why fight over words?

The 'pour-soi' and moral choice cannot exist without a mental structure, which is at the same time a sentient agency capable of controlling its behaviour, formulating reasons for action, making promises, accepting certain principles as norms of behaviour, and so on. I see that it is a difficult problem to find criteria which could show whether a given individual (say, a frog) does or does not have such a structure. But this is no reason, I submit, to argue that such structures do not exist. More important, I do not understand how 'pour-soi' could function without such a structure. A disembodied faculty of self-determination, entirely divorced of its 'en-soi' could not make moral decisions in good faith. If the two are separated and the 'pour-soi', continues alone as a vigilant self-reflection, it has no incentive to make one decision rather than another. Free of any external determination, totally devoted to abnormal discourse, why should it pursue anybody's happiness, or pay debts? Freedom to choose is not necessarily freedom to choose wisely or morally. A free spirit, unfettered by its 'en-soi' would have no idea how to make moral choices even if it wanted to. It takes at least a mental structure to make such decisions, or better, a body-and-soul human being, or better yet a human being together with his or her society.

A reconciliation of physicalism with existentialism is not possible, I am afraid. No object as described by physics is capable of self-reflection (except for the unfortunate mirrors which suggested the clumsy mental symbolism), and no object described by existentialism as 'pour-soi' does in a physical manner whatever it does 'pour-soi'. Why, therefore, should anyone want to adopt one or the other position? Neither establishes empirical truths. Physics does, but physicalism does not – it is a programme of interpretation and a unifying hypothesis. Existentialism is not even that – it is a programme of making do without any unifying hypothesis, a programme of always starting from scratch and seeing oneself every morning as a new-born baby, free as a bird. Thus for different reasons both views concur in rejecting the concept of mental structure. Would that be all that made them attractive to Rorty?

NOTES

1 Richard Rorty, *Philosophy and the Mirror of Nature* (Princeton University Press, Princeton, 1979), pp. 360f. (Hereafter, *PMN*.)
2 *PMN*, pp. 387–8.
3 *PMN*, p. 373.
4 *PMN*, p. 373.
5 *PMN*, p. 378.
6 Hilary Putnam, 'Philosophy and Our Mental Life', in *Philosophical Papers* (Cambridge University Press, Cambridge), vol. 2, p. 295.
7 *PMN*, p. 70.
8 *PMN*, p. 383.
9 *PMN*, p. 388.
10 *PMN*, pp. 24f.
11 *PMN*, pp. 192f.
12 *PMN*, pp. 131f.
13 *PMN*, pp. 165f.
14 Cf. the Antipodeans, *PMN*, pp. 70f.
15 *PMN*, p. 40.

13

Rorty, Realism and the Idea of Freedom

Roy Bhaskar

A liberal society is one which has no ideal except freedom
Rorty, 'The Contingency of Community', p. 13

Richard Rorty has given us an eloquent critique of the epistemological problematic, from which contemporary philosophy is gradually emerging. But I want to suggest that he has provided us with only a partial critique of a problem-field, to which he remains in crucial respects captive. These passing notes are not of course innocent. They are written from a particular perspective, that of a Lockean underlabouring interest in human sciences which partly do and partly do not (yet) exist – which are in the process of struggling to come into being. Such sciences would provide that sort of consciousness of our natural and social past and present as to allow us to change both ourselves and the conditions under which we live (cf. *PMN*, p. 359)[1] in such a way that 'the distinction between the reformer and the (violent) revolutionary is no longer necessary' (CC, p. 13). More specifically, I want to claim that we shall only be able 'to see how things in the broadest possible sense of the term, hang together, in the broadest possible sense of the term' (*CP*, p. xiv) from this perspective if we are committed to:

(1) an *ontologically*-oriented philosophically realist account of science, on which the world is explicitly construed, contrary to Humean ontology, as structured, differentiated and changing; and

(2) a *critical* naturalist account of the human sciences, which will sustain the idea of an explanatory critique of specific structural sources of determination and their emancipatory transformation.

Rorty remains, I am going to contend, a prisoner of the implicit ontology of the problematic he describes. My aim is to carry the dialectic of 'de-divinization' (cf. CC, p. 10) a stage or two further by conceiving reality, being, the world (precisely as it is known to us in science) as only *contingently* related to human being; and therefore as not *essentially* characterizable as either empirical or rational or in terms of any other human attribute. This is the mistake of what I call the 'epistemic fallacy': the definition of being in terms of knowledge (*RTS*, pp. 36ff.). A picture has indeed held philosophy captive.[2] It is the picture of ourselves or our insignia in any picture – the picture as invariably containing our mirror-image or mark. Philosophical post-narcissism (cf. CS, p. 12) will be evinced in the exercise of our capacity to draw non-anthropomorphic pictures of being. This is my main post-Rortian point.

But I shall also be pursuing one or two subsidiary theses. I shall argue that Rorty's remarks on science reveal an unacceptable positivist–instrumentalist and Humean–Hempelian bias, and that his account of science is based on a half-truth. Further I shall contend that *Philosophy and the Mirror of Nature* is characterized by a central tension – roughly that of Kant's '"existentialist" distinction between people as empirical selves and as moral agents' (*PMN*, p. 382), a fault-line parallel to that of the Kantian resolution of the 3rd Antimony, on which *PMN* is 'stuck fast'. Moreover, as in Kant's case, it is Rorty's ontology which is responsible for his failure to sustain an adequate account of agency and *a fortiori* of freedom as involving *inter alia* emancipation from real and scientifically knowable specific constraints rather than merely the poetic redescription of an already-determined world.

Rorty's account of science

'Kuhn himself ... occasionally makes too large concessions to the tradition, particularly when he suggests that there is a serious and unresolved problem about why the scientific enterprise has been doing so nicely lately' (*PMN*, p. 339). Rorty goes on to interpret the unease felt by Kuhn at the absence of a solution to the problem of induction as merely the expression of 'a certain inarticulate dissatisfaction' (*PMN*, p. 341). Still this does raise the question of the characterization of science. In particular in what has science been so successful lately? – in 'the prediction and control of nature' (*PMN*, p. 341; cf. p. 356). Rorty assumes that the aim of science is prediction and control – Comtean 'savoir pour prévoir, prévoir pour pouvoir'; and that explanation is deductive-subsumptive and symmetrical with prediction, i.e. Hempelian in form (*PMN*, pp. 347, 356) – a bias he shares with Habermas.[3] Such explanations presuppose of course Humean causal laws. The truth of physicalism and regularity (Humean) determinism (*PMN*, pp. 28n, 205, 354, 387) is rendered consistent with the truth of non-physicalistic statements by reference to Davidsonian theory, on which singular causal claims or heteronomic (non-strictly Humean) generalizations entail that a homonomic, strictly Humean description exists.[4] Thus Rorty is committed to a basically positivist account of the logical form of sentences in science, and of the structure of scientific theories. This in turn presupposes that the world is at least fundamentally (though not necessarily exclusively) Humean–Laplacean in form, i.e. constituted by atomistic events or states of affairs or molecular state descriptions and their *constant conjunctions*.

That Rorty can presuppose as much has to be explained by a critical lacuna in his dialectical reconstruction of the recent history of analytical philosophy of science. Roughly speaking, there have been two main axes of criticism of the standard positivist view of science of the sort against which Popperians, Wittgensteinians and Kuhnians reacted. There has been criticism of its *monistic* theory of scientific development, turning on the social, historical and/or discontinuous character of scientific knowledge – of the kind advanced by Sellars, Feyerabend and Kuhn. But there has also been criticism, from Soriven, of the *deductivist* theory of scientific structure, turning especially on the stratification of scientific knowledge. Although Rorty is aware of this line of criticism (see *PMN*, p. 168), it plays no role in his narrative.[5] It is a line which is especially salient for debates about the *Geisteswissenschaften*, where explanations conforming to the deductive-nomological model are completely unavailable[6] and where any generalizations have to be formulated 'normically', i.e. as allowing for exceptions.[7]

There are two main moments in the anti-deductivist critique of Humean and Hempelian theory. The first, whose prototype was provided by Kant's critique of Hume, which was later repeated and refined by Campbell's critique of Duhem, and then by Hesse and Harré's critique of Hempel, involves the denial that constant conjunctions are *sufficient* for causal laws, explanations, scientific theories. But it is the second on which I wish to focus here. This involves the denial that constant conjunctions are even *necessary*. This 'transcendental realist' position may be motivated by reflection on the nature of experimental and applied scientific activity (see *RTS*, C1 and C2). Analysis of experimental activity shows that the regularities necessary for the empirical identification of laws hold only under special and in general artificially produced closed conditions; but, for at least a large class of fundamental laws,[8] analysis of applied activity shows that these laws are presumed to prevail in open systems, i.e. outside the conditions which permit their empirical identification, where no constant conjunctions obtain. Such laws have to be analysed *transfactually*, i.e. as tendencies. These tendencies are of novel kinds of thing. They are the relatively enduring generative mechanisms and structures of nature, initially hypothesized in the scientific imagination but sometimes subsequently found to be real, which produce the flux of events. There are no known laws in physics that conform to the Humean form. Generalizations can be empirical, or more broadly actual, or universal, but not both – a consequence that Cartwright captures in the title of her book, *How the Laws of Physics Lie.*[9] Transcendental realism, makes possible a reformulation of the Greek action/contemplation contrast (see *PMN*, p. 11). There is 'a difference that makes a difference' between (a) 'it works because it's true' and (b) 'it's true because it works' (*CP*, p. xxix): (a) gives the gist of applied explanations in open systems, (b) of theoretical corroborations in closed systems. Rorty notes that Newtonian mechanics was doubly paradigmatic for the founders of modern philosophy – as 'a method for finding truth' and 'a model for the mechanics of inner space' (*PMN*, p. 328n). But he remains under the spell of a third effect of the celestial closure achieved by Newtonian mechanics. Namely its forming a model of phenomena as well as science, an ontological paradigm of an empirical actualist and regularity determinist cast. Galileo and Newton were misinterpreted by the Enlightenment. It is important to appreciate that in the battle between the gods and the giants (*CP*, p. xv), the friends of the Earth no less than the friends of the Forms have been wrong about science.

Reflection on experimental and applied scientific activity reveals that science is committed to a non-anthropocentric and specifically non-Humean ontology – of structures and generative mechanisms irreducible to and often out of phase with the (normally artificially contrived) patterns of events which comprise their empirical grounds. In particular, the laws of nature, as they are currently known to us, entail the (contingently counterfactual) possibility of a non-human world; that is, that they would operate even if they are unknown, just as they continue to operate (transfactually) outside the closed conditions which permit their empirical identification in science. It follows from this that statements about being cannot be reduced to or analysed in terms of statements about knowledge, so that what I have referred to as 'the epistemic fallacy' *is* a fallacy (cf. *SR*, p. 47). Accordingly, we need two dimensions in which to talk about science – an ontological or 'intransitive' dimension and an epistemological or historical sociological or 'transitive' dimension (cf. *RTS*, C1.1). The laws of nature, unlike their normally experimentally produced grounds, are not empirical, but real (tendencies). That the reality known to us in science is only contingently related to our experience of it, its knowledge and more generally human being is the only position consistent with a 'scientific realist' (*PMN*, p. 381) world-view or congruent with the Sellarsian dictum which Rorty quotes approvingly that 'science is the measure of all things, of what is that it is, and of what is not that it is not'.[10]

One consequence of the argument which establishes the transfactual and non-empirical nature of laws is that a philosophical as distinct from a scientific ontology is *irreducible* in the philosophy of science. A philosophical ontology will consist of some general account of the nature of the world, e.g. to the effect that it is structured and differentiated, whereas a scientific ontology will specify the structures which, according to the science of the day, it contains and the particular ways in which they are differentiated (see *RTS*, p. 29[11]). But a moment's reflection shows that a philosophical ontology is *inevitable* too. For one cannot talk about science – for instance about the logical form of casual laws – without implicitly presupposing something about the world known by science – about, that is to say, its ontological form, say to the effect that it is constituted by events which are constantly conjoined in space and over time. Commitment to empirical realism and in particular to the Humean theory of causal laws (empirical invariances as necessary or necessary and sufficient for laws) carries with it commitment to a (false) general account of the world.

A very damaging feature of empirical realism is the systematic tendency to conflate knowledge and being, as in the notion of the 'empirical world', or epistemological with ontological concepts or issues. Thus the transfactuality of laws is just one aspect of the existential intransitivity of objects – the condition that in general things exist (and act) independently of their descriptions (which is consistent with causal interdependency in the processes of the production of things and their descriptions, e.g. in the social domain (cf. *PON*, p. 47)). The idea of the existential intransitivity of objects (as a proposition in the intransitive dimension of the philosophy of science) is compatible with the idea of the social production of knowledge (as a proposition in the transitive dimension of the philosophy of science). Paradigmatically, we make facts and, in experimental activity, closed systems; but find out about (discover and identify) things, structures and causal laws (cf. *CL*, p. 3; *CP*, p. xxxix; *PMN*, p. 344). We could stipulate these as 'necessary truths'. But it is probably better to recognize that there is an inherent ambiguity or bipolarity in our use of terms like 'causes', 'laws', 'facts', etc., and to be prepared, whenever necessary, to disambiguate them, distinguishing a transitive (social or making) from the intransitive (ontological or finding) employment of these terms.

Kuhn provides a famous case of transitive–intransitive (epistomological–ontological) ambiguity when he notoriously says, in a passage discussed by Rorty (*PMN*, pp. 344–5), that we must learn to make sense of sentences like this: 'though the world does not change with a change of paradigm, the scientist afterward works in a different world'.[12] Once we disambiguate 'the world' into 'social, historical, transitive' and 'natural, (relatively) unchanging, intransitive' we can transcribe the sentence, without paradox, as: 'though the (natural) world does not change with a change of paradigm, the scientist afterwards works in a different (social, or cognitive) world'. I shall suggest in a moment that Rorty's argument trades in places on a similar paradox/ambiguity.

A consequence of the non-anthropocentric ontology to which science, but not Rorty, is committed is that it is not optional, but mandatory that we tell causal stories which make the laws of physics prior to and longer than the truths of biology and both of these the backdrop for human history. It is not just 'hard', but inconsistent with both the practical presuppositions and the substantive content of the sciences 'to tell a story of changing physical universes against the background of an unchanging Moral Law or poetic cannon' (*PMN*, pp. 344–5).

In any event, 'physics gives us a good background against which to tell our stories of historical change' (*PMN*, p. 345) is ambiguous in the way of Kuhn's 'world'. If physics means 'the physical world' as described by the science of physics (i.e. physics$_{id}$ – or the physical world), then it is true and unparadoxical. If, however, physics means 'the set of descriptions' of the physical world in the science of physics (i.e. physics$_{td}$ – or the science of physics), then as a rapidly changing social product it is part of the process of historical change and so cannot form a background to it. Two other instances of this ambiguity may be cited. At *PMN*, p. 342, Rorty claims that the reduction of the cognitive (fact, theory) to the non-cognitive (value, practice) would seem to ' "spiritualize" nature by making it like history or literature, something which men have *made* rather than *found*', whereas it would merely spiritualize (natural) science which has indeed been made rather than found. (The identity of nature and science only holds if one commits the epistemic fallacy or subscribes to the subject–object identity theory with which the fallacy is implicated – in which indeed it is founded.) In CS, p. 11, discussing the Nietzschean view of self-knowledge as self-creation, Rorty remarks that 'the only way to trace home the causes of one's being as one is would be to tell the story of one's causes in a new language'. He continues: 'This may sound paradoxical, because we think of causes being discovered rather than invented ... but even in the natural sciences we occasionally get genuinely new causal stories, the sort of story produced by what Kuhn calls "revolutionary science"'. However, what are told in revolutionary science are new – revolutionary – stories$_{td}$ about the causes$_{id}$ of natural phenomena. Moreover, in social life the principle of existential intransitivity holds just the same. Thus redescribing$_{td}$ the past in a revolutionary way can cause$_{id}$ radical new changes, including a new identity, self-definition or autobiography: but it cannot retrospectively cause$_{id}$ old changes, alter the past (only its interpretation). It is not surprising that Rorty should slip from transitive to intransitive uses of terms like 'cause' – it is endemic to empirical realism, the epistemological definition of being in terms of (a particular empiricist concept of) experience.

One odd feature of Rorty's account of science may be briefly mentioned. He seems to think that it may be possible to have a plurality of comprehensive closed theories of strictly Humean form: 'There are *lots* of vocabularies in the language within which one might expect to get a comprehensive theory phrased in homonomic generalizations, and science, political theory, literary criticism and the rest will, God willing, continue to create more and more such vocabularies' (*PMN*, p. 203). He seems here to be committed to a most implausible form of what might be called a 'multiple-aspect theory'.

De-divinizing ontology and the inexorability of realism

The principle of the existential intransitivity of objects, that things in general exist and act independently of their descriptions, must be complemented by the principle of the historical transitivity of knowledge, that we can only know them under particular descriptions (cf. *RTS*, p. 250; *SR*, p. 99). But it does not follow from the principle of the historical transitivity of knowledge that we cannot know that what is known (under particular descriptions) exists and acts independently of those descriptions. Rorty is correct that there is 'no inference from "one cannot give a theory-independent description of a thing" to "there are no theory-independent things"' (*PMN*, p. 279). But equally there is no inference from 'there is no way to know a thing except under a particular description' to 'there is no way to know that that thing exists (and acts) independently of that particular description'. In fact one can know that scientifically significant reality existed and acted prior to and independently of that relative latecomer science as a truth in (a result of) sciences (of cosmology and geogony, biology and anthropology) and one can know that it exists and acts independently of science as a practical presupposition of the social activity of science (and a truth in philosophy). Of course, what is known – in the discourse of philosophy – to exist and act independently of science will always be known in some more or less specific way – whether in the relatively Neanderthal forms of Peircian 'secondness' (*PMN*, p. 375) or Maine de Biran's 'intransigence'[13] or what Putnam has called '19th century . . . village atheism'[14] or in the form of a more fully elaborated ontology.

Such generic characterizations of the world can and do play a significant role in the practice of science; and some ontology, or general account of being, and hence some kind of realism, will in any event be implicitly presupposed, if it is not explicitly theorized, in a philosophical discourse on science. The crucial questions in philosophy are not whether to be a realist or an antirealist, but *what sort* of realist to be (an empirical, conceptual, transcendental, or whatever, realist); whether one explicitly theorizes or merely implicitly secretes one's realism and whether and how one decides, arrives at or absorbs one's realism. While arguing that we never encounter reality *except under a chosen description* (*CP*, p. xxxix), Rorty unwittingly inbibes and inherits Hume's and Kant's chosen descriptions of the reality known by the sciences.

Ontology is irreducible partly because different (e.g. cognitively-oriented) practices presuppose different and incompatible accounts of the world. It is not sufficient to '[explain] rationality and epistemic authority by reference to what society lets us say' (*PMN*, p. 174) precisely because 'what society lets us say' can itself always be '[placed] in the logical space of reasons, of justifying [and, we must add, criticizing] and be able to justify [and criticize] what one says' (*PMN*, p. 192). That is to say, what society or one's peers and contemporaries *ought* to let one say is always a legitimate question, especially in the case of *conflicts*, actual or potential, between different language-games, as is chronically the case in the contested and quandarous human sciences.

We can now also begin to appreciate why we need to sustain the concept of an ontological realm distinct from our current claims to knowledge of it. First, for the intelligibility of their establishment, involving, as they do, creative redescription of and active intervention in, nature. Second, for the possibility of their criticism and rational change (cf. *RTS*, p. 43). (I will deal with Rorty's claim that the transitions between normal discourses, paradigms or language-games, though caused, cannot be reasoned (CC, pp. 10–11) below.) Rorty's 'transcendentalia' (*PMN*, pp. 310–11) now become, from this perspective, necessary features of the immanent practice of the sciences. And even his welcome warnings about the dangers of reifying or hypostatizing truth become misleading (and ecologically irresponsible) if they are taken to imply that there are no real world constraints on beliefs or to license a poetic or practical Prometheanism to the effect that there are 'no non-human forces to which human beings should be responsible' (CC, p. 10).

I now want to isolate and comment on five pivotal presuppositions of Rorty's work. Rorty assumes that:

(1) Science can get by without philosophy, and in particular metaphysics and ontology.
(2) Any (philosophical) realism must be a truth-realism.

(3) The only kind of realism science needs is what Putnam calls an 'internal realism' (*PMN*, pp. 298, 341) – which is required for purposes of Whiggish historiography.

(4) The Humean theory of causal laws (at least as modified by Davidson) and the deductive-nomological accounts of explanation and prediction (and *a fortiori* their symmetry) are in order and correct.

(5) Their truth is compatible with the possibility of the *Geisteswissenschaften* and in particular the *wirkungsgeschichtliches Bewusstoein* (*PMN*, p. 359), central to the project of 'edification' and emancipatory social science alike.

None of these assumptions withstand critical scrutiny.

Rorty accepts Kant's conflation of the *a priori* and the subjective [criticized in *SR*, pp. 11ff.] (see *PMN*, pp. 8–9, 258) and thus sees the only possible locus of necessity as 'within the mind' (*PMN*, p. 189). He thus assumes that any transcendental philosophy is going to be primarily epistemological or epistemologically-oriented (*PMN*, p. 381). This prematurely forecloses the possibility of a philosophy of or for science which was no longer concerned to 'ground' knowledge or find certain foundations for it; but which was instead concerned to ask what the *world* must be like for certain characteristic (practical and discursive) social activities of science to be possible.[15] Such a philosophy would be a transcendental realism not idealism; ontologically, rather than epistemologically, geared; and unafraid of recognizing epistemically relativist implications – which are anyway quite consistent with judgementally rationalist results (*PON*, pp. 57–8).

From such a philosophical perspective, reality can be unequivocally (and no longer anthropocentrically or epistemologically) accorded to things. It would be wrong to hold, for instance, to the slogan that 'to be is to be the value of a variable'.[16] For the way things are in the world takes no particular account of how human beings are, or how they choose to represent them. Moreover, from such a perspective, (natural) necessity would, like reality, when appropriate, be unequivocally ascribed to the efficacy of causal laws and generative mechanisms, and the existence of some properties of structures and things (*RTS*, chs 3.3 and 3.5). It would reflect a superstitious anthropomorphism to believe that 'necessity resides in the way we say things, and not in the things we talk about'.[17] Also from such a perspective, there would remain no temptation to identify or treat as synonyms the 'ontological' and the 'empirical' (see e.g. *PMN*, p. 188). For such a philosophy would have a use for the category of the 'real but non-empirical', e.g. in designating the transfactual operation of causal laws prior to, outside and independently of human experience.

Finally such a transcendental philosophy would unashamedly acknowledge as a corollary of its realism, the historicity, relativity and essential
transformability of all our knowledge. Putnam's disastrous 'meta-
induction'[18] loses its force if one no longer conflates ontological realism
and epistemological absolutism and thinks of absolutism and irrationalism
as the only alternatives. Indeed, from this standpoint it should even be
welcomed – as underlining the historicity and potential transformability of
all our cognitive achievements. Rorty evades the 'relativist predicament'
(CC, p. 11) by the twin expedients of deploying an epistemic absolutism
for normal and an epistemic irrationalism for abnormal science, or more
generally discourse. In the former case he invokes Davidson's arguments
against alternative conceptual schemes and assumes that within a language-game or discourse 'everybody agrees on how to evaluate everything
everybody else says' (PMN, p. 320). In the later case he stipulates that
what is believed or said, though, like Davidsonian metaphors (CS, p. 14),
caused, cannot be reasoned – with 'the most human beings can do [being]
to manipulate the tensions within their own epoch in order to produce the
beginnings of the next epoch' (CC, p. 11). This is a counsel of despair. It
stems partly from the over-normalization of normal discourse, ignoring its
holes, silences and incommensurabilities – and also its ambiguities and
ambivalences, its open texture and rich potentialities for development.
Partly too from the failure to allow anything like immanent critique
(including the possibility of meta-critique (SR, pp. 25–6)) as a process of
rational disputation and change in the synchronic and diachronic space or
overlap between language-games, where all the interesting (and truly
dialectical) arguments take place and develop, and without which there
would be nothing very much, if at all, to say (cf. PON, p. 148).[19]

Summing up on point (1) above, then, we can reaffirm with Rorty that
there is no Archimedean point outside human history and no 'third thing'
called correspondence standing between the world and language. But that
doesn't mean that we don't need a philosophical de-divinized ontology, in
which to think (i) the contingency of our origins, of human experience and
human reason (and hence the possibility of an unexperienced or an
a-rational(ized) world); (ii) the finitude of human being (including the
uncompleted or unfinished character of human lives); and (iii) the
historicity of human knowledge (within what I have called the transitive
dimension of the philosophy of science).

Contrary to (2) above, I suggest that what is required to underlabour for
science is not an epistemologically-slanted truth realism of the sort that the
pre-1976 Putnam and the tradition have sought to provide, but an
ontologically-primed causal powers and tendencies of things realism of the
sort I sketched in RTS and Harré and Madden elaborated in *Causal*

Powers.[20] Turning to (3), there are places (e.g. at *PMN*, pp. 282, 341) where the sort of internal realist historiography which Rorty reckons a sufficient realism might appear to differ little from the account a transcendental realist might provide. But there are differences in metaphysics, ideological intent and rhetorical style. The transcendental realist is unblushingly fallibilist and historicist about science. She feels no need to be uncritical and 'complimentary' about everything that passes for knowledge or is done in science's name (contrast *PMN*, p. 298); no reason to 'buy in' to shoddy science (cf. *RTS*, p. 188); no conpunction about admitting to occasional intra-scientific perplexity or 'stuckness'. Nor does she feel under any imperative to write the story of science Whiggishly as one long continuous success story – without blemishes or periods of stasis and even regression. For she never forgets that science is something that human beings have made, in causal interaction with the things they have found, in nature.

As for (4), we have already seen that Humean and Hempelian theory are inconsistent with the practical activity and substantive content of science. (5) will be considered after the following section.

It is true that nature has no preferred way of being represented; that 'nature speaks being', like the Heideggerian 'language speaks man' (CC, p. 11), is only a metaphor. But the following should be borne in mind. Despite the indisputable formal underdetermination of theory by evidence, at any moment of time in most scientific domains most of the time, there are only one or two (if that) plausible theories consistent with the data. Theories are islands in oceans of anomolies. Second, in what might be called the 'epistemic stance' to nature,[21] we do 'read' the world, as we read the time off a clock or sentences off a page *as if* it were constituted by facts, i.e. under the descriptions of a theory (cf. *SR*, C3.6). To say that theory conditions our beliefs in epistemically significant perception is not to say that theory determines them. Theory and nature may be co-determinants of beliefs in a notional parallelogram of forces (cf. *SR*, pp. 189–91); and we may appeal to either (in propositionalized form) in a justificatory context. (In fact, Rorty allows for the control of theory by observation in the guise of 'control by less controversial over more controversial beliefs' – *PMN*, pp. 275–6n) – but beliefs of the former kind may be less controversial precisely because they were formed in or as a result of (theoretically-informed) observation.) Finally, we must never forget the immense effort that goes into that nitty-gritty practical laboratory activity which Bacon called 'twisting the lion's tail'[22] designed precisely to create or induce the conditions under which grounds for a theoretical judgement will become available. Such practical activity, comprising social transactions between human beings and their material transactions with nature, constitute the woof and warp of getting into 'the logical space of reasons, of justifying and being able to justify what one says' (*PMN*, p. 182), the staple diet of normal science.

Epistemology and anti-epistemology

The highest point reached by contemplative materialism, that is, materialism which does not comprehend sensuousness as practical activity, is the contemplation of single individuals and of civil society.

The standpoint of the old materialism is civil society; the standpoint of the new is human society, or social humanity.[23]

What is the epistemological problematic, which Rorty identifies and partially describes, but in which, in my view, he remains entrapped? For Rorty, it is a problem-field, which is also a project or quest and a theory or solution-set. The project is to identify certain foundations for knowledge, which philosophy purports to do on the basis of its special understanding of the nature of knowledge and of mind. The Cartesian–Lockean–Kantian tradition has conceived philosophy as foundational, knowledge as representational and the mental as privileged and even incorrigible. At the core of philosophy has been the quest for certainty, in response to the possibility of Cartesian (sceptical) doubt. This, in its dominant empiricist form, it has found in the immediate deliverances of sense (rather than, or sometimes as well as, in self-evident truths of reason – or their analytical proxy's, such as meanings).

Rorty's sustained polemic against foundationalism in *PMN* is accompanied by a vigorous assault on its attendant occular metaphors, mirror imagery and overseer conception of philosophy. Most of this I wholeheartedly endorse. In *PMN* he isolates one particular moment in the genesis of foundationalist epistemology of special importance. This is what I call the *ontic fallacy* (*SR*, p. 23). It consists in the effective ontologization or naturalization of knowledge, the reduction of knowledge to or its determination by being, in what may best be regarded as a species of *compulsive belief-formation* (see *PMN*, pp. 158, 374–7). (Thus Plato focused 'on the various parts of the soul and of the body being compelled in their respective ways by their respective objects': *PMN*, p. 158.) Rorty sees that this involves the dehumanization of discursive, justifying subjects and the collapse, in the alleged moment of cognition, of the *pour-soi* to the *en-soi*, of justification to para-mechanical explanation. ('It is the notion of having reality unveiled to us . . . with some unimaginable sort of immediacy which would make discourse and description superfluous' (*PMN*, p. 375).[24] But – and this is one sense in which *PMN* is based on a half-truth – Rorty does not see that it is the epistemic dual or counterpart of the ontic fallacy, namely the humanization of nature, in an anthropo-morphic, epistemological definition of being (in empiricism, in terms of the concept of experience) in the *epistemic fallacy*, which prepares the way and paves the ground for the ontologization (eternalization and diviniza-tion) of knowledge in a subject–object identity or correspondence theory. Such a theory effectively welds together the transitive or social-epistemic and intransitive or ontic dimensions of science (cf. *SR*, pp. 66, 253). On it knowledge is naturalized and being epistemoligized.

This problematic, which may be fairly called 'epistemological', has ontological and sociological conditions and consequences. The drive to certainty, powered by epistemology's sceptical foil, sets up a dialectic in which correspondence must give way to, or be philosophically underpin-ned by, identity. Similarly, accuracy of representation must pass over into immediacy of content. Then, in its dominant empiricist form, the objects intuited in experience and their constant conjunctions come, in the ideology of empirical realism, to define the world, stamp being in a Humean mould. The sociological precondition of the atomistic and uniform ontology of empirical realism is an individualism, comprised of autonomized units, conjoined (if at all) by contract, passive recipients of a given and self-evident world rather than active agents in a complex, structured and changing one. For such isolated consciousnesses, disen-gaged from material practice, their relation to their bodies, other minds, external objects and even their own past selves must become doubtful. Philosophy's task – that of the traditional 'problems of philosophy' – now becomes to reconstruct and indemnify our actual knowledge in a way congruent with these conceptions of man and being.

What explains this problematic? There seems little doubt about the role of the fundamentalist exercise. It is surely, as Rorty suggests, a misguided attempt to eternalize the normal discourse of the day (*PMN*, pp. 9–10, 333n). Moreover, it is philosophy's fundamentalist ambitions which justify its ontology. This ontology, formulated in the antiquated vocabul-ary of Newtonian and Humean mechanics is now seriously 'interferring with' (*CL*, p. 5) our efforts to investigate and change social being. What explains it? Could it be anything other than the conception of man – of single individuals in civil society – at the heart of it? Perhaps the real meaning of the epistemological project is not epistemological at all – but ontological: to reconstitute the (known) world in the self-image of bourgeois man.

If this, or something like it, is part of the meaning of the epistemological tradition which has come down to us from Descartes and Locke through Hume and Kant and their descendants, what should be said about the role of epistemology within the context of the transcendental realist philosophy of science I have been advocating here? We can approach the need for *some*, if you like, anti-traditional epistemology by reflecting on the irreducible normativity of social practice which Rorty notes (*PMN*, p. 180n). This begins to show us why we need something other than the historical sociology of knowledge in the transitive dimension of the philosophy of science – why, from the standpoint of what I have called the 'axiological imperative', namely the condition that we must act (and other than by scrutinizing the antecedents of what we will do) (*PON*, p. 87), we need an intrinsic (intentional, justifying) as well as (and, when it is efficacious, within the context of) the extrinsic (historical, explaining) aspect of science (cf. *SR*, pp. 16ff.).

I think, despite his polemics against epistemology (as normally understood[25]) *per se*, Rorty half-concedes the point when talking of the 'bifocality' of science: 'From the point of view of the group in question these subjective conditions are a combination of commonsensical practical imperatives (e.g. tribal taboos, Mill's methods) with the standard current theory about the subject. From the point of view of the historian of ideas or the anthropologist they are the empirical facts about the beliefs, desires and practices of a certain group of human beings. These are incompatible points of view, in the sense that we cannot be at both viewpoints simultaneously' (*PMN*, p. 385). An epistemology or criteriology for science is required just in so far as science is an irreducibly normative activity, oriented to specific aims (in theory, the structural explanation of manifest phenomena) and characterized by specific methods of its own (cf. *RTS*, C3).

Now, if value judgements of one sort or another are irreducible in the sciences, does this mean that they neither require nor can receive grounds other than the agreement of one's peers (cf. *PMN*, p. 176)? Certainly not. For, in the first place, a value, including a truth, judgement typically incorporates a descriptive or evidential component, alongside its prescriptive, imperatival or practical component (cf. *SR*, p. 183). To ignore the former, the descriptive ('factual' or ontological) grounds in virtue of which some belief or action is commended and recommended, could be called the emotivist or more generally *anti-naturalistic fallacy* in axiology. But can such grounds be cashed in any way other than by reference to what some community or, at the limit, agent believes about the world? Most certainly.

Outside science, a belief or action may be justified (or criticized) by reference to what the (relevant) scientific community believes. But generally *inside* (the relevant part of) science, we cannot justify, say, an explanatory claim in this way. This may be partly because what is at stake (stands in need of justification or criticism) is precisely what the community believes. But it will also be partly because at some point the explanatory query *in* science will take the form 'why is the world this way?', whereas the explanatory query *about* science will take the form 'why does the community believe such-and-such?' The answer to the former question will not consist of intellectual-cultural history or the natural sociology of belief, but of a (scientifically-) ontologically grounded, or justified, scientific explanation. Intra-scientific justifications (in the intrinsic aspect of science) will appeal to formal proofs, plausible models, decisive experiments, reliable apparatus, newly discovered phenomena, consistency with established theory and so forth. Together they will amount to a justification, couched in the terms of some substantive scientific ontology, of the explanation offered of the puzzling phenomenon, not a sociological explanation (in the extrinsic aspect of science) of that community's (or agent's) belief. To confound the two would be to commit a transposed variant of the Lockean mistake of confusing justification and explanation, which Rorty mercilessly exposes in *PMN*, C3, all over again. Of course, justifications within science are a social matter – but they require and are given ontological grounds. In failing to recognize this, Rorty has furnished us with a post-epistemological theory of knowledge without justification which matches his account of science without being. The result is just the opposite of what he intended: the epistemologization of being and the incorrigibility (uncriticizability) of what passes for truth.

The essential tension of *Philosophy and the Mirror of Nature* – or, A Tale of Two Rorty's

> Reason would overstep all its limits if it took upon itself to *explain how* pure reason can be practical. This would be identical with the task of explaining *how freedom is possible*.[26]

A pervasive tension runs through *PMN* between (α) a hard-boiled scientistic naturalism of a physicalistic determinist cast, prominent to the fore, and (ψ) an acceptance of the autonomy of the *Geisteswissenschaften* and espousal of hermeneutics, accentuated towards the aft. Indeed the book is a veritable tale of two Rorty's – tough-minded Humean versus tender-minded existentialist. Rorty's subsequent trajectory has further tautened the tension – the actualism of *PMN* culminating in the apotheosis of contingency in the 1986 Northcliffe lectures (published as CL, CS and CC). Rorty is aware of the tension in *PMN*. So it is good to have his views on the apparent (and, I shall argue, real) incompatibility set out in two series of pithy paragraphs (on pp. 354–5 and 387–9). For I want to claim that Rorty is unable to sustain either (i) an intelligible account of scientific activity (which involves, *inter alia*, causal intervention in nature to win 'epistemic access' to transfactually efficacious laws) or (ii) of the world known by science or (iii) an adequate idea of human freedom, or (iv) of the compatibility between (α) and (β).

'Physicalism is probably right in saying that we shall some day be able, "in principle", to predict every movement of a person's body (including those of his larynx and his writing hand) by reference to microstructures within his body' (*PMN*, p. 34; cf. *PMN*, pp. 28n, 204–5, 387). Against this, I am going to argue that a person's neurophysiology, or more generally physical microstructure, cannot constitute a closed system. This can be seen most easily by considering social interaction of an everyday sort. Suppose A goes into a newsagent's and says to B '*The Guardian*, please' and B hands A a copy of it. On the physicalist thesis we must suppose that for any physical movement there is a set of antecedent physical (neurophysiological, or microstructural) states sufficient for it. Call B's action 'ϕ_B'. We must now suppose either (1) that ϕ_B is determined by some set of antecedent physical states $N_1 \ldots N_n$ such that ϕ_B would have been performed without A's speech action, ϕ_A; or (2) that A's speech action, ϕ_A, as understood by B, was causally efficacious in bringing about ϕ_B.

(1) involves the supposition that B would have performed the action of handing A a copy of *The Guardian*, ϕ_B, or the movements in which it physically consists, even if A had performed some quite different action, e.g. asking for *The Independent* or a packet of chewing gum or B to marry him, or dancing a jig and even if A had not been present at all. This is absurd. But (2) involves an action of A's, as understood by B, intervening in the allegedly closed circuit constituted by B's neurophysiology (or microstructure). That is to say, it involves A's speech-act as part of a causal sequence between some prior set of neurophysiological states of B and ϕ_B – just as ϕ_B intervenes between A's contemporaneous physical states and his subsequent action, ϕ_A, of giving B 30p. (We cannot suppose that A's movement would have occurred if B had said 'Sorry, sold out' or passed him a copy of *The Sun* or slapped his face or ignored him.) So B's (and A's) neurophysiology (or microstructure) cannot constitute a closed system. Thus in the context of social interaction a person's body cannot form a closed system (cf. *PON*, pp. 104–6).

This argument may be extended to cover the broader cases of open systemic behaviour generally, animal behaviour[21] and emergent natural powers. Here I consider only the first. Suppose C takes a stroll. It starts to rain. So she opens her umbrella. We must now suppose either (1′) that C would have done so even if it had remained fine or (2′) that the allegedly deterministic chain of neurophysiological (or microstructural) states is broken – in this case, by the weather.

There is a line of last resort that the reductionist might employ at (2), (2′), namely to deny that a single person's microstructure comprises a closed system. But now physicalism loses its distinctiveness as a philosophical thesis applicable to *individual human beings* (see *PMN*, p. 387) and reduces merely to a barren form of Laplacean determinism, against which I have argued enough elsewhere (see *RTS*, esp. C2). What of (1), (1′)? It might be urged here that as a matter of fact ϕ_B and only ϕ_B will occur in response, as it appears, to ϕ_A; that given the state of B's microstructure nothing else could have occurred. What we are left with now is a bizarre variety of Leibnizian pre-established harmony of monads, in which each person's microstructure is so synchronized with every other's that it appears *just as if* they were talking and dancing, batting and bowling, laughing and crying; and so synchronized with the microstructure of every other object in the universe that it appears *just as if* they were eating and drinking, building and digging, weaving and welding.

Only an emergent powers materialism, I want to claim, can sustain the phenomenon of agency (see *PON*, 3.4–5; *RTS*, 2.5; *SR*, 2.1) and this entails the breakdown of the thesis of regularity determinism at the physical level. But we have already seen that the laws of nature, and the principles posited in scientific theories, cannot be construed as constant conjunctions – i.e. they do not have a closed systemic, regularity deterministic form. Rather, they must be taken transfactually, as real tendencies operating on and whatever (when their antecedent – stimulus and releasing – conditions are satisfied) the flux of events. Events, for their part, whether the fall of an autumn leaf, the collapse of a bridge, the purchase of a newspaper, the composition of a poem or the decline of a civilization are not determined before they are caused (cf. *RTS*, p. 107).

Rorty's next paragraph begins, 'The dangers to human freedom of such success is minimal, since the "in principle" clause allows for the probability that the determination of the initial conditions (the antecedent states of microstructures) will be too difficult to carry out except as an occasional pedagogical exercise' (*PMN*, p. 354). This is disastrous. Freedom cannot be grounded in ignorance. Or else we would have to reckon a falling man free in virtue of his ignorance of gravity or the law of fall. And most free would be the least *pour-soi* (*PMN*, p. 352), the furthest from 'the logical space of reasons, of justifying and being able to justify what one says' (*PMN*, p. 389).

Rorty continues: 'The torturers and the brainwashers are, in any case, already in as good a position to interfere with human freedom as they would wish; further scientific progress cannot improve their position'. Two brief comments. First, torturers and brainwashers achieve their results by intervening in causal series, bringing about various physical effects, ultimately sounds, inscriptions etc. – which, but for their machinations, would not *ceteris paribus* (e.g. unless those effects were overdetermined) have been forthcoming. Second, the idea that technical progress couldn't improve their position seems to me like wishful thinking. It would be rash to assume that subliminal advertising or market research were wasted. The more the manipulators know about the immediate determinants of human action (*CP*), the more successful, or so it would seem, they are likely to be.

Rorty's next paragraph may be broken down into:

(1)   'The intuition behind the traditional distinction between nature and spirit, and behind romanticism, is that we can predict what noises will come from someone's mouth without knowing what they mean'.

(2)   'Thus even if we could predict the sounds made by the community of scientific inquirers of the year 4000, we should not yet be in a position to join in their conversation.'

(3)   'This intuition is quite correct'. (*PMN*, p. 355).

Proposition (2) is quite correct. If we *were* able to predict verbal behaviour, we still might not be able to know what the agents *meant*. Thus, as Winch has pointed out, we might be able to compute the statistical probability for the occurrence of certain sounds, e.g. words in Chinese, without being able to understand what was being said[28] – and the converse is the case (cf. *PON*, p. 137). But Rorty's intuition is faulty. For the reason why we cannot in general predict the sounds or inscriptions that people make unless we know what they mean to say is because it is the latter which determines the former. It is the state of the conversation, not physiology, which will explain the sounds and marks of the community of scientific enquirers for the year 4000, though these sounds and marks must be consistent with their physiology. Just as it is the state of the economy that determines the use of machines and thus selects the initial and boundary conditions under which certain mechanical principles apply. In human agency, the agent puts matter in motion, setting the conditions for the operation of various neurophysiological and physical laws, the outcome of which is not predetermined before it has actually been caused – by the agent in the context of her bio-psycho-social life. If the concept of human agency, as manifest in such phenomena as catching buses or writing poems, as distinct from mere bodily movement, as manifest in such phenomena as catching colds and digesting cakes, is to be sustained, it must be the case that the agent is causally responsible for some but not other of her bodily movements (cf. *PON*, p. 92).

I now have enough material to attempt a diagnosis of Rorty's reconciliation of the pervasive tension of *PMN*. It is a variant of Kant's resolution of the Third Antinomy. Now this does not work for Kant, and it does not work for Rorty. The problem for Kant is how we can be held responsible for the things we do, involving as they do bodily movements (including those of our larynxes and our writing hands), if all our physical movements are fully determined by antecedent phenomenal causes. It is a problem for Rorty too. Kant has no answer to it – if we discount the idea of an original choice outside time (presumably an expedient not open to the naturalist Rorty). And whether we discount it or not, in either case, our ordinary system of causal imputation in the human world, and, with it our moral accountancy, collapses.

What prevents an adequate resolution of the antinomy for Kant is his empirical realism, his thorough-going actualism and determinism, as detailed in the Analogies, to which he is wedded in his account of the phenomenal realm. For it is this which necessitates placing 'free man' in a realm, albeit one said to be possibly real (as distinct from merely apparent), outside and beyond the purchase of science. It is the ontology implicit in Kant's account of science, as manifest in his comprehensive actualism, that prevents him sustaining an adequate account of human causal agency, and *a fortiori* of freedom as a possible property or power of embodied agents in space and time.

Rorty comes to replicate the problematic of the Kantian solution. The basic distinction he invokes is that of Kant's '"existentialist" distinction between people as empirical selves and as moral agents' (*PMN*, p. 382). We are determined as material bodies, *qua* empirical selves, but free as writing and speaking (i.e. discursive) subjects, *qua* moral agents. Actually this is not quite as he puts it, but I will justify the interpretation/ elaboration in a moment. The point for Rorty is not an ontological, so much as a linguistic one. Whereas Kant gives us an (at least) two-worlds model, Rorty gives us an (at least) two-languages model. The autonomy of the social and other less physicalistic sciences is rendered consistent with a comprehensive empirical actualism by allowing that physics (or the physical sciences) can describe every bit of the phenomenal world but that some (e.g. the human) bits of it can also be truly redescribed in a non-physicalistic way (*PMN*, pp. 28n, 205, 354, 387).

The problem for Rorty, as for Kant, is how if the lower-order level is completely determined, what is described in higher-order terms can have any effect on it. And of course the answer is that it can't. If the intentional level, at which we cite reasons for actions and offer justifications and criticisms of beliefs is merely a redescription of movements which are already sufficiently determined by antecedent physicalistic causes, then the *causal irrelevance of reasons* for the states of the phenomenal world of bodily movements and physical happenings (including the production of sounds and marks) immediately follows. Given this, both the particular reasons adduced in explanations, and the status of reason explanations in general, appear as arbitrary and the practices (from the *wirkungsgeschichtliches Bewusstsein* of edification (*PMN*, p. 359) to the creative redescriptions of strong poets (CS, pp. 11ff.)) upon which they are based as illusory (cf. *PON*, pp. 112–14).

Here again, as in Kant, it is Rorty's thorough-going actualism, determinism and deductivism which prevent an adequate account of human agency, and *a fortiori* responsibility and freedom. There is a further difference here in that the relation between reality and appearance is inverted. In Kant the phenomenal world is merely apparent, but the noumenal world is real, which is what makes freedom possible. In Rorty, on the other hand, the phenomenal actualistically described world must be taken as real, with freedom dependent on our ignorance of (or decision to hold in abeyance) those deterministic descriptions of it. But the structure of the problem-field is the same. In both cases, reason explanations become arbitrary, and the only way to change the material world is by operating on sub-social (physical) causes. Science becomes unintelligible, social science impossible and freedom cognitively unattainable.

Further considerations of the autonomy of the *Geisteswissenschaften* and Rorty's idea of freedom

> Man is always free to choose new descriptions (for, among other things, himself) (*PMN*, p. 362n)

The pivotal opposition between a phenomenal or empirical realm subject to strictly deterministic laws known to science and an intelligible realm of human being (or intentionalistic redescription) where agents are free is a familiar one. The Manichean world of late nineteenth-century German culture fused this broadly Kantian cleavage with Hegelian dichotomies to found distinctions between *Erklären* (causal explanation) and *Verstehen* (interpretative understanding), the nomothetic and the ideographic, the repeatable and the unique, the domains of nature and of history. Since then, the pivotal contrast has usually been accompanied by the claim that, in the case of the intelligible order and its denizens, science must at least be complemented (the neo-Kantian position) and at the most be replaced (the dualist anti-naturalist position) by another practice, method or approach – namely, 'hermeneutics'. The ground for hermeneutics lies in the uniquely meaningful, linguistic or conceptual character of its subject-matter, in virtue of which it is precisely intelligible. So it is with Rorty too. But before we can see this, there is some unravelling to do.

The underlying distinction for Rorty is, as we have seen,

> (A) the Kantian so-called '"existentialist" distinction between people as empirical selves and as moral agents' (*PMN*, p. 382).

It is this, or something very like this, distinction which underpins his critique of epistemology as based on a confusion of 'explanation' and 'justification' (*PMN*, C3–4) and his praise for Sellars (e.g. at *PMN*, p. 180n) for insisting on the irreducibility of norms, values and practices to facts and descriptions. (This is compatible with his critique of value-free discourse (*PMN*, p. 364)). For Rorty wants to stress the irreducible normativity of the social and defactualize the social so achieved. (Hence there are no objective (factual) constraints in social reality.) It is grounded, or so I shall argue, in the consideration that it is discourse which is distinctive of human beings: 'people *discourse* whereas things do not' (*PMN*, p. 347). Without discourse, no statement (or description) could be true or false. Also without discourse, there would be no abnormal discourse, hence no hermeneutics and no edification; no choice and therefore no *pour-soi*. It is in this sense, I have suggested, that we could sum up his reconciliation of the poles constituting the pervasive tension of *PMN* by saying that we are determined as material bodies but free as speaking and writing (discursive) subjects. In C8, (A) explicitly comes to the fore as the irreducibility of the *pour-soi* to the *en-soi*.

But before we get to C8, Kant's 'existentialist' distinction (which structures *PMN* as a whole), has already become displaced or transposed in C7 onto

> (B) the 'linguistified'[29] and Kuhnian distinction between normal and abnormal discourse.

Later, by the time of the Northcliffe lectures, this distinction has made way for, or passed over into:–

> (C) the romantic distinction between what might be called 'alter-determination' and self-creation (CS, p. 12).

But there are already clear premonitions of this in *PMN*, e.g. in the attempt to distance the romantic notion of man as self-creative from Cartesian dualism and Kantian constitution (*PMN*, pp. 346, 358). Alter-determination consists in being made rather than making oneself, and leads to stasis or replication; whereas self-creation consists in self-transformation or self-overcoming. So (C) leads readily to

(D) the Nietzschean distinction between the will to truth and the will to self-overcoming (CL, p. 5; CS, p. 12).

(C) is also the distinction between romanticism and moralism (CC, p. 14) and (D) that between philosophy and poetry.

By now the whole ontological backcloth has shifted. The comprehensive actualism of the naturalistic Rorty has given way to a celebration of contingency. (This is really only the other side of the Humean coin – they are linked in symbiotic interdependency.) Already prefigured in C8 (*PMN*, p. 381n), this familiar existentialist motif is elaborated into an ontology of the particular, idiosyncratic, accidental and unique. Thus the individuation of human beings – ideographic particulars – is to be achieved by capturing their uniqueness in a unique, and so novel way. Only in this way can we avoid the fate of being a product of some pre-existing set of programmes or formulae, and so a copy, replica or instance of a type (or universal) rather than an *individual*. (It might be argued that the concept of contingency only makes sense in relation to that of necessity, which is officially (for Quinean reasons) disallowed. But Rorty can say that his use of it is a deliberate polemical reactive one, designed to make an (anti-) philosophical point.)

(B), (C) and (D) constitute the linguistic, romantic and Nietzschean displacements of Rorty's original (in *PMN*) Kantian problematic. I am going to claim that discourse is the central unifying category in Rorty's later thought; and that it determines the progression from (A) through to (D).

In so far as it is discourse that is distinctive of human beings, we have the possibility of creating new languages (vocabularies, descriptions etc.), of unfamiliar uses of existing noises and marks (metaphors) (*CL*, p. 6), of abnormal and incommensurable, including reactive and potentially edifying (including non-constructive), discourses – and hence of *hermeneutics*. Hermeneutics is the generic term for the activity of rendering intelligible what is at present unintelligible (*PMN*, p. 321). It is the attempt to normalize discourse – that is, paradigmatically discourse (from within some normal discourse) about abnormal rather than normal discourse (*PMN*, p. 346). Hermeneutics is a kind of meta-discourse; but one which is only needed in the case of some incommensurable, and therefore (from the viewpoint of the hermeneutical enquirer) abnormal, discourse. It is the attempt to establish a 'common context of utterance' or 'mutual horizon' (*PON*, pp. 154ff.). Note that 'there is no requirement that people should be more difficult to understand than things: it is merely that hermeneutics is only needed in the case of incommensurable discourses, and that people discourse whereas things do not. What makes the difference is not discourse versus silence but incommensurable versus commensurable discourses' (*PMN*, p. 347).

In Part III of *PMN* hermeneutics is somewhat oddly counterposed to epistemology, which is thereby severed from its specific connections to science, scepticism, the theory of knowledge and philosophy. What they share in common is that they are both meta-discourses, discourses not about the world, but about our knowledge (epistemology) or discourse (hermeneutics) about the world. What differentiates them is that epistemology presupposes universal commensuration, underpinned by the figure of what I have called the 'ontic fallacy' (see p. 208 above); whereas hermeneutics does not, and in fact is necessary just when this assumption breaks down – when we must 'savour' or 'bandy about', in order to literalize or normalize, a new or different (alien) way of speaking (cf. CL, p. 6). A directly connected peculiarity is Rorty's restriction of hermeneutics to discourse about abnormal (or incommensurable normal) rather than normal discourse. This is explained by Rorty's 'overnormalization' of normal discourse (noted on p. 206 above). By contrast, I would argue that hermeneutics, or the interpretative understanding of meaningful objects, is *always* necessary in social life – and *within* it, as well as about it. (Thus there is hermeneutics in normal physics or chemistry.)

On the interpretation of Rorty I am developing, the fundamental feature of human beings, their discursivity, gives us their ontological duality: as both 'generators of new descriptions' and 'beings one hopes to be able to describe accurately', 'as both *pour-soi* and *en-soi*, as both described object and describing subject' (*PMN*, p. 378). As describing subjects, human beings can redescribe every object, including themselves, in new, including potentially abnormal (and hence incommensurable normal) ways – which is to say that because human beings are describing subjects, new, and potentially incommensurable, descriptions can become true of *any* object.

But Rorty does not clearly or explicitly distinguish the case (a) where any object (including human beings) may *change*, and so require a new, potentially incommensurable, description from the case (b) where any object (including human beings) may, though *unchanged*, be redescribed in a new, potentially incommensurable, way. To make this distinction explicitly requires disambiguating intransitive from transitive change. Thus it is characteristic of Rorty that, having allowed that 'for all we know, it may be that human creativity has dried up, and that in the future it will be the *non*human which squirms out of our conceptual net' (*PMN*, p. 351), he goes on to add that in such a case 'it is natural to start talking about an unknown language – to imagine, for example, the migrating butterflies having a language in which they describe features of the world for which Newtonian mechanics has no name' (*PMN*, p. 352).

For Rorty, then:

(1) All things may be redescribed, even if they don't change, possibly in terms of an incommensurable vocabulary.

(2) All things may exhibit novelty, and so require a new, potentially incommensurable, discourse.

(3) Only human beings can discourse (normally or abnormally, literally or metaphorically).

(4) Only human beings can overcome themselves, their past and their fellow human beings – and they do so in and by (creating a new) discourse, i.e. one in terms of a new incommensurable vocabulary.

It should be stressed that for Rorty everything is susceptible to a new, possibly incommensurable, description. He says that 'It would have been fortunate if Sartre had followed up his remark that man is the being whose essence is to have no essence by saying that this went for all other beings also' (*PMN*, pp. 361–2, n. 7). And he adds that the point is 'that man is always free to choose new descriptions (for, among other things, himself)'. But of course the addendum is not true of beings other than man. Snakes and stones, migrating butterflies and runner beans are not free to choose new descriptions. Of course some (e.g. carbon atoms, dogs) but not other (tables, chairs) kinds of things have essences (cf. *RTS*, p. 210). But can Rorty be interpreted as meaning anything other than (a) that discourse is the essence of man[30] and/or (b) that in so far as man has no specific essence (no 'species being'), he is the being whose essence, *qua* describing and redescribing subject, is to be the essence or measure of all beings, *qua* describable and redescribable objects.[31] Discourse, then, is the essence of man; and, through man, of being. This, if the interpretation is correct, is the residue of Rorty's 'linguistic turn'. It chimes in well with Gadamer's dictum that 'being is manifest in language', which itself reflects Heidegger's proposition that 'language is the house of being'.[32]

What is the connection between (A) and (B)? There is a contingent overlap between them in the sense that the science/non-science distinction gives way to the normal/abnormal discourse distinction, and as it so happens, the redescribable world of human beings (culture) is caught less well than the redescribable world of nature by the normal (scientific) discourse of the day (for any or all of reasons (i)–(iv)). Thus there is no historiographically relevant demarcation criterion, 'no deeper difference than that between what happens in "normal" and in "abnormal" discourse' – a 'distinction which cuts across [and effectively replaces] the distinction between science and nonscience' (*PMN*, p. 333). And 'that portion of the field of inquiry where we feel rather uncertain that we have the right vocabulary at hand and that portion where we feel rather certain that we do . . . does, at the moment, roughly coincide with the distinction between the fields of the *Geistes-* and the *Naturwissenschaften*' (*PMN*, p. 352).

What then becomes of freedom? It ceases to be understood merely negatively, as grounded in our ignorance of physicalistically determining laws, and becomes, through our capacity to *redescribe* that world (or relevant bits of it), something which is both positive and humanistically more recognizable – namely, the capacity to create, and choose between, different vocabularies – that is, to speak or write *abnormally*. (Thus: 'Sartre tells us we are not going to have . . . a way of seeing freedom as nature (or, less cryptically, a way of seeing our creation of, and choice between, vocabularies in the same "normal" way as we see ourselves *within* one of those vocabularies)' – *PMN*, p. 380).) Freedom then is shown in the exercise of our capacity for abnormal discourse, for instance in fantasy and metaphor. Such discourse is of course always parasitic on the weighty existence of normal, literal, public, 'stodgy' discourse (CC, p. 14). Moreover it presupposes a degree of leisure and the absence of debilitating toil or pain (CS, p. 14).

Freedom as the capacity to engage in abnormal discourse is closely linked to 'freedom as the recognition of contingency' (CS, p. 11). Recognition here consists in the use or appropriation of particular contingencies for symbolic purposes – 'which amounts to redescribing them' (CS, p. 14). However, it appears to be only the human world, where things are meaningful in character, which can be reappropriated in this way. This is particularly clear in the case of our dealings with fellow human beings. 'In coping with other persons . . . we can overcome contingency and pain . . . by appropriating and transforming their language'. But in relation to the 'non-human, the non-linguistic, we no longer have the ability to overcome contingency and pain, but only the ability to recognise [it]' (CS, p. 14). This is, as it were, a Davidsonian variant of the Vichian *facimus*. We can know the social world not so much in so far as we have made it, but in so far as we have remade or reappropriated it by redescribing it in our own terms. 'The final victory of poetry in its ancient quarrel with philosophy – the final victory of metaphors of self-creation over metaphors of discovery – would consist in our becoming reconciled to the thought that this is the only sort of power over the world which we can hope to have. For that would be the final abjuration of the notion that truth, and not just power and pain, is to be found "out there"' (CS, p. 14).

We have got slightly ahead of ourselves. So let us retrace our steps. Though determined as material bodies (which includes the movements of our larynxes and writing hands), we are free as writing and speaking (discursive) subjects – a freedom shown most signally in the exercise of our capacity for abnormal discourse. A criterion of political value flows directly from this – namely:

(B′) 'It is central to the idea of a liberal society that, in respect of words as opposed to deeds, persuasion as opposed to force, anything goes' (CC, p. 11).

What is Rorty's highest value, his *summum bonum*? It is (C) romantic self-creation, which becomes, by the time of the Northcliffe lectures, (D) Nietzschean self-overcoming. Man is the describing, redescribing being. Among the entities man can redescribe in a new, and abnormal, way is himself. By making a new, incommensurable description of herself 'stick', she makes it true; and thus 'gives birth to' (to use Harold Bloom's term) or 'creates' herself – which is to say 'overcomes' her previous or past self. Moreover, only by describing herself in a totally novel way can she capture/express her idiosyncrasy, uniqueness – or rather achieve it, i.e. achieve her individuation – for anything else would reduce her to a (more or less complex set of) formula(e), a token of a type (or set of types). Such radical self-redescription (which could be nicknamed 'me-' or 'we-' descriptions) is the highest form of description. For not only does the redescription redescribe the redescriber; but in the process of redescription – of winning it, of making it stick, of achieving recognition for it – it makes the (re)description true; so achieving the identity of subject and object, by *creating* it. This, *if* it were possible would be the historic goal of philosophy achieved in a romantic or Nietzschean mode.[33]

Man, then, by redescribing himself, a redescribing subject, in a totally new way and winning acceptance for it, creates a new identity or subjectivity for herself – and thus (potentially) for every other object in the universe too, which can be redescribed in accordance with the new image, in her own way. (For she is the genus of all genera, the *anima mundi* through which language speaks.) Self-creation by self-overcoming is the reconciliation of man as empirical self and as moral agent, as described object and describing subject; the realization of the reconciliation between nature and spirit which Kant vainly tried to achieve in *The Critique of Judgement* by recourse to a divinizing as-if, now achieved in the process of discursive self-formation. Freed from the shackles of nature by her poetic power or discursive agency, by creating new descriptions of herself or her tradition which stick, or 'take' in the community (perhaps after her death), and so become true; she overcomes, i.e. remakes, herself or her tradition. Such overcoming redescriptions are redescriptions of redescriptions of a [fully determined] physical world; and there is no criteria for their truth other than their acceptance. 'The Nietzschean substitution of self-creation for discovery substitutes a picture of the hungry generations treading each other down for a picture of humanity approaching closer and closer to the light' (CL, p. 6). On this moving staircase of history stories replace stories, and there is nothing more to this process other than the prosaic quasi-Darwinian fact that some stories which are told stick around for a while (are retold), while most do not.

Is the romantic/Nietzschean ideal – of total self-creation, full self-overcoming – possible? Clearly not. Nor does Rorty think it attainable. On the contrary, the new way of speaking can only be (a) marginal or partial and (b) recognized *post festum* and retrospectively justified; and it is (c) conditional on future acceptance, i.e. usage. (a) A total transformation would leave the discursive agent and her community without the linguistic resources to recognize or refer to her achievement; nor could it be literalized in the community unless there was some continuity or communality in usage. 'Overcoming' is always piecemeal and partial – transformation, not replacement; and it respects the existential intransitivity of the self or past to be overcome. (b) Clearly the self-overcoming discourse must be abnormal. But if it is abnormal, how can it come to be understood, i.e. normalized? Rorty's answer is that 'If it is savoured rather than spat out, the sentence may be repeated, caught up, bandied about. Then it will gradually require a habitual use, a familiar place in the language game' (CL, p. 6). I would prefer to consider the way in which something akin to a logic of analogy, metaphor and new meaning or use is implicit in our scientific, literary, artistic, political (etc.) judgements and practices. This would also be a logic of immanent critique. (c) Because the self-overcoming process must be public[34] (for Hegelian as well as Wittgensteinian reasons) 'there can be no fully Nietzschean lives . . . no lives that are not largely parasitical upon an un-redescribed past and dependent on the charity of an as yet unborn generation' (CS, p. 15).

Despite the way Rorty refuses to find an identical subject–object here, and so distances himself from the romantic and Nietzschean ideals, his account of the social world is one in which romantic/Nietzschean processes are the vital ones, with the paradigmatic human being being the strong poet (or utopian revolutionary) who manages to impose her vision, even if only marginally, retrospectively and conditionally, upon a tradition or a community. (In the former case, she becomes a member of a discontinuous series, whose fate is to be continually reappropriated in a Whiggishly continuous narrative. In the latter case, she becomes a self whose self-description 'counts' and is acknowledged in the stories which are told and repeated.) In any event, Rorty has already subscribed to one identical subject–object – that implicit in the Humean–Kantian story of the world known by (at least natural) science,[35] which remains empirical, actual and contingent – rather than real, transfactually efficacious and characterized by natural necessity (cf. *RTS*, C3.3, 5, 6). And it is that world which, I argued in the previous section, makes discursive, as much as any other socialized, open-systemic form of human agency, impossible. For such agency depends upon the agent 'making a difference' to the course of the material world.

(A) to (D) between them let us score four progressively rich degrees of freedom in Rorty.

$Freedom_0$ – as susceptibility to new descriptions, discourses. This is freedom as caprice. It depends upon the sense in which, through man, discourse speaks being – the sense in which man is 'anima mundi'.

$Freedom_1$ – as the capacity to give new descriptions, generate new discourses. This is the sense in which freedom is connected with being a moral agent, *pour-soi* and capable of justification and radical choice.

$Freedom_2$ – as the capacity to engage in metaphor, fantasy and abnormal discourse (revolutionary practice?). This is freedom as abnormal discourse – in which it is said, for instance, that the dangers to 'abnormal discourse do not come from science or naturalistic philosophy. They come from the scarcity of food and the secret police' (*PMN*, p. 389). This is linked to freedom as the recognition of contingency, the contingencies which we seize on and appropriate in poetry and fantasy. Politically it licenses the slogan that 'in words, as opposed to deeds . . . anything goes' (CC, p. 11). Its text is *On Liberty*.

$Freedom_3$ – as the capacity to generate radically new self-descriptions, and to break free from or overcome the past. This is the highest degree of freedom. It remains an individual project. Freudian or Nietzschean moral psychology cannot be used to define social goals; nor is there any bridge between a private ethic of self-becoming and a public ethic of mutual accommodation (CS, p. 12). Freedom, then, as caprice, discourse, capricious discourse and creative discourse.

How is freedom possible?

What sort of freedom is at issue here? Freedom, for example, 'from the scarcity of food and the secret police' (*PMN*, p. 389). Or from being so 'racked by pain' or 'immersed in toil' (CS, p. 14) as to be unable to engage in abnormal discourse; or from being too uneducated to be capable of edification (*PMN*, pp. 365–6); or from being too unleisured – to lack the time or the equipment – to create metaphors (CS, p. 14), fantasies or poetry or generate a new description of oneself, one's culture or one's past. This kind of freedom – $freedom_1$ – $freedom_3$ – depends, I am going to argue, upon the explanatory-emancipatory critical human sciences. Such sciences do not yet exist, but they are struggling to burst into being. We stand to them today in the same kind of position as Descartes and Hobbes stood to the infant giant of mechanics (*PMN*, p. 131). And the present notes seek to 'underlabour' for these new sciences in the way, a little later, Locke sought to underlabour for mechanics (cf. *CC*, p. 11).

How then is such freedom possible? Very briefly and schematically:

(1) The *su generis* reality and causal efficacy of social forms, on a strictly physical criterion, i.e. in terms of their making a difference to the state of the material world which would otherwise have occurred (from soil erosion and acid rain through to the production of some rather than other noises and marks) has to be recognized (cf. *PON*, p. 39).

(2) The existence of objective social structures (from languages to family or kinship systems to economic or state forms), dependent on the reproductive transformative agency of human beings, must be granted. Such structures are not created by human beings – for, they pre-exist us and their existence is a necessary condition for any intentional act. But they exist and persist only in virtue of our activity, which reproduces or transforms them. In our everyday practices of substantive *poiesis* or making, which consists in or involves the transformation, in various media, of what are to hand – (paper, a musical score, raw meat, steel) – we reproduce or transform the social world itself. In general, changes in social structures will reflect or be reflected in changes in the transformative agency which would otherwise reproduce them.

These social structures are concept-dependent, but not merely conceptual. Thus a person could not be said to be 'unemployed' or 'out of work' unless she and the other relevant agents possessed some (not necessarily correct or fully adequate) concept of that condition and were able to give some sort of account of it, i.e. to describe (or redescribe) it. But it *also* involves, for instance, her being physically excluded from certain sites, definite locations in space and time. That is to say, social life always has a material dimension (and leaves some physical trace) (cf. *PON*, p. 136).

(3) It follows from this that Rorty's distinction between 'coping with other persons' and 'coping with the non-human, the non-linguistic', namely by redescription and recognition respectively (noted on p. 221 above) needs to be reworked, on several counts. First, there is more to coping with social reality than coping with other people. There is coping with a whole host of social entities, including institutions, traditions, networks of relations and the like – which are irreducible to people.[36] In particular, it would be a mistake to think that we had overcome a social structure, like the economy, state or family, if we were successful in imposing our description of it on the community. This holds in the case of people (including ourselves) too – we need to explain and sometimes change them (ourselves) as well as to (re)describe them adequately (productively, fruitfully, etc.). Think once more of the Rortian ideal – the strong poet (or utopian revolutionary) who can redescribe the already-

determined world in accordance with their vision – who can, retrospectively, by making their descriptions of themselves or their society true (i.e. by winning acceptance for them), (re)make themselves or their society. If there are objective social and psychic (as well as natural) structures – structures which need to be tackled before or so that we can become free (even in order to do poetry) – such a victory may prove a Phyrric one.

This point may also be put by saying that there is more to normative social science than creative redescription. Rorty says, 'To see a common social practice as cruel and unjust . . . is a matter of redescription rather than discovery. It is a matter of changing vocabularies rather than of stripping away the veil of appearances from an objective reality, of experimentation with new ways of speaking rather than of overcoming "false consciousness"' (CC, p. 14). But the identification of the *source* of an experienced injustice in social reality, necessary for changing or remedying it, involves much more than redescription, even if it depends on that too centrally. It is a matter of finding and disentangling webs of relations in social life, and engaging explanatory critiques of the practices which sustain them. This may indeed often involve the detection of various types of false and otherwise unhappy consciousness (and more generally being). And this may in turn lead on to *critiques* of the vocabularies and conceptual systems in which they are expressed, and the additional social practices with which they are implicated. Moreover such explanatory critiques will lead, *ceteris paribus*, to action rationally directed to transforming, dissolving or disconnecting the structures and relations which explain the experience of injustice and the other ills theoretically–informed practice has diagnosed. Poets, like philosophers, need to think of explaining to change, rather than just reinterpreting or redescribing to edify, the world.

On the other hand, there is more to coping with nature than mere recognition – or that plus redescription. For a start, as I have already suggested, we need hermeneutics in everyday natural science and not just to render intelligible abnormal theoretical redescriptions of nature. Second, it should be stressed that just as our conscious interventions in nature (e.g. in natural science and technology) are symbolically mediated, so we intervene in nature in all our causal interactions with the world, including our dialogues with the fellow members of our kind. The social world is not a cut-off redescription of nature. Rather it is both inscribed within and in continuous dynamic causal interaction with (the rest of) nature. To fail to see this, and in particular that there are physical (natural) constraints on human social life – that is, 'non-human forces to which we must be responsible' (CC, p. 10) and responsive – is a charter for ecological disaster, if not indeed (species) suicide.

The social and the socially conditioned or affected parts of the natural world are potentially transformable by human beings. But there may be some absolutes (universals, constants) of significance for human beings – which they just have to accept or 'recognize'. For example, fundamental laws of nature, the scarcity of some natural resources, upper limits to ecologically sustainable economic growth, aspects of human nature, the fact of the finitude (if not the precise duration) of human existence. The existence of *absolute* must not be confused with the existence of *objective* structures. Social structures may be just as objective, and transfactually efficacious within their geo-historical domain, as natural laws. Moreover, both alike typically impose limits and constraints upon the kinds of action (including speech action) possible to human beings, without (normally) rigidly determining what we do within those limits or constraints (cf. *RTS*, C2.5).

The other side of the supposition that our movements are determined is the notion that our talk, discourse, is free. What does it mean, in this context, to hold that 'man is always free to choose new descriptions (for, among other things, himself)' (*PMN*, p. 362n). I have argued with Rorty (in the 'Epistemology and Anti-epistemology' section above) that we are not *compelled* or determined in our beliefs or descriptions (any more than we are in most of our other states or actions – all of which depend on or manifest themselves in or through the movements of our bodies). But it does not follow from this that nature or society does not impose *constraints* on our rationally justifiable talk. Suppose this doctrine is coupled with the collapse of the intransitive dimension, in which current theory takes the place of the ontological realm (a realm which, I have argued on p. 204 above, we need, philosophically, precisely to think the objective existence and efficacy of structures independently of our current theory of them). It is now easy to see how the notion that 'man is always free to choose new descriptions' can encourage the voluntaristic position that man is always free to choose *any* description – at any rate, any description that society, in the form of his peers (in the transitive dimension), will let him get away with – which is more or less the Rortian doctrine here (cf. *PMN*, p. 176, *passim*).[37]

Such voluntarism may not do much damage in the normal discourse of the natural sciences, but in the abnormal discourses of the social sciences and the other humanities which are already in crisis and do appeal not just to irrelevant but to absurd and patently inapplicable philosophies (like positivism (cf. *PON*, C4.2; *SR*, C3.7)), it may encourage a superficial theoretical Maoism which masks or screens the absence of real intellectual progress (or social change – where it may be a case of 'plus ça change, plus c'est la même chose'). The successful poet's life may now become an incessant succession of fleeting paradigm shifts in which even aesthetic enhancement begins to pale.

Of course these (intransitive) objective structures at work in nature and society, whether transhistorical or not, must always be described in a (transitive) more or less historically transient language, i.e. in terms of potentially transformable descriptions.[38] (But there will be objective constraints on rational linguistic change too – constraints other than those imposed by sheer poetic power, although the latter will, in context, be among them.)

(4) In virtue of the fact that efficacious reasons are causes of intentional behaviour, not just redescriptions of them, the agent's account of her reasons has a special authority, which a neo-Kantian dualism cannot ground (see *PON*, C3.2; *SR*, C2.6), but this authority is not absolute. Rather, it is subject to negotiation, as we come to understand better, both in general and in the individual case, 'how we work' (contra *PMN*, p. 258), i.e. what makes us do the apparently irrational or otherwise explanatorily interesting things which we do. (One consequence of this is that – contra *PMN*, p. 185 – language can change us, as in 'the talking cure' but also when inspired by poetry.) Unconscious motivation and tacit skills are only two of the sources of opacity in social life; others are unacknowledged conditions and unintended consequences (*SR*, C2.2). So although society is a skilled accomplishment of agents, it does not follow from this that theoretical social science (informed by participants' understanding) is redundant. The task of the theoretical social sciences will be to establish the structural conditions, consequences and contours of the phenomenologically experienced world. In some, perhaps many, cases the critical redescription and structural explanation of that experience, and the accounts given in or based on it, will be necessary.

(5) In so far as an agent is interested in preserving or extending or deepening or gaining some freedom, this will always involve trying to understand, in the sense of explaining, the character of some social or socially conditioned or affectable entity, structure or thing – in order to maintain (reproduce) or change (transform) or otherwise dissolve or defuse, or to stimulate or release it. To become or remain 'free', in the simple sense of being 'unconstrained', always *potentially* involves both a theory of those constraints and, in so far as the freedom is feasible, a practice of liberation or liberty preservation. One may be free or desire freedom, in this sense, from any kind of thing.

On the other hand, emancipation, and more especially self-emancipation, involves:

(1) a stronger sense of being 'free', namely as knowing, possessing the power and the disposition to act in or towards one's real interests (cf. *SR*, p. 170); and

(2) a stronger sense of 'liberation', namely as consisting in the

transformation of unneeded, unwanted and oppressive to needed, wanted and empowering *sources* of determination.

Emancipation, that is to say, depends upon the transformation of structures rather than just the amelioration of states of affairs. And it will, at least in the case of self-emancipation, depend in particular upon a conscious transformation in the transformative activity or praxis of the social agents concerned. As such, emancipation is *necessarily* informed by explanatory social theory.

The emancipatory social sciences may, for their part, take as their starting-point some human need or aspiration (say for poetry) and enquire into the natural (if any) and social conditions of its non-fulfilment. Or they may begin with an immanent critique of prevailing social theories or ideologies, which may move on to the explanatory critique of falsity-generating (cf. *PMN*, p. 282) or other malevolent (ill-producing) social structures (see *SR*, C2.5–7). In either case, the social sciences will be participants in a theory–practice dialectic or spiral with the emancipatory practices concerned. In this process, the kind of creative radical self or society redescriptions, to which Rorty calls our attention, may play a vital role in individuation or identity (including group and kind, i.e. species, identity) formation. And this activity of *seeing themselves under a new description which they have helped to create*, will generally figure crucially in the *transformed transformative praxis* of the self-emancipating agents.

There is no need to deny either social-scientific knowledge or a metatheory of it to make the world safe for poets. For a society (or person) that has no use for poetry will *need* it more than most; and for that it will require a kind of knowledge of its situation that only the emergent human sciences can aspire to provide. Such sciences will always depend on poets; just as poets to be free, among other things to write or speak their lines, may, in the contemporary world, have to have recourse to the explanatory sciences as well as to their redescriptive powers. As for philosophers, if they follow the sounder part of Rorty's advice and give up the search for permanent neutral ahistorical compulsive foundations of knowledge (which I have called the 'ontic fallacy'), they may find that by focusing on the historical arts and sciences and the other social practices, as they are, have come down to us and may yet develop, there is more than a little critical underlabouring (including further de-divinizing) to do.

NOTES

1 See List of Abbreviations for full references. This chapter refers to the Blackwell edition of *PMN*. 'Chapter' has been abbreviated to 'C' throughout this paper.
2 L. Wittgenstein, *Philosophical Investigations* (Basil Blackwell, Oxford, 1963), paras. 115. Cf. *PMN*, p. 12.

3 Cf. J. Habermas, *Knowledge and Human Interests* (London, 1972), p. 308.

4 The Davidsonian theory is elaborated in D. Davidson, *Essays on Actions and Events* (Oxford University Press, Oxford, 1980), especially Essays 1, 7 and 11. For a critique of it, see *RTS*, pp. 140–1.

5 Thus there is another story to tell about 'reference' besides the one told in chapter 6 of *PMN*, albeit one whose most interesting development postdates the book, namely as a story of the 'search and find' activities of scientists looking for and exploring the novel entities and structures posited by scientific theories. (See e.g. I. Hacking, *Representing and Intervening*, Cambridge University Press, 1983, and R. Harré, *Varieties of Realism*, Basil Blackwell, Oxford, 1986.) This kind of story presupposes that science has definite procedures as well as determinate results; and that it is a material practice as well as a theoretical discourse.

6 See A. Donagan, 'The Popper–Hempel Theory Reconsidered', *Philosophical Analysis and History*, ed. W. Dray (Harper & Row, New York, 1966).

7 See M. Scriven, 'Truisms as the Grounds for Historical Explanation', *Theories of History*, ed. P. Gardiner (Free Press, New York, 1959).

8 See A. Chalmers, 'Bhaskar, Cartwright and Realism in Physics', *Methodology and Science*, 20 (1987) and 'Is Bhaskar's Realism Realistic?', *Radical Philosophy*, 49 (1988).

9 N. Cartwright, *How the Laws of Physics Lie* (Oxford University Press, Oxford, 1983).

10 W. Sellars, *Science, Perception and Reality* (Routledge & Kegan Paul, London, 1963), p. 173, cited in *PMN*, p. 199.

11 Cf. W. Outhwaite, *New Philosophies of Social Science* (Macmillan, London, 1987), ch. 2.

12 See T. S. Kuhn, *The Structure of Scientific Revolutions*, 2nd edn (University of Chicago Press, Chicago, 1970), p. 121.

13 See A. Kojève, *Introduction to the Reading of Hegel* (Basic Books, New York, 1969), p. 156.

14 *Meaning and the Moral Sciences* (Routledge & Kegan Paul, London, 1978), p. 20.

15 Cf. Outhwaite, *New Philosophies*, pp. 31–5.

16 W. V. O. Quine, 'Designation and Existence', *Readings in Philosophical Analysis*, ed. H. Feigl and W. Sellars (New York, 1949), p. 50.

17 W. V. O. Quine, 'Three Grades of Modal Involvement', *Ways of Paradox* (Random House, New York, 1966), p. 174.

18 H. Putnam, *Meaning*, p. 25, discussed in *PMN*, pp. 284ff.

19 In a way nothing is more significant for understanding the political (in a broad sense) impact of Rortyism as a phenomenon than the implications of the doctrine that revolutionary change (whether in the sciences, the arts or the socio-economic-political world generally) cannot be rational.

20 R. Harré and E. Madden, *Causal Powers* (Basil Blackwell, Oxford, 1975). See also A. Sayer, *Method in Social Science* (Hutchinson, London 1984).

21 For instance, in what F. Dretske, *Seeing and Knowing* (Routledge & Kegan Paul, London, 1969), ch. 1, has called 'epistemic perception'.

22 There is some retrospective irony in this in view of Wittgenstein's famous aphorism about lions' talk.

23 K. Marx, 9th and 10th Theses on Feuerbach, *Early Writings* (Penguin, Harmondsworth, 1975), p. 423.

24 'If we could convert knowledge from something discursive, something attained by continual adjustment of ideas or words, into something as ineluctable as being shoved about, or being transfixed by a sight which leaves us speechless, then we should no longer have the responsibility for choice among competing ideas and words, theories and vocabularies' (*PMN*, pp. 375–6).

25 Rorty sometimes uses a special sense of it (discussed in the 'Further Considerations'

section below) in his Part III, where it is counterposed to hermeneutics.

26 I. Kant, *Grundlegung zur Metaphysik der Sitten*, translated as *The Moral Law* (Hutchinson, London 1948), p. 119.

27 See P. Manicas, *History and Philosophy of the Social Sciences* (Basil Blackwell, Oxford, 1987), p. 307.

28 P. Winch, *The Idea of a Social Science* (Routledge & Kegan Paul, London, 1958), p. 115. Cf. also *PMN*, p. 348.

29 This expression is taken from R. Rorty, 'Posties', *London Review of Books* 3.9.87, p. 12. It signifies here roughy the transition from epistemology to linguistic philosophy – the 'linguistic turn' (the title of an important collection of essays Rorty edited, published by University of Chicago Press, 1967). What I have been calling the 'epistemic fallacy' (see p. 198 above) is now expressed in a linguistic form as the definition of being in terms of our discourse about being – the 'linguistic fallacy' (cf. *PON*, pp. 171, 198–9).

30 In this context it is worth bearing in mind Rorty's rejection of the concept of human nature. 'Humanity' does not have 'a nature over and above the various forms of human life which history has thrown up so far' (CC, p. 13). It would surely be wiser for Rorty to argue not that there is no such thing as human nature, but (i) that it always manifests itself in some historically specific and mediated form and (ii) that it is and must always be known under some historically particular – and therefore potentially transformable – description.

31 Note the similarity with the Renaissance theme of man as the being which is the 'genus of all empirical genera', 'creatura commune', 'oculus mundi' or 'anima mundi'. See L. Colletti, *Marxism and Hegel* (New Left Books, London, 1973), ch. 11.

32 'Letter on Humanism', *Philosophy in the 20th Century*, eds W. Barret and H. Aiken (New York, 1961).

33 There is some irony in the fact that the successful strong poet (or utopian revolutionary) would thus realize the goal of, of all discourses, philosophy.

34 Though Rorty does sometimes imply the contrary: 'Any seemingly random constellation of . . . things can set the tone of a life. Any such constellation can set up an unconditional commitment to whose service a life may be devoted – a commandment no less unconditional because it may be intelligible to, at best, only one person' (CS, p. 12).

35 Even if the epistemic fallacy is now committed in a linguistically transposed mode.

36 Of course, Rorty would probably acknowledge this, but there is more than a hint of methodological individualism in *PMN* (see, e.g., p. 206).

37 Rorty's argument that the difference between the 'kooky' and the 'revolutionary' (*PMN*, p. 339) or 'fantasy' and 'genius' (CS, p. 14) is the difference between ways of speaking which, for various contingencies, just happen to 'catch on' with other people or 'take' in the community overlooks the point that, for instance, existential and other claims in the intransitive dimension, successful predictions under repeatable conditions, formal proofs, demonstrations of anomaly resolution, etc. (amongst a bundle of historically discernible criteria) have to be satisfied in a revolutionary situation in science before intellectual progress can be definitely said to have occurred. There is reason, albeit often disguised, in intellectual revolutions; and such reason does not impede, but is shown, in part, in its poetry.

38 However, Rorty tends persistently to exaggerate the degree of 'Kuhn-loss', i.e. the extent to which subjects are changed, problems are set aside or displaced rather than resolved, anomalies are repressed or forgotten instead of being cleared up or normalized, in scientific and more generally discursive change. (In this his practice is at one with his theory.) In consequence he tends to underestimate the extent to which reference is maintained (or agents continue to 'talk about' the same thing) through change.

14

Redefining Philosophy as Literature: Richard Rorty's 'Defence' of Literary Culture

Michael Fischer

In part because of the influence of deconstruction, numerous contemporary philosophers and literary critics are proclaiming the literary status of philosophy. I want here to look at the recent work of one of these writers, Richard Rorty.[1] Instead of offering a comprehensive assessment of Rorty's work, I will be trying to evaluate its importance to literary study. More specifically, I will be examining how Rorty justifies his interest in literature. I will be arguing that far from providing a powerful (and sorely needed) rationale for literary study – as Rorty at first glance seems to do – Rorty, in fact, demeans the study of literature, or fails to remedy what many see as its present aimlessness.

Rorty's redefinition of philosophy as literature can be broken down into three steps. First, he suggests that philosophers from Plato to Kant through Husserl and the logical positivists have tried to define philosophy as an autonomous, foundational discipline that arrives at the unchanging essence of knowledge and morality. These philosophers have claimed to use 'Reality's own language rather than merely the vocabulary of a time and a place'.[2] Language, for these philosophers, can be a transparent medium, a clear window, an obedient tool that allows us to see or grasp objective reality. Knowing what necessarily counts as truth entitles philosophy, on this view, to judge the seriousness and rigour of other disciplines such as the social sciences, history and literary criticism. Like Plato expelling the poets from his ideal republic, the exemplary philosopher in this tradition is a stern judge, bent on purifying thought by weeding out all that is merely literary, contingent, soft, imprecise, emotional, biased and otherwise unphilosophical.

Secondly, Rorty aligns himself with a counter-tradition that delights in undermining the magisterial image of the philosopher supposedly upheld by Kant, Husserl and the others I have mentioned. This counter-tradition includes: Hegel, who in the *Phenomenology* creates 'a new literary genre' which presumably exhibits 'the bewildering variety of vocabularies from which we can choose, and the intrinsic instability of each', making 'unforgettably clear' why the 'deep self-certainty' of each vocabulary 'lasts but a moment'[3]; Nietzsche and Foucault, who unmask the will to power beneath the pose of neutrality and superior truth; the Wittgenstein of the *Investigations*, who mocks his earlier desire in the *Tractatus* to rid philosophy of unfounded presuppositions; John Dewey and William James, whose pragmatism elides invidious distinctions between science and art; and, finally, Heidegger and Derrida, who in different ways suggest that writing leads not to absolute knowledge but to more writing. The exemplary philosopher in this tradition is not an unyielding sage but a clever conversationalist, revelling in the wordplay, allusiveness and double entendre that alarm the Platonist. In the world of these subversive philosophers, language, convention, history and politics return to haunt the rationalist tradition that tries to repress them, exposing the Platonic search for absolutes as the 'impossible attempt to step outside our skins'.[4] Instead of offering a superior way to truth, these anti-philosophers, in short, advocate setting aside, dissolving or simply forgetting about the vain quest for an atemporal, privileged vantage-point from which philosophy can monitor other uses of language.

Third, as philosophy falls in Rorty's argument, literary culture rises. (Rorty takes the label 'literary culture' from C. P. Snow's well-known *Two Cultures*.) More exactly, literature only seems marginal, frivolous and inexact when contrasted to the putative centrality, seriousness and exactitude of philosophy. Debunking the authority of philosophy accordingly rehabilitates literary culture: the philosopher-king dethroned, the poet-exiles can return to their rightful place at the centre of culture. Rorty consequently champions a 'post-philosophical', 'post-Kantian', 'post-Enlightenment' culture which, 'in an ecstacy of spiritual freedom',[5] would 'take the halo off words like "truth" and "science" and "knowledge" and "reality" rather than offering a view about the nature of the things named by these words';[6] would regard science and philosophy as genres of literature; and would let literature displace 'religion, science, and philosophy as the presiding discipline of our culture'.[7]

In order to explain my uneasiness with this last step in Rorty's argument, I need first to note my dissatisfaction with the opposition between philosophical traditions that informs steps one and two. This opposition seems to me hastily and misleadingly formulated, slanted against the rationalists whom Rorty wants to deconstruct. These philosophers, in Rorty's view, are not only embarked on a deluded quest for a rigorous account of knowledge; they are also 'neurotic',[8] 'reactionary'[9] and 'tedious'.[10] Afraid of disagreement, innovation and independence, they 'cling to' 'all the comforts of consensus' and the security of established disciplines.[11] Completely without literary pretensions,[12] they think of themselves as 'conveying a message which (in more fortunate circumstances) might have been conveyed by ostensive definition or by injecting knowledge straight into the brain'.[13] Impatient with discussion, they hope to arrive at 'true beliefs by obeying mechanical procedures' like 'a properly programmed machine'.[14] Their adversaries, by contrast, are 'more unprofessional, funnier, more allusive, sexier'.[15] As a result, 'the issue', as Rorty raises it, is 'between Socrates on the one hand and the tyrants on the other – the issue between lovers of conversation and lovers of self-deceptive rhetoric'.[16]

This portrait of rationalism seems to me a caricature, designed not to do justice to its victims but to create straw men whom Rorty can easily incinerate. Far from hoping to put an end to conversation – a crucial term in Rorty's thought to which I will return – rationalists wish it to continue. The desire to defend criteria, objectivity and progress in this tradition stems from a fear not that discussion will begin but that it will end by degenerating into a shouting match or power struggle among incommensurable perspectives. Rorty also wants constraints on discourse – to anticipate a point I will be making later – but it is not clear how he can insist on them, given his disdainful, skewed view of rationalism.

Rorty certainly does not find these constraints in literary culture! In describing literary culture, it is as if Rorty were visiting a pre-school playroom rather than overhearing a restrained conversation. Unable to engage in argument, 'operating without rules',[17] adopting a 'relaxed attitude' toward terminology, and refusing to be 'bothered by realist questions such as "Is that what the text really *says*?"',[18] literary intellectuals, as Rorty portrays them, cannot 'agree on what would count as resolving disputes, on the criteria to which all sides must appeal'.[19] In this giddy form of life, 'the true and the good and the beautiful drop out',[20] as norms, leaving critics free to engage in a kind of 'name-dropping, rapid shifting of context, and unwillingness to stay for an answer which . . . runs counter to everything that a professionalized academic discipline stands for'.[21] Similarly, the past provides 'no containing framework, no points of reference'[22] for literary intellectuals, who regard history as a kind of sandbox, full of 'material for playful experimentation'.[23] When change occurs, when a new work of literature or criticism 'succeeds', it does so, Rorty repeatedly emphasizes, '*without* argument':

> It succeeds simply by its success, not because there are good reasons why poems or novels should be written in the new way rather than the old. There is no constant vocabulary in which to describe the values to be defended or objects to be imitated, or the emotions to be expressed, or whatever, in

essays or poems or novels. The reason 'literary criticism' is 'unscientific' is just that whenever somebody tries to work up such a vocabulary he makes a fool of himself.[24]

Instead of trying to expand or satisfy the criteria that hobble analytical philosophy, literary intellectuals, in this view, abandon them.

Rorty cannot decide whether the free-wheeling literary milieu that I have been describing already dominates American culture. He frequently suggests that poets and literary critics are now legislators, despite the ineffectual complaints and absurd pretensions of the scientists and philosophers whom they have ousted from leadership. The hegemony of literary intellectuals apparently dates from the nineteenth century, when, Rorty thinks, 'imaginative literature took the place of both religion and philosophy in forming and solacing the agonized conscience of the young. Novels and poems are now the principal means by which bright youth gain a self-image. Criticism of novels is the principal form in which the acquisition of a moral character is made articulate'.[25] It follows for Rorty that 'the *weakest* way to defend the plausible claim that literature has now displaced religion, science and philosophy as the presiding discipline of our culture is by looking for a philosophical foundation for the practices of contemporary criticism'.[26] When literary critics argue for the philosophical 'seriousness' or 'truth' of their 'discipline', they resemble 'conquering warriors [who] mistakenly think to impress the populace by wrapping themselves in shabby togas stripped from the local senators'.[27] Far from providing the argumentative weapons needed to defend literary study, departments of philosophy are today 'literary' in their disorganization, their failure to settle on a fixed definition of their subject matter, and their inability to justify anything, including their own claims of authority.[28] Literary critics who seek the support of philosophy, in this view, are only being polite to the once proud discipline that they have humbled.

Many professors of literature, disappointed by dwindling enrollments, shrinking job opportunities and stagnant salaries, will be surprised to learn from Rorty that they are conquering heroes, that their depleted classrooms and budgets signal victory over the minds of 'bright youth'. As if anticipating this objection, Rorty elsewhere qualifies his proclamation of literary dominance by suggesting that the triumph of literary culture is not only unlikely but undesirable. Instead of vanquishing traditional philosophy, literary intellectuals, on this somewhat modified view, depend on traditional philosophy as a dialectical foil, in whose absence they would have nothing to say:

In a culture in which the notion of 'hard fact' – the Parmenidean notion of compulsion to truth by reality – had less of a place, the whole genre of 'modernist' writing would make no sense. The notion of 'intertextuality' would have no deliciously naughty thrill. . . . Without the foredoomed struggle of philosophers to invent a form of representation which will constrain us to truth while leaving us free to err, to find pictures where there are only games, there would be nothing to be ironic about. In a culture lacking the contrast between science and poetry [presumably the post-philosophical culture celebrated by Rorty], there would be no poetry about poetry, no writing which was a glorification of writing itself. . . . What is most distinctively modern in modern literature depends for its effect upon straight men, and especially upon philosophers who defend 'common-sense realism' against idealists, pragmatists, structuralists, and all others who impugn the distinction between the scientist and the poet. . . . If the picture picture [sic] is as absurd as I think it, it would be well that this absurdity should not become widely known. For the ironist poet owes far more to Parmenides and the tradition of Western metaphysics than does the scientist. The scientific culture could survive a loss of faith in this tradition, but the literary culture might not.[29]

Because victory over the realist would mean defeat, Rorty here hopes not for the usurpation of philosophy by literature but for endless 'crosstalk' between the two, each gaining a sense of purpose, vitality and strength from maligning the other.

Rorty thus wavers in describing the prospects of literature – in places making poets conquerors, elsewhere picturing them as ironists parasitic upon fortunately invincible philosophical straight men. I think that Rorty's vacillation on this point derives from his initial characterization of literary culture as discourse that lacks rules, a constant vocabulary, respect for history, and argumentative rigour; that fails to terminate in agreement, let alone progress; and that ignores everything an academic discipline stands for. The triumph of such an airy nothing would seem too good to be true, like a court jester replacing a king. When Rorty speaks of an influential literary text, he accordingly cannot explain its success, falling back on the tautology quoted earlier ('it succeeds simply by its success'). Unable to explain the success of a literary work, Rorty understandably does not count on literature succeeding but instead makes its victory over traditional philosophy appear not only improbable but unwelcome.

In either case, whether poets usurp philosophers or heckle a way of thinking that they cannot (and should not want to) dislodge, Rorty, in my view, exaggerates the shapelessness of the literary culture that interests him. Put more positively, though not scientists, literary critics speak a more stable vocabulary and heed firmer rules than Rorty supposes. Instead of resembling the shouting match described by Rorty, literary culture, in short, qualifies as a conversation.

In order to bring out the similarities between literary discourse and conversation, I want first to define 'conversation'. Contrasted to a certain kind of argument – a debate, for example, or a scientific paper – a conversation seems loose in structure. Participants are freer to shift topics and to digress. Similarly, the rules of a conversation – when a person speaks, for instance, and for how long – seem more flexible, generated by the discussion rather than prescribed in advance.[30] Whereas an argument aims at demonstrating a truth, often by discrediting someone else's position, a conversation is an end in itself, an instance of the interaction that it furthers.[31] Accordingly, whereas we aim at clinching or resolving an argument, we try to sustain a conversation. We consequently praise good conversationalists for their liveliness, wit and imagination, for their ability not to end the discussion but to keep it going.[32]

While a conversation may be less confining than an argument, it is nevertheless highly restrained, bound by conventions that are difficult to master (hence the frustration of parents trying to converse with one another in the presence of a talkative 4 year old). Each feature of a conversation – shifting subjects, for example, and taking turns – is governed by procedures that participants have learned (such as 'excuse me'). Similarly, despite their flexibility and open-endedness conversations have a beginning, middle and an end. There are formulas for initiating a conversation ('How are you?'), sustaining it ('This reminds me of . . .'), and ending it ('I'll see you later'). We know when these rules have been broken – when we've been interrupted, say, or lectured. Conversations, then, may not heed the more rigid, external constraints that bind arguments, but they are not for that reason lawless.

In my view, literary discourse counts as a conversation. By 'literary discourse' I mean what Rorty means by 'literature' – everything from individual literary works to literary criticism. By 'conversation' I mean the free-flowing, yet controlled, discussion that I have just described. In defining conversation, I confess that I have had in mind a well-known example of literary discourse – the plays of Shakespeare, as described in Coleridge's famous essay, 'Shakespeare's Judgment Equal to His Genius'. Here Coleridge challenges an inference similar to one made by Rorty. Because Shakespeare defies strict neoclassical guidelines for drama, Coleridge points out, critics have either praised or derided him as a 'wild', 'irregular', 'pure child of nature', 'without taste or judgment, but like the inspired idiots so much venerated in the East, uttering, amid the strangest follies, the sublimest truth'. (Similarly, I will be suggesting that because literary intellectuals break the rules of argument laid down by some philosophers, Rorty concludes that they do *'without* argument.') If this view of Shakespeare's formlessness is false (as Coleridge thinks it is), then 'it is a dangerous falsehood', for it enables a critic to praise Shakespeare 'without assigning any reason, or referring his opinion to any demonstrative principle [cf. Rorty on how literature succeeds because it succeeds]; thus leaving Shakespeare as a sort of grand lama, adored indeed, and his very excrements prized as relics, but with no authority or real influence'.

Coleridge goes on to demonstrate that 'the supposed irregularity and extravagances of Shakespeare [are] the mere dreams of a pedantry that [arraigns] the eagle because it [has] not the dimensions of a swan.'

> Imagine not that I am about to oppose genius to rules. No! . . . The spirit of poetry, like all other living powers, must of necessity circumscribe itself by rules, were it only to unite power with beauty. It must embody in order to reveal itself; but a living body is of necessity an organized one; and what is organization but the connections of parts in and for a whole, so that each part is at once end and means? . . . No work of true genius dares want its appropriate form, neither indeed is there any danger of this. As it must not, so genius cannot, be lawless: for it is even this that constitutes genius – the power of acting creatively under laws of its own origination.[33]

While Shakespeare's plays resist the 'lifeless' rules prescribed in advance by some critics, they are not for that reason disorganized. They are self-organizing.

Coleridge is here exploring the middle ground that Rorty's description of literature vacates. In its fusion of flexibility with restraint, 'living power' with 'appropriate form', Shakespeare's drama is more like a conversation than either a rigidly structured argument on the one hand or a verbal free-for-all on the other. In pointing up this parallel between literature and conversation, I am not trying to rule out other analogies for literature, such as Harold Bloom's family romance model, which shows one form, though not the only form, of textual interaction. I am also not claiming to isolate literature (as conversation) from philosophy (as argument). I would agree that philosophy is like literature, not, however, in dispensing with rules and a stable vocabulary, but in probing their limits, often in dialogues. My point, again, is that literary discourse is closer to conversation than to the chatter described by Rorty.

It might be objected that Rorty means by 'conversation' the free-wheeling discourse that he calls 'literary'. I think, however, that my use of 'conversation' matches his. Rorty is not against constraint; he only opposes the unyielding constraints presumably upheld by the Platonist or Kantian. More positively, he favours 'civility'[34] and 'the Socratic virtues', which he represents as a 'willingness to talk, to listen to other people, to weigh the consequences of our actions upon other people'.[35] Instead of cut-throat competition, he advocates 'human solidarity'[36] within 'a disciplinary matrix for ongoing work which maintains a reasonable balance between "standards" and openness'.[37] Appealing to these standards, he can distinguish 'critics of the tradition like Dewey and Heidegger from the amateur, the philistine, the mystic, or the belletrist'.[38] Finally, in practice,

Rorty takes seriously the 'realist' questions that he claims literary critics have set aside. He proposes, for example, that 'to understand Derrida, one must see his work as the latest development in [a] non-Kantian, dialectical tradition', a conclusion that Rorty supports by scrupulously quoting from Derrida's work. Rorty's point, in short, is that 'there are no constraints, on inquiry *save conversational ones*' [my emphasis[39]] – constraints that he not only defends but in practice tries to heed.

Even if it is conceded that Rorty and I mean much the same thing by 'conversation', a sympathetic reader of his work might still object that I have distorted it, in particular that I have exaggerated the shapelessness that he attributes to literary culture. Perhaps by quoting him out of context, it might be argued I have misread his intention, which is not to question the existence of restraints on literary enquiry but to challenge the effort of rationalists to base these rules in some immutable, supra-institutional realm, whether Plato's world of Being, Aristotle's human nature, or some other transcendental signified. Rorty, in this view, recognizes the necessity, even the desirability, of constraint; he argues, however, that anchoring norms outside of history freezes them and stifles creativity. Rorty thus praises literary critics not for dispensing with rules but for adopting a suitably playful or relaxed attitude towards the rules that they nonetheless follow. 'The real issue', as Rorty himself put it, is accordingly 'between those who think our culture, or purpose, or intuitions cannot be supported except conversationally, and people who still hope for other sorts of support'.[40]

This objection seems to me at odds with itself in so far as it invokes the very constraints – context, for example, and intention – that it wants to minimize. Nevertheless, this objection is important because it tries to bring Rorty's work in line with an important tendency in contemporary literary theory that is best represented by Stanley Fish, who questions not the existence of constraints on interpretation but their authority and who similarly argues that criteria cannot be supported 'except conversationally' – in Fish's terms, except by the 'interpretive community' that happens to enforce them. I cannot here examine all the reasons why Rorty doubts the possibility of 'other sorts of support', but I do want to note that in defending his 'anti-foundationalism', Rorty most often cites the 'bewildering variety' of critical vocabularies, principles and criteria. (At one point he calls them 'as plentiful as blackberries'.[41])

I think that Rorty exaggerates the diversity of these languages, but more importantly, I am not sure whether he can use their alleged instability against their cognitive claims. Elsewhere, as mentioned earlier, he sharply limits what we can say of a text that 'succeeds' – a novel, say, that acquires an apparently lasting place in the canon or a critical interpretation that becomes a standard account of an author or period. According to Rorty, we can only say that such a text succeeds; we cannot say that it succeeds because it is a just representation of general nature (to paraphrase Samuel Johnson on Shakespeare), or in the case of an interpretation, because it sheds light on the text it studies.[42] But if the enduring appeal of a text does not count *for* its truth claims, then I don't see why the merely local appeal of a text should count *against* its truth claims. Rorty cannot coherently argue that permanence is inconsequential but instability matters: instability matters only if permanence does. Both stability and instability would seem to be irrelevant to the foundationalist pretensions that Rorty wants to deflate.

Whether literary intellectuals, in Rorty's view, abandon rules or simply refuse to worry about them, Rorty's definition of literary discourse is fundamentally negative, generated by the philosophical tradition that he wants to subvert. As noted earlier, Rorty pictures literary culture as a 'deliciously naughty' and, I would add, a relatively cheap 'thrill' that sets aside everything that analytical philosophy vainly, though earnestly, seeks. But literature appears without constraints to Rorty only because it fails to heed the absolute constraints presumably valued by the Platonist. Although Rorty criticizes Platonism, his own view of literature thus perpetuates what he sees as the Platonist's all-or-nothing outlook. Rorty, to be sure, departs from Platonism when he reduces philosophy to literature, but he agrees with this tradition that literature lacks philosophical rigour, as both he and the Platonist define 'rigour'.

Despite Rorty's considerable interest in literature, he thus still allows philosophy to decide its fate. Even when literature succeeds in Rorty's argument – when it presides in triumph over the rest of our culture – literature does not win; philosophy defaults. Literature is less a force in Rorty's argument than an inert category, represented by a list of titles and names that Rorty's theory gives him no reason to analyse.[43] Instead of doing constructive work in Rorty's writings, literature, like a junk yard, just sits there, waiting to claim philosophical texts that cannot achieve what they set out to accomplish. Rorty's point, in short, is not that literature is cognitive, serious, powerful and responsible, but that philosophy (without admitting it) is like literature: imprecise, capricious and methodologically dishevelled. Instead of strengthening literature, Rorty leaves it impotent, which is why, among the consequences of Rorty's pragmatism, I do not find a convincing rationale for literary study.[44]

NOTES

Michael Fischer's 'Redefining Philosophy as Literature' first appeared in *Soundings*, 67 (1984). It is reprinted here by permission of the author.

1 I will be concentrating on *Consequences of Pragmatism* (University of Minnesota Press, Minneapolis, 1982) (hereafter, *CP*) and *Philosophy and the Mirror of Nature* (Princeton University Press, Princeton, 1979) (hereafter, *PMN*).

2 *CP*, p. xxi.

3 *CP*, p. 148.

4 *CP*, p. xix.

5 *CP*, p. 149.

6 *CP*, p. 160.

7 *CP*, p. 155.

8 *CP*, p. 161.

9 *CP*, p. 161.

10 *CP*, p. 107.

11 *CP*, pp. 152, 165.

12 *CP*, p. 103.

13 *CP*, p. 96.

14 *CP*, p. 166.

15 *CP*, p. 93.

16 *CP*, p. 169.

17 *CP*, p. 143.

18 *CP*, p. 154.

19 *CP*, p. xli.

20 *CP*, p. 66.

21 *CP*, p. 65.

22 *CP*, p. 67.

23 *CP*, p. 87. In 'Rorty's Cultural Conversation', *Raritan Review*, 3 (Summer, 1983), Frank Lentricchia astutely suggests that the hedonistic values of Rorty's 'ungrounded cultural conversation have been decisively co-opted by late capitalist economy' (p. 139). Along similar lines, Gerald Graff has analysed comparable tendencies in contemporary literary theory in *Literature Against Itself* (University of Chicago Press, Chicago, 1979).

24 *CP*, p. 142. Or he writes a book like the *Anatomy of Criticism*, Northrop Frye's attempt to arrive at a 'constant vocabulary' for literary criticism. Echoing Coleridge's fear that tributes to the 'irregularity' of literature jeopardize its 'real influence', Frye warns, 'if a critic cannot name his tools, the world is unlikely to concede much authority to his craft. We should not entrust out cars to a mechanic who lived entirely in a world of gadgets and doohickeys' (*Anatomy of Criticism*, Princeton University Press, Princeton, 1957, p. 358). In keeping with the anaology between literary discourse and conversation that I try to make below, I will not claim that Frye has succeeded in labelling once and for all the tools of the critic's trade. But I also will not say that he has made a fool of himself. Frye has made an indispensable contribution to a discussion that continues.

25 *CP*, p. 66. A similar statement occurs in *PMN*, where Rorty notes that 'by the early twentieth century the scientists had become as remote from most intellectuals as had the theologians. Poets and novelists had taken the place of both preachers and philosophers as the moral teachers of the youth' (p. 5). See also *CP*, p. 68, where Rorty registers his agreement with Harold Bloom's comment that 'the teacher of literature now in America, far more than the teacher of history or philosophy or religion, is condemned to teach the presentness of the past because history, philosophy and religion have withdrawn as agents from the Scene of Instruction'.

26 *CP*, p. 155.

27 *CP*, p. 156.

28 *CP*, pp. 217–18.

29 *CP*, pp. 136–7.

30 On the importance of improvisation to conversation (and to art) see Stanley Cavell, *Pursuits of Happiness* (Harvard University Press, Cambridge, Mass., 1981). Cavell devotes his Introduction ('Words for a Conversation') to exploring conversation as a shared concern of philosophy, criticism and film (here, seven Hollywood comedies of the thirties and forties). The films Cavell studies in this book require 'the portrayal of philosophical conversation', one indication for him that 'film exists in a state of philosophy' and 'philosophy is to be understood, however else, aesthetically' (pp. 13–14). But for Cavell 'aesthetically' does not mean casually or loosely: he wishes that our conversations about film (among which he includes his own book) will be 'as precise and resourceful' as the works of art we discuss (p. 39).

31 I hasten to add that we nevertheless can learn something in a conversation. Instruction is one product of a good conversation, though not the only one.

32 For further discussion of the differences between conversation and argument – and the metaphors used in describing each term – see George Lakoff and Mark Johnson, *Metaphors We Live By* (University of Chicago Press, Chicago, 1980), pp. 77–81.

33 Samuel Taylor Coleridge, 'Shakespeare's Judgment Equal to His Genius', in *Critical Theory Since Plato*, ed. Hazard Adams (Harcourt Brace Jovanovich, New York, 1971), pp. 460–2.

34 *CP*, p. 202.

35 *CP*, p. 172.

36 *CP*, p. 207.

37 *CP*, p. 218.

38 *CP*, p. 41.

39 *CP*, p. 165.

40 *CP*, p. 167.

41 *CP*, p. 169.

42 Along similar lines, Rorty says of science, 'The most frequently cited datum is that science *works*, *succeeds* – enables us to cure diseases, blow up cities, and the like. How, realists ask, would this be possible if some statements did not correspond to the way things are in themselves? How, pragmatists rejoin, does *that* count as an explanation?' (*CP*, p. xxiv). It seems to me that Rorty, like Fish, fails to provide a more convincing account of success than the cognitive explanation that he wants to reject. On Fish, see my *Does Deconstruction Make Any Difference?* (Bloomington: Indiana University Press, 1985), ch. 3.

43 I would contrast Rorty here to Stanley Cavell, another philosopher interested in contesting the boundaries between literature and philosophy. Unlike Rorty, Cavell does not simply cite literary texts; he analyses them, using them to expand or revise philosophy, not to illustrate its conclusions. I derive Cavell's willingness, even eagerness, to discuss literature from his respect for its cognitive seriousness. See, for example, Cavell's *The Senses of Walden* (1972; rpt. North Point Press, San Francisco, 1981) and 'The Avoidance of Love: A Reading of *King Lear*', *Must We Mean What We Say?* (1969; rpt. Cambridge University Press, Cambridge, 1976), pp. 267–353.

44 Hence my disagreement with Jonathan Culler's more optimistic reading of Rorty's work in *On Deconstruction* (Cornell University Press, Ithaca, 1982).

15

The Poetics of Personhood

Martin Hollis

The troubled history of the self – or of our present ideas of the self – goes back at least to Ancient Greece and the emergence of the city-state. Sophocles' *Antigone* shows Antigone and Creon caught between duty to the family and duty to the state. Having nowhere to stand outside the conflict, they are destroyed by it. The Chorus reflect that 'there are many strange things and none is stranger than man', the word for 'strange' being *deinon* – awesome, mysterious, out of place, anomalous. Man is indeed *deinon* in an order of nature where everything has its proper function and flourishes through its exercise and yet where the human function includes performance of irreconcilable duties. Is the anomaly peculiar to some ways of thinking about persons or is it timeless? Hegel held that the conflict was one in the reality of the ethical life of Ancient Greece and beyond the resources of that view of the world, although within the power of a Hegelian scheme. No timeless flash of mental ingenuity could have resolved it, because concepts have a history in the development of social forms which embody them. But later ethical life has a different reality, where the old anomaly can be resolved.

Hegel's reckoning is nicely balanced between, so to speak, reason and history. On the one hand, the concept of the self and, presumably, the self emerge as history permits. On the other, reason discerns the reality of the ethical life, even if only from its current perspective. This strikes just the right starting note for an essay on Rorty's view of personhood. *Philosophy and the Mirror of Nature*, in the main, dismisses any substantive notion of the self as an aberration due to place and period.[1] But there are signs that this is not the end of the matter and later writings, I shall argue, depend on

I would like to thank Tim O'Hagan for his guidance on Hegel, and also Alan Malachowski and Angus Ross for their helpful comments on an earlier draft of this essay.

there being more for reason to say. The nub will be that Rorty needs a careful and constructive account of 'self-creation', if his references to 'the conversation of mankind' and to the need for community are to carry conviction, and that the account cannot be given in the behaviourist vein which he favours. One consequence of his pragmatism will thus be to cut himself off from the fellowship of 'poets', as he terms those who speak of personhood in suitably metaphorical tones.

The recent history of the self dates from the Scientific Revolution, which took the animation out of nature. If things in nature are propelled by forces within a mechanical system of causes and effects, man becomes anomalous in a way foreign to the Greeks. If, meanwhile, the Renaissance and the Reformation have inspired a conception of human beings as individuals distinct from social roles and endowed with individual free will, the anomaly becomes acute. Descartes, seeing this with the gaze of an unclouded mind in search of truth, distinguished clearly and distinctly between mental and physical realms of being. He then posed and answered the Cartesian questions: what substance am I? What is the essence of this substance? How do I relate to my body?

The answers yielded a view of 'our glassy essence' – Rorty's witty tag for the ego of *cogito ergo sum* and *sum res cogitans* and for its alleged transparency. The *Mirror of Nature* opens with a celebrated assault on the Cartesian answers through an undermining of the Cartesian questions. There is no substance which I am, Rorty says, because there are no substances. I have no glassy essence, because there are no essences and, in particular, no definitive marks of the mental. Nothing whatever is 'glassy' in the sense of clear and distinct to an inward eye. There are no boundaries of a Cartesian sort and so none between the mental and the physical. There is no such thing as First Philosophy; in short, nothing for Descartes to liken to a tree whose roots are metaphysics, whose trunk is physics and whose three main branches are medicine, mechanics and morals. Knowledge is not the mental contemplation of substance and essence. Instead, it is a shifting, precariously consensual activity within communities in their place and time. Traditional philosophy has been a ghostly mistake.

By smashing the mirror Rorty hoped to reset the philosophical agenda on pragmatist lines unhampered by the demands of the old Search after Truth. He declared for 'the Contingency of Selfhood', the title of his 1986 article setting out 'the quarrel between poetry and philosophy, the tension between an effort to achieve self-creation by the recognition of contingency and an effort to achieve universality by the transcendence of contingency'.[2] Philosophy, represented there by Rorty's pet villains, Plato, Descartes and Kant, seeks eternal truths by self-effacing contemplation. Poetry deals not in truth but in metaphor and shows us ourselves as ineliminable creators of metaphors. In all he says about personhood,

Rorty is squarely on the side of the poets.

Although his 'philosophers' have a certain unity in their claim that Reason can reveal what is universal in the human condition, his 'poets' are a motley band, united chiefly by their opposition. They include Hegel (yet *Geist* surely embodies Reason?), Nietzsche, Freud, Heidegger and Wittgenstein, and hence some very varied refusals to transcend contingency. Thought cannot transcend its historical context; its springs lie in the unconscious mind; its proclamations are always metaphorical; its claims to truth are merely commitments to believe; its certainties are those of shared discourse; its guarantees are those of habitual social practice. Rorty speaks as if there were a thematic unity here, so that 'contingency' has a single sense. But this is at least unobvious. Try asking whether, poetically speaking, our glassy essence is an essence but not glassy, as with Freud, or glassy but not an essence, as with exitentialists, or neither, as with those who externalize the inwardness of personal knowledge. Try asking whether self-creation is a terminus to be reached or a process whose meaning and conduct is *en-soi* and *pour-soi*. One seems to find the sort of diversity, which Rorty recognizes himself in a note titled 'Postmodernist Bourgeois Liberalism', where he groups for approval pragmatists, realists, Hegelians and others.[3] To every poet there is, I venture to suggest, an opposite poet.

In that case Rorty owes us his own account of self-creation. He cannot refuse on the ground that to dissolve Descartes' presumptions is to scotch all questions about the nature of man. On the contrary, if self-creation is to be an activity in which we (communally) create our world and our understanding of it, then there is still every need for a First Philosophy, although one unlike the traditional offerings and constructed in the first person plural. The interest of Rorty's work depends on it, and, indeed, he has at least the makings of one. But they are there only in diffused and teasing form, and I shall next try to extract them.

The remarks on the self, or personhood, in the *Mirror of Nature* are largely destructive, being designed to shatter 'our glassy essence'. But his epistemological behaviourism is not altogether aimed at cashing out talk of a mental realm extensionally. Nor could it be, given the work assigned to 'the conversation of mankind' in keeping our shared world in place and moving. All the same, there are only hints about how to make an honest concept of personhood. On page 35 Rorty lists nine 'marks of the mental', which traditional philosophers have relied on, to distinguish man from other strange things. They include 'ability to act freely', 'ability to form part of our social group, to be "one of us"' and 'inability to be identified with any object "in the world"'. These three marks are described as 'items bearing on personhood' on page 37, where he promises that three later sections of the book will 'sketch the way in which I think the notion of personhood should be treated'.

'Sketch' is the operative word. The first section (IV.4) is headed 'The "'Idea' Idea"' and deploys these nested scare quotes in seeing off the idea that language is the expression of something '"inner"'. Although personhood is not mentioned, the section presumably debunks some familiar notions of it inspired by our Cartesian ways of talking about ourselves. The second (VII.4) is on 'Spirit and Nature' and contends that discussion of the *Geistes-* und *Naturwissenschaften* has been bedevilled by a lurking metaphysical assumption that, although the empirical self can be turned over to the latter, the transcendental self cannot. Once this assumption is discarded, hermeneutics can guide us in coping with as-yet-incommensurable discourses without our needing to suppose that persons are peculiar among the strange things in alien discourses which we seek to understand. The third (VIII.3), on 'Edification, Relativism and Objective Truth', urges that there is nothing final to say about the self, not even that it is an *être-pour-soi*. All that we, or any philosophy without mirrors, can do is 'to keep the conversation going', thus 'preventing man from deluding himself with the notion that he knows himself, or anything else, except under an optional description'. The three sections together discharge Rorty's promise, made on page 38, to let us see personhood for 'what I claim it is – a matter of decision rather than knowledge, an acceptance of another being into fellowship rather than a recognition of a common essence'.

Although the tenor is dismissive, there is a constructive purpose. The 'I' of *cogito* is being replaced with a 'we' of conversation, and the Cartesian mind's passive openness to universal truth is being replaced with the communal activity which results in shared belief and fellowship. This constructive theme is important because, without it, the book would be in hopeless contradictions. On the one hand, old claims to knowledge of nature or, in Platonic spirit, supernature, would be traced to the optional decisions of persons who had social authority to make them. On the other hand, on a flatly behaviourist reading, these and other decisions would not be optional but merely the customary practice of a group of persons at some place and time. The central pragmatist or 'poetic' insight that the (collective) mind is *active* in the creation of what passes for knowledge would be lost, and experience, behaviourally construed, would become the sort of inert object of experience which Rorty complains that traditional philosophers make it when treating it as a mental object. In this contradiction, poets would be left as directionless as philosophers.

To put it poetically, the web of belief needs its active spinners. It will simply be beyond our ken, unless we know it through making and remaking it. 'We' may be communal and contingent, in contrast to the individual, timeless universal ego, but 'we' is not just a dummy pronoun, and the descriptions under which we know ourselves and our creative activity are not just optional. I am confident enough that this has to be the theme not to labour the point. Since a complete demolition of 'the mental' would block all self-creation, the book needs to replace rigid categories with fluid metaphors, so that poets can converse their way forward. All the same the *Mirror of Nature* leaves two plain obstacles to progress in the conversation of mankind. Although Rorty may regard them as a misplaced residue of traditional philosophy, I shall declare them now and insist on them later.

The first is that Rorty's epistemological behaviourism is very robustly stated. The authorities cited are Quine and Wittgenstein, and the rationale is that in understanding people's behaviour we can know all there is to know about them (or us). This gives the message some ambiguity, since Quine is always definite about the need for interpretation in understanding and Wittgenstein is notably unmechanical in his notions of rule-following. So there will be scope for manoeuvre, if it becomes vital that the spinners of the web are *active*. Meanwhile, however, Rorty's behaviourism is not presented in this spirit and later texts, which I shall come to, describe the spinning in the passive voice. So there is an incipient query about what self-creation can possibly mean for an epistemological behaviourist.

Second, there is no mistaking a relativism in Rorty's undermining of the search after truth. Any simple view that thought is the prisoner of context implies, even delights in, the relativity of reason, and the book does not try to avoid being simple in this regard. This gives a consistent line, if a general scepticism about truth is intended. But Rorty plainly puts trust in 'the conversation of mankind' and, we shall find, wishes to distinguish between better and worse communities. Yet the conversation of mankind is composed of many conversations, each governed by internal criteria of sense and, metaphorically speaking, truth. Rorty seems willing to internalize all criteria, moral and alethic, to separate discourses. As soon as he wants some criterion of effective self-creation, therefore, there will be an awkward question about the limits of the relativity which he recommends.

So Rorty's dismissive remarks about the self need to be nicely judged. He cannot deal with it as in the chapter on snakes in the medieaval book on Iceland, whose chapter 21 in its entirety says that there are no snakes in Iceland. There is work for the self to do, witness his (1983) 'Postmodernist Bourgeois Liberalism'. He contends there that some societies are more morally responsible than others but adds that responsibility is a matter of being loyal to the society's own traditions and not to 'the moral law itself'. The traditions define the self – a view in contrast to Kant's or, more recently, Rawlss' hopes (in *A Theory of Justice*, although since modified) of identifying moral choice with rational choice on the part of an abstract and universal individual.[4] Hence the crux is 'to think of the moral self, the embodiment of rationality, not as one of Rawls' original choosers, somebody who can distinguish her *self* from her talents and interests and views about the good but as a network of beliefs, desires and emotions with nothing behind it – no substrate behind the attributes'.[5] There is thus a moral self. It is introduced with a destructive swipe at 'substrates' but it is there. Yet it is a 'network'. How can a network be morally responsible for a network? The next sentences only increase curiosity:

> For purposes of moral and political deliberation and conversation, a person just *is* that network, as for purposes of balistics she is a point-mass, or for purposes of chemistry a linkage of molecules. She is a network that is constantly reweaving itself in the usual Quinean manner – that is to say not by reference to general criteria (e.g. 'rules of meaning' or 'moral principles') but in the hit-or-miss way in which cells readjust themselves to meet the pressure of the environment.

Since Rorty reasserts the view that a person is 'a network that is constantly reweaving itself',[6] I take him to mean it. If so, the next question is indeed how a network, which passively adjusts to its environment, can be held morally responsible. Rorty answers by invoking 'community':

> On a Quinean view, rational behavior is just adaptive behavior of a sort which roughly parallels the behavior, in similar circumstances, of the other members of some relevant community. Irrationality, in both physics and ethics, is a matter of behavior that leads one to abandon, or be stripped of, membership in some such community.

What, then, does ethics say about communities? Rorty maintains next that there are better and worse communities, as distinguished by the self-images which they adopt by contrast to those of their neighbours. Nations, churches or movements, he says, have a collective dignity and moral justification which is 'mostly a matter of historical narratives . . . rather than of philosophical metanarratives'. Persons take their individual human dignity from their place in a dignified community.

This strikes me as a case of someone painting himself into a corner. Having said that communities cannot be judged against 'the moral law itself' (presumably part of a mere 'philosophical metanarrative'), he leaves only the test of whether they have stable, adaptive practices. By that test there is a 'moral justification' for the many viable societies which have practised slavery, subordination of ethnic groups, suppression of dissenters, the subjection of women and other illiberalities. Conversely, open societies seem to me only too likely to be fragile and to slip into authoritarian ways. Rorty tries suggesting that liberal values are a special source of adaptability because the arts 'serve to develop and modify a group's self-image by, for example, apotheosizing its heroes, diabolizing its enemies, mounting dialogues among its members, and refocusing its attention'.[7] But the making of gods and devils with the aid of the arts is an old habit of closed societies; and dialogues do not promote openness, unless focused and managed with that purpose in mind. In upshot, then, 'moral justification' turns out to be what Thrasymachos said it was in the *Republic* – the 'right' of those with power.

Rorty gets into this corner (granted that it is one) by dropping the individualist Kantian and Rawlsian tests of the proper distribution and exercise of power without offering any communitarian ones. By equating individualism with a belief in a 'substrate behind the attributes' and by ruling out access to universal moral propositions as a baseless philosophical metanarrative, he leaves himself little to work with. He might perhaps have tried to lay down guidelines for the proper conduct of that communal institution 'the conversation of mankind'. But, apparently unconcerned, he is content to internalize conversation to itself. 'We are not conversing because we have a goal but because Socratic conversation is its *own* goal' (original emphasis).[8]

Yet this notion of Socratic, or almost any, conversation is, by itself, absurd. At diplomatic cocktail parties one perhaps passes the platitudes for the sake of passing them; and encounter groups may possibly have the encounter as their goal. But, if 'Socratic' has anything to do with Socrates, the goal is wisdom. It may be a goal needing a sinuous pursuit, with some benefits of the hunt immanent in the hunt itself. But without the goal the activity is unintelligible. Rorty might consider conceding this much, I think, if he could then count on Habermas and others to specify conditions of ideal speech, where whatever emerges from the conversation is thereby as close to wisdom as we can come. Or he might maintain that Socratic conversation indeed has a goal external to its first order discourse, although one necessarily internal to its own meta-narrative. But, having classed Plato firmly among the enemy and declared wisdom an illusion, he cannot allow an objective truth to emerge even under ideal conditions; and having condemned all metanarratives, he cannot join the interpreters who find hermeneutic virtue in Plato's one. Yet, in sawing off the branches on which philosophers have sat, Rorty needs to leave himself somewhere to perch.

His reflections on personhood therefore cannot be merely negative, if 'contingency' is to stop short of a self-destructive relativism. Otherwise, by allying the poets' 'recognition of contingency' with what is local, mutable and fortuitous, he will make it impossible to speak of better and worse communities. How, then, shall one talk about personhood in a historically rooted way which allows the judging of communities? Anyone wanting an individualist answer might try Bernard Williams's distinction between 'thick' and 'thin' concepts in *Ethics and the Limits of Philosophy*.[9] Thin concepts are those, like 'good', 'right' and 'just', which belong to the philosophers' pursuit of universal and abstract truth. Thick concepts are those, like 'brutal', 'barbarous' and 'cruel', which are close enough to flesh-and-blood life to be descriptive and yet carry a moral charge. If Attila the Hun and Vlad the Impaler truly behaved as legend says, then the former was brutal and the latter cruel. This is not a matter of what counted as brutal and cruel either at the time or among those who now describe it so. Yet the moral charge is not a matter of invoking abstractions like wickedness or injustice. The task of describing and judging falls to poetic elaboration of the indifference to suffering or the pleasure taken in inflicting it. For a persuasive example, consider Amnesty reports on torture. They convey information which can be filed as statistics and which, at the same time, must be understood as evidence of the warping of our common humanity.

The implicit appeal of 'thick' concepts to a notion of personhood involves a contingency – or, if you prefer, a flesh-and-blood universality – which is not relativistic. Communities can perhaps then be ranked by how widely concepts like 'brutal', 'barbarous' and 'cruel' apply to the behaviour of their members. The snag from Rorty's point of view, however, is that the suggestion does not divide philosophers from poets. It is, rather, the old philosophical attempt to bring Plato down to earth by administering a measured dose of Aristotle, or to anchor Kant by reasserting Hume on human nature. It yields an ethics grounded in the virtues instead of in abstract principles. In this long-running quarrel about ethical motivation both parties are philosophers, and both stick to Reason through thick and thin.

Rorty's best hope of avoiding all attempts at 'the transcendence of contingency' therefore seems to me to lie in his idea that a person is 'one of us'. To be 'one of us' is not to display some universal mark of personhood but to have been 'accepted into fellowship'. Not to be 'one of us' is merely to have been 'stripped of membership' of some relevant community.

This is deliberately open-ended. For instance, koalas in pain 'writhe in quite the right way', whereas 'the pig's face is the wrong shape for the facial expressions which go with ordinary conversation. So we send pigs to the slaughter with equanimity, but form societies for the protection of koalas. This is not irrational anymore than it is irrational to extend or deny civil rights to the moronic (or foetuses, or aboriginal tribes, or martians)'.[10] Although these are described as 'borderline cases', apparently suggesting an objective area within the disputable border, Rorty means the area within the border too to be decided rather than discovered. Fellowship is thus a thoroughly culture-relative affair, the province of anthropologists, poets (and zoologists?) without scope for universal judgements by philosophers. That pigs' faces are the wrong shape is a fact as much about us. Indeed, nothing in Rorty makes it inconceivable to follow Bunthorne's advice from *Patience* to have 'a conversation *à la* Plato with a bashful young potato or a not too French French bean'. No theoretical limits are set for personhood.

What prevents the discussion merely disintegrating at this point is Rorty's faith in a connection between personhood and conversation. Chats with koalas are pretty one-sided and chats with French beans hopelessly so. That is how there can be borderline cases. So it looks as if we can use this connection to introduce an idea of progressive fellowship. One promising effect of conversation might be to widen the franchise of fellowship by making those of other sexes, races, religions and cultures 'one of us' too. Then perhaps self-creation can result from the expanding of the conversational community.

An obvious snag, however, is that communities gain and retain their identity by exclusion as much as by inclusion. In-groups define themselves against out-groups, whose existence they therefore need and may even fabricate. I see no reason to suppose that 'conversation' is, in itself, a countervailing force. It takes a special sort of conversation to encourage a broadening franchise, one with rules of discourse which have this effect. Otherwise why will Romans talk themselves into fellowship with barbarians, Jews with gentiles, gentiles with Jews, rich with poor, white with brown with black with white? Rorty seems to hope that they naturally will, but I cannot see why talk in itself tends to blur human difference, unless it has rules of discourse which emphasize human sameness, suitably enforced. Socratic or liberal rules work in this way. They are discreetly enforced, with the (disputable) warrant that they govern the process without prejudice to its results. But they embody a definite idea of Reason, of its advantages for civilized living and of the criteria for including someone (anyone) in the fellowship of rational persons. In brief they squarely conflict with Rorty's contention that personhood is 'a matter of decision rather than knowledge, an acceptance of another being into fellowship rather than a common essence'.[11] The fellowship needed for a broadening franchise is precisely one of beings who recognize a common essential sameness in others.

Rorty will not like having his poets thus restored to the bosom of philosophers conversing about reason, truth and wisdom. But they are not thereby reduced to humble silence, as there is still the vital notion of self-creation to discuss. Philosophers have traditionally been better at disciplining the mind than at understanding its *activity* in creating knowledge. There are two parts to the idea of activity. One is the replacement of mirrors with webs of belief or, less poetically, observation with interpretation, and, in general, the pragmatist consequences of the underdetermination of theory by experience. I shall not try to tackle this aspect of the current conversation of philosophers. The other is the need for active spinners of the web, or, indeed, for an active mind even in a traditional epistemology which strives to end in self-effacement. This need is perhaps plainer for the moral questions raised by the idea of being 'one of us' but it is there across the board and 'poets' can be expected to illuminate it.

That brings us back to Rorty's behaviourism, however, and to his unrelentingly passive images of persons. I would dearly like to shake him in his 'Non-Reductive Physicalism', the title of his 1987 paper in praise of Davidson. There he allies himself with Davidson and claims that objections to physicalism arise only because physicalists are carelessly prone to reductionism. If they would only behave themselves on this score, however, they would have a wholly defensible view that 'what an individual identifies as "himself" or "herself" is, for the most part, his or her beliefs and desires, rather than the organs, cells and particles which compose his or her body. Those beliefs and desires are, to be sure, physiological states under another description'.[12] The paper then restates Rorty's old theme that a person is a network which reweaves itself, as opposed to being rewoven by an agent distinct from it, like 'a master weaver so to speak'. Poets understand this best, because it has the 'truth' of a metaphor which has proved successful and does not aspire to 'truth' in the philosophers' chimerical sense.

Rorty admits that his view is 'hard to reconcile with common sense, according to which the "I" is distinct from its beliefs and desires, picks and chooses among them, etc.' He is clearly right about that. The master weaver is a well-entrenched metaphor for self-consciousness. Why exactly does Rorty regard it as a failed metaphor? I can find no good answer. The idea of an 'I' distinct from its beliefs and desires remains alive for the obvious reason that it makes apparent sense of how we experience the world, our place in it and its other inhabitants. Moreover, it is an obvious idea to turn to in explaining why even knowledge of nature cannot be the passive receipt of information. In other words it seems to me an idea which Rorty himself plainly needs. I can see why he may want to replace 'I' by 'we', but this does not affect his replacement of passive by active and self-discovery by self-creation. Common speech seems very helpful to him, and many of those whom Rorty would surely classify as poets have certainly endorsed its active forms.[13]

Futhermore, his judgement that we are dealing with a metaphor which has failed, can only belong in a discourse about the true nature of apparently creative activity. For instance, the 1987 article draws a picture (literally!) of the human condition, showing an outline individual connected to 'the body's environment' by a single two-way causal arrow. This individual, labelled 'the human body', contains only a network of neural states connected causally (one-way) to 'other physiological states'. The picture must be meant as a representation; but of what? Presumably it represents the facts about self and world under another description, a physiological and physical one. Given the title of the article ('Non-Reductive Physicalism') and what Rorty says about the optional character of descriptions, we are free to complain that the diagram is so impoverished that it cannot represent what the rich texture of poetry represents. Rorty will have to reply that the diagram contains all the ingredients of self-creation – a reply belonging to the traditional philosophical discourse of behaviourism.

Here we reach an impasse. Hermeneutic creativity by active self-interpreters will not combine with a passive physicalism. Moreover, the physicalism is too impoverished a poetic metaphor to be defended, except as a philosophical truth. Something must give. My own inclination is to return to Rorty's opening attack on the Cartesian ego and to separate the charge that the ego is too passive from the charge that it is too individual and isolated. The latter charge seems to me well directed, the former not. When Descartes' method of doubt has arrived at a clear and distinct area, then the knowing mind can fairly be compared to a mirror but only if one notes that mirroring is an activity. Kepler described science as 'thinking God's thoughts after Him' and that well catches a key element in Cartesian notions of intuition and reason. Cartesian understanding calls for an attentive and unclouded mind; but it involves thinking and interpretation. The aim is to direct the will aright, not to suppress it altogether. This mental activity differs from the kind of activity which pragmatism assigns to the mind in working an optional order into the flux of experience. But then thinking God's thoughts is a process of discovery, with no suggestion that truth is a metaphor. By pursuing the theme it should be possible to resurrect many traditional ideas under Rorty's very nose.

But that will do nothing about the solipsism threatening an ego which, even if glassy to itself, is opaque to others. Rorty's suggestion is that the self is somehow communal and that personhood is to be approached through a notion of community. How? The question invites a political answer, one denying both that a community is the sum of its individual atoms and that individuals are the creature of their community. We are thus led to the core paradox in Rousseau and the 'remarkable change in man' which his social contract brings. The contract is addressed to 'men as they are and laws as they might be'; yet it transmutes them into citizens among whom a General Will can emerge to govern their lives, while leaving each as free as before. By giving himself over entirely, man is

changed from 'a narrow stupid animal', guided by instinct, physical
impulse, desire and concern for himself alone, into a 'creature of
intelligence', guided by duty, justice, right and concern for others.
Natural liberty to grab what one can becomes civil liberty, bounded by the
General Will and legal titles to property. Slavery yields to the moral
freedom of obedience to laws we have prescribed to ourselves. If Rousseau
can walk the thin line of this paradox, perhaps Rorty can follow him in
distinguishing better from worse communities.

Rousseau's recipe makes for a society with a high risk of tyranny, if the
laws are not a true expression of the General Will, and of suffocation, if the
citizen loses all individuality in the body politic. His safeguards are
sketchy – some kind of ideal speech situation to prevent 'factions' and the
divorce of private and public will, ensured perhaps by a reasonable
equality of wealth and hence of power. But, grant him a liberal reading so
that in a community marked by a General Will people are independent of
the personal will of others without losing their individuality, and we have a
possible line on communal self-creation. The test of better or worse
communities can then be whether social relationships make for self-
expression or suffocate it.

I invoke Rousseau not to wish his solution on Rorty but for the creative
tension which he discerns among the notions of community, self and
positive freedom. The freedom of the self lies in obedience to laws which
we prescribe to ourselves. This delicate equipoise can be realized in only
some historical conditions. For, although all communities insist on some
loyalties and convictions, they differ in which, and not all permit
self-expression. The problem, then, is to identify both the equipoise and
the conditions for it. This statement of it contrasts with Rorty's remark
that the moral force of loyalties and convictions depends wholly on
whether the beliefs, desires and emotions, which buttress them, are widely
shared.[14] Rousseau was very aware that beliefs, desires and emotions can
be engineered and hence that their mere popularity is not enough. Rorty
needs to say the same, I think, but cannot, because he has left himself
nothing further to identify the loyalties and convictions with moral force.

Here it is interesting to find Hegel on Rorty's approved list of 'poets'.[15]
I began with Hegel's comment on the *Antigone* that the conflict between
civic and family duty was an objective fact about the reality of ethical life
at that time but which later forms of society could resolve. This implies a
test for ethical progress and a possibility of passing universal judgement on
the contingencies of self-creation. But when Hegel is not a 'poet' *in contrast
to* a 'philosopher'. Indeed, the same can be said of all Rorty's poets except
perhaps Nietzsche and, conversely, there is hermeneutic awareness in
Plato, Descartes and Kant, his most villainous philosophers. The terms of

'the quarrel between poetry and philosophy', as originally stated in the *Mirror of Nature* seem to me to create contrasts which Rorty might now wish to abandon.

I conclude, then, that Rorty does indeed paint himself into a corner. The poets' 'effort to achieve self-creation by the recognition of contingency' will fail without active spinners of the web and will end in tyranny or suffocation without rules to direct the communal conversation of mankind aright. His epistemological behaviourism and his relativism close the way to the promised hermeneutics. Yet Rorty's work is thoroughly revealing about the bronze age of Reason. He makes us see exactly why the golden age of systematic epistemology, with its confident universality, yielded to a silver age, where the view of the world could only be from somewhere within it. But even in a bronze postmodern age, Reason must not give up altogether. Personhood cannot be a matter of decision *rather than* knowledge nor an acceptance of another being into fellowship *rather than* a recognition of a common essence. The idea of self-creation leads into ethics and politics and thus extends the search after truth.

NOTES

1 Richard Rorty, *Philosophy and the Mirror of Nature* (Princeton University Press, Princeton, 1979).
2 Richard Rorty, 'The Contingency of Selfhood', *London Review of Books*, 8 May 1986, pp. 11–15.
3 Richard Rorty, 'Postmodernist Bourgeois Liberalism', *Journal of Philosophy*, 80/10 (1983), pp. 583–9.
4 J. Rawls, *A Theory of Justice* (Harvard University Press, Cambridge, Mass., 1971).
5 Rorty, 'Postmodernist', pp. 585f.
6 Richard Rorty, 'Non-reductive Physicalism', in *Theorie der Subjektivität*, ed. K. Cramer (Suhrkamp, Frankfurt, 1987).
7 Rorty, 'Postmodernist', p. 587.
8 Richard Rorty, *Consequences of Pragmatism* (University of Minnesota Press, Minneapolis, 1982), p. 172.
9 Bernard Williams, *Ethics and the Limits of Philosophy* (Fontana, London, 1985).
10 Rorty, *Mirror of Nature*, p. 190.
11 Ibid., p. 38.
12 Rorty, 'Non-reductive Physicalism', p. 291.
13 It will be seen that I am treating adaptability as insufficient for activity, and a network which reweaves itself without a master as something complex but passive. There is no space here for the further argument needed to make the point stick. Whether activity is or is not a sufficient degree of complex adaptability is, I suspect, one of those litmus tests which divide philosophers almost beyond final argument. But I have tried to reason the case in *Models of Man* (Cambridge University Press, Cambridge, 1987) and *The Cunning of Reason* (Cambridge University Press, Cambridge, 1988). Meanwhile, I am confident of mustering many poets on this side of it.
14 Rorty, 'Postmodernist', p. 586.
15 Rorty, 'Contingency of Selfhood'.

16

Rorty in the Epistemological Tradition

Charles Taylor

I

Richard Rorty's arresting and influential view of the tasks of philosophy is bound up with a new and challenging reading of the history of Western thought and culture. Whether this amounts to a 'meta-narrative' of the kind that Lyotard[1] and Rorty both think we should avoid, is a difficult issue that I want to sidestep for a moment. What does seem clear is that Rorty's thesis frequently finds expression in narrative. Once we believed in Truth; now we only see ourselves as knowing various truths, which don't necessarily share anything interesting in common.[2] Or, if we pay more attention to the detail: philosophy in the modern period emancipates itself from religion; there comes a stage where philosophers no longer hold to some divine source or foundation for Truth. But at first, they fail to see that this undermines all appeals to such a trans-empirical reality. It is only slowly and painfully that we arrive at the understanding that Rorty calls pragmatism.[3] And many of us have still not got the point.

The importance of narrative in the statement of this view is not an accident, or a quirk of Rorty's style. Philosophical consciousness is necessarily historical, once we get to the broader questions, such as the nature of philosophical enquiry itself. That is because our definition of a position in this domain is necessarily contrastive; we can only get clear how we think things are by drawing sharply the differences with how they have been misconceived. Clarification of our own views is inseparable from our fighting clear of the erroneous views which were handed down to us. Plato started this kind of thing, and we have never stopped. It is hard to see how we could stop, and escape altogether from this contrastive correction of our past. This correction requires a certain reading of this past, a story which validates our outlook. Hence the inescapability of narrative.

What is exciting and controversial about Rorty's narrative is the sense of a radical new departure. What is radical is the promise that we can free ourselves of a whole host of questions which have been central to philosophy hitherto: about the real nature of human beings, about the truly valid ethical standards, about truth in science, and the like. Rorty offers a great leap into non-realism: where there have hitherto been thought to be facts- or truths-of-the-matter, there turn out to be only rival languages, between which we end up plumping, if we do, because in some way one works better for us than the others.

Now I have no quarrel with narratives as such. Quite the contrary. And in perhaps a less dramatic way, I too think that we have at least the basis for new departures in philosophical thinking. What is more, many of the old errors which Rorty defines himself against are also my favourite targets. I am thinking here in particular of the mainstream epistemological tradition from Descartes to Kant. But I utterly disagree on what it means to fight clear of these. In particular, I reject Rorty's non-realism. Rather I believe that non-realism is itself one of the recurrently generated *aporiai* of the tradition we both condemn. To get free of it is to come to an uncompromising realism.[4]

This means that Rorty has to read me as being enmired in the old errors. But it also means that my reading of him is exactly symmetrical: I see him in fact as still very much a prisoner of the epistemological world-view.

How to adjudicate this issue? Right away we are brought up short by a disconcerting difficulty. Rorty seems to think that it is essential to his position that he consider this issue too as falling under his non-realist regime. So that there is no truth of the matter between us on the question whether there is a truth of the matter between views of human nature, ethics, etc. Thus in 'The Contingency of Community',[5] he repudiates the claim that certain contemporary philosophers whose work he agrees with 'have demonstrated that the philosophers of the past were mistaken'. Rather they 'provide us with redescriptions which, taken together, buttress' an alternative way of describing our predicament.

Now, I think that this claim verges on incoherence. It's not just that it doesn't fit with the tone of much of Rorty's argument, though that seems to be the case. Thus the idea that Rorty frequently denounces, that some language might prove its superiority by actually fitting the world, e.g. that 'the final vocabulary of future physics will somehow be Nature's Own',[6] seems really to be stigmatized in his work as something that is difficult to *believe*,[7] and not just as a view which is distasteful or gets in the way of some important project. But to believe something is to hold it true; and indeed, one cannot consciously manipulate one's beliefs for motives other than their seeming true to us. Where this happens – and of course it frequently does – it goes on behind the back of the thinker, and its avowal is resisted.

Moreover, there are passages where Rorty seems to be saying that some of his philosophical conclusions are hard for us to swallow; so that they are not desirable for other reasons, but presumably impose themselves because we have no reason to believe otherwise. Thus he admits that there is something we may find 'morally humiliating' in his view.

> This means that when the secret police come, when the torturers violate the innocent, there is nothing to be said to them of the form 'There is something in you which you are betraying. Though you embody the practices of a totalitarian society which will endure forever, there is something beyond these practices which condemns you.' This thought is hard to live with.[8]

Presumably one could reply here that although this 'consequence of pragmatism' might be distasteful, it is inseparably linked to the whole position. You cannot get in and out of these world-views like a cab, as Weber caustically put it.[9] You have to buy into the whole thing or not at all. But that means that we are recognizing consistency as a truth-constraint. And indeed, this seems to play an important role for Rorty. He spoke in the line quoted above of redescriptions which 'buttress' a new way of seeing things. Presumably this means at the very least 'fit properly with', and points to some constraints of consistency on the discourse of redescription. (To give 'buttress' any stronger sense would be to make the paragraph incoherent, since buttressing the new position is meant to contrast with demonstrating the falsity of the old.) And when he quotes Sellars's definition of philosophy as 'an attempt to see how things, in the broadest possible sense of the term, hang together, in the broadest possible sense of the term',[10] this too only makes sense if one recognizes such constraints; otherwise anything could 'hang together' with anything, and there would be nothing to 'attempt to *see*' here.

But then Rorty's main thesis, that one can't decide the issue between world-views by arguments evoking reason and truth, must itself repose on a strong doctrine about the self-contained nature of these world-views. Any statement of such a view can be attacked for inconsistency, and some version can be refuted, i.e. shown to be untenable, if convicted of such inconsistency. This would presumably be the fate of someone who wanted to hang on to all of Rorty's other views, even liked the idea of our being able to remake ourselves in language rather than discovering ourselves,[11] but wanted nevertheless to have something strong to say to the torturers about their violation of the human essence; (and I suspect that this motivational profile matches lots and lots of people in our culture). But nevertheless, the thesis would run, all these world-views (or maybe, all the major contenders; or maybe lots of major contenders) can be given a consistent statement which is immune to refutation.

This means that the interlocutors never reach a point where they (a) accept or find they cannot reject some things in common, which (b) sit better with one world-view rather than another. This is the picture of world-views, or 'alternative language-games'[12] as global systems, 'as closed as madness', as Merleau-Ponty put it,[13] which have within themselves the resources to redescribe everything which comes along, to re-interpret everything which might be thrown up by an opponent as contrary evidence, and hence to remain constitutionally immune to refutation. World-views are like glasses we put on our noses, and which colour everything we see.

Now, I don't thing this is a plausible view in general, though there may be some cases between utterly different cultures which begin to approach it. But beyond this, I don't think this is something you can know about in advance of trying. How could you know in general that this kind of question can't be adjudicated by reasoned argument with a view to truth? Well, you could know this if you had a lot of confidence in some general theory of what knowing was; for example, one which told us that we all only know the world mediately, through a screen of representations which each of us forms in the mind. On this view stubborn differences in representation would be unarbitrable, because no one would ever be able to get behind our pictures into contact with the world out there. This, of course, is the familiar picture of the modern epistemological tradition, which for reasons of the kind just cited frequently threw up non-realist doctrines. I harbour the dark suspicion that Rorty's confidence in his own stand on the meta-issue between us – his non-realistic reading of world-views – comes from his still being in the thrall of a latter-day variant of this picture; and this fuels my desire to hurl at him the accusation we are constantly exchanging: of being still too much enmired in the bad old ways. I want to pile up further evidence for this accusation below. But for the moment, I'd like to address the meta-issue more directly.[14]

If we don't try to decide the issue by the shotgun method of invoking the traditional epistemological Big Picture, how plausible is the scenario of closed pictures? Not very, it seems to me. First to look at a general consideration, Rorty seems to be allowing, on my interpretation above, that questions of consistency bind the two sides in the argument. If what constitutes consistency were up for grabs, then we could espouse the self-indulgent position mentioned above, and talk of remaking ourselves in our creative and personal lives, while rushing to invoke a human essence whenever the KGB or the death squads loomed.

But what makes consistency? Now there is a story which was injected into our philosophical bloodstream by the Vienna School that consistency is a matter of logic. Propositions are consistent, and they are so when they fail to contradict each other. But this doesn't get to the interesting questions. We use logical inconsistency to point up and articulate what's wrong with a position, but that's not how we identify it as wrong. For instance, we might say to a holder of the self-indulgent view: 'How nice and convenient! In your artistic and love life, you're always quoting Sartre, and rejecting any human essence. Then when you want to denounce the Junta, suddenly you're talking about their violating this essence. You can't have it both ways'.

Here we've put our interlocutor into formal contradiction with himself. He both affirms and denies that there is a human essence. He can't get away with that. But what if the rogue calmly replies, 'Of course, I stand with Sartre in denying any human essence; but what the torturers violate is not a human essence but something which is a crucial condition of human life. You're putting words in my mouth.' Everyone will recognize that this kind of move is not one I've invented out of some misanthropic fantasy, but is made all the time.

Where does the argument go from here? The self-indulger has cleared himself from the charge of formal contradiction. The accuser is still unsatisfied, because he thinks that whatever the description, you can't have 'crucial conditions' without buying into essences. His next move might be to ask the self-indulger to make the distinction. Here again, it would be easy for the rascal to find *words*. What is at stake? It is something to do with the ontology of human life: what kinds of things can you invoke in talking about human beings in the different ways we do: describing, deliberating, judging, etc.? Can you invoke something to show that a torturer is wrong, objectively wrong, which you can prevent from being invoked to show that your way of life is wrong or shallow?

The agreement about consistency which might allow me to wrestle my slippery interlocutor to the ground on this issue is more than an agreement about the laws of logic. It involves substantive agreement, if not *ex ante*, then at least as the fruit of further articulation, about substantive matters. This means, of course, that we sometimes come to disagreements about questions of consistency. And this may seem at first blush a point in favour of Rorty's view. But in fact it is not. Because (1) disagreements about consistency are clearly localized differences which sometimes arise and sometimes do not. No blanket *a priori* doctrine is available about them; we have to examine each dispute to see whether they occur; and (2) where they fail to arise, the parties are bound by common substantive elements (beliefs, or potential objects of belief, granted articulation). And where this is so, the picture of closed pictures is clearly inapplicable. Any dispute may, though no dispute must, be arbitrable in relation to these common elements.

We might put this latter point by saying that any sharp distinction between issues of consistency and issues of substantive belief, which might be invoked to explain how we can criticize beliefs on the former grounds while they remain immune to attack on the latter, has just been shown to be untenable. Either reason is powerless to criticize, even for consistency, and nothing 'hangs together' with anything; or else we have to admit that there may be substantive issues between world-views which are arbitrable by reasoned argument aiming at validity.

Rorty might here reply that he doesn't need any *a priori* argument to declare differences between language-games unarbitrable. A mere empirical observation suffices. We are always arguing about these weighty matters, and over 2500 years have not come to any agreed conclusion. Unarbitrable is just what we can't seem successfully to arbitrate. In fact, Rorty frequently evokes the poor track-record of philosophy in this respect to underpin non-realism about these perennial issues.

But this seems inadequate for two reasons. The first is that it just isn't true. There are some issues in the long history of Western thought which have been settled. For instance, a science which tried to explain inanimate nature in terms of the realization in different kinds of entity of their corresponding Form has given way to a science which explains by efficient causation, mapped by mathematical formulae. Aristotle on this issue has been buried by Galileo and Newton, and there is no looking back. Certain views are unrecoverable; nobody can even get close to marshalling good grounds for believing them any more. This goes, incidentally, for some of the bizarre ideas that Rorty loves to invoke, like the notion that the language of an adequate physics might be 'Nature's Own'. This is a distant, caricatural relation of Plato's theory of Forms, which at least in this application is beyond recall.

Absolute non-starters of this kind play an important role in Rorty's discourse, because he frequently implies that something of their range is the only alternative to his pragmatism. He trades on their deadness to good rhetorical effect, even while treating the issue surrounding them as another example of the lack of agreement in philosophy.

This shows that Rorty's belief that the world doesn't 'decide between' language-games isn't just an empirically established thesis. On the contrary, issues that have been quite conclusively decided rationally[15] are reinterpreted as having been settled on pragmatic grounds. And there is, of course, a fashionable reading of the Galilean–Newtonian revolution which does just this. It is the one associated with Kuhn's name, though I think it misinterprets grievously what he said. This interpretation takes the Kuhnian 'paradigm' as being a closed picture, confronting other equally closed pictures. On this reading, there *cannot* be a rationally justified path from Aristotle to Newton. But this reading imports the closed picture idea into the story of the scientific revolution. It doesn't find it there. People who simply review the arguments today are overwhelmingly convinced by the Newtonian side. My point is here not to show whose interpretation is correct, just to demonstrate that the view of this transition as unjustified rationally is a product of a sophisticated overall theory of knowledge, not an obvious fact demanding explanation. In fact, the epistemologist Big Picture is once more obtruding. Since Rorty invokes Kuhn in his non-realist interpretation,[16] we have additional reason to appreciate the residual hold on him of this Big Picture, and the role it plays in his thinking.[17]

The second reason is that, even for those issues which remain in vigorous dispute, there is no automatic inference from lack of consensus to unarbitrability. Disagreements may be due to deep misconceptions on one side or the other. Indeed, it is difficult to believe that any philosopher could suppose that there were no disagreements at all which arose from this source. Rorty hardly writes as one who holds that none of his opponents are confused in any way, or that their confusions play no role at all in the positions that they hold. Here again, there is no blanket verdict possible about a whole class *ex ante*; we have rather to see in examining each case what is the nature and possible resolution of disagreement.

II

What emerges from the above discussion is that the issue between Rorty and me is joined on at least three levels, which are (sometimes confusingly) related.

(1) We differ as to whether the differences between 'language games', or world-views, or global conceptions of human nature, or of science, or of ethics, are to be treated realistically or non-realistically, whether they are arbitrable in reason or not.

(2) But we also differ as to how you settle this question. Rorty seems to think that it can be settled for the whole class by some general arguments about the nature of knowledge. I think that this has to be the wrong approach. Paying careful attention to what is at stake between different such views, and how we manage to argue for and justify our positions, will show that some are in principle arbitrable; while we may have to accept that others – those which divide utterly unrelated cultures, for instance – are not. No general theory of knowledge, or of what is arbitrable-in-principle, descending from the pure heaven of philosophical argument, could upset these detailed verdicts. We would have no reason to give such a theory greater credence than these, because there is no valid source for this theory other than our best actual practice of detailed

argument and arbitrament. The general view has to be drawn from this practice.

This is not to say that a general understanding, once articulated, cannot lead us to alter our view of the nature of certain disputes. As in all such endeavours at theory in human life, there is a coming and going between detailed reading and over-all view until the (ideal moment of) 'reflective equilibrium' (to borrow Rawls's apt expression). But the new theory-induced reading of the particular case has to make better sense of this particular case. This has to be a condition on equilibrium. Rather like a psycho-analytic account is ultimately vindicated by its allowing the patient to make better sense of his life. Otherwise, in one case as in the other, theory is cut loose from all moorings and floats free in the gratuitous realm of the *a priori*.

The bad practice of the modern epistemological tradition was just the reverse of this: to develop first some conception of what knowledge and validation *had to be*. This was sometimes meant to be established by self-observation, as with the classical empiricists. But in fact, this observation was vitiated by various metaphysical prejudices, as the critiques by Heidegger, Merleau-Ponty and the later Wittgenstein in our times have amply shown. Then this henceforth unchallengeable conception was used to convince us of a great variety of counter-intuitive untruths, ranging across a wide spectrum, following the different variants of the tradition; for example, that the pain we perceive isn't really in the tooth, that the direct objects of our awareness are not things but inner representations, that our ordinary grasp of things is built out of particulate representations by some procedure of assembly (latterly computer programs are fashionably seen in this role), that we never can be sure there are Other Minds, and rather recently, that we never can determine whether our interlocutor is talking about whole rabbits or undetached rabbit parts.

Rorty's Pragmatism seems to me to fit too well into this deplorable tradition. He offers us a non-realism about the grounds for conceptual change in place of (or sometimes in addition to) the profusion of non-realisms the epistemological tradition has thrown up, from material objects, to other minds, to the meaning of my interlocutor's words. Here's where our two pictures of the possible new departures in philosophy radically diverge. I think that the great contribution of writers like Heidegger and Wittgenstein is that they carefully deconstructed the epistemological picture which 'held us captive', and allowed us to see better what we actually do, and how things actually are with us. In doing that they discredited the whole procedure of arriving *ex ante* at some view of what knowledge has to be, and then dictating to reality from that standpoint. The great vice of the tradition is that it allows epistemology to command ontology.

The most striking recent example of this can be seen in the work of philosophers like Dan Dennett, who are enamoured of the computer model in cognitive psychology. They want to deny the distinction between living beings who calculate and machines who 'calculate'; namely, that meaning and intentionality are ascribed only to the first in an underived sense, that there really is something it is to be a human or a bat, but not to be a fifth-generation computer.[18] The reason for denying this distinction is characteristically that, following their view of what it must be to observe and discover meaning or intentionality in any 'system', these would have to be ascribed to animals and computers on the same basis, i.e. that classing them as 'intentional systems' offers the best explanatory purchase on them.[19] It is significant that Rorty sides foursquare with Dennett against Nagel on this issue.[20]

Now, I believe that if one follows through on this deconstruction, and eschews *ex ante* theories of knowledge, one comes to see that the alleged grounds for a great many fashionable non-realisms dissolve. I know there is a widespread reading of Wittgenstein, which sees him as some kind of refined behaviourist, and hence as a non-realist about inner states. But I think this is an insufficiently radical reading, one which still stays too much within the epistemological picture, which only allows one to alternate between acknowledging some inner life unobservable in principle, and a non-realist reduction of all inner talk to outer behaviour (behaviourism) or explanatory principles (Dennett's solution). Wittgenstein can be more fruitfully interpreted as breaking out of this mould altogether. To follow him in overcoming epistemology is to return to an aggressive realism. Or so I believe.

I don't have time to argue this here, which is a shame, because it gets us to the heart of my first, and principal difference from Rorty. But at the moment, I'm dealing with the second, a meta-issue of how to deal with the first. And my objection to him is that he still remains too much in the bad old tradition in making his case through a global *ex ante* theory of knowledge.

This may not be immediately evident, even to him, in that he often comes across as having concluded to the unarbitrability of the traditional philosophical issues from the fact of their remaining unsettled over all these centuries. I tried to show above why this isn't adequate. When Rorty lists examples of 'alternative language-games': 'the vocabulary of ancient Athenian politics as against that of Jefferson, the moral vocabulary of St Paul as against that of Freud, the jargon of Newton versus that of Aristotle, the idiom of Blake rather than that of Dryden',[21] he throws together diverse issues. They don't properly belong together unless one accepts some very broad gauge theory of validation. Certainly the principle of unity here cannot be that there is no rational consensus on any of these, because in the absence of special pleading by an *ex ante* theory, there is no doubt that Newton has won against Aristotle.

(3) But perhaps the most striking indication of the fact that we're dealing with an *ex ante* theory is Rorty's stand on the meta-issue itself. He thinks that because he believes that disputes between alternative language-games are unarbitrable, he has in all consistency to treat this meta-claim itself as unarbitrable. This is the third issue between us, which emerges from the discussion in the previous section.

That he sees himself forced to this stand is evident in a passage like the following: 'The difficulty faced by a philosopher who, like myself is sympathetic to this suggestion (sc., that our self-redescriptions change us, rather than bringing us nearer to or farther from "an enduring, substratal human nature"), one who thinks himself as ancillary to the poet rather than to the physicist, is to avoid hinting that this suggestion gets something right, that my sort of philosophy corresponds to the way things really are'.[22]

Rorty seems to be saying here that we must be non-realistic about the meta-issue, the issue whether disputes about language-games are arbitrable in reason, because it is an *instance* of such a dispute, and we already know about the *class* that they are unarbitrable. This is the classic way of operating with *ex ante* theories.

That is what brings Rorty close to incoherence with his position on this third question. There are three levels of dispute being invoked in the argument. There are first-level differences between language games. Then there is Rorty's thesis about the non-realist status of such disputes (let's call what's at stake here the 'status issue'). Then there is the further claim about non-realism in regard to this status issue; and to challenge this is to raise a 'meta-status issue'. Now Rorty seems to argue that, since the status issue is of the same kind as any first-order dispute, its status has to be similar to theirs, and hence if they are to be understood non-realistically then so must it. In other words, deciding the status issue *ipso facto* decides the meta-status issue.

But there seems to be a crucial difficulty in deciding the meta-status issue on the basis of the status issue. For consider how we could come to a decision on the status issue. To resolve this issue we must have formed some view of how we can legitimately decide it, by rational argument or by a creative leap into persuasion. But that is precisely what is at stake in the meta-status issue. Hence this must be resolved *before* we address the status issue, and not as a corollary of its resolution.

This accounts for the disconcerting wobble in Rorty's arguments. The considerations he presents for his thesis on the status issue sound irresistibly like claims to truth. For example:

What was *glimpsed* at the end of the 18th century was that anything could be made to look good or bad, important or unimportant, useful or useless, by being redescribed. What Hegel *misdescribed* as the process of spirit gradually becoming self-conscious of its intrinsic nature was the fact that European linguistic practices were changing at a faster and faster rate, that more people were offering more radical redescriptions of more things than ever before. What the Romantics express as the claim that imagination, rather than reason, was the central human faculty was the *realization* that a talent for speaking differently, rather than for arguing well, was the chief instrument of social change.[23]

It is not just that the force of the words I've emphasized in italics suggests truth claims. It is also hard to see how the whole text would work if they were denied this status. More, it is hard to understand what the issue could be that they address if we deny them this status. How can you *opt for* the view that anything can be made to look good or bad, important or unimportant, by being redescribed, and not be *making a grievous mistake*, unless in some sense it is *so* that anything can be made to look good or bad, etc.? In contrast, we can conceive what it might mean to offer a non-realist reading of the dispute between Freud and St Paul, or even that between Aristotle and Newton, though we might vigorously reject these readings (as I would).

The simple extension to the meta-status issue of Rorty's thesis on the status issue brings his whole position close to self-refutation. It also shows up the glaring weakness of the whole procedure by global *ex ante* theories, which are then applied authoritatively across the board.

III

On my reading, the heart of Rorty's position is the claim to be able to give a general *ex ante* answer to what I have been calling the status question. This claim resembles in form while departing in content from the different *ex ante* theories which have been thrown up in what I want to call the epistemological tradition, from Descartes to Quine. Now, I believe that certain contemporary authors (e.g. Heidegger and Wittgenstein) have shown us how to deconstruct this tradition, by confronting the claims of such *ex ante* theories with our effective practices of knowing and being in a world. I naturally conclude that something similar needs to be done to Rorty's view.

What is his *ex ante* theory? It's hard to say. Officially, he shouldn't have one at all, and he often repudiates any interest in offering theories of Truth or knowledge. But the repudiation is only believable up to a point. There is the status claim itself; and the arguments he deploys for it; and then whatever is implicit in these.

I mentioned in the first section that it seemed to me that he was relying on something like the notion of world-views as closed systems, like different coloured glasses on people's noses, mutually irrefutable. This attribution may seem gratuitous, because it appears to fly in the face of Rorty's well-known rejection of the notion of 'alternative conceptual frameworks' in his paper 'The World Well Lost'.[24] But it turns out that what Rorty is arguing against here is the distinction between a single world-out-there and a plurality of conceptual schemes. It is the 'world' as a transcendent pole of all our conceivings which is meant to be 'well lost'. The ordinary, commonly received idea that there are different, mutually incompatible ways of conceiving things, between which we sometimes have to choose, is perfectly accepted by him. It is what he describes as 'alternate language-games' in the passage quoted above.

To take these games as closed in the sense of my image is to see them as (a) under constraints of consistency, while (b) being mutually immune to refutation. This means that the constraints which rule out inconsistent, self-indulgent combinations never can be invoked to show that one such whole position is inferior to another. Rorty seems to be committed to both these claims: to (a) because otherwise all distinction between positions would dissolve. One could, for instance, decide that it was groovy to hold *all* views; to (b) because otherwise the issue would be arbitrable in reason; one could demonstrate the superiority of one view over another. Moreover, this whole position is held as a general *ex ante* thesis; that is, one knows of all such disputes that (a) and (b) hold of them; and hence one can extrapolate to new cases, like the meta-status issue.

But this means that one knows in general *ex ante* that the various constraints internally recognized in each position can never serve to arbitrate between them. It is this general in principle assurance that I am trying to capture with the image of closure.[25]

Now, there is one principal line of argument, which Rorty returns to again and again in different forms, to establish his status claim, and hence this thesis of closure. This is that the only alternative to his Pragmatism is some belief in a correspondence theory, the belief that one's 'philosophy corresponds to the way things really are'.[26] This is represented as being quite untenable, even laughable; Pragmatism is the only believable alternative.

Certain suppositions seem to be made in the various invocations of this argument: (i) that the only candidate for a general account of truth is in terms of correspondence; (ii) that correspondence is to be understood in a rather simple-minded way, approaching at times a picture theory; (iii) that believers in the correspondence theory are Raving Platonists. Underlying all of this is a continuing imprisonment in the model basic to the whole epistemological tradition, which understands thinking in terms of representation.

(iii) is easily dealt with. By Raving Platonism, I mean the view that Rorty often invokes to ridicule his adversaries, such as that 'the final vocabulary of a future physics will somehow be Nature's Own', or 'that a vocabulary is somehow already out there in the world'.[27] We should consider this just as a rhetorical flourish. Rorty can't really believe that hard-faced scientific realists, who think that mechanistic materialism is literally true, subscribe to Raving Platonism.

But (ii) does rather more damage. In 'Pragmatism, Relativism, Irrationalism', Rorty seems to be glossing the correspondence theory by some kind of picturing thesis, even simpler than that of Wittgenstein's *Tractatus*.

> To say that the parts of properly analyzed true sentences are arranged in ways isomorphic to the parts of the world paired with them sounds plausible if one thinks of a sentence like 'Jupiter has moons'. It sounds slightly less plausible for 'The earth goes around the sun', less still for 'There is no such thing as natural motion', and not plausible at all for 'The universe is infinite'.[28]

But it is hard to see why the correspondence theory should be tied to such a quaint interpretation. The simple picture theory already fails to fit any negative existential proposition, like 'there are no chairs in this room', even before one gets to negations of key explanatory factors of discredited theories, like 'natural motion'. Yet there is no serious temptation to deny that the no chairs claim will be true or false in virtue of the way things are, or the nature of reality. Why should the same courtesy not be extended to the negation of natural motion? The point of the denial, I take it, is not to refuse any distinction between gravitationally induced fall and the movement of a projectile, but only to reject the explanatory account in terms of natural places. This explanatory account has been discarded, and superceded by another one which has no place for the distinction 'natural/ violent'. In so far as both accounts were attempts to offer a correct representation of the world, there seems to be no problem in saying that the second account is superior to the first just in virtue of the way things are.

Similar things could be said of the claim that there are electrons or quarks, or that there is no such thing as phlogiston or caloric. To balk at this is to slide back into the bad old non-realism of the Vienna positivists, with their untenable distinction between 'observables' and 'theoretical terms'. What is meant to be so wrong with correspondence talk here?

Rorty seems to think that it falls into one of two traps. Either it adds nothing, is just an emphatic way of saying that we accept these claims as valid. Or it is meant seriously, and then it is an attempt to invoke an unacceptable metaphysical picture, like that of the Kantian thing-in-itself, a realm of transcendent things beyond all appearances. I'll take up the first accusation in a minute. But this second alleged error puzzles me.

Kant's notion of the thing-in-itself is very much a creation of the epistemological tradition. The belief that what we are aware of immediately are appearances or representations creates the space in which we can suppose, are even invited to suppose something like a thing-in-itself. It also induces us to define it as something which we can by definition have no experience of. Once one climbs out of the *ex ante* theory which makes representation central, as e.g. Hegel did, the thing-in-itself makes no further sense.

My puzzlement is that talk of thought corresponding to reality, even to a reality independent of my representations, should be linked to the invocation of a thing-in-itself. Kant himself had the insight to see that even within the world of appearances, we cannot but operate on the understanding, which frames and shapes all our perception and scientific views, that we are dealing with a world of objects independent of us. Our entire framework understanding of our place in this world construes our representations of it as true or false by correspondence. This is the insight by which idealism is decisively refuted. The thinkers who have successfully deconstructed epistemology in our century have espoused in their own form this doctrine of Kant, while jettisoning the whole distinction between appearance and thing-in-itself. Heidegger, for instance, shows us as being at grips with a world of independent things, prior to any attempt on our part to represent them.

It is crucial to these contemporary rejections of epistemology that they no longer see our entire understanding of things as consisting in representations. The framework understanding I mentioned above, which Heidegger sometimes calls 'pre-understanding', is not itself a representation of our position in the world. It is that against the background of which I frame all my representations, and that in virtue of which I know that these are true or false because of the way things are. It has been a persistent vice of the epistemological tradition to try to assimilate this pre-understanding to the representations it frames, as though it could be exhaustively accounted for in terms of *information about* the subject and his world. The latest example of this is to be found in contemporary simulations of Artificial Intelligence, which had not surprisingly encountered an insurmountable 'frame problem'.[29]

Once you accept some view of this kind, with its conception of framed representations, there is no further problem with the proposition that the reality independent of my representations makes them true or false. And there is no temptation whatever to construe this as an invocation of things-in-themselves. It is only if one remains in the old epistemology, where representations constitute our entire understanding, and are as it were our only route to contact with the 'outside world', that this kind of talk takes on a transcendent metaphysical flavour. This is the sense of my claim above that really burying epistemology leads you back to realism.

And this is why I want to claim that Rorty is still partly trapped in the old model. It is not that he explicitly subscribes to the representational view, and indeed, he often seems to be repudiating it. It is rather that his conception of the alternatives still seem to be commanded by that view. That is, his notion of what it is to reject representationalism still seems commanded by the doctrine being rejected. So to learn that our thoughts don't correspond to things-in-themselves is to conclude that they don't correspond to anything at all. If transcendent entities don't make them true, then nothing makes them true. These were the only game in the epistemic town, and if they go the place has to be closed down. Rorty seems to be operating within the logic of the old system that linked us to transcendent reality through a screen of representations, even while distancing himself from it. Within this logic, he makes the decisive move of rejecting the transcendent; and then all the non-realist conclusions naturally follow. But they only follow if you make this move while leaving everything else unchanged. For then people with different views are construed as situated behind incompatible representations, without there being anything these representations are about which can arbitrate. They are not seen as situated in a common world, with a framework understanding partly developed dialogically, which defines for them the constraints and demands on their representations. But the question is very much whether it makes sense to scrap the transcendent without jettisoning the whole system. Rorty still seems trapped half-way.

Now Rorty might reply that he agrees perfectly well with my post-epistemological, intra-framework notion of truth as correspondence, but that this is exactly the trivial, empty use that constituted the first danger above. What have we learnt about what it is for claims to be true when we're told that they 'correspond to the facts'? Well, maybe ordinary people aren't really getting any news – it is rather Rorty's views which might surprise and scandalize them. But there still is a philosophical point to this claim. That is because this kind of truth contrasts with something. It's not all the truth there is. Here's where I'm challenging Rorty's supposition (i).

What it contrasts with is the truth of self-understanding. Just because we are partly constituted by our self-understandings, we can't construe them as of an independent object, in the way our descriptions of things are. When I move from seeing myself as being disinterestedly benevolent to understanding how much I get out of my role as benefactor; when I get beyond a view of myself as a cool loner, and understand how much I'm involved in this relationship, characteristically the emotions I'm trying to describe in each case change as well. There isn't a single independent reality, staying put through all the changes in description, like the solar system stayed there, waiting for Kepler. I'm altering myself with my new self-descriptions.

And yet, I want to say, as we all do when we're not in the grip of a philosophical theory, that one of these views can be truer, more insightful, less self-deluding than the other. My earlier view shaped me differently than my present one. But I want to describe that difference in part in epistemic terms: I was denying part of myself, or unaware of it, or deluding myself. Under the previous descriptions I *was* different; I wasn't just as I am now under the truer understanding. But what I was then was shaped by the distortion of denial more than I am now. We could say that, in this kind of case, the untruth is part of the reality described, rather than lying simply in the relation between representation and reality.

The terms in which to characterize this distortion are only available to me now that I have climbed out of it. What was being denied has flowered through its recognition, and has only become now what it had in it to be. The full reality of what was denied wasn't there then, and that is part of the reason why the terms weren't fully available. We need a concept like 'potentiality' to do justice to our cramped past.

In the last few paragraphs, I have been trying to lay out an alternative model of truth, which applies I believe in a different domain than the correspondence model does. Rorty will, of course strongly disagree. He will accept some version of the self-making by redescription. This is, indeed, one of his key doctrines.[30] But he will conclude that that excludes talking of 'truth' here in my sense, of approaching or departing from one's true self. My argument would be, if there were space to expound it, that we cannot but operate with a notion of truth; that the way we live our transitions, and struggle with potential redescriptions, unfailingly makes use of these notions of overcoming distortion, seeing through error, coming to reality, and their opposites. We can't function as agents without some such language, however much we may want to deny it in the name of some general *ex ante* view. In a conflict between these two readings, there is no doubt in my mind which ought to be given precedence; for I cannot see where any *ex ante* view can draw its credibility, if it is not in making sense of how we actually lead our lives.

Rorty and I disagree, of course, about this fundamental point. He seems to be as always drawing his inference that a representation which is not made true by some independent reality might just as well not be considered a candidate for truth at all. All of which is sensible enough on the old schema. But even if I were now to adopt his view about self-interpretation this would do nothing to deny the difference between this kind of claim and those made about the world, in say, natural science. Even if we thought there was no self-discovery but only self-making, this would still give a point by contrast with, for example, natural science, in which there precisely is discovery because there is truth-by-correspondence. So articulating the correspondence model would not be uttering something trivial and without content, even if those in the laboratories weren't aware of learning anything new.

IV

In this last section, I have been trying to come to grips with what I have called Rorty's status claim, which I see as the heart of his position. This is the view which interprets all differences between 'alternative language-games' non-realistically. This is enunciated by Rorty as a general *ex ante* view, in my language. I have been exploring his arguments for this thesis, partly in order to winkle out more insight into his *ex ante* position, and partly in order to undermine these arguments.

I don't know how successful I have been in either of these endeavours. But one thing I hope has emerged from this whole, rather rambling discussion is the inescapability of certain philosophical issues. Rorty believes that one can jettison the old epistemological view without espousing another one. One just leaves these old questions behind, like: what is the nature of knowledge? or self-understanding? of scientific truth? and moves forward into a post-philosophical world. But what the considerations I have been advancing suggest is that this move is far from being a liberation. Just trying to walk away from the old epistemology, without working out an alternative conception, seems paradoxically a formula for remaining trapped in it to some degree. But on reflection, this shouldn't surprise us. We only attain the insights we do by climbing out of old error, as I argued at the beginning. This is what justifies Rorty's narrative mode of reasoning, which is one of the strongest and most stimulating aspects of his work; it is what has enabled him to put important issues on the agenda, and make a tremendously important contribution to the contemporary discussion. But the very contrastive dimension of our thinking, which makes narrative indispensible, also prevents us from just walking away from old error, without coming to terms with it through a critique, which by its very nature engenders a new view. These philosophical questions can't be escaped. Their imprisoning distorting effect can only be neutralized by insight. To turn our back on them is to risk thraldom. We might rewrite Santayana, and say that those who ignore philosophy are condemned to relive it.

NOTES

I am grateful to Ruth Abbey for her helpful comments on an earlier draft of this paper.

1 J-P. Lyotard, *La Condition Post-moderne* (Les Editions de Minuit, Paris, 1979).
2 Richard Rorty, *The Consequences of Pragmatism* (University of Minnesota Press, Minneapolis, 1982), pp. xiii ff.
3 Rorty, *Philosophy and the Mirror of Nature* (Princeton University Press, Princeton, 1979), offers a detailed account of the genesis of Rorty's position.
4 I have explained this position at least in outline in 'Overcoming Epistemology' in *After Philosophy*, ed. R. Baynes, J. Bohman and T. MacCarthy (MIT Press, Cambridge, Mass., 1987).
5 *London Review of Books*, 24 July 1986, p. 12.
6 Rorty, *Consequences of Pragmatism*, p. xxvi.
7 E.g. in talking of 'alternative language-games', Rorty says, 'it is difficult to think of the world as making one of these better than another, of the world as deciding between them' ('The Contingency of Language', *London Review of Books*, 17 April 1986, p. 4). The normal way to take this difficulty is as one of believing the propositions cited.
8 Rorty, *Consequences of Pragmatism*, p. xliii.
9 'Politics as a Vocation', in *From Max Weber*, ed. H. H. Gerth and C. Wright Mills (Oxford University Press, New York and Oxford, 1946), p. 119.
10 Rorty, *Consequences of Pragmatism*, p. xiv.
11 Rorty, 'The Contingency of Selfhood', *London Review of Books*, 8 May 1986, pp. 11–15.
12 Rorty, 'The Contingency of Language', *London Review of Books*, 16 April 1986, p. 3.
13 Merleau-Ponty, *La Phénoménologie de la Perception* (Gallimard, Paris, 1945), p. 29.
14 I think that Bernard Williams has made a point very similar to mine very tellingly, when he says, in *Ethics and the Limits of Philosophy* (Fontana, London, 1985), pp. 137–8, that Rorty's account 'is self-defeating. If the story he tells were true, there would be no perspective from which he could express it'. In saying that the best scientific language is best not in virtue of describing a world already there, but in virtue of its being convenient or advantageous for us to adopt, 'he is trying to reoccupy the transcendental standpoint outside human speech and activity, which is precisely what he wants us to renounce'.
15 I have tried to show how this step is justified in 'Rationality' in *Rationality and Relativism*, ed. S. Lukes and M. Hollis (Basil Blackwell, Oxford, 1982), pp. 87–105. A much fuller and more convincing case is made by Alasdair MacIntyre in his 'Epistemological Crises, Dramatic Narrative and the Philosophy of Science', *The Monist*, 60.
16 See Rorty, 'The Contingency of Language'.
17 One might protest that although the Aristotle–Newton debate seems closed, the debate about how to construe this transition, realistically or anti-realistically, as I do or as Rorty does, rages on. Might *this* issue then be considered unarbitrable by reason? There is something bizarre about this suggestion. If the first-order question has been decided, it is because some intersubjectively convincing considerations of persuasive force have been recognized. The second-order issue concerns what these are, and how to classify them. But then the Rortyan arguments about their being nothing out there which our rival languages are about, and which can arbitrate between them, seem misplaced. What there has been is this process of coming to agreement on the basis of certain considerations. This is clearly something that we can get a better or worse view of, and that's why we dispute.
18 Daniel Dennett, *The Intentional Stance* (Bradford Books, MIT Press, Cambridge, Mass., 1987), ch. 8.
19 Ibid., chs 1–3.

20 Rorty, *Consequences of Pragmatism*, p. xxxiv; Nagel's position is well laid out in T. Nagel, *Mortal Questions* (Cambridge University Press, Cambridge, 1979), chs 12–14 ,and *The View from Nowhere* (Oxford University Press, New York, 1985).
21 'The Contingency of Language', p. 3.
22 Ibid.
23 Ibid. (italics added).
24 In Rorty, *Consequences of Pragmatism*, pp. 3–18.
25 Classical logical positivism had good reasons for holding that (a) could be combined with (b): consistency was purely a matter of logical compatibility, whereas different views differ in their substantive claims. But Rorty has, of course, abandoned the distinctions on which this solution rests.
26 Rorty, 'The Contingency of Language', p. 3.
27 Rorty, *Consequences of Pragmatism*, p. xxvi; 'The Contingency of Language', p. 3.
28 Rorty, *Consequences of Pragmatism*, p. 163.
29 Hubert Dreyfus and Stuart Dreyfus, *Mind over Machine* (Free Press, New York, 1986), ch. 3.
30 See Rorty, 'The Contingency of Language', and 'The Contingency of Selfhood'.

Part V

**Continuing the Conversation:
Politics and Culture**

17

The Priority of Democracy to Philosophy

Richard Rorty

Thomas Jefferson set the tone for American liberal politics when he said 'it does me no injury for my neighbour to say that there are twenty Gods or no God'.[1] His example helped make respectable the idea that politics can be separated from beliefs about matters of ultimate importance – that shared beliefs among citizens on such matters are not essential to a democratic society. Like many other figures of the Enlightenment, Jefferson assumed that a moral faculty common to the typical theist and the typical atheist suffices for civic virtue.

Many Enlightenment intellectuals were willing to go further and say that since religious beliefs turn out to be inessential for political cohesion, they should simply be discarded as mumbo jumbo – perhaps to be replaced (as in twentieth-century totalitarian Marxist states) with some sort of explicitly secular political faith that will form the moral consciousness of the citizen. Jefferson again set the tone when he refused to go that far. He thought it enough to privatize religion, to view it as irrelevant to social order but relevant to, and possibly essential for, individual perfection. Citizens of a Jeffersonian democracy can be as religious or irreligious as they please as long as they are not 'fanatical'. That is, they must abandon or modify opinions on matters of ultimate importance, the opinions that may hitherto have given sense and point to their lives, if these opinions entail public actions that cannot be justified to most of their fellow citizens.

This Jeffersonian compromise concerning the relation of spiritual perfection to public policy has two sides. Its absolutist side says that every human being, without the benefit of special revelation, has all the beliefs

I am grateful to David Levin, Michael Sandel, J. B. Schneewind and A. J. Simmons for comment on earlier drafts of this paper.

necessary for civic virtue. These beliefs spring from a universal human faculty, conscience – possession of which constitutes the specifically human essence of each human being. This is the faculty that gives the individual human dignity and rights. But there is also a pragmatic side. This side says that when the individual finds in her conscience beliefs that are relevant to public policy but incapable of defence on the basis of beliefs common to her fellow citizens, she must sacrifice her conscience on the altar of public expediency.

The tension between these two sides can be eliminated by a philosophical theory that identifies justifiability to humanity at large with truth. The Enlightenment idea of 'reason' embodies such a theory: the theory that there is a relation between the ahistorical essence of the human soul and moral truth that ensures that free and open discussion will produce 'one right answer' to moral as well as to scientific questions.[2] Such a theory guarantees that a moral belief that cannot be justified to the mass of mankind is 'irrational', and thus is not really a product of our moral faculty at all. Rather, it is a 'prejudice', a belief that comes from some other part of the soul than 'reason'. It does not share in the sanctity of conscience, for it is the product of a sort of pseudoconscience – something whose loss is no sacrifice, but a purgation.

In our century, this rationalist justification of the Enlightenment compromise has been discredited. Contemporary intellectuals have given up the Enlightenment assumption that religion, myth and tradition can be opposed to something ahistorical, something common to all human beings qua human. Anthropologists and historians of science have blurred the distinction between innate rationality and the products of acculturation. Philosophers such as Heidegger and Gadamer have given us ways of seeing human beings as historical all the way through. Other philosophers, such as Quine and Davidson, have blurred the distinction between permanent truths of reason and temporary truths of fact. Psychoanalysis has blurred the distinction between conscience and the emotions of love, hate and fear, and thus the distinction between morality and prudence. The result is to erase the picture of the self common to Greek metaphysics, Christian theology and Enlightenment rationalism: the picture of an ahistorical nature centre, the locus of human dignity, surrounded by an adventitious and inessential periphery.

The effect of erasing this picture is to break the link between truth and justifiability. This, in turn, breaks down the bridge between the two sides of the Enlightenment compromise. The effect is to polarize liberal social theory. If we stay on the absolutist side, we shall talk about inalienable 'human rights' and about 'one right answer' to moral and political dilemmas without trying to back up such talk with a theory of human nature. We shall abandon metaphysical accounts of what a right is while nevertheless insisting that everywhere, in all times and cultures, members of our species have had the same rights. But if we swing to the pragmatist side, and consider talk of 'rights' an attempt to enjoy the benefits of metaphysics without assuming the appropriate responsibilities, we shall still need something to distinguish the sort of individual conscience we respect from the sort we condemn as 'fanatical'. This can only be something relatively local and ethnocentric – the tradition of a particular community, the consensus of a particular culture. According to this view, what counts as rational or as fanatical is relative to the group to which we think it necessary to justify ourselves – to the body of shared belief that determines the reference of the word 'we'. The Kantian identification with a central transcultural and ahistorical self is thus replaced by a quasi-Hegelian identification with our own community, thought of as an historical product. For pragmatist social theory, the question of whether justifiability to the community with which we identify entails truth is simply irrelevant.

Ronald Dworkin and others who take the notion of ahistorical human 'rights' seriously serve as examples of the first, absolutist, pole. John Dewey and, as I shall shortly be arguing, John Rawls serve as examples of the second pole. But there is a third type of social theory – often dubbed 'communitarianism' – which is less easy to place. Roughly speaking, the writers tagged with this label are those who reject both the individualistic rationalism of the Enlightenment and the idea of 'rights', but, unlike the pragmatists, see this rejection as throwing doubt on the institutions and culture of the surviving democratic states. Such theorists include Robert Bellah, Alasdair MacIntyre, Michael Sandel, Charles Taylor, the early Roberto Unger, and many others. These writers share some measure of agreement with a view found in an extreme form, both in Heidegger and in Horkheimer and Adorno's *Dialectic of Enlightenment*. This is the view that liberal institutions and culture either should not or cannot survive the collapse of the philosophical justification that the Enlightenment provided for them.

There are three strands in communitarianism that need to be disentangled. First, there is the empirical prediction that no society that sets aside the idea of ahistorical moral truth in the insouciant way that Dewey recommended can survive. Horkheimer and Adorno, for example, suspect that you cannot have a moral community in a disenchanted world because toleration leads to pragmatism, and it is not clear how we can prevent 'blindly pragmatized thought' from losing 'its transcending quality and its relation to truth'.[3] They think that pragmatism was the inevitable outcome of Enlightenment rationalism and that pragmatism is not a strong enough philosophy to make moral community possible.[4] Second, there is the moral judgement that the sort of human being who is produced by liberal institutions and culture is undesirable. MacIntyre, for example, thinks that our culture – a culture he says is dominated by 'the Rich Aesthete, the Manager, and the Therapist' – is a *reductio ad absurdum* both of the philosophical views that helped create it and of those now invoked in its defence. Third, there is the claim that political institutions 'presuppose' a doctrine about the nature of human beings and that such a doctrine must, unlike Enlightenment rationalism, make clear the essentially historical character of the self. So we find writers like Taylor and Sandel saying that we need a theory of the self that incorporates Hegel's and Heidegger's sense of the self's historicity.

The first claim is a straightforward empirical, sociological-historical one about the sort of glue that is required to hold a community together. The second is a straightforward moral judgement that the advantages of contemporary liberal democracy are outweighed by the disadvantages, by the ignoble and sordid character of the culture and the individual human beings that it produces. The third claim, however, is the most puzzling and complex. I shall concentrate on this third, most puzzling, claim, although towards the end I shall return briefly to the first two.

To evaluate this third claim, we need to ask two questions. The first is whether there is any sense in which liberal democracy 'needs' philosophical justification at all. Those who share Dewey's pragmatism will say that although it may need philosophical articulation, it does not need philosophical back-up. On this view, the philosopher of liberal democracy may wish to develop a theory of the human self that comports with the institutions he or she admires. But such a philosopher is not thereby justifying these institutions by reference to more fundamental premises, but the reverse. He or she is putting politics first and tailoring a philosophy to suit. Communitarians, by contrast, often speak as though political institutions were no better than their philosophical foundations.

The second question is one that we can ask even if we put the opposition between justification and articulation to one side. It is the question of whether a conception of the self that, as Taylor says, makes 'the community constitutive of the individual'[5] does in fact comport better with liberal democracy than does the Enlightenment conception of the self. Taylor summarizes the latter as 'an ideal of disengagement' that defines a 'typically modern notion' of human dignity: 'the ability to act on one's own, without outside interference or subordination to outside authority'. On Taylor's view, as on Heidegger's, these Enlightenment notions are closely linked with characteristically modern ideas of 'efficacy, power, unperturbability'.[6] They are also closely linked with the contemporary form of the doctrine of the sacredness of the individual conscience – Dworkin's claim that appeals to rights 'trump' all other appeals. Taylor, like Heidegger, would like to substitute a less individualistic conception of what it is to be properly human – one that makes less of autonomy and more of interdependence.

I can preview what is to come by saying that I shall answer 'no' to the first question about the communitarians' third claim and 'yes' to the second. I shall be arguing that Rawls, following up on Dewey, shows us how liberal democracy can get along without philosophical presuppositions. He has thus shown us how we can disregard the third communitarian claim. But I shall also argue that communitarians like Taylor are right in saying that a conception of the self that makes the community constitutive of the self does comport well with liberal democracy. That is, if we *want* to flesh out our self-image as citizens of such a democracy with a philosophical view of the self, Taylor gives us pretty much the right view. But this sort of philosophical fleshing-out does not have the importance that writers like Horkheimer and Adorno, or Heidegger, have attributed to it.

Without further preface, I turn now to Rawls. I shall begin by pointing out that both in *A Theory of Justice* and subsequently, he has linked his own position to the Jeffersonian ideal of religious toleration. In an article called 'Justice as Fairness: Political not Metaphysical', he says that he is 'going to apply the principle of toleration to philosophy itself', and goes on to say:

> The essential point is this: as a practical political matter no general moral conception can provide the basis for a public conception of justice in a modern democratic society. The social and historical conditions of such a society have their origins in the Wars of Religion following the Reformation and the development of the principle of toleration, and in the growth of constitutional government and the institutions of large market economies. These conditions profoundly affect the requirements of a workable conception of political justice: such a conception must allow for a diversity of doctrines and the plurality of conflicting, and indeed incommensurable conceptions of the good affirmed by the members of existing democratic societies.[7]

We can think of Rawls as saying that just as the principle of religious toleration and the social thought of the Enlightenment proposed to bracket many standard theological topics when deliberating about public policy and constructing political institutions, so we need to bracket many standard topics of philosophical enquiry. For purposes of social theory, we can put aside such topics as an ahistorical human nature, the nature of selfhood, the motive of moral beahviour and the meaning of human life. We treat these as irrelevant to politics as Jefferson thought questions about the Trinity and about transubstantiation.

In so far as he adopts this stance, Rawls disarms many of the criticisms that, in the wake of Horkheimer and Adorno, have been directed at American liberalism. Rawls can agree that Jefferson and his circle shared a lot of dubious philosophical views, views that we might now wish to reject. He can even agree with Horkheimer and Adorno, as Dewey would have, that these views contained the seeds of their own destruction. But he thinks that the remedy may be not to formulate better philosophical views on the same topics, but (for purposes of political theory) benignly to neglect these topics. As he says:

> since justice as fairness is intended as a political conception of justice for a democratic society, it tries to draw solely upon basic intuitive ideas that are embedded in the political institutions of a democratic society and the public traditions of their interpretation. Justice as fairness is a political conception in part because it starts from within a certain political tradition. We hope that this political conception of justice may be at least supported by what we may call 'overlapping consensus', that is, by a consensus that includes all the opposing philosophical and religious doctrines likely to persist and gain adherents in a more or less just constitutional democratic society.[8]

Rawls thinks that 'philosophy as the search for truth about an independent metaphysical and moral order cannot ... provide a workable and shared basis for a political conception of justice in a democratic society'.[9] So he suggests that we confine ourselves to collecting, 'such settled convictions as the belief in religious toleration and the rejection of slavery' and then 'try to organize the basic intuitive ideas and principles implicit in these convictions into a coherent conception of justice'.[10]

This attitude is thoroughly historicist and antiuniversalist.[11] Rawls can wholeheartedly agree with Hegel and Dewey against Kant and can say that the Enlightenment attempt to free oneself from tradition and history, to appeal to 'Nature' or 'Reason', was self-deceptive.[12] He can see such an appeal as a misguided attempt to make philosophy do what theology failed to do. Rawls's effort to, in his words, 'stay on the surface, philosophically speaking' can be seen as taking Jefferson's avoidance of theology one step further.

On the Deweyan view I am attributing to Rawls, no such discipline as 'philosophical anthropology' is required as a preface to politics, but only history and sociology. Further, it is misleading to think of his view as Dworkin does: as 'rights-based' as opposed to 'goal-based'. For the notion of 'basis' is not in point. It is not that we know, on antecedent philosophical grounds, that it is of the essence of human beings to have rights, and then proceed to ask how a society might preserve and protect these rights. On the question of priority, as on the question of the relativity of justice to historical situations, Rawls is closer to Walzer than to Dworkin.[13] Since Rawls does not believe that for purposes of political theory, we need think of ourselves as having an essence that precedes and antedates history, he would not agree with Sandel that for these purposes, we need have an account of 'the nature of the moral subject', which is 'in some sense necessary, non-contingent and prior to any particular experience'.[14] Some of our ancestors may have required such an account, just as others of our ancestors required such an account, of their relation to their putative Creator. But *we* – we heirs of the Enlightenment for whom justice has become the first virtue – need neither. As citizens and as social theorists, we can be as indifferent to philosophical disagreements about the nature of the self as Jefferson was to theological differences about the nature of God.

This last point suggests a way of sharpening up my claim that Rawls's advocacy of philosophical toleration is a plausible extension of Jefferson's advocacy of religious toleration. Both 'religion' and 'philosophy' are vague umbrella terms, and both are subject to persuasive redefinition. When these terms are broadly enough defined, everybody, even atheists, will be said to have a religious faith (in the Tillichian sense of a 'symbol of ultimate concern'). Everybody, even those who shun metaphysics and epistemology, will be said to have 'philosophical presuppositions'.[15] But for purposes of interpreting Jefferson and Rawls, we must use narrower definitions. Let 'religion' mean, for Jefferson's purposes, disputes about the nature and the true name of God – and even about his existence.[16] Let 'philosophy' mean, for Rawls's purposes, disputes about the nature of human beings and even about whether there is such a thing as 'human nature'.[17] Using these definitions, we can say that Rawls wants views about man's nature and purpose to be detached from politics. As he says, he wants his conception of justice to 'avoid . . . claims about the essential nature and identity of persons'.[18] So presumably, he wants questions about the point of human existence, or the meaning of human life, to be reserved for private life. A liberal democracy will not only exempt opinions on such matters from legal coercion, but also aim at disengaging discussions of such questions from discussions of social policy. Yet it will use force against the individual conscience, just in so far as conscience leads individuals to act so as to threaten democratic institutions. Unlike Jefferson's, Rawls's argument against fanaticism is not that it threatens truth about the characteristics of an antecedent metaphysical and moral order by threatening free discussion, but *simply* that it threatens freedom, and thus threatens justice. Truth about the existence or nature of that order drops out.

The definition of 'philosophy' I have just suggested is not as artificial and *ad hoc* as it may appear. Intellectual historians commonly treat 'the nature of the human subject' as the topic that gradually replaced 'God' as European culture secularized itself. This has been the central topic of metaphysics and epistemology from the seventeenth century to the present, and, for better or worse, metaphysics and epistemology have been taken to be the 'core' of philosophy.[19] In so far as one thinks that political conclusions require extrapolitical grounding – that is, in so far as one thinks Rawls's method of reflective equilibrium[20] is not good enough – one will want an account of the 'authority' of those general principles.

If one feels a need for such legitimation, one will want either a religious or a philosophical preface to politics.[21] One will be likely to share Horkheimer and Adorno's fear that pragmatism is not strong enough to hold a free society together. But Rawls echoes Dewey in suggesting that in so far as justice becomes the first virtue of a society, the need for such legitimation may gradually cease to be felt. Such a society will become accustomed to the thought that social policy needs no more authority than successful accommodation among individuals, individuals who find themselves heir to the same historical traditions and faced with the same problems. It will be a society that encourages the 'end of ideology', that takes reflective equilibrium as the only method needed in discussing social policy. When such a society deliberates, when it collects the principles and intuitions to be brought into equilibrium, it will tend to discard those drawn from philosophical accounts of the self or of rationality. For such a society will view such accounts not as the foundations of political institutions, but as, at worst, philosophical mumbo jumbo, or, at best, relevant to private searches for perfection, but not to social policy.[22]

In order to spell out the contrast between Rawls's attempt to 'stay on the surface, philosophically speaking' and the traditional attempt to dig down to 'philosophical foundations of democracy'. I shall turn briefly to Sandel's *Liberalism and the Limits of Justice*. This clear and forceful book provides very elegant and cogent arguments against the attempt to use a certain conception of the self, a certain metaphysical view of what human beings are like, to legitimize liberal politics. Sandel attributes this attempt to Rawls. Many people, including myself, initially took Rawls's *Theory of Justice* to be such an attempt. We read it as a continuation of the Enlightenment attempt to ground our moral intuitions on a conception of human nature (and, more specifically, as a neo-Kantian attempt to ground them on the notion of 'rationality'). However, Rawls's writings subsequent to *A Theory of Justice* have helped us realize that we were misinterpreting his book, that we had overemphasized the Kantian and underemphasized the Hegelian and Deweyan elements. These writings make more explicit than did his book Rawls's metaphilosophical doctrine that 'what justifies a conception of justice is not its being true to an order antecedent to and given to us, but its congruence with our deeper understanding of ourselves and our aspirations, and our realization that, *given our history and the traditions embedded in our public life*, it is the most reasonable doctrine *for us*'.[23]

When reread in the light of such passages, *A Theory of Justice* no longer seems committed to a philosophical account of the human self, but only to a historico-sociological description of the way we live now.

Sandel sees Rawls as offering us 'deontology with a Humean face' – that is, a Kantian universalistic approach to social thought without the handicap of Kant's idealistic metaphysics. He thinks that this will not work, that a social theory of the sort that Rawls wants requires us to postulate the sort of self that Descartes and Kant invented to replace God – one that can be distinguished from the Kantian 'empirical self' as having various 'contingent desires, wants and ends', rather than being a mere concatenation of beliefs and desires. Since such a concatenation – what Sandel calls a 'radically situated subject'[24] – is all that Hume offers us, Sandel thinks that Rawls's project is doomed.[25] On Sandel's account, Rawls's doctrine that 'justice is the first virtue of social institutions' requires back-up from the metaphysical claim that 'teleology to the contrary, what is most essential to our personhood is not the ends we choose but our capacity to choose them. And this capacity is located in a self which must be prior to the ends it chooses'.[26]

But reading *A Theory of Justice* as political rather than metaphysical, one can see that when Rawls says that 'the self is prior to the ends which are affirmed by it',[27] he need not mean that there is an entity called 'the self' that is something distinct from the web of beliefs and desires that that self 'has'. When he says that 'we should not attempt to give form to our life by first looking to the good independently defined',[28] he is not basing this 'should' on a claim about the nature of the self. 'Should' is not to be glossed by 'because of the intrinsic nature of morality'[29] or 'because a capacity for choice is the essence of personhood', but by something like 'because *we* – we modern inheritors of the traditions of religious tolerance and constitutional government – put liberty ahead of perfection'.

This willingness to invoke what *we* do raises, as I have said, the spectres of ethnocentrism and of relativism. Because Sandel is convinced that Rawls shares Kant's fear of these spectres, he is convinced that Rawls is looking for an '"Archimedean point" from which to assess the basic structure of society' – a 'standpoint neither compromised by its implication in the world nor dissociated and so disqualified by detachment'.[30] It is just this idea that a standpoint can be 'compromised by its implication in the world' that Rawls rejects in his recent writings. Philosophically inclined communitarians like Sandel are unable to envisage a middle ground between relativism and a 'theory of the moral subject' – a theory that is not about, for example, religious tolerance and large market economies, but about human beings as such, viewed ahistorically. Rawls is trying to stake out just such a middle ground.[31] When he speaks of an 'Archimedean point', he does not mean a point outside history, but simply the kind of settled social habits that allow much latitude for further choices. He says, for example:

> The upshot of these considerations is that justice as fairness is not at the mercy, so to speak, of existing wants and interests. It sets up an Archimedean point for assessing the social system without invoking a priori considerations. The long range aim of society is settled in its main lines irrespective of the particular desires and needs of its present members. . . . There is no place for the question whether men's desires to play the role of superior or inferior might not be so great that autocratic institutions should be accepted, or whether men's perception of the religious practices of others might not be so upsetting that liberty of conscience should not be allowed.[32]

To say that there is no place for the questions that Nietzsche or Loyola would raise is not to say that the views of either are unintelligible (in the sense of 'logically incoherent' or 'conceptually confused'). Nor is it to say that they are based on an incorrect theory of the self. Nor is it *just* to say that our preferences conflict with theirs.[33] It is to say that the conflict between these men and us is so great that 'preferences' is the wrong word. It is appropriate to speak of gustatory or sexual preferences, for these do not matter to anybody but yourself and your immediate circle. But it is misleading to speak of a 'preference' for liberal democracy.

Rather, we heirs of the Enlightenment think of enemies of liberal democracy like Nietzsche or Loyola as, to use Rawls's word, 'mad'. We do so because there is no way to see them as fellow citizens of our constitutional democracy, people whose life plans might, given ingenuity and good will, be fitted with those of other citizens. They are not crazy because they have mistaken the ahistorical nature of human beings. They are crazy because the limits of sanity are set by what *we* can take seriously. This, in turn, is determined by our upbringing, our historical situation.[34]

If this short way of dealing with Nietzsche and Loyola seems shockingly ethnocentric, it is because the philosophical tradition has accustomed us to the idea that anybody who is willing to listen to reason – to hear out all the arguments – can be brought around to the truth. This view, which Kierkegaard called 'Socratism' and contrasted with the claim that our point of departure may be simply an historical event, is intertwined with the idea that the human self has a centre (a divine spark, or a truth-tracking faculty called 'reason') and that argumentation will, given time and patience, penetrate to this centre. For Rawls's purposes, we do not need this picture. We are free to see the self as centreless, as an historical contingency all the way through. Rawls neither needs nor wants to defend the priority of the right to the good as Kant defended it, by invoking a theory of the self that makes it more than an 'empirical self', more than a 'radically situated subject'. He presumably thinks of Kant as, although largely right about the nature of justice, largely wrong about the nature and function of philosophy.

More specifically, he can reject Sandel's Kantian claim that there is a 'distance between subject and situation which is necessary to any measure of detachment, is essential to the ineliminably *possessive* aspect of any coherent conception of the self'.[35] Sandel defines this aspect by saying, 'I can never fully be constituted by my attributes . . . there must always be some attributes I *have* rather than am.' On the interpretation of Rawls I am offering, we do not need a categorical distinction between the self and its situation. We can dismiss the distinction between an attribute of the self and a constituent of the self, between the self's accidents and its essence, as 'merely' metaphysical.[36] If we are inclined to philosophize, we shall want the vocabulary offered by Dewey, Heidegger, Davidson and Derrida, with its built-in cautions against metaphysics, rather than that offered by Descartes, Hume, and Kant.[37] For if we use the former vocabulary, we shall be able to see moral progress as a history of making rather than finding, of poetic achievement by 'radically situated' individuals and communities, rather than as the gradual unveiling, through the use of 'reason', or 'principles' or 'rights' or 'values'.

Sandel's claim that 'the concept of a subject given prior to and independent of its objects offers a foundation for the moral law that . . . powerfully completes the deontological vision' is true enough. But to suggest such a powerful completion to Rawls is to offer him a poisoned gift. It is like offering Jefferson an argument for religious tolerance based on exogesis of the Christian Scriptures.[38] Rejecting the assumption that the moral law needs a 'foundation' is just what distinguishes Rawls from Jefferson. It is just this that permits him to be a Deweyan naturalist who needs neither the distinction between will and intellect nor the distinction between the self's constituents and its attributes. He does not *want* a 'complete deontological vision', one that would explain *why* we should give justice priority over our conception of the good. He is filling out the consequences of the claim that it is prior, not its presuppositions.[39] Rawls is not interested in conditions for the identity of the self, but only in conditions for citizenship in a liberal society.

Suppose one grants that Rawls is not attempting a transcendetnal deduction of American liberalism or supplying philosophical foundations for democratic institutions, but simply trying to systematize the principles and intuitions typical of American liberals. Still, it may seem that the important questions raised by the critics of liberalism have been begged. Consider the claim that we liberals can simply dismiss Nietzsche and Loyola as crazy. One imagines these two rejoining that they are quite aware that their views unfit them for citizenship in a constitutional democracy and that the typical inhabitant of such a democracy would regard them as crazy. But they take these facts as further counts against constitutional democracy. They think that the kind of person created by such a democracy is not what a human being should be.

In finding a dialectical stance to adopt toward Nietzsche or Loyola, we liberal democrats are faced with a dilemma. To refuse to argue about what human beings should be like seems to show a contempt for the spirit of accommodation and tolerance, which is essential to democracy. But it is not clear how to argue for the claim that human beings ought to be liberals rather than fanatics without being driven back on a theory of human nature, on philosophy. I think that we must grasp the first horn. We have to insist that not every argument needs to be met in the terms in which it is presented. Accommodation and tolerance must stop short of a willingness to work within any vocabulary that one's interlocutor wishes to use, to take seriously any topic that he puts forward for discussion. To take this view is of a piece with dropping the idea that a single moral vocabulary and a single set of moral beliefs are appropriate for every human community everywhere, and to grant that historical developments may lead us to simply *drop* questions and the vocabulary in which those questions are posed.

Just as Jefferson refused to let the Christian Scriptures set the terms in which to discuss alternative political institutions, so we either must refuse to answer the question 'What sort of human being are you hoping to produce?' or, at least, must not let our answer to this question dictate our answer to the question 'Is justice primary?'[40] It is no more evident that democratic institutions are to be measured by the sort of person they create than that they are to be measured against divine commands. It is not evident that they are to be measured by anything more specific than the moral institutions of the particular historical community that has created those institutions. The idea that moral and political controversies should always be 'brought back to first principles' is reasonable if it means merely that we should seek common ground in the hope of attaining agreement. But it is misleading if it is taken as the claim that there is a natural order of premises from which moral and political conclusions are to be inferred – not to mention the claim that some particular interlocutor (e.g. Nietzsche or Loyola) has already discerned that order. The liberal response to the communitarians' second claim must be, therefore, that even if the typical character types of liberal democracy *are* bland, calculating, petty, and unheroic, the prevalence of such people may be a reasonable price to pay for political freedom.

The spirit of accommodation and tolerance certainly suggests that we should seek common ground with Nietzsche and Loyola, but there is no predicting where, or whether, such common ground will be found. The philosophical tradition has assumed that there are certain topics (e.g. 'What is God's will?' 'What is man?' 'What rights are intrinsic to the species?') on which everyone has, or should have, views and that these topics are prior in the order of justification to those at issue in political deliberation. This assumption goes along with the assumption that human beings have a natural centre that philosophical enquiry can locate and illuminate. By contrast, the view that human beings are centreless networks of beliefs and desires and that their vocabularies and opinions are determined by historical circumstance allows for the possibility that there may not be enough overlap between two such networks to make possible agreement about political topics, or even profitable discussion of such topics.[41] We do not conclude that Nietzsche and Loyola are crazy because they hold unusual views on certain 'fundamental' topics; rather, we conclude this only after extensive attempts at an exchange of political views have made us realize that we are not going to get anywhere.[42]

One can sum up this way of grasping the first horn of the dilemma I sketched earlier by saying that Rawls puts the democratic politics first, and philosophy second. He retains the Socratic commitment to free exchange of views without the Platonic commitment to the possibility of universal agreement – a possibility underwritten by epistemological doctrines like Plato's Theory of Recollection[43] or Kant's theory of the relation between pure and empirical concepts. He disengages the question of whether we ought to be tolerant and Socratic from the question of whether this strategy will lead to truth. He is content that it should lead to whatever intersubjective reflective equilibrium may be obtainable, given the contingent make-up of the subjects in question. Truth, viewed in the Platonic way, as the grasp of what Rawls calls 'an order antecedent to and given to us', is simply not relevant to democratic politics. So philosophy, as the explanation of the relation between such an order and human nature, is not relevant either. When the two come into conflict, democracy takes precedence over philosophy.

This conclusion may seem liable to an obvious objection. It may seem that I have been rejecting a concern with philosophical theories about the nature of men and women on the basis of just such a theory. But notice that although I have frequently said that Rawls *can be content* with a notion of the human self as a centreless web of historically conditioned beliefs and desires, I have not suggested that he *needs* such a theory. Such a theory does not offer liberal social theory a *basis*. If one *wants* a model of the human self, then this picture of a centreless web will fill the need. But for purposes of liberal social theory, one can do without such a model. One can get along with commonsense and social science, areas of discourse in which the term 'the self' rarely occurs.

If, however, one has a taste for philosophy – if one's vocation, one's private pursuit of perfection, entails constructing models of such entities as 'the self', 'knowledge', 'language', 'nature', 'God' or 'history', and then tinkering with them until they mesh with one another – one *will* want a picture of the self. Since my own vocation is of this sort, and the moral identity around which I wish to build such models is that of a citizen of a liberal democratic state, I commend the picture of the self as a centreless and contingent web to those with similar tastes and similar identities. But I would not commend it to those with a similar vocation but dissimilar moral identities – identities built, for example, around the love of God, Nietzschean self-overcoming, the accurate representation of reality as it is in itself, the quest for 'one right answer' to moral questions, or the natural superiority of a given character type. Such persons need a more complex and interesting, less simple-minded model of the self – one that meshes in complex ways with complex models of such things as 'nature' or 'history'. Nevertheless, such persons may, for pragmatic rather than moral reasons, be loyal citizens of a liberal democratic society. They may despise most of their fellow citizens, but be prepared to grant that the prevalence of such despicable character types is a lesser evil than the loss of political freedom. They may be ruefully grateful that their private senses of moral identity and the models of the human self that they develop to articulate this sense – the ways in which they deal with their aloneness – are not the concern of such a state. Rawls and Dewey have shown how the liberal state can ignore the difference between the moral identities of Glaucon and of Thrasymachus, just as it ignores the difference between the religious identities of a Catholic archbishop and a Mormon prophet.

There is, however, a flavour of paradox in this attitude towards theories of the self. One might be inclined to say that I have evaded one sort of self-referential paradox only by falling into another sort. For I am presupposing that one is at liberty to rig up a model of the self to suit oneself, to tailor it to one's politics, one's religion or one's private sense of the meaning of one's life. This, in turn, presupposes that there is no 'objective truth' about what the human self is *really* like. That, in turn, seems a claim that could be justified only on the basis of a metaphysico-epistemological view of the traditional sort. For surely if anything is the province of such a view, it is the question of what there is and is not a 'fact of the matter' about. So my argument must ultimately come back to philosophical first principles.

Here I can only say that if there were a discoverable fact of the matter about what there is a fact of the matters about, then it would doubtless be metaphysics and epistemology that would discover that meta-fact. But I think that the very idea of a 'fact of the matter' is one we would be better off without. Philosophers like Davidson and Derrida have, I think, given us good reason to think that the *physis-nomos, in se-ad nos* and objective – subjective distinctions were steps on a ladder that we can now safely throw away. The question of whether the reasons such philosophers have given for this claim are themselves metaphysico-epistemological reasons, and if not, what sort of reasons they are, strikes me as pointless and sterile. Once again, I fall back on the holist's strategy of insisting that reflective equilibrium is all we need try for – that there is no natural order of justification of beliefs, no predestined outline for argument to trace. Getting rid of the idea of such an outline seems to me one of the many benefits of a conception of the self as a centreless web. Another benefit is that questions about whom we need justify ourselves to – questions about who counts as a fanatic and who deserves an answer – can be treated as just further matters to be sorted out in the course of attaining reflective equilibrium.

I can, however, make one point to offset the air of light-minded aestheticism I am adopting towards traditional philosophical questions. This is that there is a moral purpose behind this light-mindedness. The encouragement of light-mindedness about traditional philosophical topics serves the same purposes as does the encouragement of light-mindedness about traditional theological topics. Like the rise of large market economies, the increase in literacy, the proliferation of artistic genres and the insouciant pluralism of contemporary culture, such philosophical superficiality and light-mindedness helps along the disenchantment of the world. It helps make the world's inhabitants more pragmatic, more tolerant, more liberal, more receptive to the appeal of instrumental rationality.

If one's moral identity consists in being a citizen of a liberal polity, then to encourage light-mindedness will serve one's moral purposes. Moral commitment, after all, does not require taking seriously all the matters that are, for moral reasons, taken seriously by one's fellow citizens. It may require just the opposite. It may require trying to josh them out of the habit of taking those topics so seriously. There may be serious reasons for so joshing them. More generally, we should not assume that the aesthetic is always the enemy of the moral. I should argue that in the recent history of liberal societies, the willingness to view matters aesthetically – to be content to indulge in what Schiller called 'play' and to discard what Nietzsche called 'the spirit of seriousness' – has been an important vehicle of moral progress.

I have now said everything I have to say about the third of the communitarian claims that I distinguished at the outset: the claim that the social theory of the liberal state rests on false philosophical presuppositions. I hope I have given reasons for thinking that in so far as the communitarian is a critic of liberalism, he should drop this claim and should instead develop either of the first two claims: the empirical claim that democratic institutions cannot be combined with the sense of common purpose that predemocratic societies enjoyed, or the moral judgement that the products of the liberal state are too high a price to pay for the elimination of the evils that preceded it. If communitarian critics of liberalism stuck to these two claims, they would avoid the sort of terminal wistfulness with which their books typically end. Heidegger, for example, tells us that 'we are too late for the gods, and too early for Being'. Unger ends *Knowledge and Politics* with an appeal to a *Deus absconditus*. MacIntyre ends *After Virtue* by saying that we 'are waiting not for a Godot, but for another – doubtless very different – St Benedict.'[44] Sandel ends his book by saying that liberalism 'forgets the possibility that when politics goes well, we can know a good in common that we cannot know alone', but he does not suggest a candidate for this common good.

Instead of thus suggesting that philosophical reflection, or a return to religion, might enable us to re-enchant the world, I think that communitarians should stick to the question of whether disenchantment has, on balance, done us more harm than good, or created more dangers than it has evaded. For Dewey, communal and public disenchantment is the price we pay for individual and private spiritual liberation, the kind of liberation that Emerson thought characteristically American. Dewey was as well aware as Weber that there is a price to be paid, but he thought it well worth paying. He assumed that no good achieved by earlier societies would be worth recapturing if the price were a diminution in our ability to leave people alone, to let them try out their private visions of perfection in peace. He admired the American habit of giving democracy priority over philosophy by asking, about any vision of the meaning of life, 'Would not acting out this vision interfere with the ability of others to work out their own salvation?' Giving priority to that question is no more 'natural' than giving priority to, say, MacIntyre's question 'What sorts of human beings emerge in the culture of liberalism?' or Sandel's question 'Can a community of those who put justice first ever be more than a community of strangers?' The question of which of these questions is prior to which others is, necessarily, begged by *everybody*. Nobody is being any more arbitrary than anybody else. But that is to say that nobody is being arbitrary at all. Everybody is just insisting that the beliefs and desires they hold most dear should come first in the order of discussion. That is not arbitrariness, but sincerity.

The danger of re-enchanting the world, from a Deweyan point of view, is that it might interfere with the development of what Rawls calls 'a social union of social unions',[45] some of which may be (and in Emerson's view, should be) very small indeed. For it is hard to be both enchanted with one version of the world and tolerant of all the others. I have not tried to argue the question of whether Dewey was right in this judgement of relative danger and promise. I have merely argued that such a judgement neither presupposes nor supports a theory of the self. Nor have I tried to deal with Horkheimer and Adorno's prediction that the 'dissolvent rationality' of the Enlightenment will eventually cause the liberal democracies to come unstuck.

The only thing I have to say about this prediction is that the collapse of the liberal democracies would not, in itself, provide much evidence for the claim that human societies cannot survive without widely shared opinions on matters of ultimate importance – shared conceptions of our place in the universe and our mission on earth. Perhaps they cannot survive under such conditions, but the eventual collapse of the democracies would not, in itself, show that this was the case – any more than it would show that human societies require kings or an established religion, or that political community cannot exist outside of small city-states.

Both Jefferson and Dewey described America as an 'experiment'. If the experiment fails, our descendants may learn something important. But they will not learn a philosophical truth, any more than they will learn a religious one. They will simply get some hints about what to watch for when setting up their next experiment. Even if nothing else survives from the age of the democratic revolutions, perhaps our descendants will remember that social institutions *can* be viewed as experiments in co-operation rather than as attempts to embody a universal and ahistorical order. It is hard to believe that this memory would not be worth having.

NOTES

Richard Rorty's 'The Priority of Democracy to Philosophy' first appeared in *The Virginia Statute for Religious Freedom*, ed. M. D. Peterson and R. C. Vaughan (Cambridge University Press, Cambridge, 1988). It is reprinted by permission of the publishers.

1 Thomas Jefferson, *Notes on the State of Virginia*, Query XVII, in *The Writings of Thomas Jefferson*, ed. A. A. Lipscomb and A. E. Bergh (Washington, D.C., 1905), 2: 217.
2 Jefferson included a statement of this familiar scriptural claim (roughly in the form in which it had been restated by Milton in *Areopagitica*) in the preamble to the Virginia Statute for Religious Freedom: 'truth is great and will prevail if left to herself, . . . she is the proper and sufficient antagonist to error, and has nothing to fear from the conflict, unless by human interposition disarmed of her natural weapons, free argument and debate, errors ceasing to be dangerous when it is permitted freely to contradict them' (ibid., 2: 302).
3 Max Horkheimer and Theodor W. Adorno, *Dialectic of Enlightenment* (Seabury Press, New York, 1972), p. xiii.
4 'For the Enlightenment, whatever does not conform to the rule of computation and utility is suspect. So long as it can develop undisturbed by any outward repression, there is no holding it. In the process, it treats its own ideas of human rights exactly as it does

the older universals . . . Enlightenment is totalitarian' (ibid., p. 6). This line of thought recurs repeatedly in communitarian accounts of the present state of the liberal democracies; see, for example, Robert Bellah, Richard Madsen, William Sullivan, Ann Swidler, and Steven Tipton, *Habits of the Heart: Individualism and Commitment in American Life* (University of California Press, Berkeley, 1985): 'There is a widespread feeling that the promise of the modern era is slipping away from us. A movement of enlightenment and the liberation that was to have freed us from superstition and tyranny has led in the twentieth century to a world in which ideological fanaticism and political oppression have reached extremes unknown in previous history' (p. 277).

5   Charles Taylor, *Philosophy and the Human Sciences*, vol. 2 of *Philosophical Papers* (Cambridge University Press, Cambridge, 1985), p. 8.

6   Ibid., p. 5.

7   John Rawls, 'Justice as Fairness: Political not Metaphysical', *Philosophy and Public Affairs*, 14 (1985), p. 225. Religious toleration is a constantly recurring theme in Rawls's writing. Early in *A Theory of Justice* (Harvard University Press, Cambridge, Mass., 1971), when giving examples of the sort of common opinions that a theory of justice must take into account and systematize, he cites out conviction that religious intolerance is unjust (p. 19). His example of the fact that 'a well-ordered society tends to eliminate or at least to control men's inclinations to injustice' is that 'warring and intolerant sects are much less likely to exist' (p. 247). Another relevant passage (which I shall discuss below) is his diagnosis of Ignatius Loyola's attempt to make the love of God the 'dominant good': 'Although to subordinate all our aims to one end does not strictly speaking violate the principles of rational choice . . . it still strikes us as irrational, or more likely as mad' (pp. 553–4).

8   Rawls, 'Justice as Fairness', pp. 225–6. The suggestion that there are many philosophical views that will *not* survive in such conditions is analogous to the Enlightenment suggestion that the adoption of democratic institutions will cause 'superstitious' forms of religious belief gradually to die off.

9   Ibid., p. 230.

10 Ibid.

11 For Rawls's historicism see, for example, *Theory of Justice*, p. 547. There, Rawls says that the people in the original position are assumed to know 'the general facts about society', including the fact that 'institutions are not fixed but change over time, altered by natural circumstances and the activities and conflicts of social groups'. He uses this point to rule out, as original choosers of principles of justice, those 'in a feudal or a caste system', those who are unaware of events such as the French Revolution. This is one of many passages that make clear (at least read in the light of Rawls's later work) that a great deal of knowledge that came late to the mind of Europe is present to the minds of those behind the veil of ignorance. Or, to put it another way, such passages make clear that those original choosers behind the veil exemplify a certain modern type of human being, not an ahistorical human nature. See also p. 548, where Rawls says, 'Of course in working out what the requisite principles [of justice] are, we must rely upon current knowledge as recognized by commonsense and the existing scientific consensus. We have to concede that as established beliefs change, it is possible that the principles of justice which it seems rational to choose may likewise change.'

12 See Bellah et al., *Habits of the Heart*, p. 141, for a recent restatement of this 'counter-Enlightenment' line of thought. For the authors' view of the problems created by persistence in Enlightenment rhetoric and by the prevalence of the conception of human dignity that Taylor identifies as 'distinctively modern', see p. 21: 'For most of us, it is easier to think about to get what we want than to know exactly what we should want. Thus Brian, Joe, Margaret and Wayne [some of the Americans interviewed by the

authors] are each in his or her own way confused about how to define for themselves such things as the nature of success, the meaning of freedom, and the requirements of justice. Those difficulties are in an important way created by the limitations in the common tradition of moral discourse they – and we – share.' Compare p. 290: 'the language of individualism, the primary American language of self-understanding, limits the way in which people think.'

To my mind, the authors of *Habits of the Heart* undermine their own conclusions in the passages where they point to actual moral progress being made in recent American history, notably in their discussion of the civil-rights movement. There, they say that Martin Luther King, Jr, made the struggle for freedom 'a practice of commitment within a vision of America as a community of memory' and that the response King elicited 'came from the reawakened recognition by many Americans that their own sense of self was rooted in companionship with others who, though not necessarily like themselves, nevertheless shared with them a common history and whose appeals to justice and solidarity made powerful claims on our loyalty' (p. 252). These descriptions of King's achievement seem exactly right, but they can be read as evidence that the rhetoric of the Enlightenment offers at least as many opportunities as it does obstacles for the renewal of a sense of community. The civil-rights movement combined, without much strain, the language of Christian fellowship and the 'language of individualism', about which Bellah and his colleagues are dubious.

13 See Michael Walzer, *Spheres of Justice* (Basic Books, New York, 1983), pp. 312 ff.

14 Michael Sandel, *Liberalism and the Limits of Justice* (Cambridge University Press, Cambridge, 1982), p. 49.

15 In a recent, as yet unpublished, paper, Sandel has urged that Rawls's claim that 'philosophy in the classical sense as the search for truth about a prior and independent moral order cannot provide the shared basis for a political conception of justice' presupposes the controversial metaphysical claim that there is no such order. This seems to me like saying that Jefferson was presupposing the controversial theological claim that God is not interested in the name by which he is called by human beings. Both charges are accurate, but not really to the point. Both Jefferson and Rawls would have to reply, 'I have no arguments for my dubious theological-metaphysical claim, because I do not know how to discuss such issues, and do not want to. My interest is in helping to preserve and create political institutions that will foster public indifference to such issues, while putting no restrictions on private discussion of them.' This reply, of course, begs the 'deeper' question that Sandel wants to raise, for the question of whether we *should* determine what issues to discuss on political or on 'theoretical' (e.g. theological or philosophical) grounds remains unanswered. (At the end of this paper, I briefly discuss the need for philosophers to escape from the requirement to answer questions phrased in vocabularies they wish to replace, and in more detail in 'Beyond Realism and Anti-Realism', in *Wo steht die sprachanalytische Philosophie heute?*, ed. Herta Nagl-Docekal et al. [forthcoming].)

16 Jefferson agreed with Luther that philosophers had muddied the clear waters of the gospels. See Jefferson's polemic against Plato's 'foggy mind' and his claim that 'the doctrines which flowed from the lips of Jesus himself are within the comprehension of a child; but thousands of volumes have not yet explained the Platonisms engrafted on them; and for this obvious reason, that nonsense can never be explained' (*Writings of Thomas Jefferson*, 14:149).

17 I am here using the term 'human nature' in the traditional philosophical sense in which Sartre denied that there was such a thing, rather than in the rather unusual one that Rawls gives it. Rawls distinguishes between a 'conception of the person' and a 'theory of human nature', where the former is a 'moral ideal' and the latter is provided by,

roughly, commonsense plus the social sciences. To have a theory of human nature is to have 'general facts that we take to be true enough, given the state of public knowledge in our society', facts that 'limit the feasibility of the ideals of person and society embedded in that framework' ('Kantian Constructivism in Moral Theory', *Journal of Philosophy*, 77 (1980), p. 534).

18　Rawls, 'Justice as Fairness', p. 223.

19　In fact, it has been for the worse. A view that made politics more central to philosophy and subjectivity less would both permit more effective defences of democracy than those that purport to supply it with 'foundations' and permit liberals to meet Marxists on their own, political, ground. Dewey's explicit attempt to make the central philosophical question 'What serves democracy?' rather than 'What permits us to argue for democracy?' has been, unfortunately, neglected. I try to make this point in 'Philosophy as Science, as Metaphor, and as Politics', in *The Institution of Philosophy*, ed. Avner Cohen and Marcello Dascal (Rowman & Allenfield, Totowa, NJ, forthcoming).

20　That is, give-and-take between intuitions about the desirability of particular consequences of particular actions and intuitions about general principles, with neither having the determining voice.

21　One will also, as I did on first reading Rawls, take him to be attempting to supply such legitimation by an appeal to the rationality of the choosers in the original position (the position of those who, behind a veil of ignorance that hides them from their life chances and their conceptions of the good, select from among alternative principles of justice) served simply 'to make vivid . . . the restrictions that it seems reasonable to impose on arguments for principles of justice and therefore on those principles themselves' (*Theory of Justice*, p. 18).

　　But this warning went unheeded by myself and others, in part because of an ambiguity between 'reasonable' as defined by ahistorical criteria and as meaning something like 'in accord with the moral sentiments characteristic of the heirs of the Enlightenment'. Rawls's later work has, as I have said, helped us come down on the historicist side of this ambiguity; see, for example, 'Kantian Constructivism': 'the original position is not an axiomatic (or deductive) basis from which principles most fitting to the conception of the person most likely to be held, at least implicitly, in a democratic society' (p. 572). It is tempting to suggest that one could eliminate all reference to the original position from *A Theory of Justice* without loss, but this is as daring a suggestion as that one might rewrite (as many have wished to do) Kant's *Critique of Pure Reason* without reference to the thing-in-itself. T. M. Scanlon has suggested that we can, at least, safely eliminate reference, in the description of the choosers in the original position, to an appeal to self-interest in describing the motives of those choosers. ('Contractualism and Utilitarianism', in *Utilitarianism and Beyond*, ed. Bernard Williams and Amartya Sen, Cambridge University Press, Cambridge, 1982.) Since justifiability is, more evidently than self-interest, relative to historical circumstance, Scanlon's proposal seems to be more faithful to Rawls's overall philosophical programme than Rawls's own formulation.

22　In particular, there will be no principles or intuitions concerning the universal features of human psychology relevant to motivation. Sandel thinks that since assumptions about motivation are part of the description of the original position, 'what issues at one end in a theory of justice must issue at the other in a theory of the person, or more precisely, a theory of the moral subject' (*Liberalism and the Limits of Justice*, p. 47). I would argue that if we follow Scanlon's lead (note 17) in dropping reference to self-interest in our description of the original choosers and replacing this with reference to their desire to justify their choices to their fellows, then the only 'theory of the person' we get is a sociological description of the inhabitants of contemporary liberal democracies.

23 Rawls, 'Kantian Constructivism', p. 519. Italics added.
24 Sandel, *Liberalism and the Limits of Justice*, p. 21. I have argued for the advantages of thinking of the self as just such a concatenation; see 'Postmodernist Bourgeois Liberalism', *Journal of Philosophy*, 80 (1983), pp. 583–9 and 'Freud and Moral Reflection', in *The Pragmatists' Freud*, ed. Joseph E. Smith and William Kerrigan (Johns Hopkins University Press, Baltimore, 1986). When Sandel quotes Robert Nozick and Daniel Bell as suggesting that Rawls 'ends by dissolving the self in order to preserve it' (*Liberalism and the Limits of Justice*, p. 95), I should rejoin that it may be helpful to dissolve the metaphysical self in order to preserve the political one. Less obliquely stated: it may be helpful, for purposes, of systematizing our intuitions about the priority of liberty, to treat the self as having no centre, no essence, but *merely* as a concatenation of beliefs and desires.
25 'Deontology with a Humean face either fails as deontology or recreates in the original position the disembodied subject it resolves to avoid' (ibid., p. 14).
26 Ibid., p. 19.
27 Rawls, *Theory of Justice*, p. 560.
28 Ibid.
29 It is important to note that Rawls explicitly distances himself from the idea that he is analysing the very idea of morality and from the conceptual analysis as the method of social theory (ibid., p. 130). Some of his critics have suggested that Rawls is practising 'reductive logical analysis' of the sort characteristic of 'analytic philosophy'; see, for example, William M. Sullivan, *Reconstructing Public Philosophy* (University of California Press, Berkeley, 1982), pp. 94 ff. Sullivan says that 'this ideal of reductive logical analysis lends legitimacy to the notion that moral philosophy is summed up in the task of discovering, through the analysis of moral rules, both primitive elements and governing principles that must apply to any rational moral system, *rational* here meaning "logically coherent"' (p. 96). He goes on to grant that 'Nozik and Rawls are more sensitive to the importance of history and social experience in human life than were the classic liberal thinkers' (p. 97). But this concession is too slight and is misleading. Rawls's willingness to adopt 'reflective equilibrium' rather than 'conceptual analysis' as a methodological watchword sets him apart from the epistemologically oriented moral philosophy that was dominant prior to the appearance of *A Theory of Justice*. Rawls represents a reaction against Kantian ideas of 'morality' as having an ahistorical essence, the same sort of reaction found in Hegel and in Dewey.
30 Sandel, *Liberalism and the Limits of Justice*, p. 17.
31 '. . . liberty of conscience and freedom of thought should not be founded on philosophical or ethical scepticism, nor on indifference to religious and moral interests. The principles of justice define an appropriate path between dogmatism and intolerance on the one side, and a reductionism which regards religion and morality as mere preferences on the other' (Rawls, *Theory of Justice*, p. 243). I take it that Rawls is identifying 'philosophical or ethical skepticism' with the idea that everything is just a matter of 'preference', even religion, philosophy, and morals. So we should distinguish his suggestion that we 'extend the principle of tolerance to philosophy itself' from the suggestion that we dismiss philosophy as epiphenomenal. That is the sort of suggestion that is backed up by reductionist accounts of philosophical doctrines as 'preferences' or 'wish fulfilments' or 'expressions of emotion' (see Rawls's criticism of Freudian reductionism in ibid., pp. 539 ff.). Neither psychology nor logic nor any other theoretical discipline can supply non-question-begging reasons why philosophy should be set aside, any more than philosophy can supply such reasons why theology should be set aside. But this is compatible with saying that the general course of historical experience may lead us to neglect theological topics and bring us to the point at which,

like Jefferson, we find a theological vocabulary 'meaningless' (or, more precisely, useless). I am suggesting that the course of historical experience since Jefferson's time has led us to a point at which we find much of the vocabulary of modern philosophy no longer useful.

32 Ibid., pp. 261–2.

33 The contrast between 'mere preference' and something less 'arbitrary', something more closely related to the very nature of man or of reason, is invoked by many writers who think of 'human rights' as requiring a philosophical foundation of the traditional sort. Thus my colleague David Little, commenting on my 'Solidarity or Objectivity?' (*Post-Analytic Philosophy*, ed. John Rajchman and Cornel West, Columbia University Press, New York, 1985), says 'Rorty appears to permit criticism and pressure against those societies [the ones we do not like] *if we happen to want to* criticize and pressure them in pursuit of some interest or belief we may (at the time) have, and for whatever ethnocentric reasons we may happen to hold those interests or beliefs' ('Natural Rights and Human Rights: The International Imperative', in *Natural Rights and Natural Law: The Legacy of George Mason*, ed. Robert P. Davidow, George Mason University Press, Fairfax, Va., 1986, pp. 67–122; italics in original). I would rejoin that Little's use of 'happen to want to' presupposes a dubious distinction between necessary, built-in, universal convictions (convictions that it would be 'irrational' to reject) and accidental, culturally determined convictions. It also presupposes the existence of such faculties as reason, will, and emotion, all of which the pragmatist tradition in American philosophy and the so-called existentialist tradition in European philosophy try to undercut. Dewey's *Human Nature and Conduct* and Heidegger's *Being and Time* both offer a moral psychology that avoids oppositions between 'preference' and 'reason'.

34 'Aristotle remarks that it is a peculiarity of men that they possess a sense of the just and the unjust and that their sharing a common understanding of justice makes a polis. Analogously one might say, in view of our discussion, that a common understanding of justice as fairness makes a constitutional democracy' (Rawls, *Theory of Justice*, p. 243). In the interpretations of Rawls I am offering, it is unrealistic to expect Aristotle to have developed a conception of justice as fairness, since he simply lacked the kind of historical experience that we have accumulated since his day. More generally, it is pointless to assume (with, for example, Leo Strauss) that the Greeks had already canvassed the alternatives available for social life and institutions. When we discuss justice, we cannot agree to bracket our knowledge of recent history.

35 Sandel, *Liberalism and the Limits of Justice*, p. 20.

36 We can dismiss other distinctions that Sandel draws in the same way. Examples are the distinction between a voluntarist and a cognitive account of the original position (ibid., p. 121), that between 'the identity of the subject' as the 'product' rather than the 'premise' of its agency (ibid., p. 152), and that between the question 'Who am I?' and its rival as 'the paradigmatic moral question', 'What shall I choose?' (ibid., p. 153). These distinctions are all to be analysed away as products of the 'Kantian dualisms' that Rawls praises Hegel and Dewey for having overcome.

37 For some similarities between Dewey and Heidegger with respect to anti-Cartesianism, see my 'Overcoming the Tradition', in Richard Rorty, *Consequences of Pragmatism* (University of Minnesota Press, Minneapolis, 1982). For similarities between Davidson and Derrida, see Samuel Wheeler, 'Indeterminacy of French Translation', in *Essays on 'Inquiries into Truth and Interpretation*, ed. Ernest LePore (Basil Blackwell, Oxford, 1986).

38 David Levin has pointed out to me that Jefferson was not above borrowing such arguments. I take this to show that Jefferson, like Kant, found himself in an untenable halfway position between theology and Deweyan social experimentalism.

39 Sandel takes 'the primacy of the subject' to be not only a way of filling out the deontological picture, but also a necessary condition of its correctness: 'If the claim for the primacy of justice is to succeed, if the right is to be prior to the good in the interlocking moral and foundational senses we have distinguished, then some version of the claim for the primacy of the subject must succeed as well' (*Liberalism and the Limits of Justice*, p. 7). Sandel quotes Rawls as saying that 'the essential unity of the self is already provided by the conception of the right' and takes this passage as evidence that Rawls holds a doctrine of the 'priority of the self' (ibid., p. 21). But consider the context of this sentence. Rawls says: 'The principles of justice and their realization in social forms define the bounds within which our deliberations take place. The essential unity of the self is already provided by the conception of right. Moreover, in a well-ordered society this unity is the same for all; everyone's conception of the good as given by his rational plan is a sub-plan of the larger comprehensive plan that regulates the community as a social union of social unions' (*Theory of Justice*, p. 563). The 'essential unity of the self', which is in question here, is simply the system of moral sentiments, habits and internalized traditions that is typical of the politically aware citizen of a constitutional democracy. This self is, once again, an historical product. It has nothing to do with the non-empirical self, which Kant had to postulate in the interests of Enlightenment universalism.

40 This is the kernel of truth in Dworkin's claim that Rawls rejects 'goal-based' social theory, but this point should not lead us to think that he is thereby driven back on a 'rights-based' theory.

41 But one should not press this point so far as to raise the spectre of 'untranslatable language'. As Donald Davidson has remarked, we would not recognize other organisms as actual or potential language users – or, therefore, as persons – unless there were enough overlap in belief and desire to make translation possible. The point is merely that efficient and frequent communication is only a necessary, not a sufficient, condition of agreement.

42 Further, such a conclusion is *restricted* to politics. It does not cast doubts on the ability of these men to follow the rules of logic or their ability to do many other things skilfully and well. It is thus not equivalent to the traditional philosophical charge of 'irrationality'. That charge presupposes that inability to 'see' certain truths is evidence of the lack of an organ that is essential for human functioning generally.

43 In Kierkegaard's *Philosophical Fragments*, we find the Platonic Theory of Recollection treated as the archetypal justification of 'Socratism' and thus as the symbol of all forms (especially Hegel's) of what Bernard Williams has recently called 'the rationalist theory of rationality' – the idea that one is rational only if one can appeal to universally accepted criteria, criteria whose truth and applicability all human beings can find 'in their hearts'. This is the philosophical core of the scriptural idea that 'truth is great, and will prevail', when that idea is dissociated from the Pauline idea of 'a New Being' (in the way that Kierkegaard refused to dissociate it).

44 See Jeffrey Stout's discussion of the manifold ambiguities of this conclusion in 'Virtue Among the Ruins: An Essay on MacIntyre', *Neue Zeitschrift für Systematische Theologie und Religionsphilosophie*, 26 (1984), pp. 256–73, especially, 269.

45 This is Rawls's description of 'a well-ordered society (corresponding to justice as fairness)' (*Theory of Justice*, p. 527). Sandel finds these passages metaphorical and complains that 'intersubjective and individualistic images appear in uneasy, sometimes unfelicitous combination, as if to betray the incompatible commitments contending within' (*Liberalism and the Limits of Justice*, pp. 150 ff.). He concludes that 'the moral vocabulary of community in the strong sense cannot in all cases be captured by a conception that [as Rawls has said his is] "in its theoretical basis is individualistic"'. I

am claiming that these commitments will look incompatible only if one attempts to define their philosophical presuppositions (which Rawls himself may occasionally have done too much of', and that this is a good reason for not making such attempts. Compare the Enlightenment view that attempts to sharpen up the theological presuppositions of social commitments had done more harm than good and that if theology cannot simply be discarded, it should at least be left as fuzzy (or, one might say, 'liberal') as possible. Oakeshott has a point when he insists on the value of theoretical muddle for the health of the state.

Elsewhere Rawls has claimed that 'there is no reason why a well-ordered society should encourage primarily individualistic values if this means ways of life that lead individuals to pursue their own way and to have no concern for the interests of others' ('Fairness to Goodness', *Philosophical Review*, 84 (1975), p. 550). Sandel's discussion of this passage says that it 'suggests a deeper sense in which Rawls's conception is individualistic', but his argument that this suggestion is correct is, once again, the claim that 'the Rawlsian self is not only a subject of possession, but an antecedently individuated subject' (*Liberalism and the Limits of Justice*, pp. 61 ff.). This is just the claim I have been arguing against by arguing that there is no such thing as 'the Rawlsian self' and that Rawls 'takes for granted that every individual consists of one and only one system of desires' (ibid., p. 62), but it is hard to find evidence for this claim in the texts. At worst, Rawls simplifies his presentation by imagining each of his citizens as having only one such set, but this simplifying assumption does not seem central to his view.

18

Solidarity or Singularity?
Richard Rorty between Romanticism
and Technocracy

Nancy Fraser

> Nothing can serve as a criticism of a final vocabulary save
> another such vocabulary; there is no answer to a redescription
> save a re-redescription.
>
> Richard Rorty, 'Private Irony and Liberal Hope', p. 80.[1]

Consider a somewhat cartoonish characterization of the Romantic impulse. Think of this impulse as the valorization of individual invention
understood as self-fashioning. A Romantic impulse of this sort would
lionize the figure of the extraordinary individual who does not simply play
out but rather rewrites the cultural script his socio-historical milieu has
prepared for him. It would represent this individual as a 'genius' or 'strong
poet', irrespective of the field of his inventiveness. Science, politics,
whatever – from the standpoint of the Romantic impulse, every arena of
invention would be a branch of literature in an extended sense, just as
every significant act would be an aesthetic act and every making a
self-making. Here, novelty would be valued for its own sake; it would be
the sheer difference between what is merely found or inherited, on the one
hand, and what is made or dreamed up *ex nihilo*, on the other, that would
confer value and importance. In so far as the Romantic impulse figures
such difference-making as the work of extraordinary individuals; in so far
as it treats them and their work as the source of all significant historical
change; in so far as it views history largely as the succession of such

I am grateful to Jonathan Arac for suggesting the title of this essay as well as for the invitation
which provided the occasion for writing it. I benefited from helpful discussions with
Jonathan Arac, Sandra Bartky, Jerry Graff, Carol Kay, Tom McCarthy, Linda Nicholson,
Michael Williams, Judy Wittner, and from stimulating questions from members of the
audience at The English Institute, Harvard University, August 1987.

geniuses; it becomes aestheticizing, individualist and elitist. It is, in short, the impulse to father oneself, to be *causa sui*, to separate from one's community. Thus the masculine pronoun is appropriate.[2]

Now contrast this cartoon version of the Romantic impulse with an equally cartoonish characterization of the pragmatic impulse. Take the latter to consist in an impatience with differences that do not make a difference. Take it as a distaste for baroque invention and for useless epicycles, for whatever does not get to the point. Thus, the pragmatic impulse would be goal-directed and purposive; it would care less for originality than for results. Problems solved, needs satisfied, well-being assured, these would be its emblems of value. For the Romantic's metaphorics of poetry and play, it would substitute a metaphorics of production and work. It would scorn gears that engage no mechanism, tools that serve no useful purpose, Rube Goldberg contraptions that do no real work. Indeed, from the standpoint of this impulse, words would be tools and culture an out-sized tool-kit, to be unceremoniously cast off in the event of obsolescence or rust. The pragmatic impulse, then, would be bright and busy. It would prefer the civic-mindedness of the problem-solving reformer to the narcissism of the self-fashioning poet. Its hero would be the fellow who gets the job done and makes himself useful to his society, not the one who's always preening and strutting his stuff. Moreover, the pragmatic impulse would see history as a succession of social problems posed and social problems solved, a succession that is in fact a progression. Crediting progress to the account of commonsense, technical competence and public-spiritedness, its ethos would be reformist and optimistic, its politics liberal and technocratic.

If these cartoonlike characterizations do not do justice to the complexities of the Romantic and pragmatic traditions, I trust that they none the less mark out two recognizable strands in the recent writings of Richard Rorty. These writings, in my view, are the site of a struggle between just such a Romantic impulse and a pragmatic impulse. Moreover, it is a struggle which neither impulse seems able decisively to win. Sometimes one, sometimes the other gains a temporary advantage here or there. But the overall outcome is stalemate.

It is symptomatic of Rorty's inability to resolve this contest that he oscillates among three different views of the relationship between Romanticism and pragmatism, poetry and politics. These in turn carry three different conceptions of the social role and political function of intellectuals. The first position I call the 'invisible hand' conception. It is the view that Romanticism and pragmatism are 'natural partners'. Here the 'strong poet' and the 'utopian reform politician' are simply two slightly different variants of the same species. Their respective activities are complementary if not strictly identical, providing grist for the same liberal democratic mill.

The second position I call the 'sublimity or decency?' conception. It is the view that Romanticism and pragmatism are antithetical to one another, that one has to choose between the sublime 'cruelty' of the strong poet and the beautiful 'kindness' of the political reformer. This view emphasizes the 'dark side' of Romanticism, its tendency to aestheticize politics and, so, to turn anti-democratic.

Evidently, the 'invisible hand' conception and the 'sublimity or decency?' conception are converses of one another. Thus each can be read as a critique of the other. Rorty's third position, which I call the 'partition' position, represents a compromise. If Romanticism and pragmatism are not exactly 'natural partners', but if, at the same time, one is not willing to abandon either one of them, then perhaps they can learn how to live with one another. Thus Rorty has recently outlined the terms of a truce between them, a truce which allots each its own separate sphere of influence. The Romantic impulse will have free rein in what will henceforth be 'the private sector'. But it will not be permitted any political pretensions. Pragmatism, on the other hand, will have exclusive rights to 'the public sector'. But it will be barred from entertaining any notions of radical change which could challenge the 'private' cultural hegemony of Romanticism.

An ingenious compromise, to be sure. Yet compromises based on partition are notoriously unstable. They tend not truly to resolve but only temporarily to palliate the basic source of conflict. Sooner or later, in one form or another, the latter will out.

The Sorelian temptation

Consider the role the Romantic impulse plays in Rorty's thought. Recall his insistence on the difference between vocabularies and propositions. It is precisely the tendency to confound them, to treat vocabularies as if they could be warranted like propositions, that is for him the cardinal sin of traditional philosophy. For, in Rorty's view, vocabulary choice is always underdetermined. There are no non-question-begging arguments, no reasons not already couched in some vocabulary, which could establish once and for all that one had the *right* vocabulary. To pretend otherwise is to seek the metaphysical comfort of a God's eye view.

Now consider, too, how much hinges on vocabulary shifts, in Rorty's view. The mere redistribution of truth-values across a set of propositions formulated in some taken-for-granted vocabulary is a paltry thing compared to a change in vocabulary. With vocabulary shifts, urgent questions suddenly lose their point, established practices are drastically modified, entire constellations of culture dissolve, to make room for new, heretofore unimaginable ones. Thus, vocabulary shifts are for Rorty the motor of history, the chief vehicles of intellectual and moral progress.

Consider, finally, exactly how it is, according to Rorty, that vocabulary shifts occur. A vocabulary shift is the literalization of a new metaphor, the application across the board of somebody's new way of speaking, the adoption by an entire community of some poet's idiosyncrasy. It follows that poets, in the extended sense, are 'the unacknowledged legislators of the social world'.[3] It is their chance words, coming like bolts from 'outside logical space', that determine the shape of subsequent culture and society.

The Romantic impulse in Rorty is the impulse that thrills to the sublimity of metaphor, the headiness of 'abnormal discourse'. When he is under its sway, Rorty figures the culture-hero as the poet, allowing the latter to outrank not only the priest and the philosopher but even the pragmatist's traditional heroes, the scientist and the reform-politician. In general, then, it is Rorty's Romantic impulse that dictates his 'utopian ideal' of 'an aestheticized culture', a culture with no other goal than to create 'ever more various, multi-coloured artifacts', no other purpose than 'to make life easier for poets and revolutionaries'.[4]

The Romantic impulse is fairly strong in Rorty. But it is not an impulse with which he's entirely comfortable.

And for good reason. Consider what a politics which gave free rein to the Romantic impulse would look like. Recall the individualist, elitist and aestheticist character of that impulse, its deification of the strong poet, its fetishization of creation *ex nihilo*. It takes only the squint of an eye to see here the vision of a Georges Sorel: a 'sociology' which classifies humanity into 'leaders' and 'masses'; a 'theory of action' whereby the former mold the latter by means of a sheer 'triumph of the will'; a 'philosophy of history' as an empty canvas awaiting the unfettered designs of the poet-leader.[5]

I take it that something like this Sorelian nightmare is what disturbs the sleep of Richard Rorty. For a long time now, he has been at pains to show that his own Romantic streak does not lead down this road, that his own 'utopian vision' of an 'aestheticized culture' is liberal and democratic rather than Sorelian and potentially fascistic.

The invisible hand: or, better living through chemistry and poetry

One way in which Rorty has sought to exorcize the Sorelian demon is by providing a positive political defence of his version of Romanticism. Thus he has tried to portray the Romantic dimension of his thought as compatible with, indeed even as fostering, the apparently opposing pragmatic dimension. More strongly, he has tried to show that the two dimensions are 'natural partners', that the fit between them is extremely tight and that the strong poet is the democrat personified.

The chief strategy here is to link poetizing with community-mindedness, Romantic making with social identification. Thus Rorty argues that, in giving up Kantian buttresses for liberal views, one goes from 'objectivity' to 'solidarity'. For to cease pinning our hopes on such God-substitutes as Reason, Human Nature and the Moral Law is to start pinning them on one another.[6]

Likewise, Rorty claims that the aesthetic stance and the moral stance are not antithetical to one another. On the contrary, they are not even distinct. For in adopting the aesthetic attitude, one 'dedeifies' or disenchants the world, thereby promoting tolerance, liberalism and instrumental reason.[7] The refusal to mortgage culture-making to ahistorical authorities liberates us for 'experimentalism' in politics, for that simultaneously utopian and down-to-earth sort of 'social engineering' that is the very soul of moral progress.

Moreover, claims Rorty, to treat the strong poet as one's hero and role model is 'to adopt an identity which suits one for citizenship in an ideally liberal state'.[8] For there is a 'fairly tight' fit, supposedly, between the freedom of intellectuals and 'the diminution of cruelty'.[9] We only see practices of earlier ages as cruel and unjust because we have learnt how to redescribe them. And we have only done that by virtue of vocabulary shifts owing to the metaphors of poets. Thus, contrary to initial appearances, it is not really elitist to 'treat democratic societies as existing for the sake of intellectuals'.[10] On the contrary, only by making society safe for poets can we ensure that language keeps changing. And only by ensuring that language keeps changing can we prevent the normalization of current practices which might later look cruel and unjust. Thus, to make society safe for poets is to help make it safe for everyone.

Finally, claims Rorty, a culture organized for the sake of poetry and play would foster 'decency' and 'kindness'. It would diminish or equalize the liability to a specifically human form of suffering, namely, the humiliation that comes from being redescribed in someone else's terms while one's own vocabulary is peremptorily dismissed. The best safeguard against this sort of cruelty is an awareness of other people's vocabularies. Such an awareness in turn is best acquired by reading lots of books. Thus a culture that fostered a cosmopolitan literary intelligentsia would promote the greatest happiness of the greatest number.[11]

In short, Rorty claims that cultural innovation and social justice go together. They are united in the liberationist metaphorics of liberal societies, where history is figured as a succession of emancipations: serfs from lords, slaves from plantation owners, colonies from empires, labour from the unlimited power of capital. Since both are dominated by these images of opening-up, Romanticism in the arts goes with democracy in politics.[12]

In all these arguments, what is really at stake is the accusation of elitism. Rorty seeks to rebut the charge that a Romantic politics must elevate liberty over equality, sacrificing the greatest happiness of the greatest number on the altar of the strong poet. His general approach is to invoke a version of the old trickle-down argument: liberty in the arts fosters equality in society; what's good for poets is good for workers, peasants and the hard-core unemployed.

Here, then, is the Rorty who has sought a seamless joining of Romanticism and pragmatism. Adopting an 'invisible hand' strategy, he has tried to show that aesthetic play and liberal reformist politics are but two sides of the same coin. That what promotes one will also promote the other. That we can have Better Living through the Marriage of Chemistry and Poetry.

These arguments do not represent Rorty at his most persuasive. On the contrary, they tend to raise far more questions than they answer. For example: is to say goodbye to objectivity really to say hello to solidarity? Surely there is no relation of logical entailment between anti-essentialism and loyalty to one's society. Nor is there even any contingent psychological or historical connection, if modern Western societies are considered any measure. Moreover, why assume a quasi-Durkheimian view according to which society is integrated by way of a single monolithic and all-encompassing solidarity? Why not assume rather a quasi-Marxian view according to which modern capitalist societies contain a plurality of overlapping and competing solidarities?

Next, is it really the case that societies which produce the best literature are also the most egalitarian? Do poets' interests and workers' interests really coincide so perfectly? And what about women's interests, given that, Rorty's use of the feminine pronoun notwithstanding, his poets are always figured as sons seeking to displace their cultural fathers? Moreover, does poetizing really dovetail so neatly with social engineering? How does the down-to-earth, results-oriented character of the latter square with the extravagant playfulness of the former? For that matter, why is 'social engineering' the preferred conception of political practice? And why is equality cast in terms of 'kindness' and 'decency'? Why is it made to hinge on a virtue of the literary intelligentsia, on the latter's supposed inclination to forebear humiliating others? Why is equality not instead considered in terms of equal participation in poetizing, culture-making and politics?

Sublimity or decency? or, the dark side of Romanticism

As usual, no one states the case against the invisible hand 'solution' better than Rorty himself. Recently, he has acknowledged that there is a 'dark side' of Romanticism, a side he now designates as 'ironism'. By 'ironism', Rorty means the modernist literary intellectual's project of fashioning the best possible self by continual redescription. Identifying himself as such an ironist, Rorty wonders whether it really is possible to combine 'the pleasures of redescription' with sensitivity to 'the sufferings of those being redescribed'. He fears that the ironist demand for maximum cultural freedom may indeed be elitist, compatible with indifference to the sufferings of non-poets. Ironism, he concedes, is by definition reactive, requiring a non-ironist public culture from which to be alienated. Thus, even in a post-metaphysical culture, ironism cannot be the generalized attitude of the entire social collectivity. It can only be the attitude of one stratum of society, a literary intelligentsia or cultural elite. Moreover, there is no denying that ironism can be cruel. It delights in redescribing others instead of taking them in their own terms. There is no question but that this is often humiliating, as when a child's favourite possessions are set next to those of a richer child and thereby made to seem insignificant. To make matters worse, the ironist cannot claim that, in redescribing others, he is uncovering their true selves and interests, thereby empowering them and setting them free. Only the metaphysically minded politician can promise that. It follows that, even were the ironist to profess support for liberal politics, he could not be very 'dynamic' or 'progressive'.[13]

Considerations like these lead Rorty to a dramatic reversal of his earlier view. Now he no longer assumes that to substitute making for finding is to serve one's community, that to say goodbye to objectivity is to say hello to solidarity. On the contrary, Rorty now discerns a 'selfish', anti-social motive in Romanticism, one that represents the very antithesis of communal identification. He finds that the Romantic's search for the sublime is fueled by a desire for disaffiliation, a need to 'cut loose from the tribe'. Thus, behind the strong poet's love for what is original and wholly new lurks a secret contempt for what is familiar and widely shared. This is especially disturbing when what is familiar and shared is a commitment to democracy. In a culture supposedly already organized around a metaphorics of liberation and social reform, to seek new, more vivid, less hackneyed metaphors is to court political disaster.

Thus Rorty voices a new worry that Romanticism and pragmatism do not mix. Whereas pragmatism is community-minded, democratic and kind, Romanticism now seems selfish, elitist and cruel. Whereas the pragmatist aims to solve the problems and meet the needs of his ordinary fellow citizens, the Romantic ironist is more likely to dismiss these as trite, uninteresting and insufficiently radical.

Thus, *soi-disant* Left-wing poststructuralists are deluded in thinking they 'serve the wretched of the earth' by rejecting the currently disseminated liberal political vocabulary. On the contrary, what they really do is express the traditional vanguardist contempt for their fellow human beings. Heideggerians, deconstructionists, neo-Marxists, Foucaultians and assorted New Leftists – these are not differences that make a difference. All are potential Sorelians who confuse the ironist-intellectual's special yen for the sublime with society's general need for the merely beautiful.[14]

It is in this vein that Rorty has recently taken care explicitly to distinguish the pragmatic and the Romantic conceptions of philosophy. He argues that Romanticism and pragmatism represent two distinct reactions against metaphysics and that they ought not to be conflated with one another. Granted, both reject the traditional view of 'philosophy as science', as the search, that is, for a permanent neutral matrix for enquiry. But whereas Romanticism wants to replace this with a view of 'philosophy as metaphor', pragmatism prefers to substitute the view of 'philosophy as politics'. It follows that the two approaches differ sharply in their views of the ideal person: on the metaphor view this must be the poet, while on the political view it is the social worker and the engineer. Granted, both perspectives are holistic; both distinguish abnormal discourse from normal discourse, the invention of a new metaphor from its literalization or social application. But they part ways over the value of turning live metaphors into dead metaphors by disseminating them in the service of society. For the Romantic, this sort of applied poetry is the vilest hack work, while for the pragmatist it is exactly what the best metaphors are made for. It follows that the two views entail very different social attitudes. On the Romantic view, the social world exists for the sake of the poet. On the pragmatic view, on the other hand, the poet exists for the sake of the social world.[15]

In this rather more complicated scenario, then, there are not one but rather two alternatives to objectivity. Only one of these leads to solidarity and democracy, while the other leads to vanguardism if not to fascism.

Here Rorty frames the issue as Romanticism versus pragmatism. He treats the two impulses as antithetical to one another, and he forces a choice. Romanticism or pragmatism? Sublimity or decency? Strong poetry or dead metaphors? Self-fashioning or social responsibility? One cannot have it both ways.

Or can one?

The partition position

In his most recent essays, Rorty refuses to choose between sublimity and decency, Romanticism and pragmatism. He has instead contrived a new formulation aimed at letting him have it both ways: he will split the difference between Romanticism and pragmatism along a divide between private and public life.

The idea is that two things that cannot be fused into one may none the less coexist side by side, if clear and sharp boundaries are drawn between them. Now, sublimity cannot be fused with decency, nor strong poetry with social responsibility. But if each were allotted its own separate sphere and barred from interfering with the other, then they might just make passably good neighbours.

This, then, is the strategy of Rorty's partition position: to bifurcate the map of culture down the middle. On one side will be public life, the preserve of pragmatism, the sphere where utility and solidarity predominate. On the other side will be private life, the preserve of Romanticism, the sphere of self-discovery, sublimity and irony. In the public sphere, one's duty to one's community takes precedence; social hope, decency and the greatest happiness of the greatest number are the order of the day. In the private sphere, by contrast, the reigning cause is one's duty to oneself; here, one may disaffiliate from the community, attend to the fashioning of one's self and, so, deal with one's 'aloneness'.[16]

Thus Rorty wishes to preserve both ecstasy and utility, 'the urge to think the Unthinkable' and 'enthusiasm for the French Revolution'.[17] But only by strictly isolating them from one another. Indeed, he now claims that it is the desire to overcome the implacable split between public and private life that is at the root of many theoretical and political difficulties. This desire, it turns out, is common to metaphysics and its ironist critique, to Marxism and to various non-Marxist forms of radical politics. It is what led even the later Heidegger astray, causing him to confound what was actually his private need to get free of some local, personal authority figures named Plato, Aristotle and Kant with the destiny of the West.[18]

Rorty claims that there is a lesson to be learnt from the difficulties of all these opponents of liberalism: when irony goes public, it gets into trouble. Thus, ironist theory has to stay private if it is to stay sane.[19]

It turns out, happily, that there is a way to neutralize the non-liberal political implications of radical thought. It is to deny that radical thought has any political implications. So Heidegger was simply mistaken in imagining his work has any public relevance. Ditto for all those would-be leftists who aim to make political hay of deconstruction, postmodernism, Foucaultianism and neo-Marxism. In fact, the sole use of ironist theory is a private one: to bolster the self-image and aid the self-fashioning of the literary intelligentsia.

Clearly, the partition position entails a revised view of the social role and political function of intellectuals. The strong poet as heretofore conceived must be domesticated, cut down to size and made fit for private life. He must become the aesthete,[20] a figure denuded of public ambition and turned inward. Thus the intellectual will be king in the castle of his own self-fashioning, but he will no longer legislate for the social world. Strictly speaking, indeed, the intellectual will have no social role or political function.

It is a measure of the domesticated status of Rorty's aesthete that he may only pursue sublimity on his 'own time, and within the limits set by *On Liberty*'.[21] He may think ironic thoughts involving cruel redescriptions within the privacy of his own narcissistic sphere. But he must not act on them in ways which might cause pain or humiliation to others. This means that the aesthete must have a bifurcated final vocabulary, a vocabulary split into a public sector and a private sector. The private sector of the aesthete's final vocabulary will be large and luxuriant, containing all manner of colourful and potentially cruel terms for redescribing others. The public sector of his vocabulary, on the other hand, will be smaller, consisting in a few flexible terms like 'kindness' and 'decency' which express his commitment to the politics of liberalism.[22]

The partition position represents a new and extremely interesting development in Rorty's thinking. It is his most sophisticated effort to date to take seriously the problem of reconciling Romanticism and pragmatism. And yet this position is seriously flawed. It stands or falls with the possibility of drawing a sharp boundary between public and private life. But is this really possible? Is it really possible to distinguish redescriptions which affect actions with consequences for others from those which either do not affect actions at all or which affect only actions with no consequences for others?[23] Surely, many cultural developments that occur at some remove from processes officially designated as political are none the less public. And official-political public spheres are by no means impermeable to developments in cultural public spheres, since cultural processes help shape identities which in turn affect political affiliations. Moreover, the social movements of the last hundred or so years have taught us to see the power-laden and therefore political character of interactions which classical liberalism considered private. Workers' movements, for example, especially as clarified by Marxist theory, have taught us that the economic is political. Likewise, women's movements, as illuminated by feminist theory, have taught us that the domestic and the personal are political. Finally, a whole range of New Left social movements, as illuminated by Gramscian, Foucaultian and, yes, even by Althusserian theory, have taught us that the cultural, the medical, the educational – everything that Hannah Arendt called 'the social', as distinct from the private and the public – that all this, too, is political.[24] Yet Rorty's partition position requires us to bury these insights, to turn our backs on the last hundred years of social history. It requires us, in addition, to privatize theory. Feminists, especially, will want to resist this last requirement, lest we see our theory go the way of our housework.

Abnormal discourse reconsidered

None of Rorty's three positions represents a satisfactory resolution of the tension between pragmatism and Romanticism. The invisible-hand position fails because to say goodbye to objectivity is not necessarily to say hello to a single, unitary solidarity; and because what's good for poets is not necessarily good for workers, peasants and the hard-core unemployed. The sublimity or decency position fails because not all radical theorizing is elitist, anti-democratic and opposed to collective concerns and political life. Finally, the partition position fails because final vocabularies do not neatly divide into public and private sectors; nor do actions neatly divide into private or public.

If none of the three proffered solutions is adequate, then it may be worth reconsidering the terms of the original dilemma. We might take a closer look at the categories and assumptions that inform Rorty's thinking about culture and politics.

Begin with the key distinction in Rorty's framework, the contrast between normal discourse and abnormal discourse. In fact, Rorty oscillates between two views of abnormal discourse. The first view is the one developed in *Philosophy and the Mirror of Nature* and it is derived from the work of Thomas Kuhn. It is the simple negation of the discourse of normal science, that is, of discourse in which interlocutors share a sense of what counts as a problem or question, as a well-formed or serious hypothesis and as a good reason or argument. Abnormal discourse, then, is discourse in which such matters are up for grabs. It involves a plurality of differentiatible if not incommensurable voices and it consists in an exchange among them that is lively if somewhat disorderly. Call this 'the polylogic conception' of abnormal discourse.

Now contrast the polylogic conception with another conception of abnormal discourse which is also found in Rorty, a monologic conception. The monologic view is the Romantic-individualist view in which abnormal discourse is the prerogative of the strong poet and the ironist theorist. It is a discourse that consists in a solitary voice crying out into the night against an utterly undifferentiated background. The only conceivable response to this voice is uncomprehending rejection or identificatory imitation. There is no room for a reply that could qualify as a different voice. There is no room for interaction.

Clearly, these two different conceptions of abnormal discourse correspond to the two different impulses I identified earlier. The monologic view develops under the spur of Rorty's Romantic impulse, while the polylogic view is fed by his pragmatic impulse. In addition, the monologic view maps onto Rorty's notions of radical theory-*cum*-strong poetry and privacy, while the polylogic view maps onto his notions of practice, politics and publicity.

At one level, this mapping makes good sense. It seems that Rorty is perfectly right to want a polylogic politics instead of a monologic politics – indeed, to reject a monologic politics as an oxymoron. However, at another level, there is something profoundly disturbing here. It is the sharply dichotomous character of the resulting map of culture, the abstract and unmediated opposition between poetry and politics, theory and practice, individual and community.

Consider the impact of the monologic conception of abnormal discourse on the various regions of Rorty's map of social space. The monologic conception, we have seen, is individualistic, elitist and anti-social. Moreover, it is associated by Rorty with radical theorizing, which is itself treated as a species of poetizing. As a result, radical theorizing assumes individualistic connotations, becoming the very antithesis of collective action and political practice. Radical theory, in other words, gets inflected as a sphere apart from collective life, a sphere of privacy and of individual self-fashioning. It becomes aestheticized, narcissized and bourgeoisified, a preserve where strivings for transcendence are quarantined, rendered safe because rendered sterile.

Now, this privatized, narcissistic conception of radical theory has two important social consequences. First, there can be no legitimate cultural politics, no genuinely political struggle for cultural hegemony; there can only be Oedipal revolts of genius sons against genius fathers. Second, there can be no politically relevant radical theory, no link between theory and political practice; there can only be apolitical ironist theory and atheoretical reformist practice. Thus both culture and theory get depoliticized.

The privatization of radical theory takes its toll, too, on the shape of the political. In Rorty's hands, politics assumes an overly communitarian and solidary character, as if in reaction against the extreme egotism and individualism of his conception of theory. Thus, we can supposedly go straight from objectivity to solidarity, from the metaphysical comfort of traditional philosophy to the communitarian comfort of a single 'we'. Here, Rorty homogenizes social space, assuming, tendentiously, that there are no deep social cleavages capable of generating conflicting solidarities and opposing 'we's'. It follows from this assumed absence of fundamental social antagonisms that politics is a matter of everyone pulling together to solve a common set of problems. Thus social engineering can replace political struggle. Disconnected tinkerings with a succession of allegedly discrete social problems can replace transformation of the basic institutional structure. And the expert social-problem-solver and top – down reformer can replace the organized social movement of people collectively articulating their own interests and aspirations, as the political agent gets typified by the social worker or the engineer instead of by, say, the members of the National Welfare Rights Organization or of the Clamshell Alliance. Moreover, with no deep rifts or pervasive axes of domination, practice can float entirely free of theory. If there are no mechanisms of subordination inscribed in the basic institutional framework of society, then *a fortiori* there can be no need to theorize them. Thus politics can be detheoreticized.

Clearly, this cultural map presupposes a substantive political diagnosis, one with which I shall later take issue. But it also possesses a noteworthy formal feature: Rorty's conceptions of politics and of theory are obverses of one another. If theory is hyperindividualized and depoliticized, then politics is hypercommunalized and detheoreticized. As theory becomes pure *poesis*, then politics approaches pure *techne*. Moreover, as theory is made the preserve of pure transcendence, then politics is banalized, emptied of radicalism and of desire. Finally, as theory becomes the production *ex nihilo* of new metaphors, then politics must be merely their literalization; it must be application only, never invention.

It is paradoxical that such a dichotomous picture should be the upshot of a body of thought that aimed to soften received dichotomies like theory versus practice, aesthetic versus moral, science versus literature. It is also paradoxical that what was supposed to be a political polylogue comes increasingly to resemble a monologue.

Consider that Rorty makes non-liberal, oppositional discourses non-political by definition. Such discourses are associated by him with Romanticism, the quest for the uncharted. They are made the prerogative of free-floating intellectuals who are 'bored' with widely disseminated vocabularies and who crave 'the new' and 'the interesting'. Radical discourses, then, are inflected as a turning-away from the concerns of collective life. Thus Rorty casts the motive for oppositional discourse as aesthetic and apolitical. He casts the subject of such discourses as the lone, alienated, heroic individual. And he casts the object or topic of radical discourses as something other than the needs and problems of the social collectivity.

With radical discourses thus aestheticized and individualized, indeed oedipalized and masculinized, political discourse, in turn, is implicitly deradicalized. Political discourse in fact is restricted by Rorty to those who speak the language of bourgeois liberalism. Whoever departs from that vocabulary simply lacks any sense of solidarity. Likewise, it turns out that the adherents of bourgeois liberalism have a monopoly on talk about community needs and social problems. Whoever eschews the liberal idiom must be talking about something else. About, say, individual salvation.

Thus, in Rorty's recent essays social solidarity and non-liberal discourses are seen as antithetical to one another. Discourse rooted in solidarity and oriented to collective concerns is restricted to liberal problem-solving. Non-liberal discourse, on the other hand, is reduced to aestheticism, apoliticism and Romantic individualism.

Clearly, this way of mapping the discursive terrain effects some significant exclusions. There is no place in Rorty's framework for *political* motivations for the invention of new idioms, no place for idioms invented to overcome the enforced silencing or muting of disadvantaged social groups. Similarly, there is no place for *collective* subjects of non-liberal discourses, hence, no place for radical discourse communities that contest dominant discourses. Finally, there is no place for *non-liberal* interpretations of social needs and collective concerns, hence, no place for, say, socialist-feminist politics. In sum, there is no place in Rorty's framework for genuinely radical political discourses rooted in *oppositional* solidarities.

Thus, Rorty ends up supposing there is only one legitimate political vocabulary, thereby betraying his own professed commitment to a polylogical politics. This, too, is a paradoxical result for a thought that seemed always to insist on the decisive importance of vocabulary choice for the framing of issues.

In any case and whatever his intentions, by dichotomizing private and public, singular individual and homogeneous community, Rorty cuts out the ground for the possibility of democratic radical politics.

How can we build this possibility back into the picture? How can we retrieve a version of pragmatism that is compatible with radical democracy, polylogic abnormal political discourse and socialist-feminist politics?

Towards a democratic-socialist-feminist pragmatism: a recipe

Rorty has recently summarized the aim of his latest round of essays: 'to separate . . . "postmodernism" from political radicalism, polemics against "the metaphysics of presence" from polemics against "bourgeois ideology", criticisms of Enlightenment rationalism and universalism from criticisms of liberal, reformist, political thought'.[25]

In contrast, I would like to summarize *my* aim in the present chapter: to

separate pragmatism from cold-war liberalism, polemics against traditional foundationalist philosophy from polemics against social theory, criticisms of Romantic Sorelian politics from criticisms of radical democratic-
socialist-feminist politics.

Let me conclude by sketching roughly how such a separation can be
effected. Since the point is to show that one can indeed put asunder what
Rorty hath joined together, my sketch will be a recipe for an alternative
combination, a democratic-socialist-feminist pragmatism.[26]

Begin with the sort of zero-degree pragmatism which is compatible with
a wide variety of substantive political views, with socialist-feminism as
well as bourgeois liberalism. This pragmatism is simply anti-essentialism
with respect to traditional philosophical concepts like truth and reason,
human nature and morality.[27] It implies an appreciation of the historical
and socially constructed character of such categories and of the practices
they get their sense from, thereby suggesting at least the abstract
possibility of social change. This sort of zero-degree pragmatism is a
useful, though hardly all-sufficing, ingredient of socialist-feminism.

Then, add the kind of zero-degree holism which combines easily with
radical democratic politics. This holism is simply the sense of the
difference between the frame of a social practice and a move within it. It
implies an appreciation of the way background institutions and habits
prestructure the foreground possibilities available to individuals in social
life. This zero-degree holism does not necessarily lead to conservative
politics. On the contrary, it is a necessary ingredient for any politics that
aspires to radical social transformation as opposed to simple amelioration.

Next, add a keen sense of the decisive importance of language in
political life. Mix with the pragmatism and the holism until you get a
distinction between making a political claim in a taken-for-granted
vocabulary and switching to a different vocabulary. This distinction clears
a space for those far-reaching redescriptions of social life at the heart of
every new political vision, from bourgeois liberalism to Marxism to
contemporary feminism. This distinction also allows for contestatory
interactions among competing political vocabularies. It thus makes conceivable the sort of robust, polylogic, abnormal discourse which is
essential to radical democratic politics in a multicultural society.

Next, add a view of contemporary societies as neither hyperindividualized nor hypercommunitarian. This view should allow for social divisions
capable of generating multiple, competing solidarities and multiple,
competing political vocabularies. It should allow also for inequality and
for power. Thus it should distinguish dominant from subordinated
solidarities, hegemonic from counter-hegemonic vocabularies. This view
of society should be mixed with the preceding ingredients to get a keen
sense of social contestation.

Contestation, in turn, should be broadly conceived to include struggle over cultural meanings and social identities as well as over more narrowly traditional political stakes like electoral office and legislation. It should encompass struggles for cultural hegemony, the power to construct authoritative definitions of social situations and legitimate interpretations of social needs. This broad sense of contestation allows for a politics of culture that cuts across traditional divisions between public and private life. It allows also for the possibility of radical democratic social movements: broad, informally organized, collective formations wherein politics and poetry form an unbroken continuum as struggles for social justice shade into the unleashing of creativity.

Next, add a view of social change as neither determined by an autonomous logic of history nor as simply contingent and utterly inexplicable. Consider the agents of historical change to be social movements rather than extraordinary individuals. Avoid a rigid, dichotomous opposition between playing the game in the same old way and starting completely from scratch; between boring, stable, frozen normality and the sudden, novel bolt from the blue. Avoid, also, a dichotomy between sheer invention and mere application, between the heretofore undreamt of and its routinization. Instead, see these extremes as mediated in the social practice of social movements. See such practice as spanning the gulf between the old and the new, as application that is always at the same time invention. This allows for the possibility of a radical politics that is not Sorelian, not the expression of the elitist and masculinist will to the Wholly Other. It allows for the possibility of a radical democratic politics in which immanent critique and transfigurative desire mingle with one another.

Next, add the view that, multiplicity and contestation notwithstanding, contemporary societies are organized around a basic institutional framework. Of course, any precise characterization of the structure of this framework will suppose contestable political commitments and a contestable political vocabulary. Nonetheless, suppose that among the candidates for core elements of this framework are things like the following: an organization of social production for private profit rather than for human need; a gender-based division of social labour that separates privatized childrearing from recognized and remunerated work; gender and race-segmented paid labour markets that generate a marginalized underclass; a system of nation-states that engage in crisis-management in the form of segmented social-welfare concessions and subsidized war production.

Now, add to this the possibility that the basic institutional framework of society could be unjust, that it could work to the systematic detriment of some social groups and to the systematic profit of others. Stir with the preceding ingredients to get a sense of the possible political uses of a critical social theory. Consider, for example, the utility of a theory that could specify links among apparently discrete social problems via the basic institutional structure, thereby showing 'how things, in the broadest sense, hang together, in the broadest sense'.[28] Or consider the utility of a social theory able to distinguish system-conforming reforms that perpetuate injustices, on the one hand, from radical and empowering social changes, on the other hand.

Next, add some distinctions among different kinds of theories. Distinguish, for example, traditional, ahistorical foundationalist theories, as in Epistemology or Moral Philosophy, from the ironist pragmatic meta-theories which provide their critique. Then distinguish both of these from a third kind of theory, to wit, first-order, substantive social theory that is non-foundational, fallibilistic and historically specific. Now use these distinctions to avoid throwing out the baby of critical social theory with the bathwater of traditional philosophy. Use them, also, to avoid conflating social theory with Heideggerian bathos, private irony or Oedipal hijinks. Instead, use these distinctions to make room for politically relevant radical social theory and thus for theoretically informed radical democratic politics.

Then, add a non-Leninist, non-vanguardist conception of the role of intellectuals in radical Left-wing democratic politics. Think of such intellectuals first and foremost as members of social groups and as participants in social movements. Think of them, in other words, as occupying specifiable locations in social space rather than as free-floating individuals who are beyond ideology. Think of them, in addition, as having acquired as a result of the social division of labour some politically useful occupational skills, for example, the ability to show how the welfare system institutionalizes the feminization of poverty or how a poem orientalizes its subject. Think of them as potentially capable of utilizing these skills both in specialized institutions like universities and in the various larger cultural and political public spheres. Think of them, thus, as participants on several fronts in struggles for cultural hegemony. Think of them, also, alas, as mightily subject to delusions of grandeur and as needing to remain in close contact with their political comrades who are not intellectuals by profession in order to remain sane, level-headed and honest.

Combine all these ingredients with a non-individualist, non-elitist, non-masculinist utopian vision. Articulate this utopian vision in terms of relations among human beings, instead of in terms of individuals considered as separate monads. Imagine new relations of work and play, citizenship and parenthood, friendship and love. Then consider what sort of institutional framework would be needed to foster such relations. Situate these relations in the institutional framework of a classless, multicultural society without racism, sexism or heterosexism, an international society of decentralized, democratic, self-managing collectivities.

Combine all the above ingredients and season to taste with social hope. Concoct just the right mix of pessimism of the intellect and optimism of the will.

NOTES

1 In Richard Rorty, *Contingency, Irony, and Solidarity* (Cambridge University Press, Cambridge, 1989).

2 It is worth recalling that one of Rorty's heroes is Harold Bloom, especially the Bloom of *The Anxiety of Influence*. My own view of the masculinist character of Rorty's Romantic impulse has been influenced by the feminist critique of Bloom by Sandra M. Gilbert and Susan Gubar in *The Madwoman in the Attic: The Woman Writer and the Nineteenth-Century Literary Imagination* (Yale University Press, New Haven, 1979).

3 This is Rorty echoing Shelley. 'Philosophy as Science, as Metaphor and as Politics'. In *The Institution of Philosophy: A Discipline in Crisis?*, ed. Avner Cohen and Marcelo Descal (Open Court Publishers, La Salle, IL, 1989) pp. 13–35.

4 Richard Rorty, 'The Contingency of Community', *London Review of Books*, 24 July 1986, pp. 11, 13.

5 The choice of Sorel as the personification of this possibility is mine, not Rorty's. He tends rather to represent it with Lenin. In my view, Lenin is far less appropriate here than Sorel. The 'sociology', 'theory of action' and 'philosophy of history' I have sketched bear little resemblance to Lenin's and much to Sorel's. Moreover, Sorel's much greater ambiguity in terms of standard notions of 'right' and 'left' better captures the flavour of the sort of political Romanticism I am trying to characterize here. Finally, Rorty's choice of Lenin as the personification of Romanticism run amok is an anti-Marxist political gesture which I do not wish to repeat. In general, Rorty shows no awareness of the tradition of Western Marxism nor of attempts within Marxism to find alternatives to vanguardist conceptions of the relation between theory and practice.

6 Richard Rorty, 'Solidarity or Objectivity', in *Post-Analytic Philosophy*, ed. John Rajchman and Cornel West (Columbia University Press, New York, 1985), pp. 3–19.

7 Richard Rorty, 'The Priority of Democracy to Philosophy', in *The Virginia Statute of Religious Freedom*, ed. Merrill Peterson and Robert Vaughan (Cambridge University Press, Cambridge, 1988), pp. 39–40. See also 'From Logic to Language to Play', *Proceedings and Addresses of the American Philosophical Association*, 59 (1986), pp. 747–53.

8 Rorty, 'The Contingency of Community', p. 14.

9 Ibid.

10 Ibid.

11 Rorty, 'Private Irony and Liberal Hope', pp. 89, 94–95.

12 Ibid.

13 Ibid., pp. 87–91.

14 Richard Rorty, 'Habermas and Lyotard on Postmodernity', in *Habermas and Modernity*, ed. Richard J. Bernstein (Harvard University Press, Cambridge, Mass., 1985). 'Method, Social Science and Social Hope', in Richard Rorty, *Consequences of Pragmatism: Essays 1972–1980* (University of Minnesota Press, Minneapolis, 1982). 'Thugs and Theorists: A Reply to Bernstein', *Political Theory*, 15/4 (November 1987), pp. 564–80.

15 Rorty, 'Philosophy as Science, as Metaphor and as Politics'.

16 Rorty, 'The Priority of Democracy to Philosophy', p. 37.
17 Rorty, 'Habermas and Lyotard on Postmodernity'.
18 Rorty, 'Self-creation and Affiliation: Proust, Nietzsche, and Heidegger', in *Contingency, Irony and Solidarity*, pp. 100, 110, 114, 118–121.
19 Ibid., p. 120.
20 I am grateful to Michael Williams for the suggestion that Rorty's view of the intellectual here is that of the aesthete.
21 Rorty, 'Posties', *London Review of Books*, 3 September 1987), p. 11.
22 Rorty, 'Private Irony and Liberal Hope', pp. 92–93.
23 This problem is posed but by no means resolved in Mill's *On Liberty*.
24 To insist on the power-laden and therefore political character of these matters is not necessarily to authorize unlimited state intervention. One can favour, instead, the use of non-governmental counterpowers like social movements and democratic political associations. This is the view of many feminists, including myself, with respect to pornography: pornography that is harmful to women in a diffuse rather than a direct way is better opposed via boycotts, pickets, counter-propaganda and consciousness-raising than by state censorship.
25 Rorty, 'Thugs and Theorists', p. 564.
26 The recipe form has a number of advantages, not least of which is a certain gender resonance. In choosing this genre, I am taking seriously Rorty's implicit assimilation of theorizing to housework. For me, however, this means deprivatizing housework rather than privatizing theory. It also suggests a non-technocratic and more genuinely pragmatic view of the relation between theory and practice, since cooks are expected to vary recipes in accordance with trial and error, inspiration and the conjunctural state of the larder. Finally, the receipe form has the advantage of positing the outcome as a concoction rather than as a system or synthesis. It thus avoids those hyperbolic forms of theoretical totalization of which the democratic left has rightly grown suspicious.
27 Rorty, 'Pragmatism, Relativism and Irrationalism', in *Consequences of Pragmatism*, p. 162.
28 This is one of Rorty's favourite positive characterizations of philosophy. He attributes the characterization to Wilfred Sellars.

19

Conversational Politics: Rorty's Pragmatist Apology for Liberalism

Jo Burrows

Even those who are largely in sympathy with Rorty's negative diagnosis of analytical philosophy in *Philosophy and the Mirror of Nature* (henceforth, *PMN*) might have some reservations concerning the political implications of his positive recommendations in the final sections of that book. Rorty seems to think that what he calls 'conversation' – the attempt to produce interesting descriptions – is, in the end, the only legitimate goal of philosophy,[1] and that philosophers, themselves, will be better placed to make a significant contribution to culture if they set aside the so-called 'perennial problems', thereby abandoning the search for 'foundations', 'universal principles', 'absolute truth', and so on. They will be 'better placed', because only then will they have freed themselves from the stale vocabularies of their tradition. For Rorty, 'conversation' is essentially a creative endeavour, akin, at its best, to poetry; and, as such, it requires language which is fresh.

This whole line of thought has its attractions, especially since it might inspire imaginative changes within, for instance, the curricula of universities. But such changes may be arbitrary. Furthermore, when it comes to applying Rorty's way of thinking *outside* the sphere of academic repositionings, the reader of *PMN* might well be left wondering about the *political* upshot. What are the political preconditions for conversational practices? Are these practices 'benign' (i.e. non-confrontational), and if so, how can this be squared with political reality? Are the limitations on the selection of the subject-matter of conversation analogous to the constraints on the choice of theme for a poem or novel? Is participation likely to be restricted to those fortunate enough to be able to view their

I would like to thank Richard Sexton, Barrie Powell and especially Alan Malachowski for comments on an earlier draft of this paper.

lives 'ironically', in a spirit of Derridean playfulness? In short, what
determines the style and content of conversation, and who gets to take
part?

If *PMN* were all we had to go on, then we would be restricted to voicing
our misgivings in this highly speculative form. In that work, Rorty leaves
us guessing as to the political details of his position. More recently,
however, Rorty has begun to flesh out his conception of the political
nature of post-philosophical culture.[2] In various essays focused on this
very theme and on the role of political theory, he provides us with an
opportunity to test out our initial suspicions, and hopefully to make any
criticisms better informed and more refined.

In this chapter, I will argue that despite some of the potentially
liberating promises of his rhetoric, there are important tensions and
anomalies in Rorty's position which have yet to be resolved. And, that
furthermore, it is not clear that these difficulties can be handled properly
within the framework of ideas Rorty has formulated to date. In other
words, the above questions still need to be addressed.

I begin with a very brief summary of Rorty's overall approach; mainly
to record some sympathy with it. I then move on to more detailed
discussion of the difficulties he faces in the political arena. Here, I start
with his notion of 'contingency', and then, after raising some issues
concerning ideology, I turn to some of the problems underlying his
pragmatism. This attempt to meet Rorty on his own ground leads to some
rather banal conclusions. I wind things up by shifting perspective in order
to look at Rorty's position through the eyes of a 'political contender', and
this engages some more urgent critical considerations.

II

In *PMN* Rorty criticizes the 'analytical tradition' in philosophy for being
largely 'Cartesian' in outlook and practice. He argues that its misguided
search for overarching theories and 'foundations' has produced little of
practical value. Rorty makes some telling points against the moribund
aspects of this tradition.[3] But, although there is much to admire in Rorty's
bold attempts to break through what he, and others, take to be a
fundamental impasse (what Bernstein has aptly called 'the grand Either/
Or dilemma of modern philosophers'[4]), suspicions may be aroused when
he extends this manoeuvre into the political sphere. For here, he seems to
be making the mistake of applying what works in some areas of discourse
to discourse *in general* – thus perpetrating the very same sort of crime for
which he indicts the great reductivist theorists of the analytical tradition;
namely, that of trying to construct a meta-story within which all problems

can be commensurated, if not solved. My own view is that while Rorty *has* achieved worthwhile results in challenging specific features of the analytical tradition in philosophy, he has overstretched his resources when handling political issues. His deconstructive onslaught loses momentum when it reaches the stubborn difficulties of political life.

Rorty's paper 'Thugs and Theories' (henceforth, TT) is a deliberate political rejoinder to complaints made by Bernstein and other thinkers about his previous paper entitled 'The Priority of Democracy to Philosophy' (reprinted this volume, ch. 17). TT is revealing in two ways. First, because he has been pressed to meet various political objections (such as the charge of 'conservatism'), Rorty makes an effort to defend his *defoundationalist* critique of political theory more explicitly. And, second, in making this defence, Rorty puts his political cards on the table, leaving the reader in little doubt as to his own allegiances. These considerations – the second of which would otherwise be of no interest here – set things up for us to highlight the tensions between Rorty's desire to hold firm to liberal beliefs and his concurrent motivation for wanting to deconstruct political theory and do away with ideology.

On first reading, TT may well strike the reader as politically naïve, and to a surprising degree. It might even look as if Rorty is *perpetuating* ideology rather than overcoming it as he intends. Here, the following kind of remark is likely to make our ears prick up:

> I do not think that old-fashioned cold war liberalism needs any apologies. It will need them only if new evidence shows that Soviet Imperialism never existed, or no longer exists, or if somebody comes up with a better alternative for dealing with it than the Cold War.[5]

This is perhaps a rather loaded quotation to begin with, but there are others in the same vein, and it illustrates why we might have some preliminary cause for suspicion. Rorty actually speaks as if the identification of Soviet Imperialism is a *purely factual matter* and as if the Cold War is simply one effective way of dealing with the appropriate states of affairs (a way of 'facing up to the facts'). I will return to this issue soon, meanwhile it will be sufficient to note the sort of remark that Rorty thinks can be made on a 'non-ideological' basis.

III

In the spirit of American pragmatism, Rorty upholds Dewey as one who showed us how to 'start with our social hopes and work down from there to theories about the standard philosophical topics . . . without becoming "irrationalist" or "relativist"'.[6] This respect for Dewey fits in with Rorty's view that liberalism cannot (and need not) be justified, or 'legitimated', in any deep, philosophical sense, that 'theory' alone cannot privilege it above other political stances.[7] Our identification with liberalism, or any other political system for that matter, should be based on our particular, local, circumstances and the practical upshot. After all: 'There is nothing sacred about either the free market or about central planning; the proper balance between the two is a matter of experimental tinkering.'[8]

In 'Postmodernist Bourgeoise Liberalism',[9] Rorty concedes (to the Marxist objection) that 'Bourgeoise Liberal institutions and practices are possible and justifiable only in certain historical and especially economic conditions'.[10] Turning this to his own advantage, he argues that his own commitment to liberalism is a mere 'contingent', historical matter. What he wants to make clear here (and in TT) is presumably that in parading his own liberalism, he is not attempting to produce a grant justificatory defence of it. He merely wants to contrast bourgeoise liberalism – 'the attempt to fulfil the hopes of the North Atlantic Bourgeoisie' – with 'Philosophical Liberalism, a collection of Kantian principles thought to justify us in having those hopes'.[11] That is to say, he is concerned to drive home the difference between subscribing to liberalism simply because it is the 'best pragmatic option', given the historical circumstances, and subscribing to it because it can somehow be shown to be 'absolutely correct' on philosophical grounds.

But the question that is raised now is: does Rorty's pragmatic approach to liberalism stand up to scrutiny? No doubt there is a sense in which we can all share political beliefs, hopes and dreams without committing ourselves in any ultimate justificatory way. We can, for instance, view our everyday political aspirations with a certain degree of irony, when we 'stand back' and 'reflect' that 'in the end nothing really matters, etc.'. More philosophically, we might agree with Rorty that there is no Archimedean point from which to privilege one kind of political discourse over another. In other words, we might be inclined to agree that there are sometimes reasons for thinking that 'everything is contingent', or, as Rorty puts it (alluding to Roberto Unger), 'It's all Politics'.[12]

However, this sort of easy-going, relativistic contingency does not seem to be what Rorty is after despite his frequent pleas for a more light-hearted approach. The common (everyday) ability to view our situation contingently is surely going to seem pretty trivial on his account if it is simply the ability to recognize that one's viewpoint is one among many which could be taken up. Rorty therefore needs to make more of his notion of 'contingency' if he is to distinguish it from 'everyday relativism' (and indeed relativism *per se*, the sceptical counterpart of foundationalism in the analytical tradition). Furthermore, he would no doubt want to argue that those who view their life-projects in this contingent light, by reflecting on their own position *vis-à-vis* that of others are not really being 'contingent' in his sense of having properly divested their beliefs of all non-contingent, legitimating associations. One of Rorty's problems with this 'commonsensical' view of contingency might be its whole vocabulary of 'standing back' and 'reflecting'. After all, such terms have a natural Archimedean ring to them. And even their casual use is likely to smuggle in something like a rational, impersonal, vantage-point in the midst of the most relativistic-sounding claims. Moreover, to try to build something philosophically substantial out of such commonsense conceptions is surely to risk portraying the individual as someone who exists *prior* to any community, who makes history rather than being shaped and formed by it.

There are three fairly distinct levels of discourse operating in this discussion which can now be identified: the commonsense level, the philosophical level and Rorty's level (which we are trying to pin down). It is clear that Rorty wants to avoid the second level since he believes it to embody some rather foolish ambitions concerning 'theoretical justification', and so on. And, we have suggested reasons why he might want to avoid the first, but does he really need to?

Perhaps Rorty does not have to make more out of 'contingency' – perhaps his position should be assimilated to the 'commonsense' perspective. Perhaps he can learn to live with the incipient metaphysical leanings of that way of looking at things. The everyday vocabulary of 'standing back' and 'reflecting' does, after all, express one of the main characteristics of liberalism (contingent or otherwise).[13] Since Rorty espouses liberalism without wanting to make a big philosophical deal out of his political beliefs, maybe his best bet is simply to blend them back in with commonly held beliefs. That appears to be an option; we will consider its drawbacks presently. Meanwhile, we should not ignore the possibility that Rorty might even be able to make his peace with *philosophical* liberalism. His belief that he can take a 'laid back', contingent, stance – without ultimate philosophical commitment is, itself, reminiscent (some might say constitutive) of philosophical defences of liberal pluralism. One can detect in Rorty's views the familiar liberal reliance on notions like 'free choice', 'tolerance', 'agnosticism about the good life', 'checks and balances', and so on. This links him with the Enlightenment outlook which Rorty claims to have meta-outlived.

The problem here is that not only does this option leave Rorty with little to say that is distinctive, but it is, as we shall see, incongruous with his desire to do away with ideology. Given the 'pluralistic' nature of liberal beliefs and convictions (certainly in the Humean version of liberalism which Rorty avows),[14] we might wonder whether his notion of 'contingency' is really a notion which 'makes a difference'. How can we distinguish *contingently* held beliefs from *philosophically-grounded* beliefs? And, just how is one to tell the difference between a person who views her beliefs ironically, in the appropriate contingent manner, using all the right tools in Rorty's 'philosophical' debunking kit, and the urbane, sceptical person in a liberal society who simply asserts things like: 'Everything is relative (contingent)', 'One view is as good as another in the end', 'I could believe something else tomorrow – I believe what I believe until something better comes along', 'I choose my values – the state only interferes', 'Those who try to force ideology down our throats are only trying to show that they have all the answers, that they know what is best for us', and 'I just do what works, *they* get into ideology/politics'. When we examine the latter claims, it does not seem feasible to argue that because the beliefs involved are (supposedly) held contingently, they operate outside ideology, in some politically (or theoretically) neutral territory. On the contrary, there would be a good case here for saying that the attitudes so expressed just *are* what liberal ideology comes down to.[15]

Of course, Rorty need not accept, and might well challenge, our divisions of discourse here. He prefers a liberalism which has been stripped of high theory, and is thus likely to regard the classical liberal thinkers as being at their best when they are simply trying to make 'commonsense' liberal beliefs 'look good', without adding any special philosophical ingredients. On this understanding, we can collapse philosophical liberalism into commonsense liberalism. What is wrong, we might ask, with Rorty then identifying his own position with that which emerges here?

Since it amounts to a position where plain liberalism has been made to look good, we can call the emergent position 'sophisticated liberalism'. Assume that Rorty holds this position, and that his answer to the problems of not having anything philosophically distinctive to say is that what is unique about his position is that it manifests the insight that actually there is not much to be said that is distinctive! Does this let Rorty off the hook? Well, as we have already intimated, it leaves him in a weak and complacent position with regard to the question of ideology.

Just because sophisticated liberalism professes to be non-ideological, does not mean that it *is* non-ideological.[16] This should not need saying, but Rorty's stance provokes it. Rorty seems quite happy to take a line very close to that taken by the 'End of Ideology' movement in the 1950s, whose advocates became notorious for their smug, cagey attitudes towards their own theoretical and ideological presuppositions. In his well-known paper 'The End of Ideology and the End of the End of Ideology', MacIntyre argued forcefully that this movement was itself ideological.[17] Indeed, a prominent feature of liberal rhetoric has been the staking of strong claims to ideological neutrality, along with a tendency to see 'totalizing', ideological monsters lurking in every alternative creed. Rorty seems to be speaking in roughly the same vein, if with some 'sophistication'. Can he deflect our present complaints by continuing to play the pragmatist card?

Rorty himself might respond to this question by pointing out that the 'pragmatist card' is not a *separate* card, and that we have misrepresented his position by focusing on the notion of contingency in isolation from what he has to say about pragmatism and politics. This would be fair comment, but I will try to show that the pragmatist framework Rorty appeals to actually makes his idea of contingency seem even less viable, politically speaking, than we have made it out to be so far. In 'Is Patriotism a Virtue',[18] MacIntyre plausibly cites North America as a land (and culture) whose *Sittlichkeit* just is *Moralitat* (where these Hegelian terms stand for 'contingently shared values' and 'values which are grounded in some grander way', respectively). The point I want to take up here is that perhaps shared values (in Rorty's sense of the values defining 'we liberals') might turn out to be indistinguishable from *Moralitat*, that is from values which are grounded in some more universal manner. We raised this point earlier, but now we can put it into a pragmatist context. Contingently held beliefs can display the same external features, and have the same practical political outcome, as 'grounded beliefs'. Furthermore, in daily affairs, we may care little whether the people we are dealing with invest in their beliefs to any deep, metaphysical, justificatory extent – or indeed whether they view their politics with irony. We may simply want to know what their next move is going to be, what their plan of action is. Suppose Rorty wants to take this line – after all, when writing about political pragmatism, he tends to place a lot of weight on the capacity to anticipate what the opposition is up to: 'the fate of democracy and of socialism' should be seen 'as largely a matter of who shoots who first, or whose agents co-opt which revolution first'?[19]

As we have set things up, the pragmatist context of Rorty's political claims needs to resolve two main difficulties: (i) it has to show what marks out 'contingency', and (ii) it has to show how ideology can be overcome. We have just indicated that Rorty might resolve (i) by not worrying too much about theoretical distinctions between ways in which political beliefs are held – that again he might be content to assimilate 'contingency' to 'groundedness' (or *vice versa*), and concentrate instead on the notion of 'practical consequences'. Our second difficulty concerning the question of ideology is not so easily dispensed with. Indeed, the sticking point of (ii) involves Rorty's very dependence on the latter notion of 'practical consequences'. Often political issues cannot even be *identified* pragmatically, that is non-ideologically. Yet Rorty's pragmatic approach leans heavily on the possibility of doing just that. His use of the phrase 'We liberals' is defended 'by reference to a view of current political dangers and options'. A common factor, too, in the eight liberal tenets Rorty outlines in TT is the contention that political problems can be identified in a similarly 'pragmatic' fashion:

> Whether Soviet Imperialism is a threat is a paradigm of a non-ideological, unphilosophical, straightforwardly empirical question. It is a matter about what will happen if such and such other things happen (if NATO collapses, if S. Africa goes communist etc.).[20]

He even goes so far as to suggest not just that this sort of question cannot be answered by 'improving one's philosophical sophistication', but that the thing to do instead is to read the appropriate intelligence reports 'about what the Politburo said'.[21]

What is most surprising here (apart from the apparent naïvety again) is that Rorty's keen nose for 'theory-ladeness' – which functioned so efficiently during his discussions of epistemology in *PMN* seems to let him down when he tackles the subject of politics. Why is he led to think that such pardigmatically political phenomena as 'intelligence reports' are ideologically neutral, or at least can be treated as such?

There are two plausible answers. The short answer is that by taking liberalism as a non-ideological 'given', Rorty can then consider intelligence reports about the 'Soviet threat' to be empirical descriptions. This answer has an equally brief accompanying explanation as to why Rorty opted for liberalism in the first place. Since he feels so strongly that there is no way to elevate oneself above local beliefs in order to 'judge and/or justify' them, he was bound to go for some form of North American liberalism. And since the only justification he does have respect for – pragmatism – provides no such means of 'elevation' either, there is a sense in which it is bound to support his decision. Here, it only requires the assumption that the liberalism available to Rorty has *some* advantageous practical consequences for it to appear that his liberalism and his pragmatism were made for one another.

The second, longer, but more charitable, answer to our puzzlement posits a line of argument about pragmatism and politics which explains away Rorty's apparent lack of sensitivity to the presence of ideological elements in what he regards as empirical phenomena. It is not easy to reconstruct this argument directly from Rorty's own work, but the argument has been stated boldly by Gordon Graham in his paper, 'Beyond Ideology: Politics and Pragmatism'.[22] If we take it that something like Graham's argument is behind Rorty's casual approach, this removes the veneer of naïvety from Rorty's claims, and thus makes some of them less startling. It does not, however, afford him much protection against objections connected with (ii) above (that is the problem of how ideology can be overcome); Graham's argument is, itself, vulnerable on this score. And, it is not very difficult to show why.

IV

Graham makes a suitable ally for Rorty because he also wants us to set aside ideological considerations, and 'choose the policy that works best'. Graham maintains that 'a pragmatic approach to political action is possible because we can have political ends in the shape of problems and formulate solutions to them without recourse to ideology'. Like Rorty, he thinks that the identification of political problems is a fairly straightforward, empirical exercise, that it is *means* rather than ends which are generally in dispute. This is not the place for a detailed discussion of Graham's position, but the following quotations should be sufficient to indicate the Rortyan spirit of the kind of 'pragmatism of the moment' that Graham advocates:

> We can conduct political argument on the grounds of what will or will not be successful. . . . Political action is possible without recourse to grand conceptions of history and society. . . . The pragmatist operates with no conception of history or vision of the future. . . . The pragmatist policy is neither short term nor long term. It is simply needed for the moment and just how long that moment is . . . is something contingent circumstances will determine.

Such claims however, amount to no more than 'hand-waving' rhetoric without more substantial support. Graham seems to think they can be so supported by an argument along these lines:

> Many important political problems can be identified on an empirical basis – that is, independently of ideological concerns; and, if such problems have a solution, this need not involve ideology either. From the evidence which supports this claim, we can draw the general conclusion that ideological considerations are neither necessary nor sufficient for either the identification or resolution of typical political problems. And, correlatively, pragmatic considerations are necessary and sufficient in both respects.

What is wrong with this argument? The major weakness is that it is vulnerable to counter-examples. Even the cases which Graham thinks will most obviously provide evidence in favour of his premises can be challenged in this way.

Graham is quite confident that there are many central cases which support his way of looking at things: 'Riots, wars, famines, epidemics, civil strife, economic stagnation and so on are all problems with which those in charge of the state must deal regardless of their ideological views'. However, even these cases can be disputed. If we examine them closely, then Graham's 'What shall we do? Do something about these problems' approach falters. According to Graham, we have here some *prima facie* evidence for the existence of 'ideology-transcendent ends', together with handy criteria for assessing the means of attaining such ends (Is *x* the right means? Will it: Stop the riots, end the war, feed the hungry? . . . and so on). But, this very assumption about agreement on ends presupposes a middle-of-the-road liberal perspective. Take the case of war. Graham says that in this instance, 'The criteria of political success are plain – such steps as will bring the war to an end are those that should be taken'. Why, we might ask should war be considered a bad thing in itself, something we would naturally want to bring to an end? When one thinks of 'political agents' who regard themselves as 'freedom fighters' or who consider the whole ethos of 'the rich North Atlantic democracies' to be fundamentally corrupting, one can imagine a desire on the part 'of those in charge of the state' (or those seeking this power on behalf of a significant proportion of a population) for a situation of perpetual warfare. And certainly, to bring things down to earth, it would be presumptuous to attempt to sit at a negotiating table with Iran and Iraq or Israel and the PLO (not to mention Nicaragua and the Contras or South Africa and the ANC) and try to push the Graham line on war. Of course, it is possible for Graham to reshuffle the cards so that these examples fit a pragmatist scheme of things – but to do so (and this is my main point here) he will have to take into account the ideological background. When it comes down to specific historical situations, 'contingent circumstances' do not hand us 'the problem of war' on a plate, as a non-ideologically given problem. Similar considerations make 'famine' (where not-so-middle-of-the-road liberals might argue that there is no obligation to take action) and 'economic stagnation' (witness the debates as to whether unemployment is a problem about which those 'in charge of the state' should do something) less than convincing illustrations of the practical possibility of political pragmatism.

In meeting Rorty on his own ground, and following through various moves that he could make to accommodate criticisms, we have ended up with the rather bland conclusion that despite his protests to the contrary, Rorty is peddling liberal ideology. If we now shift our ground and look at Rorty's position through the eyes of what we might call a 'political contender', then some more urgent conclusions can be drawn. My purpose is not to endorse the position of the contender, but rather to use it as a means of showing that there is something inherently unsatisfactory about Rorty's position.

V

If we were to end on a 'Rorty-is-peddling-liberal-ideology' note, he could simply admit to the charge, and then argue, in a 'fair-minded', pragmatic, sort of way, that perhaps liberalism is not such a bad system to be peddling ideology for. Then we would be at stalemate. If, however, we take up the perspective of someone who has good reason to contend for (say) a new political set-up, then irrespective of the merits, or otherwise, of liberalism *in situ*, it begins to look as if Rorty is surreptitiously narrowing down the options, and doing this in a way which belies the even-handed gloss of his ideology. Here is how things might look from this perspective:

(1) The liberal, being already part of a dominant status quo, can *afford* to take things lightly on the theoretical front in just the ways Rorty recommends (i.e. engage in ironic/contingent discursive practices, treat the 'opposition' hermeneutically and not worry too much about ideological presuppositions).[23]

(2) What puts the Rortyan liberal in the position described in (1) is not just a personal choice about what attitude to take towards theory, ideology, metaphysics, foundationalism, or whatever, but material circumstances of advantage in the historical-economic-political situation of the world at large.[24]

(3) Despite gestures towards 'openness', 'pluralism', 'sensitivity to persuasion', and so on, the liberal set-up as apologized for by Rorty does not cater for the political contender. The phenomena that such a contender is likely to be concerned about just do not show up in the liberal scheme of things in ways which match the contender's own conception (and perhaps first-hand experience) of them. For instance, in the favourite liberal models of 'contracts', 'bargaining', 'free-markets', and such, unsavoury phenomena like inequality, injustice and personal greed are either screened out initially or later explained away at an abstract level. And then, the best that seems to be on offer at the concrete level where such phenomena are manifested in poverty, exploitation and worse, is either a patronizing assurance that some such unwelcome phenomena must be accepted as brute facts (it's just a matter of chance that the political contender is on the receiving end – 'blame is not part of the game' here) or the hypothetical consolation that eventually everything will even out if everyone just keeps 'playing according to the rules'.[25]

(4) In the picture Rorty presents, any worthwhile resources for advocating a transformation in the direction of the political contender's view of things seem to be wiped out. Or to put it in Rortyan terms, the political contender may see the need for a radical redescription of things (e.g. one which shows the 'game' (of, say, international trade) to be

rigged, and 'fair play' to be a sham), but any redescription the political contender tries to provide will only gain credence if it fits in with the Rortyan liberal outlook. Conveniently, any attempt to point out 'real' inaccuracies in the liberal picture can be labelled 'metaphysical scare-mongering', in line with the Rortyan reaction to all projects which involve the purported 'unmasking' of underlying realities.

(5) Further to (4), the Rortyan approach can make alternative pragmatic options look ideologically unsound. Since there is no way to show 'how things really are' on the Rortyan understanding, there is no way to appeal to facts which undermine the liberal picture. Any such appeal by the political contender can be marginalized by making it appear 'ideological' in a prejorative sense. The possibility that a political contender might need guidance from a theory which competes with the liberal outlook (where such a contender needs to abstract from the current situation, and then generalize about flaws in the liberal set-up on the basis of this abstraction) can all too easily be ruled out in this way.[26] Rorty's call for 'fresh language' amounts to no more than a call for more frequent shufflings of the pack, where pragmatic counter-theories have been treated like 'jokers' and discarded before play commenced.

These points which tend to emerge when we view Rorty'a position through the eyes of a political contender support two important critical observations on his whole approach to politics. First, on the practical front, Rorty's pragmatism is very limited in scope. His recommendations might well strike a political contender as being a home-made recipe for disaster (or, closer to the point perhaps, a recipe for 'continuing the disaster') and, more generally they lack credibility as anything other than tenets of North American liberal ideology because they fail to extend beyond an articulation of a rather self-satisfied outlook from within which it is bound to appear that *all* political theorizing on behalf of radically competing outlooks must be ideological rather than pragmatic. Rorty's failure to appreciate the *pragmatic* potential of socialist theory independent of the Soviet threat,[27] and his heavy-handed treatment of Marxism in general seem to be products of this kind of liberal self-satisfaction.[28] Second, Rorty advocates some fairly negative conclusions about the utility of political theory, but his grounds for doing so are ideological. He presumably sees himself as promoting a self-effacing role for theory on grounds which are both pragmatically and philosophically compelling. But, as we have stressed, the pragmatic support for his conclusions is limited – strictly speaking it applies only within a liberal framework. And, on his own understanding, philosophy can provide no decisive verdict (not even, perhaps, the verdict that it can provide no decisive verdict on political matters). Liberalism has a way of swallowing up political differences and spitting out apologies which suit its own purposes. For, as MacIntyre puts it:

> Liberalism . . . is often successful in pre-empting the debate by reformulat-
> ing quarrels and conflicts with liberalism, putting in question this or that
> particular set of attitudes or policies, but not the fundamental tenets of
> liberalism with respect to individuals and the expression of their preferences
> . . . the contemporary debates within modern political systems are almost
> exclusively between conservative liberals, liberal liberals and radical liberals.
> There is little place in such political systems for the criticism of the system
> itself, that is, for putting liberalism in question.[29]

Rorty writes as if there are non-ideological reasons for not 'putting liberalism in question', but it is not clear what these reasons amount to in the end. This makes his 'apology' for liberalism disappointing to those of us who are looking for ways in which to construct political theories to meet the demands of the times rather than the reduced ambitions of the 'Alexanderian culture of social and historical thought that now flourishes in the North Atlantic democracies'.

NOTES

1 See *Philosophy and the Mirror of Nature* (Basil Blackwell, Oxford, 1982), p. 378. 'To see keeping a conversation going as a sufficient aim of philosophy, to see wisdom as consisting in the ability to sustain a conversation, is to see human beings as generators of new descriptions rather than beings one hopes to be able to describe accurately'. See also Rorty's references to this process as one of edification (p. 360) – that is, 'The project of finding new, better, more interesting, more fruitful ways of speaking', where 'the quest for truth is just one among many ways in which one might be edified', and 'the search for objective knowledge . . . one human project among others'.

2 See, for instance, 'The Priority of Democracy to Philosophy' (ch. 17 of this volume); 'Postmodernist Borgeoise Liberalism', *The Journal of Philosophy*, 80 (Oct. 1983), pp. 583–9; 'Thugs and Theorists', *Political Theory*, 15 (Nov. 1987), pp. 564–80; *Contingency, Irony and Solidarity* (Cambridge University Press, Cambridge, 1988); and 'Unger, Castoriadas and the Romance of a National Future', *Northwestern University Law Review* (1988). In this chapter, however, I shall be referring mainly to 'Thugs and Theories'.

3 Anette Baier, whose work Rorty acknowledges, makes analogously convincing comments about moral theory. See her 'Doing without Moral Theory?', in *Postures of the Mind: Essays on Mind and Morals* (Methuen, London, 1985), p. 228.

4 According to Bernstein, the dilemma is this: 'Either there is some basic foundational constraint or we are confronted with intellectual and moral chaos'. He sees Rorty as 'not advocating that we take sides on this fundamental dichotomy that has shaped the Cartesian–Lockean–Kantian tradition', but rather as trying to 'help us see through it, and set it aside'. See Richard Bernstein 'Philosophy and the Conversation of Mankind', as reprinted in Bernstein, *Philosophical Profiles* (Polity Press, Cambridge, 1986).

5 See Rorty, 'Thugs and Theories', p. 18, n. 25: 'My project was not to make this sort of liberalism look better, but to take it for granted and discuss another subject: what sort of culture might lie at the end of the road which we liberal intellectuals have been travelling

since the Enlightenment?' Rorty also takes the line that old-fashioned cold-war liberalism does not need any apologies in response to Bernstein's pointed criticism that his 'celebration of a new tolerant jouissance' is 'little more than an ideological apologia for an old-fashioned version of cold-war liberalism dressed up in postmodern discourse'. (Richard Bernstein, 'One Step Forward, Two Steps Backward: Richard Rorty on Liberal Democracy and Philosophy'.)

6 See Rorty, 'Thugs and Theories', p. 15, n. 20.

7 Ibid., p. 14, n. 17.

8 Ibid., p. 4. This is in keeping with his comment that 'We should think of politics as one of the experimental rather than the theoretical disciplines.'

9 Reprinted in *Praxis and Hermeneutics*, ed. R. Hollinger (University of Notre Dame Press, Notre Dame, 1985).

10 Ibid., p. 216.

11 Ibid., p. 216. Rorty's picture of Kant as a 'foundationalist' tends to degenerate into caricature; for a less rigid, 'defoundationalist' view of Kant, see some of O. O'Neill's interesting work on Kantian political theory, especially 'The Public Use of Reason', *Political Theory*, 14/4 (Nov. 1986).

12 See Rorty, 'Thugs and Theories, p. 15, n. 20, and also Roberto Unger's interpretation of 'It's All Politics', in *Social Theory: Its Situation and Its Task: A Critical Introduction to Politics, a Work in Constructive Social Theory* (Cambridge University Press, Cambridge, 1987). See especially pp. 148–9, on contingent practical politics.

13 For a related discussion of liberalism, see the work of John Rawls, a philosopher who has contributed to the recent debate – between contingency and foundationalism – which is already in danger of losing its point. (See Amy Gutman, 'Communitarian Critics of Liberalism', *Philosophy and Public Affairs* (1985). Rawls's *A Theory of Justice* has often been criticized for presupposing a rational individual who is able to stand back (in the Original Position) and abstract from all social and contingent particulars, and even history itself (see Sandel's *Liberalism and the Limits of Justice*, Cambridge University Press, Cambridge, 1982, for such objections). Rorty would obviously be reluctant to identify with a Rawls who, on this interpretation, seems to follow in the wake of 'Kantian transcendentalism'. But since, Rawls's 'pragmatic turn', in his most recent interpretation of his own work (see e.g. 'Justice as Fairness: Political, Not Metaphysical', *Philosophy and Public Affairs*, 1985), Rorty now shares much of Rawls's outlook. Rawls makes the appropriate adjustments, defends the Original Position on the grounds of a thought experiment, makes the priority of justice a *contingent priority* of 'we liberals' and thereby exorcizes any metaphysical ghosts. This kind of relativistic concessionary Hegelianism – whereby we preface our discourse with the cautionary 'we liberals' tag in order to deflect charges of *universalism* – is of course strikingly similar to Rorty's approach in his recent work on political theory. Interestingly for our purposes, however, Rawls does not appear to see his position as a non-philosophical one.

14 See 'Thugs and Theories', p. 18, n. 24, where Rorty argues, 'I should like the sentiments of pity and tolerance to take the place of belief systems or the commitment to rationality . . . in bonding liberal societies together. I want a meta-ethics which follows up on Hume, rather than on Kant.'

15 Implicit in much commonsense liberal discourse, it seems, is a positivistic fact–value distinction – which privileges the individual chooser as freely endowed with subjective preferences (emotive choices), which 'objective' reason and or 'factual' considerations cannot arbitrate between. If Rorty's position is assimilated to commonsense liberalism, then how will he be rid of its corresponding positivistic associations (as well as its emotivist instrumentality towards means and ends)?

16 Richard Bernstein argues a similar point about the End of Ideology Movement in his

336   *Conversational Politics*

paper, 'One Step Forward, Two Steps Backward'; see also TT p. 18, and Christopher Norris's *Contest of Faculties* (Methuen, London, 1985), esp. Introduction.

17 In A. MacIntyre, *Against the Self-Images of the Age* (Duckworth, London, 1971). The End of Ideology Movement can be seen as arising out of the 1950s spirit, in which American liberals saw themselves as balanced neutrally between the totalizing world ideologies of the Second World War. Liberalism was therefore considered to occupy a middle ground which could fit everything of value in the opposing ideologies into its own pluralistic and 'eminently sensible', 'open to suggestions' model.

18 Philosophy Department, University of Kansas. O'Neill in her paper 'Ethical Reasoning and Ideological Pluralism', *Ethics*, July 1988, makes a similar and cogent reference to this comment by MacIntyre.

19 TT, p. 10.

20 See TT, pp. 18, 21, where Rorty denies that differences on empirical issues are ideological (i.e. whether Soviet imperialism is a threat, or whether the system still works etc.).

21 TT, p. 18.

22 See Gordon Graham, 'Beyond Ideology: Politics and Pragmatism', Dubrovnik Conference: Survival of the Planet, 1987. I am not suggesting here that Rorty and Graham would themselves want to identify with one another's respective positions.

23 Liberals can afford to be complacent about liberal foundations and (thereby) deconstruct 'the tradition'; that is, 'put less value on being in touch with reality' (*PMN*, p. 365). They have already reaped its intellectual fruits. Rorty himself makes a related point when he argues that abnormal or reactive (existential) discourse is parasitic upon normal discourse and that 'edifying' philosophers are 'intentionally peripheral', that is they know that 'their work loses its point when the period they were reacting against is over' (see *PMN*, pp. 370, 365). If, contrary to its own self-image, postmodern discourse is dependent upon some fixed ground from which to take an edifying ironic stance, the relevant question for us becomes one of how those at a different stage (perhaps earlier, or disadvantaged, or both – e.g. Third World peoples or women) can be similarly confident without first achieving Enlightenment-type norms (and/or material gains) that they can react against. Sandra Harding makes this point in reference to epistemology. She asks, 'Should feminists be willing to give up the political benefits which can accrue from believing that we are producing a new, less biased, more accurate social science? . . . Is it premature for women to be willing to give up what they hever had. . . . Perhaps only those who have had access to the benefits of the Enlightenment can "give up" those benefits'. Sandra Harding, 'Conclusion: Epistemological Questions', in *Feminism and Methodology*, ed. Sandra Harding (Open University Press, Milton Keynes, 1987), pp. 188–9, also p. 183. See also Rorty's remarks on being 'hermeneutic about the opposition', *PMN*, p. 364.

24 Liberals in the North Atlantic Hemisphere can afford to take their political situation for granted since the underlying material circumstances of advantage will tend to exist whatever 'theoretical' stance the individual takes up. Whereas, the Third World contender may have to fight for his or her basic economic structure before gaining the appropriate political set-up.

25 Furthermore, to argue that there are structural constraints and inequalities in the international economic system where the balance is weighted against the Third World (and perhaps even the Soviet Union, given the capitalistic nature of the international game) is not to make any correlative claims that Western capitalism is inherently wrong. Nor is it to focus merely on evils 'integral' to liberal society as Rorty assumes leftist critics do (see TT, pp. 8, 9). It is merely to point out the constraints on liberalism – for instance that there may be only limited opportunities at any one time, in liberal societies.

26 The contender, outside the liberal consensus, will tend to look suspiciously metaphysical on Rorty's model, since she will be viewed as being committed to some absolute critique which claims to undercut all other forms of practice or discourse by providing more secure foundations, which are closer to reality or which better represent 'our interests' etc. (and/or give us a privileged understanding of the world). She is viewed as *confrontational* rather than edifying. The political contender may need some form of theoretical critique. The freedom-fighter cannot be merely edifying. She has to act as if her beliefs are correct. How else does she motivate herself and or mobilize others to act? One doesn't lead a war of liberation by arguing that we are fighting for a particular cause because it looks good, or because it's what people like us do or how we choose to describe ourselves. One argues that we are fighting this war to liberate the people, to lead them to a better state of affairs, to overcome injustice, and so on. This is indeed a pragmatic decision, but it is based on that of believing in the truth or a better state of affairs.

27 By ignoring fundamental economic and social constraints in the international 'game', Rorty tends to oversimplify the role of socialism and various Third World political movements. He is prone to see red (TT, p. 6) in what may only be socialist rhetoric, or even actually liberal demands which have been mistaken as 'socialist'. All too often, 'socialism' is used as a negative descriptive term to keep at bay those peripheral players (or potential players) who are contending for places which do not exist for them – if such contenders flood the system, Western standards will be threatened. In short, not everyone can have their 'democratic claims' satisfied. Where a 'peripheral' country may pose an economic threat, for instance in the case of Nicaragua, it may be expedient to talk in terms of 'reds'. In Nicaragua, the hope for social and democratic reforms may well be what spells out danger for US (economic) interests, since if other Central American countries were to follow suit and also ask for what the West has, this would place too great a burden on the limited resources of the international economic pie. The threat here, then, is not a Soviet one or even a Marxist threat independent of the Soviet Union, but 'liberal demands' made by those on the periphery competing for scarce resources and a fair chance in the international game. (If the Soviet Union looks hopefully towards a better outcome in Nicaragua, it does not follow that Nicaragua looks hopefully towards the Soviet Union. Aid, as Rorty would acknowledge, will be accepted from any country who will offer it, including the Soviet Union – this is an entirely pragmatic decision). Because it is so difficult for Third World countries to break into Northern monopolies, more drastic measures are required merely to achieve the basic democratic freedoms that the West can take for granted (e.g. placing tariffs, not letting money go outside the country, keeping skilled workers in the country, forming co-operatives, discouraging cash crops that may only benefit the rich, etc. – all measures that are labelled 'socialist' when enacted by 'peripheral' countries and 'pragmatic' when carried out by Northern countries, as witnessed by the US deficit and placing tariffs against Third World goods).

28 Rorty, in keeping with the liberal tradition, agrees with Bell that, 'What was useful in Marxism has been absorbed into the social democratic Deweyan tradition and the residue can be safely neglected' (see note 17 above; see also TT, pp. 14–15, where Dewey and Weber are described as absorbing everything useful out of Marxism). He thus dismisses Marxism as an 'amiable, but fruitless, exercise in nostalgia'. 'We see no point trying to work a political vocabulary developed in the middle of the nineteenth century than in trying to rework one developed in the middle of the fourteenth century BC' (TT, p. 14). But this surely begs some questions, since one could equally argue liberal doctrine is outdated and no longer adequate for the modern-day world. (Certainly with the Third World now on the political agenda, we ought to be looking for an entirely

338   *Conversational Politics*

new political system which accommodates East and West, North and South.)

As we pointed out earlier, Rorty tends to oversimplify left-wing politics, as he does socialist theory independent of the Soviet case, by overemphasizing the necessatarian deterministic aspects of classical Marxism and thereby undermining its, at times, powerful role as a pragmatic social critique (serving up what Unger might call a context-shattering anti-deep structure enterprise).

Rorty is probably right to oppose what he sees as the over-theoretical, textual Romanticism of much 'continental' political theory, viewing it as offering no practical alternative to liberal (pluralistic) pragmatism. But he is surely wrong to pose the only alternative to the liberal tradition as being 'a dreadful, pompous, useless, mishmash of Marx, Adorno, Derrida, Foucault and Lacan', thereby trying to win his argument by default on the grounds that Marxism has been appropriated by over-theoretical, or abstract, continental academics. Here Rorty ignores pragmatic socialist alternatives which have been worked out in the Frankfurt critical studies movement, as well as feminist groups, small-scale (grass-roots), participatory groups and by Third World developmental practitioners, and so on. If Marxism embodies the 'metaphysics of presence' (TT, p. 16), it is not surprising, that Rorty should think that some 'continental' philosophers have misappropriated Marxism, especially if they hope to use it as a political weapon. Rorty's message here seems to be that 'deconstruction' can be used to suit liberal purposes, thus blending in with Rawls and Dewey, but not for anything which *contends* with liberalism. C. Norris quite rightly points out that given Rorty's interpretation here, Marxists would be justified in thinking the 'American deconstruction movement' to be reactionary (Norris, *Contest of Faculties*).

29 Alistair MacIntyre, *Whose Justice: Which Rationality* (Duckworth, London, 1988), p. 392.

20

Biting the Bullet: Rorty on Private and Public Morality

Charles B. Guignon and David R. Hiley

Liberal democracy and the new pragmatism

It is tempting to think of Rorty's recent writings on moral and social theory[1] as merely an attempt to work out the consequences of his critique of foundational epistemology for other 'areas' of philosophy. But it makes more sense, we believe, to see these new writings as making explicit the moral and social commitments that have motivated his critique of epistemology-centred philosophy from the outset. The worry expressed near the end of *Philosophy and the Mirror of Nature* – that traditional philosophy's search for final solutions to questions about truth, rationality and knowledge could lead to the 'freezing-over of culture' and the 'dehumanization of human beings'[2] – seems to reflect the moral concerns that drive the argumentation of the whole book. As Rorty sees it, the Platonic quest for a final, rationally justified consensus based on access to an eternal Truth is actually a manifestation of what Nietzsche called a 'craving for metaphysical comfort': the desire to close off inquiry, to calcify a privileged set of descriptions, and to 'escape our humanity' by becoming properly programed machines.

Rorty's anti-foundationalist pragmatism, in contrast, is supposed to avoid these 'dehumanizing' tendencies in traditional philosophy. By reminding us of the contingency of our community and of our own identity as humans, it reaffirms our freedom, and promises a 'renewed sense of community'. It shows us that 'what matters is our loyalty to other human beings clinging together against the dark, not our hope of getting things right'.[3] What speaks in favour of adopting the pragmatic stand-point, then, is the hope that we mortal millions living alone may reach out across the estranging sea and achieve true solidarity if only we come to see our community as something we *make* in the free interplay of diverse voices, not something we *find* by discovering our human nature. The pragmatist point of view offers a 'way of strengthening liberal institutions'[4] by encouraging diversity, tolerance and freedom.

At the same time, however, the critique of foundationalism dictates a particular vision of the ideal liberal democratic culture, an ideal Rorty calls 'postmodernist bourgeois liberalism' or 'aestheticized culture'. This ideal culture will abandon any attempt at grounding itself in terms of a conception of the moral law or 'the good for man'; it will give up 'the idea that intellectual or political progress is rational' in the sense of satisfying neutral criteria; and it will accept that 'anything goes' so long as change is achieved by persuasion rather than by force.[5] It is a culture which takes as its hero the 'strong poet' who spins off imaginative redescriptions of our predicament rather than the scientist who tries to ground our practices in facts. The ideal culture Rorty envisions 'has no ideal except freedom, no goal except a willingness to see how [free and open] encounters go and to abide by the outcome . . ., and no purpose except to make life easier for poets and revolutionaries.'[6] Understanding itself as a human artifact, as an ungrounded product of optional metaphors, it has no other aim than to maximize freedom and diversity in order to foster 'the creation of ever more various and multi-coloured artifacts'.[7]

It is important to see how Rorty is led to this vision of an ideal form of life. In his view, the critique of foundationalism initiated by Nietzsche has shown us that we have no access to timeless truths about the nature of reality. Our beliefs about the world and our self-interpretations are always preshaped by a background of understanding built into our culture's linguistic practices. As we are initiated into the forms of life of the public world, we soak up the outlook on things and the norms and standards for acting which are laid out in advance by our culture's language. The force of what Rorty calls his 'Hegelian historicism' is to lead us to see that this background of understanding constantly shifts through time, 'new forms of life constantly killing off old forms'.[8] At any given time, however, there will be a shared background of 'normal discourse' circulating in the public world. Normal discourse is defined as discourse conducted within 'an agreed-upon set of conventions about what counts as a relevant contribution, what counts as answering a question, what counts as having a good argument for that answer or a good criticism of it'.[9] It is distinguished from 'abnormal discourse' defined as 'the sort of discourse which sounds strange to the ears of a given audience.'[10]

In terms of this distinction, the illusion of traditional philosophy is seen to lie in the belief that philosophy can step outside of all normal discourse in order to ground our practices in transcendental, ahistorical truths. But there can be no such external vantage-point. Our moral convictions, for instance, cannot be justified by recourse to a moral law independent of our current beliefs and practices. Instead, 'morality' refers to what a particular group happens to commend, and the only goods are those goods internal to the practices of the group. Given this 'internalist' view of morality, there can be no 'higher' standpoint for judging the worthiness of our practices. But neither is there any need for such justification. Rorty sees the awareness of 'Hegelian historicism' as leading to a 'mild ethnocentrism', the view that 'we have to start from where we are', that 'we must, in practice, privilege our own group',[11] and that we must accept as true whatever is the outcome of normal discourse within our community at the present time. Enquiry can only start from 'the way *we* live now', and so 'we can only rationally change some of our beliefs by holding most of our beliefs constant'.[12] For us, as residents of 'the rich North Atlantic democracies', this means that we must start from the convictions and values internal to our liberal democratic society. There is no basis for such loyalties aside from the fact that they are shared by the group with which we identify. The convictions central to our liberal society include our commitment to freedom, tolerance, pluralism, procedural justice and the 'Jewish and Christian element in our tradition' which even 'free-loading atheists' can invoke.[13] The ungrounded background ideals of our liberal society provide the bedrock from which moral and political reflection begins.

Rorty's prescription for achieving an ideal liberal culture thus starts out from the 'normal discourse' of our current liberal democratic society. But he is also aware of the need to respond to recent criticisms of liberalism before he can adopt it as the bedrock for his reflections on morality and society. The main thrust of these criticisms is that precisely the conception of human nature which made possible liberalism's success against tyranny, superstition and authority make it ill-suited to serving the goals of individual freedom and reciprocity which motivated it. Rorty considers three types of criticism launched against liberalism: first, the charge made by social researchers that the individualism engendered by liberalism undermines social commitment and produces self-defeating strategies for self-fulfilment;[14] second, the moral charge that liberal society produces undesirable or reprehensible social types (what MacIntyre calls 'the rich aesthete, the manager and the therapist', and Charles Taylor calls 'strategic calculators' or 'simple weighers');[15] and, third, claims that liberalism is incoherent because it leads to relativism or requires for its justification an untenable view of human nature.[16] Rorty's response to the first, empirical charge is to suggest it is overstated – that actual moral progress shows that liberalism 'offers at least as many opportunities as it does obstacles for the renewal of a sense of community'[17] – and his reply to the moral objection is to say that, although liberalism may produce ignoble individuals, this may be a price well worth paying for freedom and greater cultural diversity. We will return to Rorty's replies to the first two objections in the last section; his answer to the third line of criticism is of special interest for clarifying his current project.

Rorty's response to the charge that liberalism is incoherent because it leads to relativism and is grounded in an untenable view of human nature is to claim that the demand for non-relativistic grounding makes sense only within an Enlightenment rationalist vocabulary which is 'obsolete' in our postmodern world. The vocabulary of Enlightenment rationalism and the 'scientized culture' it inaugurated was, of course, crucial at the beginnings of liberal democracy. But, given the upshot of anti-foundationalism, this vocabulary 'has become an impediment to the progress of democratic societies'[18] and should be replaced. What this means will become evident if we consider the significance of what Rorty calls 'the ubiquity of language'. This is the claim that 'all problems, topics, and distinctions are language-relative – the results of our having chosen to use a certain vocabulary'.[19] Since all criteria of truth and all standards for conducting enquiry are predefined by the language-game we have chosen to play, and since there are no vocabulary-neutral criteria for assessing different vocabularies, we are free to spin off new vocabularies whenever they might seem useful. It is, in fact, this capacity for 'linguistic innovation', this ability to create new vocabularies, that is 'what is most important for human life'.[20] Rorty therefore offers what he calls an 'apologetics' for liberal society, where 'apologetics' is defined as 'a way of describing old institutions and practices in a new, more useful way'.[21] This new vocabulary drops the outdated notions of objective truth and rational justification that were central to the old scientized culture, and instead promotes an aestheticized culture which glorifies the creation of new vocabularies as what is most valuable for moral and intellectual progress. The vocabulary of an aestheticized culture, Rorty thinks, is better equipped to articulate the liberal ideals of freedom and pluralism. By emphasizing the value of an ever-expanding repertoire of alternative descriptions, this culture sees its goal as protecting 'the poets and the utopian fantasts, the people who do not talk as we do . . . [in order to] ensure that its language keeps changing'.[22] It is a culture which does not try to normalize abnormal discourse.

From the standpoint of this apologetics, the third criticism of liberalism simply dissolves. Since there is no such thing as 'human nature' independent of what our latest vocabularies put in play, there can be no such thing as grounding a society in a view of human nature. And since all justification is 'relative' in the banal sense that beliefs 'can only be justified to people who hold certain other beliefs',[23] the charge of relativism – the claim that liberalism is incoherent because it cannot justify the morally privileged status it accords to freedom – has no impact. Rorty agrees with

Joseph Schumpeter that 'what distinguishes a civilized man from a barbarian' is the ability 'to realize the relative validity of one's convictions and yet stand for them unflinchingly'.[24] If all justification is relative to a particular vocabulary, and if there is no way to justify the choice of one vocabulary over another, we would do best to simply drop the old distinctions between absolute and relative, and between rational and irrational. It is the mark of a 'mature' liberal society that one will 'stand unflinchingly for one's moral convictions' while acknowledging that there is no ground for those convictions independent of the convictions themselves.

Needless to say, Rorty is aware of the risks accompanying such an aestheticized culture. In his essay, 'Nineteenth-Century Idealism and Twentieth-Century Textualism', he considers the possibility that the 'anything-goes' attitude of pragmatism might license types of literary criticism which 'substitute inhuman intertextuality for human influence' and might thereby isolate literary culture from common human concerns. As opposed to these 'inhumanist' approaches to literature, Rorty favours a more humanistic style of criticism which 'preserves our sense of a common human finitude' and nurtures an 'identification with the struggle of finite men'. But he admits he does 'not know how to back up this preference with argument'. 'To do so', he says, 'would involve a full-scale discussion of the possibility of combining private fulfilment, self-realization, with public morality, a concern for justice'.[25]

This concern for connecting private fulfilment and public morality points to the agenda for Rorty's latest writings on moral and social issues. He envisions a transformed cultural life which will abandon the Enlightenment dream of forging a bond between views of the self and society, and instead will maintain a sharp distinction between 'a private ethic of self-creation and a public ethic of mutual accommodation', recognizing that 'there is no bridge between them'.[26] The good for the individual can be nothing other than an untrammelled freedom for self-enlargement through spinning off idiosyncratic self-descriptions. And the good for the group, understood as 'a band of eccentrics collaborating for the purposes of mutual protection rather than a band of fellow-spirits united by a goal',[27] is a commitment to tolerance together with whatever system of procedural justice is currently in place in our society. Rorty describes as an 'ideal world order' an 'intricately-textured collage of private narcissism and public pragmatism'.[28]

What is most admirable about Rorty, we feel, is the courage, integrity and clear-sightedness with which he bites the bullet and draws out the inevitable consequences of anti-foundationalism for moral and social thought. He is willing to stand unflinchingly for the ideals of liberal society while both undercutting their traditional supports and acknowledging that there is a price to be paid. But what we find admirable we also find deeply troubling. We might ask: is this a culture we would *want to* stand for unflinchingly? Is Rorty's vision of an ideal culture coherent? Before turning to these questions, it will be necessary to fill out Rorty's post-foundationalist picture of the self and morality to clarify the motivation for his recommendations. This will involve examining one key strand in Rorty's anti-foundationalism, the primarily continental movement called 'decentring the subject'. After looking at a last-ditch effort to formulate a post-foundationalist view of the self in some recent 'hermeneutic' philosophies, we will lay out Rorty's minimalist picture of the self and his defence of 'self-enlargement' as the character ideal best suited to a postmodern culture. In the last section we will turn to an assessment of Rorty's stance on moral and social issues.

Decentring the subject: beyond hermeneutics

Rorty's recommendations for a new cultural life depend on his pragmatic anti-foundationalist conclusions. We have already noted how Rorty's 'Hegelian historicism' and 'ubiquity of language' claim suggest that there is no way to step outside our vocabularies in order to ground them in timeless truths about human nature. On the one hand, our sense of who we are and of what is worth pursuing in life are preshaped by the normal language-games we absorb in becoming participants in an historical culture. On the other hand, the fact that there are no privileged vocabularies means that it is up to us to take over and reshape current public ways of speaking as we see fit. The thorough-going pragmatist realizes that new ways of speaking can 'help us get what we want',[29] and that there are no prior constraints on how we describe things. Although it is always possible in principle to make currently discordant vocabularies commensurable, there is no reason to seek such commensuration. Rather, we should 'let a hundred flowers bloom' in the hope of creating new forms of intellectual life. The antidote to the 'freezing-over of culture' is to create an environment in which new forms of abnormal discourse constantly spring up.

These anti-foundationalist conclusions contribute to the current movement toward 'decentring the subject'. Since our self-understanding is a by-product of historically generated vocabularies, there is no 'fact of the matter' concerning what it is to be a human being discoverable through intuition, pure reason or scientific observation. We exist as, so to speak, intersections of transient, public interpretations. There is nothing which 'has' these interpretations, just as there is no uninterpreted reality these interpretations are *of* – in H. L. Dreyfus' formulation, we are 'interpretation all the way down'. Regarded as a crossing-point of public interpretations, the 'I' begins to look like a construct. Jonathan Culler sums up this decentring trend: 'As it is deconstructed, broken down into component systems that are all trans-subjective, the self or subject comes to appear more and more as a construct: the result of systems of convention. When man speaks, he artfully "complies with language"; language speaks through him, as does desire and society ... The "I" is not something given; it comes to exist ... as that which is seen and addressed by others.'[30]

The decentred picture of the self is apparent in Heidegger's obscure one-liner, 'Man does not speak; rather, language speaks man'. The suggestion here is that human speech is always guided in advance by inherited ways of speaking which operate behind the speakers' backs. We exist, according to Heidegger, as a 'clearing' or 'opening' in which the interpretations of our historical culture come to be interwoven. Sartre echoes this reading of the self by defining the *pour-soi* as 'nothingness'. Our self-understanding is always predelineated by a public background of interpretations which defines our 'facticity', including the possible roles, vocations and status relations we can take over. But we always have the ability to 'surpass' or 'transcend' that facticity by transforming its significance in our freely chosen projects. In this sense we are always *more than* what we are as facticity: as self-constituting beings, we are never just objects with fixed sets of attributes.

One consequence of this decentring of the subject is that it undermines what R. C. Solomon calls 'the transcendental pretence' – the belief that we can discover timeless truths about the human condition by examining our latest, historically-shaped perspectives. It helps dispel the illusion 'that deep down beneath all the texts, there is something which is not just one more text but that to which various texts are trying to be "adequate".'[31] The decentred view of the self also opens up the possibility of an 'exuberant Nietzschean playfulness'[32] with respect to ourselves. Nietzsche promotes 'the ideal of a spirit who plays naïvely – that is, not deliberately but from overflowing power and abundance – with all that was hitherto called holy, good, untouchable, divine.'[33] Instead of pursuing a final truth, the healthy person sees 'that every *elevation of man* brings with it the overcoming of narrower interpretations; that every strengthening and increase of power opens up new perspectives and means believing in new horizons'.[34] To become 'human beings who are new, unique, incomparable, who give themselves laws', we must '*destroy* the world that counts for real, so-called "*reality*"', and create 'new names ... in order to create in the long run new "things".'[35] The ideal of self-creation through creating new vocabularies is guided solely by aesthetic criteria: '*One thing is needful*. To "give style" to one's character ... In the end, when the work is finished, it becomes evident how the constraint of a single taste governed and formed everything large and small. Whether this taste is good or bad is less important than one might suppose, if only it was a single taste!'[36]

Rorty's characterization of the self reflects this trend towards decentring the subject. Since we explain agency by reference to beliefs, desires and feelings, it is best, for the 'purposes of moral and political deliberation and conversation', to see the self as 'a network of beliefs, desires, and emotions with nothing behind it – no substrate behind the attributes'. A person 'just *is* that network', 'a network that is constantly reweaving itself' in a hit-or-miss way to meet the pressures of the environment.[37] The picture of the self as a web of beliefs and desires, together with the awareness that we freely constitute ourselves from the linguistic materials made available in our cultural world, leads Rorty to adopt a Nietzschean experimentalist and aestheticist picture of the mature self in a postmodern age. The will to 'create ourselves as a work of art', in Foucault's words, is motivated not by Nietzsche's crypto-metaphysical 'will to power', but by a more Sartrean sense that we realize our humanity by expressing our freedom. For Sartre, it is bad faith to think that there are prior constraints on our freedom. When faced with a moral dilemma, for instance, one can only 'invent', leap one way rather than another. It is self-deception to think one's choice is guided by moral principles, for in choosing one's action one simultaneously chooses the vocabulary of moral reflection in which that choice appears justified. Our facticity does not constrain us, since it is always up to us to decide what our concrete situation in the world means: 'facticity is everywhere, but inapprehensible', Sartre says; 'I never encounter anything except my responsibility'.[38] Although Rorty renounces Sartre's attempt to build a 'metaphysics of nothingness' from this view of the self, he is clearly in sympathy with Sartre's sense that we are most human when we are most creative.

To see ourselves as self-reweaving webs of beliefs and desires, drawing on and transforming the optional vocabularies and metaphors available in the public world, is to see that the best stance to take towards ourselves is 'a spirit of playfulness and irony'.[39] This is a stance which rejects the onerous 'spirit of seriousness' of the tradition and instead turns to creativity aimed at growth and stimulation. At the same time, however, Rorty rejects the unwarranted *ressentiment* against the bourgeoisie found in Nietzsche, Sartre and Foucault. We have every reason to 'celebrate bourgeois capitalist society as the best polity actualized so far',[40] and to dedicate ourselves to realizing that society's ideals while rejecting its pretensions to transcendental grounding. We should, in Derrida's phrase, learn to 'inhabit the old structures in new ways'.

Before turning to Rorty's recommendations for a postmodern way of looking at the self, it will be helpful to consider an attempt, found in recent 'hermeneutic' writers,[41] to salvage a notion of a centred self after the demise of foundationalism. The hermeneutic approach accepts most of the conclusions of anti-foundationalism: since we have no access to uninterpreted 'facts' about ourselves, it is best to think of the self as a web of self-interpretations drawn from the vocabularies circulating in our historical context. But it also holds that self-interpreting activity and historicity themselves provide the resources for formulating an account of the self as unified and focused. Heidegger's conception of philosophy as involving a 'two-fold task' provides the model for the two key moves generally found in the hermeneutic strategy.[42] The first move is to claim that even though all interpretations are shaped by historically shifting vocabularies, there is nevertheless what Heidegger calls an underlying 'essential structure' of self-interpreting activity which can be identified by phenomenology or by reflection on our ordinary ways of describing ourselves. This quasi-Kantian 'formalist' move is supposed to reveal the conditions for the possibility of any interpretation whatsoever. The move appears in Heidegger's account of the ongoing 'happening' of our lives as rooted in the 'formal existential totality' of human 'temporality'. According to this reading of human existence as a 'life-course' or 'life-history', the temporal flow of life 'between birth and death' has a unified formal structure determined by 'thrownness' and 'futurity'. On the one hand, we find ourselves thrown into a concrete historical context which lays out the range of possible interpretations we can take over in being agents in the world. On the other hand, action has a teleological structure – it is directed toward realizing goals in the future. In Heidegger's view, the fact that life is finite – that it *will be* completed because we are 'being-toward-death' – reveals that we have an overriding goal which is to organize our lives into a coherent and unified totality. The essential structures of human activity – our rootedness in a cultural context and our goal-directedness – therefore ensure the unity of life and direct us towards living a particular sort of life.

The second move in the hermeneutic strategy is to describe our cultural and historical context in such a way as to show that it embodies a meaningful action-guiding 'content' for filling in the formal temporal structure. This 'contextualist' move appears in Heidegger's description of the self as rooted in a 'heritage' – a background of living traditions which provide us with an understanding of ourselves as co-participants in the joint venture of realizing our culture's 'destiny'. If we can recover the most binding goals of our cultural heritage, we will gain a sense of the 'essential decisions' facing us as a people. By retrieving these 'primordial' historical possibilities, we will also have a basis for criticizing the fads and fancies of the 'Today'.[43] Our 'historicity' therefore makes it possible to formulate meaningful goals for our future and to engage in a critical dialogue with the present in the light of alternative ideals revealed by our heritage.

History is contingent to the extent that it might have turned out differently, but it is also binding on us in so far as it defines who we are and who we can be.

The hermeneutic strategy points to a particular ideal of a more centred, integrated way of living – an ideal of 'self-focusing'. Our everyday existence, Heidegger claims, is characterized by 'falling' and 'inauthenticity'. We tend to be dispersed, distracted, caught up in trivial pursuits and preoccupied with the demands of the present. Everyday life slips into mere means–ends calculations with no overarching sense of where life is going or of what is truly worth pursuing. We sink into mindless conformism, drifting into current cultural practices, with no sense of viable alternatives. As a result, our lives lack genuine continuity, coherence and orientation. To become 'authentic', according to Heidegger, is to grasp the deepest possibilities for self-interpretation made accessible by one's culture, and to dedicate oneself to realizing those aims for the future. An authentic individual has the equipment for criticizing the present because he or she grasps alternative visions of the goal of life made accessible by our historical traditions. The life of such a person is defined by what Charles Taylor calls self-defining 'strong evaluations' which give direction to choice and action.[44] Understood in this way, life can be seen as having what MacIntyre calls 'the unity of a narrative quest', a quest aimed at realizing those 'future possibilities which the past has made available to the present'.[45] Hermeneutic writers generally follow Heidegger in suggesting that this 'self-focused' form of life carries with it a sense of responsibility to the wider community: a willingness to see others as ends rather than as means, and a recognition that one's own life-history is indebted to and bound up with the unfolding project of the wider community.

Rorty regards the hermeneutic strategy as a failure of nerve, as a retreat from following anti-foundationalism through to its inevitable conclusions. In his view, both the formalist and contextualist moves are red herrings. The attempt to discover 'essential structures' of life by phenomenology or by insight into our own agency still operates on the assumption that we can gain access to timeless truths about the human condition. If all self-interpretations are by-products of current language-games, however, then our interpretations of our own agency or of our own self-interpreting activity are either ephemeral images shaped by our present vocabularies or vestiges of a metaphysical tradition we would do well to discard. Even if we could detect such formal structures, they would be empty and uninformative unless interpreted by us in some way. In particular, the attempt to pinpoint some significance in the fact that our lives lie 'between birth and death' is an illusion. What our lives add up to is not something *we* decide; on the contrary, we depend 'on the charity of as yet unborn generations' to determine whether our actions accomplished something or were mere exercises in futility. For Rorty, life 'cannot be completed because there is nothing to complete: there is only a web of relations to be rewoven, a web which time lengthens every day'. To recognize the upshot of the decentring of the self is to see life as 'a tissue of contingent relations, a web which stretches backward and forward through past and future time', not 'something capable of being seen steady and whole'.[46]

The contextualist attempt to treat history as loaded down with binding values that impart direction to life is also a non-starter. What we inherit from our tradition is not a set of action-guiding directives, but rather a plurality of conflicting interpretations of our *telos*. How we hear this cacophony of voices and what we choose to make of it is largely up to us. In Rorty's view, any random constellation of events and images 'can set up an unconditional commandment to whose service a life may be devoted',[47] and the tradition provides no absolute criterion for judging the worthiness of such commitments. The most humans can do at any given time is 'manipulate the tensions within their own epoch in order to produce the beginnings of the next epoch',[48] hoping for the best.

Rorty is especially suspicious of teleological views of history which see human existence as directed towards some larger, totalizing goals beyond the causal contingencies of history. Some hermeneutic thinkers suggest that, because historians can select what is relevant from the past only on the basis of some sense of where history as a whole is going, we must presuppose a teleological vision of history as moving towards a final consensus or towards the realization of the finest goals of our civilization. Rorty, in contrast, sees the need for selection in writing history as showing, at most, that historiography is a matter of starting from our current ethnocentric sense of what is good about ourselves, and then casting about for a vocabulary suitable for describing 'the past events which made these good things possible'.[49] There is no exit from our current interests and vaguely formulated hopes to any sort of insight into the true *telos* of history. Instead of longing for the comfort of a future consensus or nostalgically pining for a time when our *telos* seemed written in the sky, we would do better to drop all 'grand metanarratives' and treat our intellectual past 'as material for playful experimentation rather than as imposing tasks and responsibilities upon us'.[50] The value of history lies in providing us with a stock of 'anecdote and convention' for explaining our choices *post festum*; only the intellectual historians of the next century will know for sure where we really were going.

Rorty generally seems intent on demystifying the jargon of 'authenticity'. If the upshot of anti-foundationalism is that we should think of ourselves as a 'clearing' in Heidegger's sense, then invidious comparisons between self-focusing and dispersal beg all the interesting questions. Looked at differently, what is called 'dispersal' might be seen as the kind of playful experimentalism which provides stimulation and growth. Instead of criticizing modern aestheticism and instrumental reason, Rorty recommends a more upbeat 'light-minded aestheticism' and 'philosophical superficiality' which 'helps make the world's inhabitants more pragmatic, more tolerant, more liberal, more receptive to the appeal of Weberian instrumental rationality'.[51] And instead of trying to hem in our freedom and creativity by linking our actions to 'essential structures' or 'living traditions', we should create an environment which encourages curiosity, self-assertion, imaginative redescriptions of the past, and unconstrained utopian fantasies about the future.

Private morality as self-enlargement

Rorty's conception of our post-foundationalist predicament paves the way to his recommendations for a new way of looking at the self and morality. First, the decentred picture of the self as a space of self-elaboration undermines traditional hierarchical views of humans which distinguish reason from appetite, a core from a periphery, a deep self from what is superficial, or the essential from the accidental. If we are only webs of beliefs and desires constantly reweaving ourselves from materials drawn from the surrounding culture, then the ideal of 'being true to what one really is' must be dropped. Second, given the internalist view of moral goods as defined solely by existing practices and institutions, there is no longer any way to draw the traditional distinction between prudence and morality. For if 'good' can refer only to the goals currently accepted within the practices of a society, then there is no way to distinguish instrumental-ist means–ends calculations aimed at achieving the ends of practical activities – mere shrewdness in handling practical affairs – from obeying the Moral Law or realizing the proper function of humans. Instead of seeing the morality/prudence distinction as a distinction between what is demanded by morality and what seems advisable in morally-neutral situations, we should think of it as 'the difference between an appeal to the interests of the community and an appeal to our private, possibly conflicting interests'.[52]

Rorty therefore proposes a new way of carving up the conceptual field of moral philosophy. We should distinguish private morality, the 'private ethic of self-creation', from public morality, the 'public ethic of mutual accommodation'. Private morality deals solely with the individual's concern for developing his or her own character, with striving for personal self-realization. The private 'search for perfection in oneself' should be set off from the concerns of public morality: 'the attempt to be just in one's treatment of others', the sort of concern which is 'codifiable in statutes and maxims'.[53] As we noted above, the interests of public morality are adequately handled by the principles of procedural justice already built into our current liberal democratic society. What is needed in the arena of public morality is not more theory but more hard work in making sure those principles extend equally to all. The concerns of private morality, in contrast, have no bearing whatsoever on public morality.

The key figure in defining the issues of private morality for our age, Rorty suggests, is Freud. In 'Freud and Moral Reflection', Rorty distinguishes three ways of seeing the self. The traditional view regarded humans as a 'natural kind', and saw the self as having a centre with an inbuilt function and set of obligations defined by its membership in the human species. This traditional view was eventually displaced by the view of the self as a centreless machine which accompanied modern science's 'mechanization of the world picture'. Although some have felt that this mechanized view of the self has important moral repercussions, Rorty thinks it has no real significance for morality. Since the chief characteristic of machines is that they have no predetermined use, to think of ourselves as machines is just to think that 'it is up to us to invent a use for ourselves'. The mechanization of nature 'made protopragmatists of most people', Rorty claims; they became accustomed to describing themselves as machines for purposes of prediction and control while using a different vocabulary for talking about themselves as moral agents. What the mechanical view did was to free us from the idea that the self has an 'essence' or 'centre' that determines how we should talk about it.

The view of the self Freud gives us, in contrast, has changed our self-image and our understanding of morality. What Freud adds to the mechanized picture of the self is the suggestion that there are different, mostly unconscious 'quasi selves' or 'persons' within us who are causing us to do things. This leads to the unnerving thought that, in Freud's words, 'we are "lived" by unknown and uncontrollable forces'.[54] Freud's view decentres the self in a much more radical way than the picture of the self as a centreless mechanism. Drawing on Davidson's reading of Freud, Rorty claims that if we think of a person as 'a coherent and plausible set of beliefs and desires', and if we think of irrational behaviour as a matter of being caused to act by sets of beliefs and desires which conflict with 'our better judgement', then it will be natural to think that our bodies play host to 'two or more persons' who are entering into causal relations with one another, though 'they do not, normally, have conversational relations',[55] We are divided or 'partitioned' selves whose inner space is populated by different person-analogues – different 'internally coherent clusters of belief and desire' – in constant causal interaction but without the internal coherence to form a single, unified person.

This Freudian picture of the self as, in Nietzsche's words, habouring within itself 'not "one immortal soul," but *many mortal souls*'[56] – this picture does transform our moral self-understanding. By letting us see ourselves as made up of different persons, each person having a different language-game with its own inbuilt interpretations, criteria and standards, it lets us see our 'conscience' as '*just* another story' about how things are, with no privileged status in giving us directions as to how we should act. We can see that there are no correct answers to the questions, 'What did happen to me in the past?' or 'What sort of person am I now?' independent of optional vocabularies spoken by different inner persons. As a result, we are freed up to interpret ourselves in any way we like.

This sense of ourselves as a space for the interplay of optional vocabularies of self-interpretation points to a new kind of character-ideal for shaping our private morality. The traditional character-ideal, according to Rorty, is the ideal of 'self-purification'. It is the 'ascetic ideal' of peeling away everything accidental in order to get in touch with one's true self – the ideal of willing one thing, of being resolute, of becoming a simpler, more transparent being. The ideal of self-purification expresses the desire to find a centre that will hold, a commitment or ultimate concern that focuses one's life into a coherent narrative unity, or a rational life-plan according to which one can engineer the bits of life into a perfectly functioning mechanism. Its model is the *agon* – the core self, the protagonist, struggling heroically against the antagonistic appetites, passions or inclinations.

The character-ideal which makes the best sense in the light of Freud is what Rorty calls the ideal of 'self-enlargement'. This is the desire to expand one's possibilities and to multiply one's perspectives through curiosity and constant learning. It is an 'aesthetic ideal' found in Nietzsche (when we strip away his attachment to the idea of 'becoming what one is'), and it is shared by de Sade, Byron and Hegel. Self-enlargement is achieved through the enrichment of language, 'the development of richer, fuller ways of formulating one's desires and hopes, and thus making those desires and hopes themselves – and thereby onself – richer and fuller'.[57] Its approach to life is experimental – *bricolage* rather than engineering, a matter of monkeying around with the bits and pieces on hand – and it is guided solely by personal aesthetic criteria. Its model is ludic – playful inventiveness and spontaneity, freed from the heavy-handed 'spirit of seriousness' of the tradition. Whereas the literary mode for self-purification seems to be what Frye calls the 'tragic' – the possible or real exclusion of the solitary individual who stands alone – the literary mode for self-enlargement is the 'comic', the promise of inclusion in the *bon homie* of a tolerant community where every identity is mistaken and every attachment is temporary.[58]

In Rorty's view, Freud's transformation of our self-image opens up new possibilities for the aesthetic life by letting us 'see ourselves as centreless, as random assemblages of contingent and idiosyncratic needs rather than as more or less adequate exemplifications of a common human essence'.[59] This shift from an ethics of purity to one of self-enrichment, he feels, is a gain for our culture. Freud helps us to 'become increasingly ironic, playful, free, and inventive in our choice of self-descriptions'; he shows us how to 'slough off the idea that we have a true self' which imposes moral demands on us; and he enables us to 'think of moral reflection and sophistication as a matter of self-creation rather than self-knowledge'.[60] Freud's 'major legacy' is the 'increased ability of the syncretic, ironic, nominalist intellectual' to play with 'religious, moral, scientific, literary, philosophical and psychoanalytic vocabularies without asking the question, "And which of these shows us how things really are?"'[61] Rorty clearly commends the values usually associated with the Freudian outlook: increased manoeuvrability through recognition of our own malleability, maturity understood as 'a nominalistic, ironic, view of oneself', and a 'tolerance for ambiguities' which is supposed to lead, in Rieff's words, to 'a genuinely stable character in an unstable time'.[62] From this standpoint, moral reflection is more a matter of spinning off vocabularies of self-assessment and trying them on for size than of looking for a moral straitjacket to keep oneself in check.

In response to those who criticize the sort of 'culture of narcissism' that might follow from the acceptance of this ideal, Rorty asks us to weigh the costs against possible gains. There is, first of all, a gain in freedom: to recognize our contingency, to see that there are no suprahuman directives guiding our choices, is to see that we are free to 'construct our own private vocabularies of moral deliberation'[63] unhampered by external constraints. This gain in freedom helps to undercut the kinds of fanaticism and rigidity which are the real enemies of democracy. A culture whose sole ideal is self-enlargement would also seem to encourage a more tolerant 'live-and-let-live' attitude. Freud's picture of conscience and the sense of duty as accidental episodes from one's past which have been internalized and organized according to an optional and dispensable story-line helps us lighten up on ourselves and see our own sense of duty as an idiosyncratic story rather than as a quasi-divine imperative. This more laid-back attitude towards ourselves can steer us to a less judgemental attitude towards others. We can see the 'Kantian dutiful fulfiller of universal obligations' and the playful Nietzschean experimentalist as 'exemplifying two out of many forms of adaptation, two out of many strategies for coping with the contingencies of one's upbringing'.[64] Freud 'shows us how to see every human life as a poem', how to see sexual perversion, extreme cruelty or obsession 'as the private poem of the pervert, the sadist or the lunatic:

as richly-textured and "redolent of moral memories" as our own life'.[65]

A further advantage is that a culture dominated by individuals seeking self-enlargement would breed greater diversity. Such a culture would accept that 'something pointless or ridiculous or vile to society can become the crucial element in the individual's sense of who she is', and that no interpretation of the point of life is privileged over any other.[66] Finally, such a culture would free us from the oppressive teleology of the Western tradition by acknowledging that there are countless narrative strategies and genres for emplotting events in order to storyize one's life. Narratives of our life that enable us to see our own solitary existence as geared into a larger historical narrative are worth having because they impart 'a Romantic sense of grandeur to our existence', but there is no reason to believe in a meta-narrative underlying and directing the course of history. Generally, Rorty believes that a private morality dedicated to self-enlargement comports best with our liberal democratic ideals; that is, our commitment to an open society understood as an arena for expressing divergent views, trying out new ideas, and blending conflicting values. The pursuer of self-enlargement, who sees the 'strong poet' as the highest cultural hero, is 'the ideal citizen of such an ideal state'.[67]

Rorty feels he can take a fairly blasé attitude towards charges of 'decisionism' and moral relativism. Our 'allegiance to social institutions . . . [is] no more arbitrary than choices of friends or heroes.'[68] If we see ourselves as seamless webs of beliefs and desires, there is no place for 'decisionism' understood as gratuitous leaps of will, for 'there is no such thing as getting outside the web which constitutes oneself, looking down upon it, and deciding in favour of one portion of it rather than another'.[69] To think one can just choose a set of interpretations is to presuppose a distinction between a self which decides and a self which happens to have certain interpretations – an assumption ruled out by the holistic and minimalist picture of the self.

Charges of moral relativism and irrationalism can also be trivialized. If saying beliefs are 'relative' means that they can only be justified to people who hold certain other beliefs, then the term 'relativism' has 'no contrastive force'.[70] The distinction between 'rational conviction' and 'conviction brought about by (mere) causes rather than by reasons' makes sense only *within* particular vocabularies with their pregiven standards and criteria of rationality. When it comes to adopting different vocabularies of moral reflection, there are no neutral criteria to which we might appeal, and so the distinction between 'rational' and 'irrational' has no application. Because 'what counts as cruelty and injustice is a matter of the language that is spoken', to find that a practice is cruel is 'a matter of redescription rather than of discovery'.[71] When we Americans ask how our forebears could have condoned the cruelties of slavery, 'the right answer is that they

. . . were using a language which was built around this practice, a language different from the one in which we are now condemning it'.[72] And if our descendants come to accept fascism, then 'fascism will be the truth of man', and there will be no objective way to judge them wrong.[73] To grant the anti-foundationalist conclusion that there can be no such thing as grounding a language-as-a-whole except by reference to what comes 'to *seem* clearly better' at some future point in history is to see that the charge of relativism is senseless. As clear-headed ethnocentrists, we can – and, indeed, *must* – congratulate ourselves on our current moral practices and tell ourselves stories about how we are better people than the slave-owners of the past or the fascists of the future. But it would be self-deception to think we do so on the basis of access to truths about human dignity or the moral law that they lack.

The limits of pragmatism

Part of the appeal of Rorty's views on moral and social issues lies in his defence of 'standing unflinchingly' for our ideals without succumbing to the temptations of the transcendental pretence. He proposes a way of making sense of both our concern with personal fulfilment and our commitment to social justice by carefully distinguishing the private and public spheres of life. Our 'existentialist' concern for freedom, growth and creativity is backed up by the minimalist picture of the self as a space of self-elaboration which can freely generate new self-interpretations – and hence new ways of being human – by creating innovative forms of abnormal discourse. And our 'communitarian' sense of being 'one of us' – of identifying with a community and remaining loyal to its practices and goals – is backed up by the recognition that abnormal discourse is possible only against a background of normal discourse which defines our shared identity.

Yet, Rorty holds, neither the existentialist nor the communitarian strands depends on any philosophical theories or arguments in the traditional sense. His apologetics presents 'a circular justification of our practices' which 'makes one feature of our culture look good by citing still another'.[74] Although the minimalist, decentred picture of the self looks good together with certain liberal democratic ideals, Rorty is not claiming that this picture is the 'truth' about humans. For 'one is at liberty to rig up a model of the self to suit oneself',[75] and alternative models of the self can be evaluated only in terms of their pay-off for our culture. If we are to confront Rorty on his own pragmatist turf, then, we should begin by pressing the kinds of empirical and moral questions mentioned in the first section: is Rorty's aestheticized culture in fact 'a way of strengthening liberal institutions'? Does it offer a vision of a better, worthier form of life?

We might begin to reflect on the consequences of Rorty's pragmatism by unravelling some of the implications of the existentialist strand in his thought: the ideal of greater freedom through self-enlargement, or what he calls 'private narcissism'. One risk here is that such a life style might tend to aggravate certain underlying tensions and problems in our contemporary society. In recent years, psychotherapists have been reporting a decline in the classical neuroses which Freudian analysis was originally designed to treat, and an increase in 'disorders of the self' which are manifested in 'feelings of meaningless, feelings of emptiness, pervasive depression, lack of sustaining interests, goals, ideals and values, and feelings of unrelatedness'.[76] Today's therapists are sought out for help with 'empty lives lacking zest and joy and seeking escape through addiction to drugs or alcohol, to perversion or delinquency – and even to frenzied life styles, whether in business or the arts'.[77] The feeling is widespread that Freudian clinical techniques are of little use in treating problems of the self.[78] These disorders are rooted not in an overbearing cultural superego but in such social factors as 'the lack of stable ideologies and values ... or an atmosphere of disillusionment and cynicism in the surrounding society'.[79] And they are self-perpetuating in so far as parents who lack a coherent sense of self are unable to relate to their children as autonomous selves, with the result that these children grow up with the same disorders and pass them on to their children.[80] The upshot has been made familiar by Christopher Lasch: a 'culture of narcissism' tending towards social fragmentation, lack of sustaining commitment, cynicism, privatism and self-preoccupation.

Rorty might claim with some plausibility that these social ills arise from the sense of loss that accompanies the breakdown of older religious and Enlightenment ideals, and that a fully Nietzschean aestheticized culture will be freed from such feelings of loss. But it seems more likely that Rorty's vision of a culture devoted to a 'spirit of playfulness and irony' would exacerbate rather than resolve disorders of the self. To see why this is so, we might consider Nietzsche's own diagnosis of the detached attitude which follows from an over-developed historical consciousness. The 'modern man who continuously has the feast of a world exhibition prepared for him by his historical artists', Nietzsche suggests, 'has become a spectator merely enjoying himself'. Through this detached stance, 'an age acquires the dangerous disposition of irony with regard to itself, and from this the still more dangerous one of cynicism: in this, however, it ripens even more into clever egoistic practice through which the vital strength is paralyzed and finally destroyed'.[81] Nietzsche also describes the dangers inherent in 'the faith of the Americans today': 'The individual becomes convinced that he can do just about anything and *can manage almost any role*, and everybody experiments with himself, improvises, makes new experiments, enjoys his experiments; and all nature ceases and becomes art.' The outcome, according to Nietzsche, is that life comes to be seen as mere role-playing: 'whenever a human being begins to discover how he is playing a role and how he *can* be an actor, he *becomes* an actor', and consequently the 'strength to build becomes paralyzed; the courage to make plans that encompass the distant future is discouraged'.[82]

Nietzsche's worry is that treating all life-goals as optional roles or as transient historical impositions will undermine the ability to take social responsibilities and projects seriously, breeding cynicism, egoism and ultimately impotence. Seen in this light, there is no reason to believe that a culture in which the pursuit of individual freedom and the recognition of historical contingency became the norm would lead to greater civic responsibility, solidarity or social hope. Rorty's confidence that it would seems to depend on the assumption that people will naturally tend to produce good works if they are enlightened and given enough freedom. But this confidence is empirically suspect if the increase in a sense of the contingency of all beliefs and practices in fact leads to cynicism and detachment. And it relies on the very sort of assumption about human nature Rorty rejects.

At times, however, Rorty seems to be saying that aestheticized culture should be the ideal not of everyone, but only of poets and intellectuals. The highest good of such a culture, he suggests, is to protect the poets and fantasts – to 'safeguard the freedom of a leisured elite' – in the belief that fostering new forms of abnormal discourse 'is the only thing which our society can do to ensure that its language keeps changing'.[83] On this reading, however, Rorty's view is not only undemocratically elitist, it is naïve in its faith that poets and intellectuals will serve us well if they are given enough rope. Behind Rorty's thinking there appears to be some version of the rudimentary classical liberal belief that a society designed as a neutral matrix to promote freedom, where freedom is understood as negative liberty, will naturally lead to the public good. But this belief made sense only given a substantive view about human nature which seems untenable today.

Rorty's trust that his version of an aestheticized culture will at least pay its own way in terms of the types of moral individuals it produces also seems suspect. A great deal of the plausibility of Rorty's vision of the ideal state rests on the communitarian strand in his thought: the claim that there is a background of shared normal discourse, including the discourse of our public morality, which underwrites our ethnocentric respect for the goods embodied in our practices. Our current discourse provides us with what Rorty calls 'vocabularies of moral reflection' – vocabularies containing terms like 'magnanimous, a true Christian, decent, cowardly, God-

fearing', and so on – from which we draw our self-evaluations and our
ability to praise and criticize others.[84] This common language of aspiration
and assessment lets us identify with our group and exclude those whose
utterances are too abnormal.

What is questionable here, however, is whether precisely *this* sort of
normal moral discourse will survive and continue to exert a pull on us if we
evolve into a fully aestheticized culture. For it seems that Rorty's 'private
morality' is morality in name only. We saw that a full-blooded Nietzschean aestheticism, stripped of its ties to what Rorty regards as a
crypto-metaphysical notion of the will to power, holds that the only thing
needful is 'to "give style" to one's character', where it is irrelevant
whether the taste governing one's life is good or bad. There is no pre-given
moral map for assessing the outcome of experiments or for guiding one's
aesthetic tastes. As Nehamas points out, however, 'The fully integrated
person [Nietzsche] so admires may well be morally repulsive.'[85] In fact,
the Nietzschean character-ideal has no necessary connection to morality
whatsoever. Rorty's own praise for 'the private poem of the pervert, the
sadist or the lunatic', and his disparaging picture of 'the unselfish,
unselfconscious, unimaginative, decent, honest, dutiful person' who is
'notoriously dull',[86] suggest not so much a new way of looking at morality
as a way of dissolving it. A culture dedicated to aestheticist self-
enlargement may well come to drop the concerns of morality altogether.
Our current vocabularies of moral reflection give us meaningful tools for
moral assessment only because terms like 'magnanimous' and 'a true
Christian' come to us already tagged with their normal moral import. But
it is not clear why they should continue to have this import, or why the
'moral/immoral' distinction should continue to have any special significance for us, in a fully aestheticized culture.

It seems, then, that the existentialist strand in Rorty's thought subverts
the communitarian concerns that underlie it. People generally 'stand
unflinchingly' for their convictions because they see those convictions as
pointing to a good life. If they were to adopt an internalist view of goods,
seeing them merely as the ends of a group's current practices, and if they
saw these practices as contingent and temporary, it is not obvious that they
would continue to stand unflinchingly for their convictions. To do so
would require a kind of Sartrean decisionistic 'leap of the absurd' which
could go in any direction. If, alternatively, Rorty is addressing his
recommendations solely to poets and intellectuals, then his notion of an
ideal culture seems to point the way to a cultural elite – a band of
free-floating intellectuals and kibitzing dilettantes, bound together by
clever conversation over brandies and cigars after dinner, with nothing at
stake other than keeping the conversation going and protecting the leisure

of the theory class. On either alternative, the strong sense of community Rorty hopes for is not likely to follow.

At the same time, however, the communitarian strand in Rorty's thought tends to undermine the existentialist ideal of unhampered self-creativity. For if 'language speaks us' in such a way that dense and opaque linguistic codes are constantly operating behind our backs, then the whole notion of greater freedom through more talk looks suspect. We then seem to be confronted with an unattractive choice: either we uncritically accept the status quo, or we engage in the kind of Foucauldian directionless 'permanent critique of the present' which Rorty criticizes as a product of *ressentiment*. Rorty hopes to protect both our individualistic commitment to personal freedom and our communal concern for solidarity by making a sharp distinction between private and public life. But it is not clear such a distinction is consistent with the goals of a liberal democracy, or that it even makes sense. An individual's self-descriptions are realized in his or her agency in the public world, and public practices and institutions impact on the individual's capacities for self-fulfilment. It is the task of moral and social philosophy to clarify these bonds between civic responsibility and meaningful freedom.

The split between the existentialist and communitarian strands in Rorty's thought reflects a deeper tension in his picture of our human situation. On the one hand, his Hegelian historicism tells us that we are always caught up within a normalized culture and historical context which pre-shapes our outlook and values. Since there is no exit from our embeddedness in a concrete context, we must operate within what might be called an 'insider's perspective' on ourselves and our community. On the other hand, the notion of the ubiquity of language encourages us to adopt an 'outsider's perspective' with respect to ourselves and our historical culture. When we realize that existing vocabularies and goods are contingent by-products of our current practices, the door is opened to shopping around for new goods and to cooking up new vocabularies 'to help us get what we want.'

Now this bifocal vision on our situation seems to produce a type of 'ego-splitting': the self regarded as an 'empirio-transcendental doublet'. We are holistic webs of beliefs and desires engaged in an interminable process of reweaving, yet it is also up to us 'to invent a use for ourselves', to undertake the task of 'what Bloom calls "giving birth to oneself"'[87] by inventing new metaphors and self-descriptions. This implies a distinction between an 'I' who is the web and an 'I' who reweaves and recreates the web. Similarly, we are social selves who cannot help but feel loyal to our group, yet we always have the ability to step back and decide what that social identity means to us. At one moment we are swept away by faith in our capacity for 'moral and intellectual progress' through imaginative redescriptions of the plight of the oppressed; at the next we see all discourse as directionless literary 'play'. Rorty's ideal of self-enlargement actually seems to advocate an outsider's perspective on ourselves, encouraging us to speak a new vocabulary in which, instead of saying 'Manipulating others is wrong' or 'Slavery is bad', we will be able to say, 'My superego is telling a story according to which manipulating others is wrong' or 'Our group currently holds the view that slavery is bad.' Yet somehow we are simultaneously supposed to keep believing that these things really *are* wrong.

The split perspective also gives Rorty a suspicious facility in evading objections. In response to Sandel's charge that liberalism is self-defeating because it cannot account for its own dedication to freedom, Rorty adopts an insider's perspective and says that Sandel's mistake is to assume 'that we liberals ought to be able to rise above the contingencies of history and see the kind of individual freedom which the modern liberal state offers its citizens as just one more value'. But there can be no 'higher standpoint from which we can scrutinize competing values to see which are morally privileged'.[88] As insiders in a liberal democracy, we just *must* accept freedom as one of our highest values. Similarly, Rorty can reply to charges that we are breeding morally reprehensible moral types by suggesting that, as the rich aesthetes, managers and therapists we are, it is hard to see these types as all that bad.

Yet he replies to other objections by shifting ground to an outsider's perspective. In response to realists who hold that we have access to an insight into what we are as agents, Rorty recommends '"stepping back" in the historicist manner of Heidegger and Dewey, or the quasi-anthropological manner of Foucault', instead of trying to safeguard the tradition or make ourselves 'even more deeply Western'.[89] To those who feel that intellectual history fails to capture philosophy's concern with achieving knowledge, Rorty recommends 'adopting a sociological view of the distinction between knowledge and opinion', treating it as a matter of how much deviance a group allows with respect to holding views.[90] Generally, the rule seems to be that we must be insiders when it comes to thinking about our public practices and outsiders when it comes to looking at philosophy. If it turns out, however, that our public practices embody quasi-philosophical beliefs – if, for instance, the man on the street believes that our love of freedom is justified or that there are things we can know – then Rorty's detached outsider's irony will bleed into and transform our practices.

We might also take a closer look at where Rorty himself stands when he articulates his position. So long as he was merely criticizing traditional foundationalist philosophy, he could be 'content to have *no* answer to the question "Where do you stand when you say all these terrible things about other people?" [91] But when he is presenting his own views, he must take responsibility for where he stands. It seems that his cool observations on the inevitable outcome of anti-foundationalism and his recommendations for re-engineering our culture to promote a more light-minded, insouciant, ironic attitude presuppose a quasi-sociological outsider's stance towards our cultural life. From this stance of bemused detachment, it is possible to see our current cultural commitments as optional and dispensable, and to imagine a form of life in which moral reflection is a matter of playing with contingent vocabularies. But it becomes difficult to make sense of why we have the commitments we have or why we should take one path into the future rather than another. The detached standpoint, itself a product of modern science and the Enlightenment, encourages us to think of freedom from constraint and mutual accommodation as the highest possible goods by concealing or trivializing other goods of our community such as civic responsibility, sacrifice, integrity, social service, moderation, self-discipline, civility and brotherly love.

These limitations of Rorty's pragmatism suggests to us that the hermeneutic strategy deserves reconsideration. Hermeneutic thinkers generally insist on holding firmly to the insider's perspective. Recognizing our 'situated freedom' and our historicity, our task is seen as critically evaluating our current commitments in the light of the possibilities laid out by the past in order to articulate meaningful goals for the future. And this task, it could be argued, is better undertaken by individuals who take self-focusing rather than self-enlargement as their character-ideal.

NOTES

1   Especially Richard Rorty, 'The Contingency of Selfhood', *London Review of Books*, 8 May 1986; 'The Contingency of Community', *London Review of Books*, 24 July 1986; and 'Freud and Moral Reflection', in *Pragmatism's Freud: The Moral Disposition of Psychoanalysis*, eds Joseph H. Smith and William Kerrigan (The Johns Hopkins Press, Baltimore, 1986).

2   Richard Rorty, *Philosophy and the Mirror of Nature* (Princeton University Press, Princeton, 1979), p. 377.

3   Richard Rorty, *Consequences of Pragmatism* (University of Minnesota Press, Minneapolis, 1982), p. 166.

4   Rorty, 'Contingency of Community', p. 13.

5   Ibid., pp. 10–11.

6   Ibid., p. 13.

7   Ibid., p. 11.

8   Richard Rorty, 'The Contingency of Language', *London Review of Books*, 17 April 1986, p. 6.

9   Rorty, *Mirror of Nature*, p. 320.

10 Richard Rorty, 'A Reply to Six Critics', *Analyse & Kritik*, 6 (1984), p. 86.

11 Richard Rorty, 'Solidarity or Objectivity?' in *Post-Analytic Philosophy*, eds John Rajchman and Cornel West (Columbia University Press, New York, 1985), p. 12.

12 Richard Rorty, 'Le Cosmpolitisme sans Emancipation: en Réponse à Jean-François Lyotard', *Critique* (1985), p. 570.

13 Richard Rorty, 'Postmodernist Bourgeois Liberalism', in *Hermeneutics and Praxis*, ed. Robert Hollinger (Notre Dame University Press, Notre Dame, 1985), p. 220.

14 Christopher Lasch, *The Culture of Narcissism* (W. W. Norton, New York, 1979); and *The Minimal Self: Psychic Survival in Troubled Times* (W. W. Norton, New York, 1984); Daniel Yankelovich, *New Rules: Searching for Self-Fulfilment in a World Turned Upside Down* (Random House, New York, 1981); Robert Bellah, Richard Madsen, William Sullivan, Ann Swidler and Stephen Tipton, *Habits of the Heart: Individualism and Commitment in American Life* (University of California Press, Berkeley, 1985).

15 Alasdair MacIntyre, *After Virtue* (Notre Dame University Press, Notre Dame, 1981); Charles Taylor, *Philosophical Papers*, 2 vols (Cambridge University Press, Cambridge, 1985).

16 Michael Sandel, *Liberalism and the Limits of Justice* (Cambridge University Press, Cambridge, 1982).

17 Richard Rorty 'The Priority of Democracy to Philosophy', ch. 17 of the present volume.

18 'The Contingency of Community', p. 10.

19 *Consequences of Pragmatism*, p. 140.

20 Ibid., p. 142.

21 'The Contingency of Community', p. 10.

22 Ibid., p. 14.

23 Ibid., p. 10.

24 Ibid.

25 *Consequences of Pragmatism*, p. 158.

26 'The Contingency of Selfhood', p. 12.

27 'The Contingency of Community', p. 13.

28 Richard Rorty, 'On Ethnocentrism: A Reply to Clifford Geertz', *Michigan Quarterly Review*, 25 (1986), pp. 533–4.

29 *Consequences of Pragmatism*, p. 150.

30 Jonathan Culler, *Ferdinand de Saussure* (Penguin, New York, 1976), p. 82.

31 *Consequences of Pragmatism*, p. xxxvii.

32 'The Contingency of Selfhood', p. 14.

33 Friedrich Nietzsche, *The Gay Science*, tr. Walter Kaufmann (Vintage Books, New York, 1974), s. 382.

34 Friedrich Nietzsche, *The Will to Power*, tr. Walter Kaufmann and R. J. Hollingdale (Vintage Books, New York, 1968), s. 616.

35 Nietzsche, *The Gay Science*, ss 335, 58.

36 Ibid., s. 290.

37 'Postmodernist Bourgeois Liberalism', p. 217.

38 Jane-Paul Sartre, *Essays in Existentialism*, ed. Wade Baskin (The Citadel Press, Secaucus, 1974), pp. 67–8.

39 'The Contingency of Selfhood', p. 14.

40 *Consequences of Pragmatism*, p. 210n.

41 Under this label we would include such self-styled hermeneutic thinkers as Dilthey, Heidegger, Gadamer, H. L. Dreyfus and Charles Taylor, as well as such like-minded thinkers as Habermas, MacIntyre and Robert Bellah. As will become evident, Rorty's description of his own position as 'hermeneutic' in *Philosophy and the Mirror of Nature* is, from our standpoint, a misnomer.

42 Martin Heidegger, *Being and Time*, tr. John Macquarrie and Edward Robison (Harper

& Row, New York, 1962), s. 6; see also Charles Guignon, *Heidegger and the Problem of Knowledge* (Hackett, Indianapolis, 1983), ss 6 and 16.

43 Heidegger, *Being and Time*, p. 449.
44 Taylor, *Philosophical Papers*, vol. I, especially chs 1 and 4.
45 MacIntyre, *After Virtue*, pp. 203, 207.
46 'The Contingency of Selfhood', pp. 14–15.
47 Ibid., p. 11.
48 'The Contingency of Community', p. 11.
49 Ibid., p. 11.
50 *Consequences of Pragmatism*, p. 87.
51 'The Priority of Democracy to Philosophy', p. 39.
52 'The Contingency of Community', p. 13.
53 'Freud and Moral Reflection', p. 10.
54 Freud, *The Ego and the Id*, tr. Joan Riviere (W. W. Norton, New York, 1962), p. 13.
55 'Freud and Moral Reflection', pp. 4–5.
56 Nietzsche, *Human All-too-human*, tr. R. J. Hollingdale (Cambridge University Press, Cambridge, 1986), II, 17.
57 'Freud and Moral Reflection', p. 11.
58 Northrop Frye, *Anatomy of Criticism* (Princeton University Press, Princeton, 1957), First Essay.
59 'Freud and Moral Reflection', p. 12.
60 Ibid., p. 12.
61 Ibid., p. 15.
62 Ibid., p. 9.
63 'The Contingency of Selfhood', p. 12.
64 Ibid.
65 Ibid., p. 14.
66 Ibid.
67 'The Contingency of Community', p. 11.
68 Ibid., p. 11.
69 'A Reply to Six Critics', p. 95.
70 'The Contingency of Community', p. 10.
71 Ibid., p. 14.
72 Ibid.
73 *Consequences of Pragmatism*, p. xlii.
74 'The Contingency of Community', p. 13.
75 'The Priority of Democracy to Philosophy', p. 278 above.
76 Morris N. Eagle, *Recent Developments in Psychoanalysis: A Critical Evaluation* (McGraw-Hill, New York, 1984), p. 73.
77 Ernest S. Wolf, '"Irrationality" in a Psychoanalytic Psychology of the Self', in *The Self: Psychological and Philosophical Issues*, ed. Theodore Mischel (Basil Blackwell, Oxford, 1977), pp. 203–4.
78 See Heinz Kohut, *The Restoration of the Self* (International Universities Press, New York, 1977), ch. 1.
79 Eagle, *Recent Developments in Psychoanalysis*, p. 73.
80 See Alice Miller, *The Drama of the Gifted Child: The Search for the True Self* (Basic Books, New York, 1981).
81 Friedrich Nietzsche, *On the Advantage and Disadvantage of History for Life*, tr. Peter Preuss (Hackett, Indianapolis, 1980), p. 28.
82 Nietzsche, *The Gay Science*, s. 356.
83 'The Contingency of Community', p. 14.

84   'Freud and Moral Reflection', pp. 11–12.
85   Alexander Nehamas, *Nietzsche: Life as Literature* (Harvard University Press, Cambridge, Mass., 1985), p. 167.
86   'The Contingency of Community', pp. 14, 13.
87   'The Contingency of Selfhood', p. 12.
88   'The Contingency of Community', p. 11.
89   *Consequences of Pragmatism*, p. xxxi.
90   Richard Rorty, 'The Historiography of Philosophy: Four Genres', in *Philosophy in History*, eds Richard Rorty, J. B. Schneewind and Quentin Skinner (Cambridge University Press, Cambridge, 1984), p. 66.
91   *Consequences of Pragmatism*, p. 150.

On Teaching Rorty

Philosophy and the Mirror of Nature is an engaging, provocative and, in various ways, difficult work. As such it clearly merits a course of academic study in its own right. This appendix is intended to stimulate ideas as to how such a course might be profitably taught, and to highlight some of the unique problems *PMN* poses for teachers. However, the suggestions made here are no more than tentative. They await modification or improvement by teachers, students and general readers alike. Needless to say, the editor welcomes further advice on this matter.

General comment: narrative

PMN presents an astute narrative assessment of a long and complex tradition in philosophical thought. Thus perhaps one of the biggest initial problems it raises for those who want to render it digestible for academic study is the problem of getting a 'narrative fix' on its own contents. The pitfalls are obvious: any 'summary' is likely to overlook vital twists in the plot, whereas any 'in depth' commentary is simply going to turn out too unwieldy. The best 'compromise' is probably to try to convey a picture of the overall aims of *PMN*, and then to consider specific themes in detailed case studies which focus on the issue of whether those aims have been achieved.

Preparing students

In his discussion of Rorty's 'refurbishment of pragmatism',[1] C. G. Prado points out: 'Teaching Rorty is difficult. Students respond favourably, but superficially, to his critique. They consider it iconoclastic and exciting, but few of them have had the time to feel the grip of what he rejects. They may appreciate in an abstract way that it is unproductive to do epistemology but few can feel *liberated* by Rorty's critique because they have not been captives of Bernstein's "Cartesian Anxiety"'.[2] Similarly, in an informal report to the editor of his own experience of teaching *PMN* to undergraduates at the University of East Anglia, Alan Hobbs writes, '*The Mirror of Nature* is designed as an exorcism of ghosts. For students to profit from the book, their minds must therefore first be haunted. Without suitably muscled ghosts with which to do battle, the excitement of the exorcism is missing'.[3] Prado and Hobbs signal an important moral for teaching strategy: since in philosophy a 'walkover' is rarely a good result, teachers need to ensure that students at least recognize the strengths and virtues of the ideas Rorty is trying to undermine.

If prospective students have had little exposure to the positive side of the kind of 'traditional philosophy' Rorty is criticizing, then sections of *Reading Rorty* (*RR*) can be appropriated for the purpose of building up the muscles of their ghosts. Here are some examples of how thematic case studies might be matched up with 'responses' from *RR*:

Philosophy of Mind:	*PMN*, chs 1 and 2; *RR*, Hornsby, Hollis.
Epistemology:	*PMN*, ch. 3; *RR*, Yolton, Vision, Davidson, Malachowski, Taylor.
Philosophy of Language:	*PMN*, ch. 6; *RR*, Houghton, Clark.
Truth:	*PMN*, *passim*; CC, Introduction; *RR*, Vision, Heal, Davidson.
Pragmatism:	*PMN*, *passim*; CC, Introduction; *RR*, Williams, Vision, Heal.
Post-philosophical Culture:	*PMN*, chs 7 and 8; *RR*, Sorell, Fischer, Fraser, Burrows, Guignon and Hiley.

The References, Bibliography and Index of *RR* will facilitate finer-grained matchings of this kind up to graduate level where the reading load can obviously be increased considerably.

Widening horizons

To make the most of *PMN*, students not only need to appreciate the nature of the tradition it opposes, but they should have some 'feel' for the 'extra-traditional' approaches it alludes to. The problem here, of course, is to determine just how much time to devote to 'extra-traditional' considerations (and, indeed, how to divide up the time so devoted). Though 'solutions' will have to depend on the inclinations and areas of competence of individual teachers, the following bibliographical suggestions can be made with *PMN* in mind.

Central figures

Descartes, Locke, Hume and Kant are key thinkers in the 'epistemology-centred' tradition Rorty opposes. The literature on each of these philosophers is vast, but these works are particularly suitable for study in partnership with *PMN*:

Descartes: *Descartes' Meditations on First Philosophy with Selections from Objections and Replies*, tr. J. Cottingham (Cambridge University Press, Cambridge, 1986).

B. Williams, *Descartes* (Pelican, London, 1978).

Locke: J. W. Yolton (ed.), *The Locke Reader* (Cambridge University Press, Cambridge, 1977).

J. W. Yolton, *Locke: An Introduction* (Basil Blackwell, Oxford, 1985).
R. S. Woolhouse, *Locke's Philosophy of Science and Knowledge* (Basil Blackwell, Oxford, 1971).

Hume: B. Stroud, *Hume* (Routledge & Kegan Paul, London, 1977).

Kant: N. Rescher, *Kant's Theory of Knowledge and Reality* (University Press of America, Washington D.C., 1983).

Quine, Davidson and Sellars are also central to *PMN*, and useful work on their philosophy can be found in:

Quine: R. F. Gibson, *The Philosophy of W. V. Quine: An Expository Essay* (University of South Florida Press, 1988).

Davidson: E. LePore (ed.), *Truth And Interpretation: Perspectives On The Philosophy Of Donald Davidson* (Basil Blackwell, 1986); see esp. Rorty's contribution.

Sellars: H. Castañeda (ed.), *Action, Knowledge And Reality: Studies in Honour of Wilfred Sellars* (Boss-Merril, New York, 1975).

Peripheral Thinkers

Rorty cites three key figures in this connection: Dewey, Heidegger and Wittgenstein. However, Hegel and Nietzsche are equally important for an understanding of Rorty's stance. Introductory material on all five thinkers is now available in abundance, but these works are particularly suited for reading in conjunction with *PMN*:

Hegel:	C. Taylor, *Hegel And Modern Society* (Cambridge University Press, Cambridge, 1979).
	R. C. Solomon, *In the Spirit of Hegel* (Oxford University Press, Oxford, 1983), ch. 6.
Nietzsche:	R. Schacht, *Nietzsche* (Routledge & Kegan Paul, London, 1983).
Dewey:	J. Tiles, *Dewey* (Routledge & Kegan Paul, London, 1988).
Heidegger:	C. Guignon, *Heidegger and the Problem of Knowledge* (Hackett, Indianapolis, 1983).
Wittgenstein:	A. C. Grayling, *Wittgenstein* (Oxford University Press, Oxford, 1988).
	Richard Rorty, 'Keeping Philosophy Pure', in *CC*.

Pragmatism

This subject is well served by the volume on Dewey mentioned above (see Tiles's remarks on Rorty), and by further volumes in the same series on James (G. Bird) and Peirce (C. Hookway) respectively. Students can also be referred to: I. Scheffler, *Four Pragmatists* (Routledge & Kegan Paul, London, 1974); M. K. Moritz, *Contemporary Analytic Philosophy* (Macmillan, London, 1981), ch. 2; and Rorty's 'Comments On Sleeper and Edel', *Transactions of the Charles S. Peirce Society*, 21 (1985), pp. 40–8 (see also the papers by Sleeper and by Edel in this same issue). The work of Quine and Davidson is also relevant in this connection.

Hermeneutics

K. Mueller-Vollmer (ed.), *The Hermeneutics Reader* (Basil Blackwell, Oxford, 1986); R. Hollinger (ed.), *Hermeneutics and Praxis* (University of Notre Dame Press, Notre Dame, 1985); Hans-Georg Gadamer, *Philosophical Hermeneutics* (University of California Press, Berkeley, 1977) (students may find the Editor's Introduction particularly useful in this case); and B. R. Wachterhouser (ed.), *Hermeneutics and Modern Philosophy* (State University of New York Press, 1986).

Continental Philosophy

C. Norris, *The Deconstructive Turn* (Methuen, London, 1983); P. Dews, *Logics of Disintegration* (Verso, London, 1981); H. J. Silverman (ed.), *Philosophy and Non-Philosophy Since Merleau-Ponty* (Routledge, Chapman and Hall, 1988); J. Habermas, *The Philosophical Discourse of Modernity* (MIT Press, Cambridge, Mass., 1987); D. C. Hoy (ed.), *Foucault: A Critical Reader* (Basil Blackwell, Oxford, 1986); C. Norris, *Derrida* (Fontana, London, 1987); and R. C. Solomon, *Continental Philosophy Since 1750* (Oxford University Press, Oxford, 1988).

Meeting Rorty's challenge

Our suggestions as to how Rorty might be taught have been, in a sense, rather conservative. On the one hand, there is a story about minds, truth, knowledge, language and the like, as told within a certain tradition in philosophy; on the other hand, there is a 'counter-story' as told by Rorty – and then, squarely in the middle, playing the role of adjudicator or would-be neutral commentator, is the philosophy teacher. This tactic of standing back and playing a tradition and Rorty off against one another can be productive, especially if classic texts such as those of Descartes, Locke, Kant and Hume are dipped into for comparison with Rorty's interpretation of them, and if the 'horizon' is also widened to include 'extra-traditional' material. But, it is liable to gloss over the *radical* nature of *PMN* which makes the book a challenge to the very ideas of philosophical adjudication or conceptual neutrality. Thus, even if a conservative approach is preferred, the teacher should at least address the issue of whether *PMN* requires *special* treatment on account of its radical content. Can its rhetorical qualities, its reassessment of the order of importance of philosophical figures, its political implications, its historical dimension and its denial of the existence of 'perennial problems' be catered for by orthodox approaches?

Interesting material which may help with the latter question can be found in: R. J. Bernstein, *Philosophical Profiles* (Polity Press, Cambridge, 1986); R. J. Bernstein, *Beyond Objectivism and Relativism* (University of Pennsylvania Press, Philadelphia, 1983); J. Rajchman and C. West (eds), *Post-Analytic Philosophy* (Columbia University Press, New York, 1985); C. Norris, *Contest of Faculties* (Methuen, London, 1985); and C. G. Prado, *The Limits of Pragmatism* (Humanities Press, New York, 1987).

Stimulating views on *historical* approaches to philosophy are voiced by a number of thinkers in R. Rorty, J. B. Scheewind and Q. Skinner (eds), *Philosophy in History* (Cambridge University Press, Cambridge, 1984).[4] And, for thought-provoking views on, as Alan Hobbs puts it, 'the dangers and excitements of philosophical life without philosophical tools', see Rorty's own post-*PMN* work, especially *Contingency, Irony and Solidarity* (Cambridge University Press, Cambridge, 1988).

Some teachers may find that rather than failing to meet with Rorty's challenge, their views on philosophy actually seem to outstrip that challenge, making *PMN* seem *insufficiently* radical. The responses of Fraser and Burrows in *Reading Rorty* tackle alleged *political* shortcomings in Rorty's outlook. Other critics have noted that *PMN* lacks a *feminist* perspective. Rorty appears to have sympathy with this complaint, but apart from making fun of what he takes to be the 'macho self-image' of analytic philosophy, he has not tried to answer it in detail. Useful ideas on how feminist thought might be brought to bear on the main concerns of *PMN* can be derived from: S. Benhabib and D. Cornell (eds), *Feminism As Critique* (Polity Press, Cambridge, 1987); M. Griffiths and M. Whitford, *Feminist Perspectives in Philosophy* (Macmillan, London, 1988); and S. Harding, *Discovering Reality: Feminist Perspectives On Epistemology, Metaphysics, Methodology and Philosophy* (Reidel, Dordrecht, 1983).

Finally, graduates may benefit from comparisons between *PMN* and other reactions to the 'Analytic Tradition', as found in L. J. Cohen's, *The Dialogue of Reason* (Clarendon Press, Oxford, 1986); H. Wang, *Beyond Analytic Philosophy* (MIT Press, Cambridge, Mass., 1986); A. MacIntyre, *After Virtue*, 2nd edn (Duckworth, London, 1985); and S. Rosen, *The Limits of Analysis* (Basic Books, New York, 1980).

NOTES

1 C. G. Prado, *The Limits of Pragmatism* (Humanities Press, New York, 1987).

2 See R. J. Bernstein, *Beyond Objectivism and Relativism* (Basil Blackwell, Oxford, 1983), esp. pp. 16–20.

3 I am grateful to Hobbs for showing me some of his lecture notes; he is not responsible for the use I have made of them in this appendix.

4 See also 'An Historicist View of Teaching Philosophy', *Teaching Philosophy*, 7 (1984), pp. 313–23.

Bibliography of the Works of Richard Rorty

Books

(ed.): *The Linguistic Turn*. Chicago: University of Chicago Press, 1967.

(co-ed.): *Exegesis and Argument: Essays in Greek Philosophy presented to Gregory Vlastos*. Amsterdam: Van Gorcum, 1973.

Philosophy and the Mirror of Nature. Princeton: Princeton University Press, 1979 (trans. Chinese, French, German, Italian, Spanish, Portuguese).

Consequences of Pragmatism. Minneapolis: University of Minnesota Press, 1982 (trans. French, Italian, Japanese).

(co-ed): *Philosophy in History*. Cambridge: Cambridge University Press, 1985.

Solidarität und Objectivität (in German translation). Ditzingen: Reclam Verlag, 1988 (contains: (1) Solidarity or Objectivity? (2) The Priority of Democracy to Philosophy; (3) Freud and Moral Reflection).

Philosophy: Its End and its New Hope (in Japanese translation). Tokyo: Iwanami Shoten, 1988 (contains: (1) Science as Solidarity; (2) Texts and Lumps; (3) Pragmatism without Method; (4) The Historiography of Philosophy: Four Genres; (5) The Priority of Democracy to Philosophy; (6) Pragmatism, Davidson, and Truth).

Contingency, Irony, and Solidarity. Cambridge: Cambridge University Press, 1988 (trans. forthcoming in 1989: German, Italian).

Objectivity, Relativism and Truth: Philosophical Papers I. Cambridge: Cambridge University Press, forthcoming.

Essays on Heidegger and Others: Philosophical Papers II. Cambridge: Cambridge University Press, forthcoming.

Articles and reviews

1959

Review of *Experience and the Analytic: A Reconsideration of Empiricism*, by Alan Pasch. *International Journal of Ethics (Ethics)*, 70 (Oct. 1959): 75–7.

1960

Review of *John Dewey: His Thought and Influence*, ed. John Blewett. *Teacher's College Record*, 62 (Oct. 1960): 88–9.

Review of *Modern Science and Human Freedom*, by David L. Miller. *International Journal of Ethics (Ethics)*, 70 (Apr. 1960): 248–9.

1961

Pragmatism, Categories and Language. *Philosophical Review*, 70 (Apr. 1961): 197–223.

Recent Metaphilosophy. *Review of Metaphysics*, 15 (Dec. 1961): 299–318.

The Limits of Reductionism. In *Experience, Existence and the Good*, ed. I. C. Lieb. Carbondale: Southern Illinois University Press, 1961.

Review of *Introduction to the Philosophy of History*, by Raymond Aron. *The New Leader*, 25 Dec. 1961: 18–19.

1962

Review of *American Pragmatism: Peirce, James and Dewey*, by Edward C. Moore. *International Journal of Ethics (Ethics)*, 72 (Jan. 1962): 146–7.

Review of *The Value Judgement*, by W. D. Lamont. *Journal For the Scientific Study of Religion*, 2 (Fall 1962): 139–40.

Realism, Categories, and the 'Linguistic Turn'. *International Philosophical Quarterly*, 2 (May 1962): 307–22.

1963

Review of *Utopian Essays and Practical Proposals*, by Paul Goodman. *Teacher's College Record*, 64 (May 1963): 743–4.

The Subjectivist Principle and the Linguistic Turn. In *Alfred North Whitehead: Essays on His Philosophy*, ed. George L. Kline. Englewood Cliffs, NJ: Prentice-Hall, 1963.

Matter and Event. In *The Concept of Matter*, ed. Ernan McMullin. (Notre Dame: Notre Dame University Press, 1963): 497–524. A revised version appears in *Explorations in Whitehead's Philosophy*, ed. L. Ford and G. Kline.

Empiricism, Extensionalism and Reductionism. *Mind*, 72 (Apr. 1963): 176–86.

Review of *Understanding Whitehead*, by Victor Lowe. *Journal Of Philosophy*, 60 (25 Apr. 1963): 246–51.

Review of *Reason and Analysis*, by Brand Blanshard. *Journal Of Philosophy*, 60 (12 Sept. 1963): 551–7.

Comments on Prof. Hartshorne's Paper. *Journal Of Philosophy*, 60 (10 Oct. 1963): 606–8.

1964

Review of *Chauncy Wright and the Foundations of Pragmatism*, by Edward H. Madden. *PHilosophical Review*, 73 (Apr. 1964): 287–9.

Untitled in *Philosophical Interrogations*, ed. Beatrice and Sidney Rome. Eastbourne: Holt, Rinehart & Winston, 1964).

Review of *Clarity is not enough: Essays in Criticism of Linguistic Philosophy*, by H. D. Lewis. *International Philosophical Quarterly*, 4 (1964): 623–4.

1965

Mind–Body Identity, Privacy, and Categories. *Review of Metaphysics*, 19 (Sept. 1965): 24–54. Also in *Philosophy of Mind*, ed. S. Hampshire (???); and in *Materialism and the Mind–Body Problem*, ed. David M. Rosenthal, Englewood Cliffs, NJ: Prentice-Hall,

Bibliography 373

1971); and in *Modern Materialism: Readings on Mind–Body Identity*, ed. John O'Connor, New York: Harcourt, Brace & World, 1969.

1966

Aristotle. *The American Peoples' Encyclopedia*, ed. Walter D. Scott. Spencer, 1966.
Review of *Charles Peirce and Scholastic Realism: A Study of Peirce's Relation to John Duns Scotus*, by John F. Boler. *Philosophical Review*, 75 (Jan. 1966): 116–19.

1967

Introduction. In *The Linguistic Turn*, ed. Richard Rorty. Chicago: University of Chicago Press, 1967.
Intuition. In *The Encyclopedia of Philosophy*, ed. Paul Edwards. New York: Macmillan and Free Press, 1967, vol. 4: 204–12.
Relations, Internal and External. In *The Encyclopedia of Philosophy*, ed. Paul Edwards. New York: Macmillan and Free Press, 1967, vol. 7: 125–33.
Review of *Metaphysics, Reference and Language*, by James W. Cornman. *Journal of Philosophy*, 64 (23 Nov. 1967): 770–4.
Do Analysts and Metaphysicians Disagree? *Proceedings of The Catholic Philosophical Association*, 41 (1967): 39–53.

1970

Review of *Science and Metaphysics: Variations on Kantian Themes*, by Wilfrid Sellars. *Philosophy*, 45 (Mar. 1970): 66–70.
In Defence of Eliminative Materialism. *Review of Metaphysics*, 24 (Sept. 1970): 112–21. Also in *Materialism and the Mind–Body Problem*, ed. David M. Rosenthal. Englewood Cliffs, NJ: Prentice-Hall, 1971
Strawson's Objectivity Argument. *Review of Metaphysics*, 24 (Dec. 1970): 207–44.
Cartesian Epistemology and Changes in Ontology. In *Contemporary American Philosophy*, ed. John E. Smith, New York: Humanities Press, 1970.
Incorrigibility as the Mark of the Mental. *Journal of Philosophy*, 67 (25 June 1970): 399–429.
Wittgenstein, Privileged Access, and Incommunicability. *American Philosophical Quarterly*, 7 (July 1970): 192–205.

1971

Verificationism and Transcendental Arguments. *Nous*, 5 (Fall 1971): 3–14.
Review of *The Origins of Pragmatism: Studies in the Philosophy of Charles Sanders Peirce and William James*, by A. J. Ayer. *Philosophical Review*, 80 (Jan, 1971): 96–100.

1972

Functionalism, Machines and Incorribibility. *Journal Of Philosophy*, 69 (20 Apr. 1972): 203–20.
Dennett on Awareness. *Philosophical Studies*, 23 (Apr. 1972): 153–62.
The World Well Lost. *Journal of Philosophy*, 69 (26 Oct. 1972): 649–65. (*Consequences of Pragmatism*, ch. 1).
Review of *Nihilism*, by Stanley Rosen. *The Philosophy Forum*, 11 (1972): 102–8.
Indeterminacy of Translation and of Truth. *Synthese*, 23 (Mar. 1972): 443–62.

1973

Criteria and Necessity. *Nous*, 7 (Nov. 1973): 313–29.
Genus as Matter: A Reading of Metaphysics Z-H. In *Exegenesis and Argument: Essays in Greek Philosophy Presented to Gregory Vlastos*, eds R. Rorty, E. N. Lee, A. P. O. Mourelatos. Assen: Van Gorcum, 1973.

1974

More on Incorrigibility. *Canadian Journal of Philosophy*, 4 (Sept. 1974): 195–7.
Matter as Goo: Comments on Grene's Paper. *Synthese*, 25 (Sept. 1974): 71–7.

1976

Keeping Philosophy Pure. *The Yale Review*, 65 (Spring 1976): 336–56. (*Consequences of Pragmatism*, ch. 2).
Realism and Reference. *The Monist*, 59 (July, 1976): 321–40.
Realism and Necessity: Milton Fisk's *Nature and Necessity*. *Nous* 10 (1976): 345–54.
Overcoming the Tradition: Heidegger and Dewey. *Review of Metaphysics*, 30 (Dec. 1976): 280–305. (*Consequences of Pragmatism*, ch. 3).
Professionalized Philosophy and Transcendendalist Culture. *The Georgia Review*, 30 (1976): 757–69. (*Consequences of Pragmatism*, ch. 4).
Review of *On Human Conduct*, by Michael Oakeshott, and *Knowledge and Politics*, by Roberto Mangabiera Unger. *Social Theory and Practice*, 4 (Fall 1976): 107–15.

1977

Wittgensteinian Philosophy and Empirical Psychology. *Philosophical Studies*, 31 (Mar. 1977): 151–72.
Dewey's Metaphysics. In *New Studies In The Philosophy of John Dewey*, ed. Steven Cahn. Hanover: University of New England Press, 1977). (*Consequences of Pragmatism*, ch. 5).
Review of *Why Does Language Matter to Philosophy?* by Ian Hacking. *Journal of Philosophy*, 74 (July, 1977): 416–32.
Derrida on Language, Being and Abnormal Philosophy. *Journal of Philosophy*, 74 (Nov. 1977): 673–81.

1978

Epistemological Behaviourism and the De-Transcendentalization of Analytic Philosophy. *Neue Hefte Für Philosophie*, 14 (1978): 117–42. Also in *Hermeneutics and Praxis*, ed. Robert Hollinger, Notre Dame: University of Notre Dame Press, 1985.
A Middle Ground between Neurons and Holograms? *The Behavioural and Brain Sciences*, 2 (1978): 248.
Philosophy as a Kind of Writing: An Essay on Derrida. *New Literary History*, 10 (Autumn 1978): 141–60. (*Consequences of Pragmatism*, ch. 6).
From Epistemology to Hermeneutics. *Acta Philosophica Fennica*, 30 (1978): 11–30. (*Philosophy and the Mirror of Nature*, ch. 7) (trans. French).

1979

Transcendental Argument, Self-reference, and Pragmatism. In *Transcendental Arguments and*

Science, eds Peter Bieri, Rolf-P. Hortsman, Lorenz Kruger. Dordrecht: D. Reidel, 1979.
The Unnaturalness of Epistemology. In *Body, Mind and Method: Essays in Honor of Virgil C. Aldrich*, eds Donald Gustafson, Bangs Tapscott. Dordrecht: D. Reidel, 1979.

1980

Pragmatism, Relativism and Irrationalism. *Proceedings And Addresses of the American Philosophical Association*, 53 (Aug. 1980): 719–38. (*Consequences of Pragmatism*, ch. 9).
Idealism, Holism, and the 'Paradox of Knowledge'. In *The Philosophy of Brand Blanshard*, ed. P. A. Schilpp. (La Salle, Ill., 1980).
Kripke vs. Kant. Review of *Naming and Necessity*, by Saul Kripke. *London Review of Books*, 4 Sept. 1980: 4–5.
On Worldmaking. Review of *Ways of Worldmaking*, by Nelson Goodman. *The Yale Review*, 69 (1980): 276–9.
Reply to Dreyfus and Taylor. *Review of Metaphysics*, 34 (Sept. 1980): 39–46.
(with Dreyfus and Taylor) A Discussion. *Review of Metaphysics*, 34 (Sept. 1980): 47–55.
Searle and the Secret Powers of the Brain. *The Behavioural and Brain Sciences*, 3 (1980): 445–6.
Freud, Morality and Hermeneutics. *New Literary History*, 12 (Autumn 1980): 177–85.

1981

Is There a Problem about Fictional Discourse? *Funktionen Des Fictiven: Poetic und Hermeneutik*, 10 (Munich: Fink Verlag, 1981). (*Consequences of Pragmatism*, ch. 7).
Review of *American Sociology and Pragmatism*, by J. D. Lewis and R. L. Smith. *Review of Metaphysics*, 35 (1981): 147.
Reply to Professor Yolton. *Philosophical Books*, 22 (1981): 134–5.
Nineteenth-Century Idealism and Twentieth-Century Textualism. *The Monist*, 64 (1981): 155–74. (*Consequences of Pragmatism*, ch. 8).
From Epistemology to Romance: Cavell on Scepticism. *Review of Metaphysics*, 34 (1981): 759–74. (*Consequences of Pragmatism*, ch. 10).
Beyond Nietzsche and Marx. Review of three books by or about Foucault. *London Review of Books*, 19 Feb. 1981: 5–6.
Method, Social Science, and Social Hope. *The Canadian Journal of Philosophy*, 11 (1981): 569–88. (*Consequences of Pragmatism*, ch. 11) (trans. French).
Being Business. Review of *A Heidegger Critique*, by Roger Waterhouse. *Times Literary Supplement*, 3 July 1981: 760.
Review of *The Calling of Sociology and Other Essays*, by Edward Shils. *Review of Metaphysics*, 35 (1981): 167–8.

1982

Philosophy in America Today. *The American Scholar*, 51 (1982): 183–200. (*Consequences of Pragmatism*, ch. 12) (trans. German, Hungarian).
From Philosophy to Post-Philosophy (interview). *Radical Philosophy* (Autumn 1982): 10–11 (trans. German).
Persuasive Philosophy. Review of *Philosophical Explanations*, by Robert Nozick. *London Review of Books*, 20 May 1982: 10–11.
Introduction. In *Consequences of Pragmatism*. Minneapolis: University of Minnesota Press, 1982. Reprinted as: Pragmatism and Philosophy, in *After Philosophy*, ed. K. Bayles, J.

Bohman and T. McCarthy, 1987). Abridged version appeared as: The Fate of Philosophy, *The New Republic*, 18 Oct. 1982: 28–34.

Contemporary Philosophy of Mind. *Synthese*, 53 (Nov. 1982): 323–48. Reprinted as: Mind as Ineffable, in *Mind in Nature*, ed. Richard Elvee, Nobel Conference 17, 1982: 60–95.

Comments on Dennett. *Synthese*, 53 (Nov. 1982): 181–7.

Brute and Raw Experience. Review of *Philosophy in the Twentieth Century*, by A. J. Ayer. *The New Republic*, 6 Dec. 1982: 33–6.

Hermeneutics, General Studies, and Teaching, *Synergos*, 2 (1982): 1–15.

1983

Unsoundness in Perspective. Review of *Nietzsche*, by R. Schacht; and *Nietzsche and Philosophy*, by G. DeLeuze. *Times Literary Supplement*, 17 June 1983: 619–20.

Against Belatedness. Review of *The Legitimacy of the Modern Age*, by Hans Blumenberg. *The London Review of Books*, 16 June 1983: 3–5.

What Are Philosophers For? *The Center Magazine* (Sept./Oct. 1983): 40–4.

Pragmatism without Method. In *Sidney Hook: Philosopher of Democracy and Humanism*, ed. Paul Kurtz. Buffalo: Prometheus Books, 1983 (trans. Japanese).

Postmodernist Bourgeois Liberalism. *The Journal of Philosophy*, 80 (Oct. 1983): 583–9.

The Pragmatist. Review of *A Stroll with William James*, by Jacques Barzun. *The New Republic*, 9 May 1983: 32–4.

1984

A Reply to Six Critics. *Analyse & Kritik*, 6 (June 1984): 78–98.

Habermas and Lyotard on Post-Modernity. *Praxis International*, 4 (Apr. 1984): 32–44. Also in *Habermas and Post-Modernity*, ed. R. J. Bernstein. Cambridge: Polity Press, 1985: 161–76 (trans. French, Portuguese).

Heidegger Wider den Pragmatisten. *Neue Hefte für Philosophie*, 23 (1984): 1–22.

Deconstruction and Circumvention. *Critical Inquiry*, 11 (Sept. 1984): 1–23.

Solidarity or Objectivity. *Nanzan Review of American Studies*, 6 (1984): 1–19. Also in *Post-Analytic Philosophy*, ed. John Rajchman and Cornel West, New York: Columbia University Press, 1985. Presented as: Relativism, the Howison Lecture at UC Berkeley, 31 Jan. 1983 (trans. Chinese, French, Italian, German).

Signposts Along the Way that Reason Went. Review of *Margins of Philosophy*, by Jacques Derrida. *London Review of Books*, 16 Feb. 1984: 5–6.

(with Schneewind and Skinner) Introduction. In *Philosophy in History*, ed. R. Rorty, J. B. Schneewind and Q. Skinner. Cambridge: Cambridge University Press, 1984).

The Historiography of Philosophy: Four Genres. In *Philosophy in History*, ed. R. Rorty, J. B. Schneewind and Q. Skinner. Cambridge: Cambridge University Press, 1984) (trans. Hungarian, Italian, Japanese).

What's It All About?. Review of *Intentionality*, by John Searle. *London Review of Books*, 17 May 1984: 3–4.

Life at the end of Inquiry. Review of *Realism and Reason: Philosophical Papers III*, by Hilary Putnam. *London Review of Books*, 2 Aug. 1984: 6–7.

1985

Feeling His Way. Review of *The War Diaries of Jean-Paul Sartre November 1939–March 1940. The New Republic*, 15 April 1985: 32–4.

The Humanities: Asking Better Questions, Doing More Things (interview). *Federation Review*, 8 (Mar./Apr. 1985): 15–19.

Comments on Sleeper and Edel. *Transactions of The Charles S. Peirce Society*, 21 (Winter 1985): 40–8.

Le Cosmopolitanisme sans Emancipation: Réponse a Jean-François Lyotard. *Critique* (May 1985): 569–80, 584.

Review of *Traditional and Analytical Philosophy: Lectures on the Philosophy of Language*, by Ernst Tugendhort. *Journal of Philosophy*, 82 (1985): 720–9.

Philosophy without principles, *Critical Inquiry*, 11 (Mar. 1985): 132–8.

Texts and Lumps. *New Literary History*, 17 (1985): 1–15 (trans. Japanese).

Absolutely Non-Absolute. Review of *Philosophical Papers*, by Charles Taylor. *Times Literary Supplement*, 6 Dec. 1985: 1379–80.

1986

The Contingency of Language. *London Review of Books*, 17 April 1986: 3–6.

The Contingency of Selfhood. *London Review of Books*, 8 May 1986: 11–14.

The Contingency of Community. *London Review of Books*, 24 July 1986: 10–14.

Freud and Moral Reflection. In *Pragmatism's Freud: The Moral Disposition of Psychoanalysis*, ed. Joseph H. Smith and William Kerrigan. Baltimore: Johns Hopkins University Press, 1986 (trans. German).

Should Hume Be Answered or Bypassed? In *Human Nature and Natural Knowledge: Essays Presented to Marjorie Grene*, ed. A. Donegan. Dordrecht: D. Reidel, 1986.

From Logic to Language to Play. *Proceedings and Addresses of the American Philosophical Association*, 59 (1986): 747–53 (trans. Spanish).

The Higher Nominalism in a Nutshell: A Reply to Henry Staten. *Critical Inquiry*, 12 (1986): 462–6.

On Ethnocentrism: A Reply to Clifford Geertz. *Michigan Quarterly Review*, 25 (1986): 525–34.

Sex and the Single Thinker. Review of *Sexual Desire: A Moral Philosophy of the Erotic*, by Roger Scruton. *The New Republic*, 2 June 1986: 34–7.

Pragmatism, Davidson and Truth. In *Truth and Interpretation: Perspectives on the Philosophy of Donald Davidson*, ed. E. LePore. Oxford: Basil Blackwell, 1986 (trans. Japanese).

Foucault and Epistemology. In *Foucault: A Critical Reader*, ed. D. C. Hoy. Oxford: Basil Blackwell, 1986.

Comments on Toulmin's 'Conceptual Communities and Rational Conversation'. *Archivio di Filosofia* (1986): 189–93.

Freedom as Higher than Being. *Working Papers: Critique of Modernity* (ed. Robert Langbaum), 1 (Apr. 1986): 16–26.

Beyond Realism and Anti-Realism. In *Wo steht die Analytische Philosophie heute?*, ed. Ludwig Nagl and Richard Heinrich. Weiner Reihe: Themen Der Philosophie, R. Oldenbourg Verlag, Munich, 1986).

Introduction. In *John Dewey: The Later Works, vol. 8: 1933*, ed. Jo Ann Boydston. Carbondale: Southern Illinois University Press, 1986.

Interview with Richard Rorty (interview) [South African]. *Journal of Literary Studies/Tydskrif Vir Literatuurwetenskap*, 2 (Nov. 1986): 9–13.

1987

Non-Reductive Physicalism. In *Theorie der Subjecktivitat*, ed. Monrad Cramer, et al. Frankfurt: Suhrkamp, 1987 (trans. Chinese, Danish).

Thugs and Theorists: A Reply to Bernstein. *Political Theory*, 15 (Nov. 1987): 564–80 (trans. French).

Unfamiliar Noises: Hesse and Davidson on Metaphor. *Proceedings of the Aristotelian Society*, Suppl. vol. 61 (1987): 283–96.

Posties. Review of *Der Philosophische Diskurs der Moderne*, by Jurgen Habermas. *London Review of Books*, 3 Sept. 1987: 11–12.

Waren die Gesetze Newtons schon vor Newton Wahr? In *Jahrbuch des Wissenschaftkollegs zu Berlin*, 1987 (trans. Italian).

Nominalismo e Conestualismo. Alfabeta, 9 (Sept. 1987): 11–12.

Science as Solidarity. In *The Rhetoric of the Human Science*, ed. John S. Nelson, A. Megill and D. N. McCloskey. Madison: University of Wisconsin Press, 1987 (trans. Japanese, Italian).

1988

The Priority of Democracy to Philosophy. In *The Virginia Statute of Religious Freedom*, ed. Merill Peterson and Robert Vaughan. Cambridge: Cambridge University Press, 1988 (trans. Danish, French, German, Italian, Japanese, Serbo-Croatian, Spanish).

Is Natural Science a Natural Kind? In *Construction and Constraint: The Shaping of Scientific Rationality*, ed. E. McMullin. Notre Dame: Notre Dame University Press, 1988.

Unger, Castoriadis and the Romance of a National Future. *Northwestern University Law Review* (trans. Spanish).

Representation, Social Practice, and Truth. *Philosophical Studies*.

I Professori Sono Meglio dei Torturatori (interview). *Alpfabeta*, 10 (Mar. 1988): 5.

That Old-Time Philosophy. *The New Republic* (on Allen Bloom), 4 April 1988: 28–33 (trans. French).

Taking Philosophy Seriously. Review of *Heidegger et le Nazisme*, by Victor Farias. *The New Republic*, 11 April 1988: 31–4.

Philosophy as Science, as Metaphor, and as Politics. In *The Institution of Philosophy*, ed. Avner Cohen and Marcello Dascal. Rowand & Allenfield, 1988 (trans. German).

1989

Two Meanings of 'Logocentrism': A Reply to Norris. In *Redrawing the Lines: Analytic Philosophy, Deconstruction and Literary Theory*, ed. Reed Way Dasenbrock. Minneapolis: University of Minnesota Press, 1989.

Is Derrida a Transcendental Philosopher? *Yale Journal of Criticism*, 1989.

Moral Identity and Private Autonomy. In a volume of proceedings of a Foucault conference, ed. François Ewald. Paris: Editions de Seuil, forthcoming.

Index

382 *Index*

Reading Rorty

For Holly